Lords of the Lebanese Marches: Violence and Narrative in an Arab Society

MICHAEL GILSENAN

Lords of the Lebanese Marches looks at relations between different forms of power, violence and hierarchy in Akkar, the northernmost province of Lebanon, during the 1970s. Often regarded as 'backward' and 'feudal', in reality this area was controlled mainly by groups with important roles in government and business in Beirut. The most 'feudal' landowners had often done most to introduce capitalist methods to their estates and 'backwardness' was a condition produced by this form of political and social control.

Using both material collected during his stay in Akkar and a variety of historical sources, Gilsenan analyses the practices that guaranteed the rule of the large landowners and traces shifts in the discourses of domination in the area. He also examines the importance of narratives and rhetoric in constituting social honour, collective biography and shared memory/forgetting. The result is an exceptionally lively account of how changes in hierarchy were expressed in ironic commentary on the narratives of idealized masculinity and violence, how subversive laughter and humour counterpointed the heroic ethic of challenge and revenge, and how peasant narratives both countered and reproduced the values of hierarchy.

Michael Gilsenan is Professor of Anthropology and Near Eastern Languages and Literatures at New York University and is Emeritus Fellow at Magdalen College, Oxford. He was Khaled bin Abdullah al-Saud Professor for the Study of the Contemporary Arab World at Oxford University from 1984–95. He is author of *Recognizing Islam: Religion and Society in the Modern Middle East* (1990).

Lords of the Lebanese Marches

Violence and Narrative in an Arab Society

MICHAEL GILSENAN

University of California Press

BERKELEY   LOS ANGELES

University of California Press
Berkeley and Los Angeles, California

Published by arrangement with I.B.Tauris Publishers

© 1996 by I.B.Tauris and Co

Cataloging-in-Publication data on file with the Library of Congress

ISBN 0–520–20589–8; 0–520–20590–1 (pbk.)

Printed in the United Kingdom

9 8 7 6 5 4 3 2 1

Contents

CONTENTS

Plates

Acknowledgements

This book, so long in the writing, would never have been finished were it not for the patient, supportive, cajoling confidence of friends over many years: Nick Blatchley, Jenny Buckman, Terry and Caroline Burke, Felicity Edholm, Richard Fardon, Haim Hazan, Dymphna Hermans, Edward Hower, Benjamin Kilborne, Julian and Annick Laite, Alison Lurie, Jeremy Macdonald, Joe and Anne McDonald, Tim Mitchell, Regina Nadelson, Robin and Doka Ostle, Alain and Bernice Ricard, Raoul Weexsteen and Isabelle Champetier de Ribes, and many others. Anna Enayat showed a patience as great as her editorial eye was perceptive. Nabil Beyhum and Fawaz Trabulsi have unstintingly shared their profound and imaginative understandings of Lebanese society with me over the most difficult of times for anyone who cared for Lebanon. In my early years of research Fuad Khury, Ibrahim Ibrahim and Selim Nasr were generous with their help to a beginner. Tarif Khalidi has nudged me along, in his warm and inimitable way. Nadim Shehadi, Fida Nasrallah and everyone associated with the Centre for Lebanese Studies at Oxford have been always ready to draw my attention to material I might easily have missed. Lila Abu Lughod, John Davis, John Nightingale, Frank Romany and Robert Smith gave me the attentiveness of friends and valuable critical readings of sections of the manuscript, as well as a readiness to engage with and help me define my project. Bernard O'Donoghue read the whole of an early draft and standing at his own special poet's angle to the universe offered a different perspective on my writing – for his and Heather's hospitality and gallous Irish evenings many thanks. Working with Maha Azzam, Christine Daniels, Bénédicte Dembour, Tony Free, Julian Johansen, Nawaf Kabbara, John McGovern, Reem Saad and Martin Stokes has been an enormous pleasure and benefit to me. Robert Malley, with whom I also worked, and John Affeldt enjoyed old armagnac and have been good companions. Flagg Miller helped me greatly in proof reading.

Colleagues in many universities have discussed seminar papers I have given and tried to get me to rethink my approaches. I owe a particular debt to those at seminars in Oxford, at the Anthropology Department of University College London and at the University of London, to Robert Ilbert and his department at the University of Aix-Marseille, to Jean Hannoyer and the CERMOC group in Amman and Beirut, and to Françoise and Jean Métral and their colleagues in Lyon. Raymond and Marie-Jo Jamous in Paris have been hosts, friends, and discussants of some of my work. Terry Wright gave me valuable advice on the selection of photographs. Peter Hayward of the Department of Geography at Oxford provided his much appreciated expertise for the maps and drawings.

The Emir Khaled bin Abdallah al Saud established a Chair in Contemporary Arab Studies at Magdalen College, Oxford and that this book was finished in such ideal surroundings I owe to his generosity and the College's fellowship.

The fieldwork on which the book is based was funded by the then Social Science Research Council. The project was established at Manchester University and the late Emrys Peters, head of the Department of Anthropology at Manchester, kindly invited me to participate in the group of researchers.

Gale Duggan edited the manuscript and taught me the creative terrors of the word 'rewrite'. Her extraordinary tact, unerring eye and gentle insistence on making the book truer to its subject have contributed enormously to whatever virtues it has. I am most grateful to her and to Dug Duggan for their understanding and friendship over many years.

Neville Symington and Isabel Menzies Lyth brought their own fieldwork to bear on my own experience. The book shows many marks of their deconstructions and constructions of narratives, interpretations and memories. Their extraordinary capacities for creative, disturbing, questioning listening were and are of great importance for me.

I thank all those in Akkar who made my stay possible, tolerated the presence of someone who never really defined his purposes in ways that made local sense, and taught me what it was to be totally out of my depth. Many went out of their way to help me and to share aspects of their lives with me. Many died later in the Lebanese wars and this book is dedicated to them all. If I mention Abu Walid by name, it is because even in the context of the Lebanese wars his murder was hideously gratuitous. It obliterated a man of integrity and generosity who lived a life constantly shadowed by bloodshed in his own family.

Three deaths have defined the past few years as I was rewriting this manuscript. My brother Terry was killed in Saudi Arabia in a car crash in December 1988, which threw memory brutally into turmoil and was an awful blow to the family. Albert Hourani, my mentor in the study of Arab societies, died in early 1993. He had encouraged me to go into social anthropology when I was a student many years ago and he never wavered in his support, often seeing my life and possible avenues of exploration far more clearly than I did. He did – and it is a consoling thought – go through the penultimate version of the manuscript late in 1992 and furnished me with a reading of characteristic precision, wisdom and encouragement. My mother died in January 1994. Her patient impatience to see the next book was not this time rewarded. Her pride in what I did through often difficult years moved me and I remember her here long before I have come to terms with the loss.

Michael Gilsenan, Magdalen College, Oxford, 1994

Preface

This book is a study of practices of power in a Lebanese social setting in which hierarchy, domination and contest were basic premises of life. Violence, in many different forms, was much practised and violent events were much narrated. In 1971–72 I worked in Akkar, a rural area of Lebanon controlled by large landholders known as *beys*,[1] men who frequently had close connections with state apparatuses or held state office. Though the region was regarded as the periphery of the Lebanese periphery in economic and cultural terms, it was always linked through the beys with wider sets of political relations. They claimed to be of one descent group established in the region as tax collectors and military controllers by the Ottoman Empire since the seventeenth or eighteenth century. The genealogies of their 'houses' were records of that descent, but were also associated with accounts of the accumulation and loss of lands in struggles for dominance locally and in relation to the state. Indeed, they frequently for all purposes *were* the state in the experience of local people.

The beys used the families of small landholders, the *aghawat* or aghas, as their administrators and strong-arm men to control the *fellahin* sharecroppers and labourers and to confront rival lords. Such controls varied from physical coercion, expulsion from dwellings, seizure of produce and the threat of expropriation of means of production and livelihood, through debt and usury, to sharecropping agreements and long-standing labour association.

Land appropriation or purchase from indebted less successful landlords, the dispossession of cultivators, the imposition of labour and sometimes sexual services, the acquisition of luxury properties and consumption goods in Tripoli and Beirut, all were common themes in the discourse of the landlords' 'naked' power. Local accounts, state reports over a fifty-year period and contemporary newspapers represented overt physical coercion and other kinds of violence as essential, and essentially visible characteristics of class relations and hierarchy. They also represented the system of power as 'traditional', 'feudal' and unchanging, even if any given family might gain or lose political and economic influence in battles with rivals.

My aim is to examine the processes which historically constituted such a social universe.

Violence, reputation, name, fear: stories and narratives of powerful men were produced in and played an important part producing hierarchy in social life. At the extreme such men were said to show a sovereign pleasure in violating others by deed and word arbitrarily, gratuitously, 'just like that', without any reason but their own personal will and pleasure. This notion of an absolute (and absolutist) freedom of action, unconstrained by any custom, tradition or morality, was important in the imagination and indeed experience of power, as if it were the immanent property of persons and the motivating force in social relations.

Narratives contextualized and partially constituted relations of contest and dominance in the everyday world. They were crucial in persons' experiences of different dimensions of power, history and social identity. When I first began my work, I found that listening to often repeated accounts of the deeds of a powerful bey or feared agha created a very homogeneous, tauto-logical discourse. Famous men were men who achieved fame. Narrative circles reinforced the sense of personal force and domination from above. Only as time went on did I begin to appreciate how important it was to look at what was not told, who could not narrate, who might not author his own history, what spaces were occupied by the defeated, forgotten, unconsidered, in-significant. It was only once these considerations emerged that I could begin to appreciate that the practices of overt, self-evident, public power required many processes less immediate to sight.

I had no access to women's lives or narratives, which therefore remain unheard in this book. Men spoke only obliquely or in formal terms of women, when they spoke of them at all, a set of practices itself highly significant of gender relations. Sexual honour, *sharaf*, was certainly important in maintaining family and personal integrity. Its violation through more or less public sexual exploitation of poor women labourers on the estates, women who in any case were dishonoured by appearing in a dependent role before the eyes of men, was part of a system of relations of hierarchy. On the other hand, I heard of very few cases where confrontation between men derived from a dispute over sexual dishonour. The workings of narratives of violence and power are specifically a male preserve and they are my focus here.

Readers may be surprised to find that a book on any aspect of Lebanese society does not discuss religion and 'confessions', the term often used in English for the religious categories by which the Lebanese state formally classified the population. The specific area in which I worked was almost entirely Sunni, though in other parts of Akkar there were Maronite and Greek Orthodox populations. Certainly the major landowners made alliances with other notables and men of power who might be of other confessions. The Lebanese political system, with its constituencies electing lists constructed according to the supposed confessional balance of its population, required such alliances. Yet, as readers will see, confession did not enter in any central way into the themes which I examine, an absence that was certainly contrary to my own initial assumptions.

Part One of the book begins with a panoramic view over the landscape of Akkar as if through the eyes of a major landlord and politician surveying his domains from the balcony of his palace. I use this image to establish one important element of the discourse and imagination of power – that of the all-seeing figure who imposes his will upon those beneath his gaze. The landscape is not a natural phenomenon, but almost a function of his gaze; it is a political and economic set of relations, mapped out in landownership and histories of contested possession known to all. This 'top-down' view of power is interrogated and its social force analysed throughout the rest of the book.

Chapter 2 treats my arrival in the village and the way in which my anomalous project was greeted by some of the young men with a visit to that same palace balcony. That visit, and the unexpected presence/absence of the man of power, was the first indication of the instability of power and the obstacles to the reproduction of social position over the generations. Chapter 3 gives the reader a social sketch of Akkar and the village in which I mostly worked, detailing the occupations and incomes of families and setting out the empirical context of the research.

Part Two, 'State and Local Narratives', begins with a discussion of the relations of narrative and violence. The three following chapters are similarly structured and deal with closely related topics: how different states and their officials, Ottoman, French and Lebanese, defined and sought to act upon the region. For all the officials, Akkar was the type case of the Marches, the wild frontier zone, inhabited by people who could barely be said to have any kind of culture. I consider their observations and rhetoric in the context of how they perceived the relation of this isolated peripheral region to their political centres. State enquiries were meant to be instruments in the control and classification of this savage space, even though their effects were in fact very limited. Official reports, spread over the years from 1916 to 1960, are counterpointed with material drawn from contemporary research and with villagers' histories of the same periods.

Part Three, 'The Weight of the Ancestors', continues with the related theme of different constructions of the past in the present. I take narratives of the famine of the First World War by the aghas and *fellahin* and demonstrate the tensions and oppositions between them. These chapters, 8 and 9, examine hunger, eating and being eaten as a metaphor of power. They concern the power to speak and narrate one's own changing or unchanging place in the world. I also focus attention upon historical changes in the often fraught relations of fathers and sons, uncles and nephews, and show the ideology of male family solidarity as highly unstable and ambivalent.

Part Four, 'Marvellous Stories, Dirty Deeds', employs narratives of violence to work through the practices of power, social honour and dishonour. I focus on what in Scots and Irish are called 'gallous' or 'brilliant' stories of acts that to others might be nothing but 'dirty deeds';[2] parricide that both did, and did not occur; violence as the way of changing relations and catalysing narratives which might be marvellous and carry their own transforming magic, but risked having their social spells broken; the delights of telling stories 'for their own sake'; the eruption of comedy out of high seriousness, and the reverse; 'lies' that enabled truths to be revealed, or drew persons into their own and others' fantasies, or served as instruments of control.

People took endless pleasure in creating narratives out of their own and others' biographies, and in 'revealing' the narratives of others as nothing but 'talk', 'lies', or dirty deeds that should not be talked about at all. Narrative was a battleground of histories, reputations and identities. Being 'heard of' and 'spoken of' were crucial qualities in the operations of domination. But narratives were therefore also liable to variation, being turned into comedy or parody of claims to honourable behaviour. Instability of apparently fixed meanings and the reversing of styles of telling from serious to comic, often with a spontaneous abruptness that would leave me almost literally gasping, became an 'ordinary' experience. Improvisatory skill in rhetorical play, like the closely allied readiness to act in a sudden moment of challenge, was a matter of high practical value. Spontaneity flashed forth from existing patterns of dominance in whose microscopic readings some were far more expert than others; those patterns might grow or be moulded by a moment of genius in ad libbing. Awareness of the constraints and freedoms of such transformations was crucial to successful intervention.

The following chapters in Part Four trace out the trajectories of acts of violence embedded in social histories and relations, frequently having to do with questions of property and the service of a particular landlord. Such acts became part of a narrative chain of events, linked to others, that had effects persisting for many years. Groups and persons had to find ways of 'avoiding' each other, which required a fine apprehension of where one might or might not be at what moment, and who was at risk from whom; or they had to know where to seek out an intended victim; or how to react to a split-second encounter of unexpected confrontation. Relations of fathers and sons, younger and older generations, were intricately bound up with violence. The young men were both the essential force of a descent group and a danger to it if they could not be controlled. Rather than being used by the fathers, they might refuse control or drive situations farther than their elders intended. Generational relations, as Part Three shows, were subject to inherent tensions.

Chapters 15 and 16 form Part Five, 'Imperatives of Work', and end the book with a discussion of the impact upon social life of wage work and the labour market with its own, less immediate and personal violence and fears. The demands of earning an income in the rapidly changing circumstances of the Lebanon of the 1960s and early 1970s, when the services sector of the economy became overwhelmingly dominant, had complex effects on the region. 'Work' had taken on new significance. Young men now had to find wages, and the provision of work for them could be one very important way in which a leader could stake his claims to their loyalty against rivals and the older generation. The building site in Beirut or Tripoli, with its dumper trucks, bulldozers and high cranes, was becoming the foundation of young men's lives as much as agriculture.

Generational relations, once again, were relations of ambiguity and of interests that might be perceived as contradictory. The sons of great landlords might think of little but how to sell off land or the olive harvest to enjoy the extravagance of consumer pleasures in Beirut and abroad. Their fathers' insistence on the importance of acting and holding property collectively might have little effect. Young aghas felt that their fathers demanded of them codes of behaviour which they both had to obey, but which in a changing world were extraordinarily difficult, if not impossible to follow. The gap between language and social realities was often seen as acute. Yet at the same time, the capacity for violence by individual or group had not lost its meaning in Lebanese society and politics. Strong-arm men, bodyguards, chauffeurs with guns were all needed. Likely lads who also drove tractors and harvesters were recruited, for wages, suits and dark glasses. Kalashnikovs were increasingly within the financial reach of even relatively poor families, including the cultivators who had hitherto been outgunned.

At the same time there were those who represented themselves as seeking to stay apart from the public world of aggressive masculinity. For them, work and wages were a way to a less risky and less family-dominated existence. They wanted to live 'in the house, untroubled', a wish very contrary to the ideals of men ever ready to defend their social honour 'out there' and leaving the home to women. Others might deride such a wish as merely a rationalization of social insignificance, or an attempt to disguise lack of status.

Lebanese society in the 1960s and early 1970s was marked by what many perceived as increasingly fundamental divisions of class, wealth, political ideology and patterns of consumption – divisions which all manifested themselves locally. Though I did not know it, the period of the Lebanese wars would begin only four years later.

1. The palace of Muhammad al-Abboud

PART ONE

The Rule of the Lords from the Snow to the Sea

CHAPTER ONE

Figures in a Landscape: One

From his place high on the open balcony of the palace the Minister looks down over the tight clusters of flat-roofed village dwellings that stretch out in a thin ribbon along the hill immediately below him. His gaze follows the ordered lines of the olive trees covering the wide, fertile valley the village of Berqayl commands and moves on over the low hills that descend gently on their other side to the coastal plain. The Mediterranean sea, bright in the sunset, stretches beyond to a horizon lost in the summer haze. His eyes move right and north, over the sweeping curve of the broad bay and the widening plain towards the Syrian frontier twenty kilometres distant. The mountains are at his back.

Muhammad al Abboud spends most of his time in Beirut, now only two and a half hours away to the south by car, for he is very much a man of the city. Residing for the most part in the Lebanese capital, he has the tastes and way of life of any notable of the *haute bourgeoisie*. The luxury of his country mansion is part of the urban lifestyle of a well-known politician, businessman and large landlord whose centre of operations is Beirut. He has only recently constructed its five-storied ostentatious splendour, the sharp gables of its great red-tiled roof visible from far away and dwarfing every other building, its presence dominating the landscape.

The rows of tall, rectangular windows that look out onto the landscape on every side are open to allow the evening breezes to flow through the spacious rooms. The shutters, which during the day have shielded the interior from the sun, are folded back in trim ranks against the grey walls. This building is a powerful testimony to the Minister's own position among the political élite of the centre and a spectacular break with the native architecture of Berqayl, a break which says much about that other, superior world of great landowners and men of power which he inhabits.

Muhammad al Abboud returns on regular visits to his domains and the seat of his political power and – as on this early June summer evening in 1953 – takes his ease for a while up here on the balcony. He must receive clients, organize an electoral campaign, greet distinguished visitors, reckon the harvests from his estates, and show allies and opponents how significant is the web of interests and personal relations of which he is the centre. But before he addresses the serious business demanding his attention, his custom is to sit for a while in this favourite spot overlooking the heart of the village and the broad expanse of Akkar, the northernmost frontier marches of Lebanon.

The Minister sees. His gaze from the top of the high concrete mansion is itself a sign and instrument of power. For a man who has *markaz* – social standing and place – the notions of 'looking over', and even more 'looking into', are part of the idiom and practice of knowing and controlling the lives of others in the social hierarchy. To sit here demonstrates his superior place as much as does the building itself. He is above others.

The Minister is seen. The men who have come in from a long day of harvesting and sit chatting by the wide-spreading plane tree that shelters the spring and the old mosque below know he is above them. No hidden observer, he imposes his visibility upon them whether they wish it or not. They are aware of his presence. Powerful men mean to be in view, are expected to be in view, personally seen by inferiors who are both socially and in this case physically *below*.

Muhammad al Abboud is not alone. His personal entourage – servants, attendants and armed bodyguards – is always close at hand. One of them is with him on the balcony, an honoured companion, the *murafiq*, by whom lords are customarily accompanied. Another is preparing coffee. Others wait below within earshot. The murafiq wears the baggy *shirwal* trousers and shirt with its drawstring tightened at the neck worn by all the villagers. His lord, habitually dressed in a suit and tie, makes only one aristocratic concession to the appearances of traditional clothing in an elegant flowing outer garment, the *abba*.

The two men talk together confidentially and easily. The companion speaks in a harsh, direct voice, states his views bluntly, and gestures emphatically as is typical of men in his position – men accustomed to issuing orders, overseeing labourers, confronting the challenges of rivals, hunting alone in the mountains. The Minister's voice is softer, much closer to the educated intonations of the capital than to the heavier accent of the Akkari. They make a strongly contrasting pair, but much binds them together. Theirs is a privileged encounter, the lord and the murafiq sharing in the beauty and excellence of status honour.

The Minister always addresses his companion by the courtesy title of *agha*, a Turkish rank below that of bey and pasha but here used as a mark of prestige and standing. Muhammad al Abboud knows the two agha descent groups, Beit Khalid and Beit Abd as-Salam, very well. The former are somewhat less important for his interests, since many of them have moved down to Tripoli over the years and become part of the life and economy of the city. They are now more at home in the urban world of small businesses and white-collar jobs. Still, they keep their houses in the village and the *mukhtar* is one of their number, an indication of their continuing significance in the community. The Minister therefore needs their votes and their support in disputes, so he is careful to guard their interests. Beit Abd as-Salam, the 'cousin' house of Beit Khalid with which it shares a genealogy going back to a single common founder, has remained resident in Akkar itself and has its social base in the village. Men of this group, like his companion on the balcony, possess small or medium-size land holdings across the plain into Syria, as well as acting as companions, gunmen and administrators for the beys. They are the most immediate allies in defence of the landed interest.

The Minister and his companion know very well that much binds them together as the dominant landed strata. The aghas need the wider power of the great landowners as guarantor for the whole system and for their own more local interests. The lords in their turn need the aghas, not least as an apparatus to discipline and organize labour over the wide areas of the latifundia in a world in which violence and the threat of violence are vital to maintaining the estates.

Yet each man knows, too, that much holds them apart. Certain tensions characterize this crucial relationship between beys and aghas. Beit Abd as-Salam and Beit Khalid can mobilize a considerable number of armed men, far more than the members of the beys' families of Berqayl, the Minister's village and that of his ancestors for two hundred years. Their united force could easily triumph in any serious local dispute with a lord's house. Had they not driven one important bey's family from Berqayl years ago after a dispute over his exercise of authority? Muhammad al Abboud and his murafiq remember that story well.

Both the Minister and his companion also recall how, only a few years ago after the Second World War, the lords of Berqayl had tried to use a few of the more promising of the young *fellahin* or labourers of the village as bodyguards and labour bosses. The move was instantly interpreted by the aghas as a manoeuvre designed to infringe on their monopoly of such positions and the social power going with them. Beit Abd as-Salam and Beit Khalid mobilized at once. There were confrontations, the most dramatic being in the great reception room of the Minister's own father himself. Blunt words were spoken, threats made. The lords quietly withdrew their plan, defeated. But only for the time being. They might try again, playing on fellah hostility to the aghas who are the men most directly involved in the day-to-day relations of domination on the estates. Less dramatically, but perhaps most significant of all, the beys continue to buy up the land of any agha who is compelled by economic necessity to sell, and in this way too they undercut their allies' social independence.

The agha groups are also divided by their loyalties to the houses of rival lords. These rivalries are often acute, involving bitter quarrels over property and the control of labour. Individual aghas become identified with their bey's interests, and may defend that interest with force of arms against their own kin. One young agha of Beit Abd as-Salam has already killed another from a different branch of the same beit because of a dispute between their respective lords, and the blood feud that has followed continues to pose great problems to the descent group as a whole.

None the less, both sides do have vested interests to preserve. Muhammad al Abboud appreciates the significance of the aghas' practical and political support, and always extends the most courteous of treatments to his formidable murafiq. For this is a man who is well known locally, a man of whom stories are told, because he has been involved in violent encounters with the men of other beys seeking to encroach on the lord's domain.

Their conversation in the pleasant coolness of a summer evening is thus one in which a certain intimacy is founded on a practical sense of interests both closely allied and clearly distinct. Each man is acutely sensitive to the underlying currents of this vital relationship. Their talk is relaxed, but to the point. The Minister must continually gather information and stay in touch with key issues: the two men are concerned about problems organizing production in one of his villages; the marriage that is being arranged for one of the young beys of another village which prompts them to contrast the marriage strategies of one bey's house with those of another; and the continuing, threatening activity of the lord's main political rival in the Akkar.

The companion has the right to a certain familiarity with Muhammad al Abboud. He has earned it by his service. He does not hesitate to complain that the Minister has mishandled a troublesome situation in one of his villages, to correct him on points of local detail, to contradict him outright, or to say what his father would do in these circumstances. Such familiarity has its own etiquette. The companion is meticulous in his use of the title of 'bey', that Turkish rank which together with 'pasha' is still applied to the landowners who owe the foundations of their power to incorporation in the Ottoman military and tax administration during the eighteenth century. It is always 'Muhammad Bey' here. The companion's observation of the decorum of rank marks the social distinctions, for he in turn receives the appropriate indications of respect from the lord.

The Minister's *qahwaji*, his coffee-maker and a member of another branch of Beit Abd as-Salam, is grinding the coffee. As this is not a formal occasion he does not use the elaborate percussive rhythms beaten out with the large ceremonial wooden mortar and pestle kept for feasts and receptions, but works expertly with the metal bowl and grinder. He wears the ornamental waistcoat and Arab cord and draped black cloth headdress he always puts on when his master is in residence. He is known by the fellahin as a harsh man in his control over the agricultural labourers in his charge and is used to intimidating anyone who shows signs of giving trouble.

The Minister's *nargalji* comes and goes, tending the hubble-bubble pipes (*nargileh*). He also is an agha by family, but of only a small and relatively insignificant branch. He changes the charcoals, or remakes the cone of tobacco which must be neither too wet nor too dry, too tightly nor too loosely packed on the clay head. Another pipe is needed if the first fails to draw properly. He must alter the water level a little. Things must be done properly, forms must be preserved, and he joins discreetly in the ebb and flow of the evening quartet, making his own contribution to the exchange of news, gossip, and evaluation.

So the lord is at ease on his palace balcony. The villagers below can see him quietly smoking the water pipe. That act, too, is an important detail in the spectacle of appropriate forms of power. In Beirut he smokes cigars – he had smoked one when photographed for the newspaper – as is customary for the wealthy modern politician. But here in the village his nargileh is the appropriate sign of his status. The sword and lance, which once indicated men of rank, have now vanished. But the nargileh remains a traditional object of display which men like the Minister use to show their standing. Indeed, in formal receptions in the salon on the first floor, the elaborate leisurely and judicious rituals of the water pipe play an important part in the aesthetics of interaction and the marking of social station. At such times the Minister uses a nargileh with a long decorated stem fitting closely into a fine old Bohemian crystal or Damascene painted glass base. Servants place water pipes in front of prestigious guests, the relative height of the tall, silver-coloured stem and the beauty of the glass indicating every man's degree of importance. Each of the more ornate crystal vessels has its own history and genealogy. It is expected that in answer to a respectful question from a visitor or the deferential comment of a dependent the owner will explain how it had belonged to such a bey who inherited it from such a pasha who in turn …

Seated on his balcony, the Minister uses a simple nargileh: just a small flask of plain white glass and a short-stemmed pipe. Though on view, he is also 'on his own' and more elaborate signs of rank are unnecessary. It suffices that he is smoking the water pipe in relaxed enjoyment of personal comfort, and in the sight of all.

The prayer beads Muhammad al Abboud turns in his hand are simple too, perhaps hardly more than a black-beaded string. In the grandeur of the expensively furnished salon of the mansion or in Beirut, by contrast, he prefers the beads of semi-precious stone with the gold tassle to flip casually from side to side over the back of his fingers. Like the nargileh, valued rosaries have a known genealogy – they have been in the hand of such a lord or sheikh and before him such another – and they are a fit subject of conventional polite enquiry and appreciation. Some men are known to collect particularly fine rosaries, and the lord may graciously lend his to a guest while they talk. On his balcony, with only his attendants around him, less ostentation is required.

A cool breeze blowing up the steep narrow valley overlooked by the great house brings relief from the day's close summer heat. Muhammad al Abboud savours the broad, panoramic view of village, hills, plain, sea and mountain. The panorama is all the more pleasant as he and his father own and directly exploit much of what he surveys in tranquillity from his high vantage point. It is indeed very much 'his view'. Moreover, only a lord is said to 'have a view', for such a concept is in itself alien to the world of the labourers and marks a superior social position and taste formed by high status in the Lebanese political élite, as well as by that French education so characteristic of the upper class.

Status and power have come to the Minister thanks to the efforts of a far-sighted father: aggressive in land acquisition, consistent in alliance with the French during the League of Nations Mandate period between the two World Wars, and shrewd in urban investment, a father who has made himself a key figure in northern Lebanese politics. This formidable emblem of landlord power, Abboud Bey Abd ar-Razzaq, has a reputation for ruthless and arbitrary rule among the labourers, the fellahin. But not only with them.

All the villagers talk about Abboud. Many narratives tell of his single-mindedness, cunning and violence in the drive to land acquisition, the displacement of rivals, the command of the labour force. Abboud Bey has made himself into a great and dominant landowner, though he inherited little from his father, and he has done it, they say, with as much violence as entrepreneurial shrewdness: hadn't Abboud shot dead a worker on the scaffolding round his house to show off his new rifle? Don't men still talk of the boy whose head was smashed open on a wall because the lord was furious at some imagined lack of respect? Remember how close he and the French officer were, the officer who used Abboud's men to put down local protests with no mercy?

There is much in this vein to relate, to repeat in the evenings when men gather together and recount key moments of collective life. For just as a man who achieves power is always 'on view' and makes himself visible, so he is talked about and makes himself the central figure in the ways in which men give accounts of their world to each other. He creates events and acts upon others 'as he wishes' and according to his will: that at least is how figures of power are imagined and how men speak of them. They 'respect' Abboud. They fear him.

The great bey is old now and yet more unpredictable. Even some of the aghas say that he has become a 'tyrant', a *zalim*, in his advanced years, though they will never use that word in front of the lower orders and woe betide a fellah who dares to be heard judging Abboud with such a term. That increased arbitrariness of act and temper only strengthens villagers' fear, that emotion which is so central to the way in which power is practised, represented and narrated here. When men reckon the events of the past and narrate the significant deeds and crucial moments of their shared histories the name of Abboud looms over their narrative landscape as does the mansion of his son over the village.

Of that son there are quite other and more routine, everyday accounts. Muhammad al Abboud is not the charismatic founder of the family power.

He is the businessman who takes on the major tasks of consolidating and administering what his still active father has achieved. He does not have the glamour of the man who has made himself into the greatest force in the region. The son is an inheritor, not a founder, the rule rather than the exception; he continues the enterprise rather than blazing the trail. As an only son he has been forced into his role and he does it well, but no one pretends that Muhammad al Abboud is more than the competent scion of Abboud Abd ar-Razzaq and has achieved his position because of dynastic transmission rather than by any startling individual capacity for the acquisition of power. So though villagers 'respect' this man who can exercise such control over their lives, that control is not so personal, vivid and immediate as that of Abboud himself. There are few typical narratives of the Minister's acts, for he represents and is represented as a different kind of leader. Yet the two distinct biographies complement and combine with each other to form one great story of success in the accumulation of property and influence, a story which can be compared with those of other great Lebanese political notables.

But there is one critical problem which no amount of power can resolve. Muhammad al Abboud is an only son. Still worse, he himself has no son. The future thus depends entirely on him. There is no group of brothers to guard the patrimony, divide the many tasks and run the political machine. The patrilineal line of succession is threatened just when its influence is at its height. If anything were to happen to him now, years of acquisition and alliance would go for nothing. Should he die, when he dies, what will become of that power so shrewdly accumulated? That is the shadow over the landscape.

The Minister glances to his right and sees his father's dwelling only a short distance away. The son has constructed his palace adjacent to Abboud Abd ar-Razzaq's elegant white stucco and blue country chateau half hidden in the trees. It is typical of the region that males of one family cluster together. Whether beys, aghas or labourers, fathers, sons and brothers build close together and share a space set off from others. The contrasting styles of the two palaces mirror the evolution of taste of two generations of power and command; both are utterly distinct from all other buildings, including the fortress-like stone constructions of the other lords. But they obey the common rule: that of male family unity in space.

The Minister therefore has the freedom and the special perspective from which to take the landscape, his landscape, as aesthetically pleasing. For his property extends 'from the snow to the sea' as the local idiom has it to express the grand sweep of a lord's power (*min at-talg ila-l bahr*). These moments of conspicuous relaxation are brief intervals in his relentless political and social competition with other leading beys. But they are also part of that same relentless competition. People expect him to show himself 'at his ease'. He must play the part as it is inscribed in the discourse of power. Villagers who pass below know many stories of men of honour whose ostentatious insouciance challenged dangerous opponents. In such narratives the hero, as if he had not a care in the world, seats himself in some pleasing spot in the sight of all, daring them to come for him 'if they are real men'. The place on the lofty balcony, as everyone knows, must be vigorously defended against rivals for local and national power.

To be on view and to show oneself always asserts some element of challenge, whether faint or strong. A man claiming respect stands against and over others. He is ready to be challenged in turn, and the higher the place the greater the fall. The challenge may be economic, or electoral, or even mortal. The Minister's chair is, after all, within easy rifle shot from the hill across the wadi. The risk is present here in his village, even though minimal, a faint but constant hint of menace to the figure so conspicuously surveying the world below.

Directly behind him rises the mountain, the region known as the Jurd. Stripped over the years of its covering of trees, it is rocky and scrub-dotted, its soil washed off by the heavy winter and spring storms. Only a few pines remain, for Akkar was stripped of much of its woodlands by Ottoman military and civil engineers before their defeat and withdrawal from the Lebanon in 1918. Once common, mulberry trees disappeared when the silk industry, of only limited importance in Akkar, collapsed in the following decade. Other trees were felled – by administrators for the French League of Nations Mandate in the 1920s and 1930s, and after them, by the British forces at the end of the Second World War; then by Lebanese businessmen seeking a commodity to exploit and finding ill-paid forest guards only too happy to aid them for a few lira; and finally, by poor cultivators who scavenged and cut what was left for fuel and building, their goats completing the destruction.

The highest villages are at 1,500 metres, and the route is only newly paved (a *route asphaltée de 3ème classe* as the tourist map has it – not that there are any tourists). One can now make the journey down in an hour or so by vehicle but there are as yet few cars, buses or lorries. Most traffic is still on foot or by donkey. Heavy snows, bitter winds and brutal cold limit passage during the winter months of the year.

At the top of the road and identified as the heart of the Jurd region lies a cluster of large villages, entirely Sunni Muslim like the Minister's own. Two of these, the most important, Fneidek and Michmich, are well known to Muhammad al Abboud for the independence of their clan organization. These mountain shepherds do battle regularly for summer sheep pasture with the herders of the Beqa'a valley who come up the eastern slopes to compete for the grasses of the high plateau. They are also ready to confront the agents of the relatively new Lebanese state, which is in any case dependent on local power holders for any authority it may have. The army and gendarmerie have little control in the Jurd. No officer with any sense or experience takes his patrols there unless invited and backed by notables and men of influence. Those who too zealously pursue a 'brigand' or an 'outlaw' meet heavier fire than they themselves command, or find the village empty of *shebab*, the arms-bearing men. The misguided patrol then has to get back down the precipitous track faster than the shepherds can come after it. The officer is blamed for his stupidity, not praised for dedication to the rule of law. Since such outlaws are not infrequently in the pay of a lord and carry out his dirty work for him, the wretched officer also risks offending the mighty and losing his position altogether.

To the established families of Tripoli, the main city of north Lebanon and urban centre for Akkar, 'the mountain' is the epitome of unregenerate 'tribalism' and savage 'backwardness'. The warrior figures of the Jurd with their upturned moustaches, rifles and bandoliers seem the very type of archaic traditionalism. They represent the polar opposite of city values and are the subject of a certain mocking humour. But to the people of the foothills and plain, the Jurd signifies something more precise, and more immediate: clanship, autonomous self-help, heavily armed men, forces to be feared and not easily restrained. Men of the higher villages sometimes 'come down' on the lower settlements in a raid or in furtherance of some political dispute. Most seriously, they can cut the water supply to the lower settlements. The state gives little protection against these mountain communities who live very different lives from the small cultivators and labourers. Only powerful lords such as the Minister can ensure that relations with the Jurd remain relatively stable.

As a great Akkari landlord and political notable Muhammad al Abboud has good reason to be well acquainted with the Jurd and knowledgeable about its social composition. He cannot afford any easy stereotypes of wild shepherd warriors. His family has holdings up there in the mountain. He knows how the clans are organized, which are dominant, the power of the religious sheikhs, who own the flocks and can mobilize the violence groups, who are the subordinate poor cultivators and sharecroppers. More to the point, at this moment he has particular political questions in mind: Which village will support him in the forthcoming elections only a few days away? Which clan or fraction of a clan opposes him and why? Can they be bought, can a deal be struck? Who should be chosen as his local 'keys' able to deliver labourers for harvests, voters at elections, armed groups to protect and intimidate? Such information, constantly assessed and reassessed, is vital to his hold on regional influence in an ever-more competitive environment of national and local politics.

The need to enhance his support in the villages of the Jurd is more pressing than it has ever been. Two years ago, in 1951, the Minister had the bitter and unusual experience of losing a parliamentary election, the first time either his father or he had been defeated. His supporters allege fraud and corruption, as they are bound to do. Defeat was a major blow for a man whose father, Abboud Abd ar-Razzaq, has five times been elected a deputy for his region. The Minister has himself assumed the succession since making his entry in the elections of 1937. Twice he has been Minister of National

Security and once the Minister of Finance. This is therefore a critical period for him. In the upcoming elections in North Lebanon, to be held on 25 July, there will be only one slot for a Sunni Muslim candidate instead of the more usual two on the regional list, and he will have a powerful opponent in the bey who has so recently beaten him.

National politics are at a crucial stage. So too is the Minister's career. There is a new President determined to exercise to the full the wide powers the constitution grants him, and the successful rival lord is his close ally. The Minister has chosen to remain loyal to the previous incumbent with whom he has been long associated, so he has lost a vital link to power. He has never had to face hostility from the head of state before. Such hostility can easily cost even a man as important as Muhammad al Abboud his seat, given the capacity of the security apparatuses to intervene in the electoral process. Out of power, it is far more difficult for him to gain access to all the resources and benefits which office-holders routinely use to reward supporters and maintain networks and alliances. He needs to make enormous efforts, political and financial, to recapture his position.

The President, who has a reputation for being a skilled operator, wants to reduce the number of deputies from sixty-six to forty-four and to pack the reduced National Assembly with his supporters. That is why the regional list has been changed. The political pressure is intense. The Minister must therefore pay particular attention to every electoral possibility in every village of Akkar, while never for a moment neglecting his alliances with political notables in the North as a whole and in the capital.

Small wonder that Muhammad al Abboud and his murafiq carefully analyse the shifting allegiances of the Jurd. Those villages have many votes. In addition, they are part of that wider area known as the *Qayta'* in which his own village is situated. This is his political home territory and ought to be the bedrock of his support. The Minister has to keep alive his relations with major clans in these mountain settlements. He must receive and visit, make gifts calculated exactly to the degree of status and obligation appropriate, offer lavish hospitality, pay out money to those who can simply be bought. And he has to fund expenses for client families who run their own reception rooms where his name will be praised, followings mobilized, conflicts mediated, and favours or jobs distributed. The Jurd is demanding.

How very differently the Minister assesses the villages of the plain and the foothills. Here are the beys' personal centres of power and control, directly under their sway. What is important about a *dai'a*, village, to the Minister is the family or families of lords to whom it 'belongs'. That is its identifying factor – the name of the bey with whom it is associated through narratives of the past, residence and property.

In the beys' shared narrative of how they came to be identified with different villages of the Akkar, they speak of themselves as originally a single large descent group of both ethnic and geographical outsiders. They say they are of Kurdish descent and thus formerly, like the Circassian aghas, both non-Arabic speaking and from a distant region. They have detailed genealogies back to the founding ancestor, Shadid, who, they say, first set foot in the region and pitched his tents on the plain in the eighteenth century. Paintings of elaborate family trees with elegant calligraphy inscribing the names of each branch hang on the walls of more than one residence to show this ancestry in all its complexity of different descent groups from the first founder. The collective memory is framed and exhibited as claim and proof of title and dominance (though many of the lords know only the most general lines of descent of their own group).

The beys tell a story in which they have imposed themselves on the Akkar and its different groups of inhabitants by a combination of external force and imperial fiat, for their ranks of bey and pasha come from the Ottoman authorities who appointed them as military power and tax farmers for the troublesome region of the Akkar marches. Muhammad al Abboud can thus map out the distribution of the settlements in terms of Ottoman administrative divisions and the territories of these family branches, reading the landscape as a changing set of personal names and histories. The name of his own village for example, Berqayl, denotes to all the area's inhabitants a centre of important rival estate owners: the House or Beit of his grandfather Muhammad Pasha Muhammad and the rival Beit of Mustapha Bey define the wider social meaning of the word. They make Berqayl what it has often been called, a capital of the great landlords.

The landless of the plain and foothills, the fellahin, are for the most part direct personal subjects of the lords' power, poor sharecroppers and agricultural labourers with none of the independent violence groups and resources of the major mountain clans. They are bound to their dai'a by subsistence needs and the ramified power of the lords, not by some primordial sentiment or memory. The fellahin do not claim a history prior to the coming of the beys or have a pride in some autochthonous status as the original people of the Akkar. But there are some who say that over the years they were deprived of rights they used to have to work common land in a share system by the lords and that they were victims of the beys' manipulations of land law under the Ottoman and French administrations. Fellahin stories, however diffuse and anonymous, therefore carry a moral commentary on the injustice of prevailing social relations of hierarchy which bind them to the lords.

Such poor cultivators have narratives that are the complementary opposite of those accounting for the beys' power: they too speak of coming in 'from outside', but as dependent and servile populations. Inhabitants of a satellite settlement which exists only a short distance up the mountain road near the Minister's palace have a not untypical story of being 'brought in a long time ago' from, they think, either Syria or Palestine to work on the estates. Many agricultural workers have these kinds of bald narratives of origin that place them as arriving from an unspecific 'somewhere else' at that equally unspecific 'long time ago', quite often as part of a non-Arab group such as the Turkmen, or as nomads and transhumants, or as landless workers from other regions.

In the beys' discourse of descent, status honour and power, the fellahin are represented as hapless instruments of the lords' will and not as agents with their own social role in history. In their own discourse, fellahin speak in the passive voice as people brought to a village as the objects of the landlords' power and violence.

The experience of domination is central to the social definition of space and settlement. To both lords and the subordinate strata the very idea of a dai'a is bound up with that of control and a hierarchy imposed upon heterogeneous populations through force. There is nothing romantic or nostalgic about 'the village' in such a context to any social class. For the beys it means power, labour and, increasingly, votes. The phrases in which power and property are expressed make this very clear – one bey 'has seventeen villages', a second 'five', and a third 'eleven and he shares three of them with another lord'. This is the language of Muhammad al Abboud.

There are some exceptions. One or two Christian villages have an anomalous prosperity, for *émigrés* who have made good overseas have remitted money to their families and built impressive houses quite uncharacteristically luxurious for the region. But emigration overseas has not been structurally significant in Akkar as it has become in the area of Mount Lebanon to the south where many have established themselves overseas in trade and business, and send vital and considerable remittances back home. Relatively few Akkaris have taken the routes to South America, the United States and West Africa which successive waves of mainly Christian migrants of the Kisrwan and Metn districts of Mount Lebanon initiated.

The beys' political control, the relative insulation from the economic and social transformations which had such an effect on central parts of the country from the 1820s onwards, and the absence in the Akkar of those links with France or England that have been so important for the evolution of modern Lebanese history, have combined to reinforce the quasi-isolation of the region.

The lords are happy to do everything they can to preserve this social and cultural backwardness to maintain local domination and their own autonomy from the centre. They have done little to encourage any form of modernization, preferring a population which depends as totally as possible upon their authority. Few dai'a have schools, clinics, post offices, sewage and drainage, piped water or electricity. The beys see to that by their influence in the National Assembly and the Ministries.

Many of the villages of Akkar are situated in the foothills on the spring line, or on small *tall* or hills that rise here and there above the plain. The former location offers shelter from the strength of the winds which blow fiercely in the winter and water for the village from the outlets on the spring line. The latter attests to the problems of building on the plain itself. There are many rivers and runoffs, the water table is high, and wide areas often flooded in the past before the recent irrigation and drainage works somewhat improved the situation. Passage for caravans, men and animals was very difficult. The plain was marshy, and malarial.

Nineteenth- and early twentieth-century travellers complained also about problems of security: horsemen swept down quickly from the overlooking hills; brigandage threatened the merchants' caravans. Control of routes was, and is, a vital resource for the beys. Berqayl has a double advantage: its position in the foothills at the junction of plain and mountain enabling it to cut access to and from the high villages if there is a dispute, and its easy access to the main road leading up from Tripoli. This route divides at Abde, one branch swinging up the coast to Banyas, Tartous and Lattakia, the other heading inland through the small provincial administrative centre of Halba as the main link to Homs, Hama, and ultimately Aleppo. Berqayl is therefore well placed in the strategic geography of the area.

The whole of the Akkar plain is a contested space, a marches frontier region. Different groups have battled throughout history to control the key route linking the great cities of Tripoli and Homs which cuts a broad path between the last summits of the Lebanese mountain to its south and the Alawite mountain visible to the north. Crusaders used this entry way into northern Syria; the ruins of their fortifications recall their presence in the long line of outsiders who imposed themselves here. A military interpretation of landscape is natural to its inhabitants; force determines social geography.

No one knows this better than the Minister. The military significance of the Akkar is part of his family and personal experience. The history of the beys, the one that they themselves recount, begins with their implantation in the region in the eighteenth century to keep order for the Ottoman Empire and to subdue rebellions by communities of Shi'a who then dominated the plain, or by the peasants of the Alawite mountain to the north. Years later the Minister's father performed similar services for the French during the Mandate (1919–43). Military power and estate formation have been integrally linked in their family history. Space must be read in these terms of domination and control of land and populations.

Geographically, socially, the coastal plain itself on this side of the Lebanese frontier – the *sahel* – has been an emptiness, an absence: the Ottomans classified it as *rif*, 'country', precisely because of the absence of towns. Habitation is still very sparse. The miserable conglomerations of huts and shelters in places like Masoudiya are scarcely more than temporary and convenient sites to the beys, locations for their most impoverished labourers 'brought in from Syria' to work the heavy, poorly drained soils. Other labour is supplied from the beys own villages on a daily basis, men and women going down at dawn and returning at dusk, depending on the seasons, their own needs as subsistence cultivators and sharecroppers, and the demands of the landlords. They make the plain productive.

The beys established their main latifundist control further north, where the plain (bisected by the modern border with Syria) broadens out and sweeps inland away from the coast. Problems of flooding and travel were always much less acute in that more distant area on the other side of the Nahr al Kabir river that now marks the international boundary. Yet even there the population is scattered in small settlements, not in large villages. The wood and earth habitations are meagre and usually the property, like the tools and animals, of the beys. But the ground is fertile and easily worked, and experimentation with new crops has already been tried during the French Mandate. Cotton proved highly successful until international market factors killed it off. There is room for innovation.

The Minister spends little time in the northern landholdings. Those large tracts are mostly his father's property, and, in any case, in Syria and therefore not part of his electoral calculations. As businessman and landlord the plain exists for him in accounts and measures of produce. Muhammad al Abboud sees the sahel as a source of new economic opportunities. The financial needs of a politician are great and getting greater. He must lead the luxurious lifestyle appropriate to a member of the ruling class, and that means maximizing the value of the landholdings. Like his father, therefore, he is always planning how their estates can be made more productive and profitable as a business enterprise. There is scope for mechanization and raising the very low level of technology employed in the traditional extensive cultivation of cereals. He is starting to use more machinery. Some of the younger aghas are becoming drivers and mechanics able to operate the new tractors and harvesters, so he is developing a reservoir of skilled labour.

If the water resources can be better harnessed, as they are beginning to be, then land there will become far more valuable. Irrigation can transform land use and land prices, sometimes dramatically. A man of power like the Minister is in a position to ensure that state irrigation programmes benefit his properties and not those of other owners. French agronomists in the 1920s testified to the potential of the area and drew up reports for the Mandate officials that pictured Akkar as ripe for development.

The changes in production methods and investment in new crops after the Second World War promise much higher returns. Muhammad al Abboud's father, a great entrepreneur, has been among the first to see the importance of switching to methods and relations more characteristic of capitalist farming. He was the one who planted those ordered groves of olive trees that stretch out in straight lines over the valley and hills below Berqayl, for he appreciated how much more profitable a systematic and organized production of olives might be than simply using the land for cereals. His son has learnt the lesson. He, too, has no time for the traditional patterns of cultivation and, unlike some of the less far-sighted and less wealthy beys, has worked to transform the running of the estates.

The plain has also attracted investment from the well-to-do merchant class of Tripoli; Muhammad al Abboud knows them all. Their holdings have usually been gained from beys who, by sticking to traditional methods, have failed to maintain sufficient production to sustain themselves in their urban lifestyle and have been forced to sell their lands. The new owners threaten the social and economic dominance of the lords as they acquire control of larger areas of the plain. Everyone speaks with a certain condescension of those landless families of lords who now occupy modest apartments in Tripoli and spend their time trying in vain to cobble together enough income to appear to keep up a status they no longer possess, reduced to the position of clients and dependents on their more successful cousins.

The Minister therefore has many reasons for planning to make the sahel a more rationally exploited economic resource. His murafiq companion may speak enthusiastically of the days when the beys exercised their horses down there on the flat land, as their grooms still do in this region famous for its riders and bloodstock, but the Minister is concerned with the future and with a different kind of world.

Extensive agriculture based on grain cultivation using old techniques, implements, modes of labour organization and accounting will therefore no longer suffice in a rapidly changing Lebanon where the Akkar appears as an impoverished peripheral zone, literally and figuratively 'on the borders'. Increasing profitability on the estate can be translated into diversification of investment in urban property and business companies, essential given the general trends of the Lebanese economy and society. Business and the professions are beginning to dominate more and more. Landownership has been slowly losing some of its social importance for membership in the political élite and the National Assembly. Muhammad al Abboud's father had grasped that reality more quickly than most of his peers. How else have the château and the palace been built? How else has electoral success – until this last worrying reverse of 1951 – been achieved?

Land means labour and the control of labour. In a thinly populated region such control has always been a preoccupation for the beys and a source of competition between them. In his villages and domains the Minister, like all the major lords, uses different arrangments: sharecroppers with various kinds of tenancies, small leaseholders, a rural proletariat with nothing but their labour power to sell in exchange for subsistence, and day labourers usually from the Alawite mountain at harvest time.

Across the wadi and the cemetery to his left is that area of Berqayl called the *Zawiya*, the main quarter of the labourers. Men say it is the oldest part of the village. The word itself designates a centre or meeting place, devoted in this case to the shrine of a long-dead local holy man, Seyyid Omar. Though no centre exists today, still the name remains for the area of the village identified with the fellahin. The holy man's resting place is not a focus of a *mulid* celebration to mark his birth or death day, and no collective social occasions take place at the low, domed shrine. Here, too, the power of the

beys has excluded any public, communal marking of identity around a figure
so closely associated with the peasant quarter and a time before the coming
of the lords. Yet individuals and families still visit the Seyyid's tomb, visible
in the upper part of the cemetery above the road. Fellahin men and women
come to its cramped and dusty space, empty but for the low, rectangular
grave, to ask for blessing, favour, fertility, a cure, protection from harm. The
holy man represents a spiritual hierarchy from which, in contrast to the
worldly order, they may hope for blessing in their marginal lives.

To be a fellah is a classification of status indicating that a person is born
into the lowest social stratum, not a description of their occupation. Fellahin
are at the bottom of the social hierarchy in the village and throughout Akkar,
regarded by the Minister and his peers as mere instruments in the system of
the beys' dominion.

To Muhammad al Abboud on his balcony, the narrow earth paths that
separate one cluster of houses from another are invisible. The Zawiya appears
as an undifferentiated mass of stone shelters clinging tight and huddled to
the hill. None of the houses have electricity, nor running water. None of the
inhabitants are educated in any formal way. A few of them have learnt the
Quran, or parts of it, by heart from a couple of the self-taught older men
who claim to be from a family of 'sheikhs'. One such sheikh is known to
have several books of a religious kind in his house, but he is unique.
Familiarity with any books, let alone those dealing with the power of religion,
is rare.

The Minister knows what he needs to know of the names, marriages,
incomes and loyalties of all those living over there on the hill. He knows the
different 'houses' or family groups of the fellahin by name. But he does not
regard them as 'houses' in the honorific sense. Some of these groups are
very small, only two or three individual dwellings and no more than a dozen
or so people. Others are much larger. The houses of some fellah beits are
packed close together, others are much more scattered. A few have established
themselves in the valley below the village. All are tied to him and the other
beys by the need for access to land, for work and for protection from
arbitrary actions at the hands of the overseers and administrators, or from
a rival lord.

Companions and servants keep the Minister well informed with the
practical knowledge of relevant daily affairs among the fellahin. It is a
traditional attribute of a great bey to 'know everything', and Muhammad al
Abboud's father is particularly notorious among the labourers for his extraordinary awareness of every aspect of his domains, even, they say, of each
individual sheep.

Only exceptional circumstances take the Minister to the Zawiya personally
– fellahin come to him and not vice versa – but he is aware of the residence
areas of each group in the tightly packed primitive houses clustered on either
side of the road that winds in a long S-bend down from the mountain. He

can see their dwellings on the higher part of the hill; further down the slope, houses are hidden from his sight by the curve of the land and by the almond trees whose delicate white blossoms make the village look so beautiful in the springtime.

The Minister deals regularly with the fellahin, though usually through his deputies and organizers. Sharecroppers or day labourers, the fellahin harvest cereals, almonds and olives; they plough and sow or apply fertilizer (including the recent chemical fertilizer that is part of the change in methods of certain landowners). Some move down to the coast for the spring and summer months to cultivate, and then come back up to the village for winter. Others prune the olive trees, act as watchmen, herd sheep and goats or cows. They build the houses and animal pens; they work a lord's land-clearing project, or make new paths, or maintain the shallow terraces of olive trees on the low hills opposite. They are donkey or camel drovers plying back and forth between the village and the plain. Many will perform most or all of these tasks while working small subsistence plots of their own, if they have them.

Until recently the beys could exact obligatory labour service, a *corvée*, taxes, 'offerings' to the lords and other customary dues; that was how the road to the village from the plain had been built. A fellah would still find it extremely difficult to refuse any demand Muhammad al Abboud chooses to make on his time and effort. He might be beaten and the shirt ripped from his back for his presumption.

Women and children are at the lords' command too: they are even cheaper than the men. Groups of women from the poorer families of this village and the neighbouring one just to the south bring in the grain or maize harvests, along with boys and girls from eight or nine years old and upwards. Such families cannot afford to restrict their women to the house or to prohibit them from the public work others regard as shameful. Nor can they do anything about the sexual use and abuse their masters are said to inflict. Such is the power, the *saitara*, of the great lords.

A few of the labourers have become aware of the increasing competition for their votes at elections. Thanks to the rivalry between powerful lords, space is slowly, very slowly, opening up for any fellah who has the requisite nerve and adroitness to try to use the lords' need for labour and his family's votes for the possibility of a little cash. Here, too, he risks harsh penalties. He may easily lose his work altogether to Alawite labourers brought over from Syria in gangs and paid by the day at rates lower than those for Lebanese. People who show signs of getting above themselves are dealt with by the Minister's strong-arm men. And now that the Minister is engaged in the bitter struggle to regain his seat in the Assembly, against the wishes of the new President, he is making sure that his men carry out maximum supervision of the fellahin.

Muhammad al Abboud's eyes travel down from the Zawiya and over the bare-sided hill of the village cemetery only a few hundred metres away from his palace. On the far side of the road the fellahin are buried in the customary unmarked graves. On this side and above, ranks of elaborate headstones mark the tombs of the pashas and beys of the village, carved with the deceased's titles in ornamental calligraphy, his status recorded by the form of turban or headdress on the stone. The Minister has often accompanied his father to the crowded funerals of relatives and rivals, and attended the elaborate receptions for distinguished guests who come from all over Lebanon to the last rites of a great landowner.

Permanence, hierarchy, monuments and inscriptions: the aristocracy imposes itself on the space of the dead too. Not only that. His father has a plan to build a large mosque with a dome and tall minaret on the hill by the beys' tombs. Visible for miles to any traveller coming to Berqayl or passing along the routes across the plain, it will stand just across the wadi from the two palaces, a fitting emblem of Abboud Abd ar-Razzaq's eminence. The son can see the large square plot quite clearly from his balcony. The new mosque will be situated to the front, and within its high-walled compound will be a separate tomb for his father that will look for all the world like a shrine itself. But unlike the almost invisible tomb of the holy man whose shape it takes, it will be a shrine of earthly power. The highly visible form is unlike the graves of any other of the lords; Abboud will truly be set apart from and above all the great landowners, in death as in life. The 'house' of Muhammad Pasha Muhammad, the grandfather of Abboud Abd ar-Razzaq, will constitute its own central space on the landscape, in death as in life. No doubt in the fullness of time the Minister, too, will be buried in the same splendid mosque enclosure.

Directly below is the heart of the village, where the incoming tracks and paths meet by the spring and the old mosque. People refer to this space with the same word they use for the whole village, 'the dai'a', for it is the spatial core of Berqayl. The Minister can see anyone who approaches it from the plain, for they are bound to come to this single point of entry. Any stranger will be noticed, and if necessary challenged. The Friday prayers gather the men of the village there, regardless of status, every week. All funeral processions halt at the old mosque. Animals are watered at the spring gushing forth at the road's edge. The beys' cars are washed there. At certain times of day when the men are working, women come to fill water cans and jars and to enjoy their possession of an area at other periods closed to them.

The fortress dwellings of the other beys, including the Minister's ancestors, lie just above this socially central space on the hill to the south and at a lower level than Abboud Abd ar-Razzaq's blue and white stucco palace. One or two cars are parked where horses are tethered to heavy iron rings on the outer walls of these old buildings, but there is little other obvious sign of change. Like the Minister, the lords come and go to the village from Tripoli or Beirut depending on the season and specific political or agricultural purposes. Family heads keep an open *manzul* or reception room when they are in the village: it is obligatory for any lord with pretension to social importance, and the cost is high. Summer is the period when a bey most often resides at his place of origin, combining business with the appropriate lifestyle of one who keeps a great house in his village as well as his urban residence.

Below the great palace and to his right the Minister can see the aghas' solid, rectangular houses built in large, carefully cut stone, clearly lined up facing each other in that part of the village known simply as *al Hara*, 'the quarter'. Further down are two other small groups of agha family houses in the same style. Those are called 'the garden', *al Bustan*, divided into the 'upper' and the 'lower'. Further away to the right along the line of the hill is the *Marouche*, an agglomeration of houses belonging to one particular descent group of the aghas, also closely linked to the lords.

In practice these men stand as much for 'Berqayl' and the ways in which that name signifies a whole web of property and power across the landscape as do the beys. In the day-to-day world of the estates, the aghas are the most familiar and visible figures of a power they both embody and organize. They are not often in the village. Attending on the lord may take them to Beirut, Tripoli or Damascus as necessary. But their main activities concern the extensive Akkar plain. The Minister's companion, Mahmud Muhammad, is seldom in Berqayl save in winter months when there is less to do on the estates.

The aghas have a relation to Berqayl distinct from that of either the beys or the fellahin. The dai'a need not be the actual site of their property, activity or chief residence. They know as much, if not more, about the Syrian villages and the small towns of the coast, where some of them have their lands, as they do about the dai'a in its narrowly defined geographical sense. In the village their houses are ranked in lines and form quarters named and recognized by all. Yet at any given moment the exigencies of the great domains and their own holdings scatter them over a wide area. As a result, they have acquired a breadth of social knowledge and experience that is part of their value to the lords, and an asset to themselves.

The Minister needs the aghas' knowledge and social networks, their agricultural expertise, their capacity for violence. Since Muhammad al Abboud is an only son, and he has no male child, the dynasty is peculiarly vulnerable to physical threat. He always has his escort, as well as his servants, and the rifles or revolvers the companions wear are not only marks of status and necessary for the show of force, though they are certainly that. They are for use. Weapons are a visible sign of the personal power the lord wields, a sign to opponents of the force he can direct in service of his interests and necessary protection to his person. Competition for political dominance is growing more and more acute in independent Lebanon and it is not only in the political and economic spheres that the position of a leader may be challenged.

The French have now gone, and his father's alliance with the Mandate authority no longer underpins the family position, though the estates have been built up and investment diversified. The Minister is forging his own alliances, not least with other important Muslim and Christian leaders of North Lebanon and Beirut. But he is aware of the very personal nature of power in Lebanese politics, and of the dangers of political rivalry. The companions and bodyguards may have to be used, as any Lebanese politician knows.

There is much political work to be done. The next elections are getting closer. The last defeat is a warning of vulnerability. Muhammad al Abboud risks exclusion from the benefits of wider political authority and perhaps even the loss of a large share of power over the region where his father and he have played major roles over the past fifty years. With the President against him too, he must make his greatest effort to mobilize support. His followers are optimistic. They say that it is clear that he will win with a large majority if he is the Sunni candidate, and – is there a hint of unease? – that his opponents know it.

After sunset. It is time to preside in his reception room. Men are gathering to see him, to ask for favours, pledge support, attend instructions. They are waiting for him. The Minister rises to his feet, passes from the sight of those below as he crosses the roof, and goes downstairs.

CHAPTER TWO

Figures in a Landscape: Two

In the Presence of the Minister

April, 1971. The heavy shape of a tall, sharp-roofed building on the hill above us was the first thing I saw on the night of my arrival in the village. We were at the end of our two-hour journey from Beirut. Torrents of spring rain were falling as I struggled to follow the curve in the narrow road in the darkness. Guided by directions from my companion, I swung the old Volkswagen Beetle round the sharp S-bend circling a huge plane tree and then immediately left through an entrance in a wall on to an upward sloping patch of rough ground.

Before me were two adjoined houses with flat façades and flat roofs. Raw concrete stairways led to entrances on the either side. Each house was dark and shuttered, and each was built over ground-floor levels that looked like stables or storerooms below. The house on the left would be mine. It belonged to a minor bey who had not used it for some years and I would rent it for 150 Lebanese lira (LL) a month. Climbing the steps, I again became aware of the large, gabled mansion in the darkness over us. I remember that an irreverent thought of Hitchcock's *Psycho,* with its gothic dwelling and a mad Anthony Perkins, came to my mind, a facetious distraction from my real nervousness now that I was 'in the village'.

The dark form – there was no light visible anywhere – loomed up on the hill only fifty yards or so above my new rented home. My companion, Ahmad Khalid Abdulla, told me that this imposing mansion had belonged to someone called Muhammad al Abboud, who was now dead. Preoccupied by my arrival in a strange place of which I knew virtually nothing, I forgot the name at once. Besides, anxiety, lack of confidence, and exasperation at my failure to grasp much of what to my ears was the heavy local dialect so different from my now faltering Egyptian Arabic, inhibited further enquiries.

I had an additional reason for distraction. My companion had asked me to stop briefly as we drove through the northern districts of Beirut at the start of our night drive to Akkar. He had only been away for a couple of minutes, and returned with a new Belgian revolver. Belgian revolvers were the best, he said, handling its heavy, loaded weight with some pride. He had explained that it was for my protection; a man had to carry one, and with him there I had no reason to fear any 'problems'. I had been uneasy. He was

a short, stocky man, red-haired, not obviously prepossessing, and to me
largely incomprehensible. His confident references to 'protection' had not
reassured me. Protection from what? Since I had never handled a revolver
in my life, the idea that it might from now on be a routine presence and
object of discussion disconcerted me.

When we had come, through the driving rain and on flooded roads, to a
night roadblock 20 kilometres north of Tripoli manned by the notoriously
tough 16th brigade of the security forces, all Ahmad Khalid's confidence
vanished instantly. He panicked. We had no permit for the revolver – permit?
Nobody had mentioned a permit to me before – and being caught with the
gun would mean serious trouble. What could we do, what could we do?
Suddenly, without any warning, he stuffed the gun down between my back
and the driving seat saying that as a foreigner I would not be searched. I was
at once scared, furious at his loss of nerve, my total loss of control of the
situation, and in no mood to appreciate that he might have been right about
our only hope.

I had not been searched. The soldiers had little interest in us and waved
us on without my having to utter a word or offer my passport for inspection.
The gun was put back in its chastened user's pocket. Was this the man who
would guarantee my protection? Were those friends and contacts in Beirut
who had warned against the wildness and violence of the region perhaps not
merely showing the sophisticates' stereotype of the rural backwater but
referring to reported realities, and was I already even farther out of my
depth than I had imagined? It was my first lesson in the rhetoric of manliness
and its sometimes comic realities, though I did not realize that at the time.

We took the right-hand fork where the main coast road divides, following
the route that moves inland from the coast and leads to the Syrian border
and the cities of Homs and Hama beyond. Only a few hundred yards further
on Ahmad Khalid indicated a sharp right-hand turn on to a narrow road that
was difficult to follow in the bad visibility because of the heavy rain and
tricky to navigate with its lack of curbs or markings and the ditches and trees
on either side. We passed through a village after a mile or so, and then up
over a line of foothills into more open country through regularly planted
lines of olive trees. A mile or two more, and we were in Berqayl.

I had come to carry out anthropological fieldwork in the Lebanon and
had recently settled on the idea of doing research in the Akkar. A Lebanese
friend whom I had first got to know when we were both at Harvard in 1967
had found me a contact in Beirut, a businessman, who could 'broker' my
entry to a village in the region. I was particularly grateful because it had
proved difficult to find out much about Akkar from published sources which
were scanty and, apart from the Institut de Recherche et de Formation en
vue de Développement (IRFED) government development report volumes
of 1960 and a few newspaper denunciations of 'feudal' tyranny, uninformative.[1]
My contact's father, also a businessman, was from the only really wealthy

village up there in the far north, a population of Greek Orthodox whose wealth was based on several generations of successful emigration to the Americas. The old man, who appeared to be in his seventies and spoke only Arabic, was still trustee for a now deceased great landlord's estate. The dead man was from a large Sunni Muslim group of families who regarded themselves as coming ultimately from one ancestor back in the eighteenth century. They were called the Mir'abis and dominated landholding in Akkar, a region in which the majority of the population were Sunnis, though there were also Greek Orthodox and Maronites.

The father told me that my entry could only be through 'the beys', as the landlords were called. I could not simply turn up in a place and make my presence known to the appropriate officials or important persons. Furthermore, it was appropriate for me to have a 'companion' to whom I should pay 150LL a month to act as attendant with formal responsibility for my well-being. He nodded towards a man sitting smiling in the corner of the room: Ahmad Khalid Abdullah. Since I was single this man's wife would cook and wash for me, those were two of the services for which I was paying. But first I had to meet the widow of the great landlord, for it was she who now owned the estate. My protector or 'companion', Ahmad, worked for her as a bodyguard and labour organizer and his attachment to me would be a mark of the link that guaranteed my presence. Her approval was essential.

I had gone to her luxury apartment in Beirut. The idea that I would live in the village seemed to amuse her. Why would an Englishman want to spend all his time in Akkar? Attempts to explain my interest in social history and anthropological research had not noticeably diminished her amusement. What could I possible study up there with those people? Wouldn't I find far more to concern me here in Beirut, in the capital, not to mention a social life which the village could not conceivably provide? I would surely be terribly bored. Clearly she found it a bizarre, if apparently harmless, project.

A boy of fourteen or so entered the room. His mother introduced him: 'my son Muhammad'. He was on holiday from his school in Switzerland. I was slightly puzzled that he should be sent away for education, given the range of excellent private schools to which Lebanese of that class could send their children, but thought no more about it. The boy was reserved, as is proper and polite before adults and strangers. He and I did not talk to each other beyond the initial greetings, also correct etiquette in the circumstances, and he soon left us.

The interview over, the lord's widow indicated to me that my stay in this particular village might take place under her aegis. The old agent had already told me that if I wanted to work in the north, this was the only arrangement he could make. He had thought of another village, quite near to the one I was to go to and the seat of a member of the National Assembly, but had decided against it, for reasons I was never to discover. So, if I was determined to go to Akkar, Berqayl was the only choice.

I was indeed determined, though I knew it would seem a slightly odd choice to some colleagues. My head of department in Manchester University, Emrys Peters, who only the previous year had himself worked in Beit Mary, a Maronite village in the mountains just above Beirut, urged me to study a Druze community and to interest myself particularly in their religious life and practices. This would in some sense have been a continuation of themes in my doctoral research in Egypt on Sufi brotherhoods carried out in 1964–66. But quite apart from my feeling that such a project might sound fine in theory yet turn out to be extremely hard in practice, I had had enough of studying 'religion'. I felt out of my depth, deeply uncertain about whether I had understood anything at all about Sufi groups, and suffocated by the weight of other peoples' certainties and symbols. I wanted to do something quite different.

I found far more interesting the possibility of doing research in a region described in the Lebanese newspapers, surveys and reports as *the* archetypally 'feudal' and 'underdeveloped' area of modern Lebanon. The workings of what sounded like an extreme form of political domination had not been studied. I wondered how a social universe of what were sometimes called latifundia of great landlords and dependent labourers – a universe to whose poverty, overt coercion and violence the newspapers made reference – related to the very different world of a rapidly developing Beirut and to the powers of the political centre. Sociological instinct told me that words like 'traditional' and 'feudal' concealed more than they revealed, and that the region was probably not at all the unchanging, archaic world it was portrayed as being.

I had sympathies with 'the left' in politics. The Palestine Liberation Organization, already a major force in Lebanon, had become a central figure in radical discourse at that period and I was reading about its struggle in what was called Third World literature. Accounts in the local Lebanese press of exploitation and of peasant revolts against landlords in Akkar had an obvious interest for me, all the more as I had been much impressed by comparative work on landlord–peasant relations in the modern world. 'Under-development' seemed more to be what certain states, classes or groups did to others than merely the abstract and politically neutral condition of those who were neither 'modern' nor 'western' in modernization theory. Influenced also by my reading of Max Weber more than by any other intellectual source, I wanted to study the processes of power and status honour which character-ized the latifundia. Much political economy appeared to me to be economistic and to leave out the political dimensions, as well as paying only limited attention to small-scale empirical research.

In the light of these interests, south Lebanon was one possible area for research, for it, too, was characterized by 'feudal' landowners and an agrarian regime of great harshness. But Lebanese colleagues counselled me against such a choice, suggesting that it was too politically difficult, given the significance of Palestinian settlement there, local tensions, and occasional raids by the Israelis. Akkar, I thought, would be the place to go.

On our arrival at Berqayl that night we were met by a couple of my companion's small children, and another man who looked to be very poor. It was explained that he worked as a labourer for the woman landowner I had met in Beirut. He had no teeth and I found his speech impossible to comprehend. We all took warm milk and bread and spent what to me was an excruciatingly awkward hour in the chilly bare house sitting together, an hour in which I could make virtually no contribution to the desultory talk. I at last felt able to say that I would like to go to sleep and they all left.

Next morning, my first in the village, I was woken before sunrise by what turned out to be two camel drovers who kept their beasts' feed in the ground-floor storage space below my bedroom. Still tired I wandered into the empty kitchen but realized that I had no way of making tea as there was neither stove nor kettle, nor indeed any cutlery or crockery. I looked out of the back windows of my bare, four-room house and up the stony hill behind and had my first shock. The building above me, the enormous villa I had glimpsed last night, which dominated Berqayl and the valley below, was only an empty concrete shell beneath its sharp angled, red-tiled roof. There were no doors, window-frames or shutters. It was open to the winds. I could see the mountain slope through the window-gaps in its walls.

A child about six years old banged on the door and asked me to come down to see his father, my companion. I had tea and bread with him at his house only two minutes away from my own, and noted how basic the family dwelling was. A rough stone wall enclosing a small unpaved courtyard in front of two rooms built in the same stone and mud. Up an open staircase on the right-hand side one reached another room whose window faced the Zawiya, furnished with five or six wooden-armed chairs covered with cheap material. This was the space where visitors were received.

I returned to my new home. Half a dozen young men arrived shortly after, climbing up the flight of steps and walking along the narrow balcony to knock at the tall double doors. They were led by my companion's eldest son, a quiet, self-contained person of eighteen or so whose task it was to escort me everywhere and answer any of my needs. I realized that they were performing a social duty. As a visitor I would be constantly attended and should never be left 'alone', that would be a shameful lack of good manners on their part. These young men, late adolescents mostly, were responsible for carrying out the wishes of their elders and for fulfilling the necessary tasks of hospitality. They were here to attend me, as well as to satisfy their curiosity to see what this bey's house looked like and to assess its, and his, social standing. They did not seem to think too much of either.

All were intrigued by the stranger's arrival, appropriately deferential, but puzzled by what I could possibly be doing there. It seemed fairly obvious that they were even more puzzled after my attempted explanations. What could one study *here*? I was aware that I was not making any sense with my talk of 'history', and lied, saying that I was working for a doctorate, in the hope that that would at least serve as a goal and reason for my presence. Not only was I then trapped with the guilty feeling of having lied, but if anything my story made the bafflement greater. No one could see how Akkar could possibly be linked with a foreign university sending someone out to 'study', let alone for something called a 'doctorate'. There was 'nothing here', they said. How I could find the situation of 'interest' and what interest I might have in doing so was as puzzling as ever. But they were far too polite to persist.

We were speaking in Arabic, and the information that no one in the village spoke either English or French pleased me. It meant I would have no choice but to learn local idioms without having a privileged interlocuter with whom I would be tempted to speak my own languages. At the same time this linguistic imperative intimidated me because I was missing so much of what was said and felt a fool, given that I had spent two years in Egypt and had a degree in classical Arabic from Oxford. I did note, however, that they referred to themselves in a derogatory way as 'stupid' and 'uneducated'; other people in Lebanon spoke several languages and were knowledgeable, but they were just 'without learning'. One or two of them, my companion's son among them, was doing the *brevet*, and would learn their results very shortly. But others had apparently dropped out of school.

They took the opportunity to inspect the four bare rooms of my living space, empty but for a bed in the bedroom, a side table, two small round-backed armchairs of a certain age with musty pink covers in the sitting room, a large wooden desk with a single drawer in what must have once been a dining area next to the kitchen, and the kitchen itself off which there were the shower and the toilet. The floors, in what looked like a kind of imitation marble, had no coverings. The main reception room, some twenty feet square, had no furnishings save for the armchairs. The large windows all had shutters and ornamental iron grills. From the front I could look directly out on to the great tree by the old mosque and the centre of the village a hundred yards below. A single electric lightbulb hung down unshaded from the centre of the ceiling of each room. The shower, with its slender cylindrical wood-burning stove, provoked surprised comment – they had never seen one in the village before and wondered if it functioned properly, which it did. The kitchen tap worked, but I would need butagaz and a gas ring if I wanted coffee, which in any case someone else would always offer to make for me. Clearly nobody had lived here for some time.

The young men told me that the house was usually kept closed like the one adjoining it, which was also owned by a bey, the brother of my landlord. There was some derisive joking about the latter, but I could not catch the point of it and felt worse about my lack of comprehension of the accent and idioms. My own Egyptian accent was commented on and they talked about the Egyptian films they went to see in Tripoli from time to time.

I, of course, had difficulty remembering everybody's name. Their references to who was what kind of family relative to whom were too quick for me to keep in my head. A typical start to fieldwork.

The young men offered to show me the palace above, using the Arabic word *dar* appropriate for such grandeur, however incongruous the term now seemed given its condition. We climbed up the rocky ground from the back door of my new home to the ponderous grey structure. When we entered the building the shebab, the lads, began joking and starting mock arguments with each other, allowing themselves behaviour which they had, up to that point, suppressed in front of the high-status newcomer. Some ran from floor to floor of the completely bare building, calling out and laughing.

All the furniture, fixtures and decorations had disappeared. The piping had been ripped out, the wiring too. The place was just a concrete shell. Paradoxically, it looked as if the construction had only just been completed and was ready now to be taken over by the new owner.

I was baffled by the reality of its still inexplicable desolation. The lads were talking about the thefts from the building by a young man they obviously knew: 'What a devil he is, he'd steal anything.' One or two said that it was dishonourable to behave in that way; it was shameful. They got little response to their piety.

We climbed up four stories to the roof balcony where, they told me, the great bey Muhammad al Abboud used to sit looking out over the village years ago. The shebab all knew the name and the story, for their fathers and elder brothers had told them. They were too young to remember the Minister personally yet they spoke of him with a certain familiarity: 'This is where he had his seat. Up here on the summer evenings' one said to me, though I as yet had little idea of who this vanished figure might have been or what he represented. 'He was the lord of the whole village', said another, '*rabb ad-dai'a kullha*'. The grandiose ring of the phrase lodged it in my mind and, later that night, in my notes. I was far too unfamiliar with the language to realize that it was part of the conventional rhetorics of power and boasting.

We walked back across the balcony and down the stairs to the floor below. There was an atmosphere I could not quite grasp – of daring? – an odd excitement, even unease? Then I realized that there was one room, and only one, which still had doors. Why was it so different? One young man opened the doors, and they stood respectfully back for me to enter first.

I went in to discover a small room that was quite dark, though shafts of sunlight came in round the door jambs that faced on to the wadi outside. The air was grey and heavy with concrete dust. In the centre, and so large that I had to squeeze past it, was a coffin resting on a couple of trestles and covered by a silk Lebanese flag. 'That's his casket', said my companion's son, 'Muhammad al Abboud'.

'He was a Minister and very powerful', another told me. 'They knew he was going to win the election and they killed him', he went on, trying to provide an account that would seem satisfactory to a stranger whose incredulity and shock must have been apparent. 'It was years ago, in 1953.' He had the matter-of-fact air of one repeating a narrative so common it need not be spoken save to a foreigner like myself.

There was not much time either for reflection or to collect myself. One young man grabbed the flag and tried to smother a friend with it. They both ran out, one shouting mock menaces, the other screaming with what seemed a real terror. Another grinned and said that the victim, a young corporal in the army, was notorious for his fear of death; why, he wouldn't even shake the hand of the *imam* who washes the dead because he was afraid of pollution. But he was caught and mercilessly shrouded in the red and white silk with the green cedar of Lebanon at its centre. His howls and the shebab's peals of laughter echoed up and down the grey dusty stairs, through the hallways and the huge naked concrete reception room.

When the horseplay had subsided the shebab elaborated their version of the assassination for me: Muhammad al Abboud was going to win in the elections of 1953, everyone knew that. There was only one Sunni seat, instead of the rather more usual two for the region after a radical reduction in the number of deputies. His opponent, who had won the previous election, and the new President, who was also against him, were desperate when they saw defeat looming. They suggested a meeting to resolve the issue, and to try to persuade the Minister to withdraw as a candidate. It was a trap, said the young men with great conviction. His enemies had a plan. If Muhammad al Abboud came down the steps of the Presidential Palace with the other candidate after the meeting, that would mean that he had agreed to withdraw. If he refused, he would be left to come down alone, and what would follow would follow.

The Minister came down alone. A follower of his rival was waiting at the foot of the steps and shot him. The Minister died a day or two later. The whole thing was set up, they could assure me of that: 'Everyone knew.'[2]

The murdered man's father, a great bey called Abboud Abd ar-Razzaq, had decreed that the son was not to be buried until vengeance was taken. In cases of honour, the adolescents explained, men interred the body but left the funeral rites unfinished until the blood of revenge had been shed. There were no ceremonies of Quran reading on the third, seventh and fortieth days as is customary. They let their beards grow, and gave all the signs of intent to act to avenge their house. In this exceptional case the body was still unburied, eighteen years after the killing.

Abboud had married again, despite his advanced age, a teenage bride from an agha's family that possessed lands on the plain. She had born him a son who was named Muhammad after his murdered half-brother. The boy was being educated abroad 'for his safety'. 'They' might try to kill him too, for sons grow up with the heavy duty of avenging fathers and may be a danger to be eliminated.

Six years after Muhammad al Abboud's murder, in 1958, Abboud himself died from wounds received during the 'Civil War' of that year, attacked as he was driven through Beirut by his chauffeur and bodyguard.[3] 'No one knows who did it,' said the young men. He was buried in the grounds of his large mosque on the other side of the wadi opposite his son's villa. Abboud's château, just adjacent to the palace, was also now empty and derelict.

The elegant woman in her luxury apartment, the fourteen-year-old boy, and the Beirut interview now become clear. His name, 'Muhammad', was that of the Minister, and his schooling in Switzerland was for reasons more than simple education. My companion Ahmad Khalid worked for the widow of Abboud Abd ar-Razzaq. I was here in Berqayl by her authorization.

One of the lads replaced the flag on the coffin. The doors were shut again, and we left.

The terrified victim who had been wrapped in the flag was described to me as a fellah, from one of the 'peasant' beits or 'houses' by origin. The others were 'all of one beit', Beit Abd as-Salam, and they classified themselves as 'aghas'. Within Beit Abd as-Salam there were four smaller units, each also called beit. The young aghas explained that the village was made up of three social strata in a strict hierarchy. At the top were the beys or landlords, three major families of beys whose houses were in a cluster not far above my own. But they all lived in Tripoli or Beirut and only came to the village for visits, 'politics', or to take a direct look at the administration of their holdings. Next came the aghas themselves, who were closely associated with the ruling groups. Some owned land, one was mentioned as owning 'a lot', and most had been or still were companions or estate bailiffs for the beys. They married strictly from among their agha stratum, and there were a couple of senior men who dealt with what one of the young men called 'external affairs' outside the village, and a larger number of elders who had major influence over any local or internal disputes in which aghas might be involved. Finally there were the fellahin, whom they defined as just workers and labourers, 'poor people'. They mostly 'had nothing' and there were ten or eleven beits which married between each other. 'Fellah', clearly, was a pejorative term for those without social honour.

The day quickly turned into a bewildering series of introductions and meetings as I was taken round various houses. The young men obviously had instructions that I should be escorted to meet their seniors. Some of the men of the beit were away in Tripoli, some were in the army and posted to other regions and I was told that I would have a chance to meet them when they returned to the village. Others were down on the plain working. But they returned in the evening and I was taken on another round of formal visits until nearly eleven o'clock.

It was only much later that night, exhausted as much by the nervous strain of being assessed as by the ferocious concentration necessary to try to grasp who any of my interlocuters were and what they were saying, that I had a moment to gather my thoughts and jumbled impressions together. My companion's eldest son, the quiet and self-possessed teenager, accompanied me everywhere as surrogate for his father and would not consider leaving the house until it seemed that I was actually going to sleep.[4] As long as I sat at the desk trying to scribble down notes while not in fact knowing even quite where to start, his role was to stay in attendance. Eventually I was able to usher him out.

I went back to writing in my red reporter's notebooks. The villa with its presence and absence, its living force and its dead, its fullness and emptiness, preoccupied my thoughts, then as now. It stands at the entry to this book as a mark of the problematic character of power in that universe. Built to demonstrate the domination of a dynasty and its continuity over time, the building seemed to show how unstable and provisional power might be, its reproduction in the next generation brutally cut short. Violence and the narrative of violence were enshrined on the landscape. Akkar was thus initially framed for me as an arena for personal, even murderous, contest between individual men of property for a place in the national state.

The force of that construction for a long time made it difficult for me to see another order of the problematics of power: what were the conditions which made possible and deeply plausible such narratives of coercion and social order produced by the will, pleasure and acts of the great lords?

Moving through the Story

The empty mansion was the site of my first participatory experience in the village of narratives as social action. The social circumstances of the narrative occasion were relatively simple, if locally unusual: multiple narrators, young and not yet fully adult males drawn from both agha and fellah families, addressing a foreigner of higher, if somewhat indeterminate status, with whom they had no previous acquaintance. The place was central to the narration. The building's concrete space materially anchored my responses as the young men transported me physically and indexically through the story: the view over the landscape from this balcony here, down those stairs, through these doors, in that flag-covered coffin.

The account proceeded through the real time of our movement from place to place, the time of telling the story, and through its own tenses and modes (which I here give in English as I 'translated' them at the time to myself and in my notes, and not in the Arabic of the original): the Minister 'used to' sit here, he 'was killed' just before the elections of 1953, the coffin 'is' here, it 'would be interred' if revenge 'were taken'.[5]

Memory thus took an active, collective form in the empty villa with its single, closed room. Past articulated present. The narration looked forward as well as back, to different imaginable futures as well as a remembered past that was part of the contemporary historical imagination of the community.

It passed from the generalized time of 'he used to sit here' in his village palace, to the specific instant and place of the shooting on the steps of the Presidential Palace in the heart of the capital, to some moment in the yet-to-come when the motive power which the coffin's apparent stillness contained would be activated, realized in an act of vengeance.[6] Then, and only then, the body might be buried, released from its extraordinary hiatus between heaven and earth. The Minister would be moved to his proper location in the grave. His death could be socially and ritually accomplished. Those upon whom the obligation had fallen would achieve social purification. And, on the same instant, they would be compelled to assume that watchfulness against the other's attack, and to make those calculations of strategies and risks that formed part of the taken-for-granted of such narratives.

Or perhaps – an unspoken possibility only explicitly alluded to later by opponents of the house of Abboud – 'nothing' might happen. No revenge killing, no new act renewing the exchange of violence, the coffin not motivating but becoming a shaming mark of unfulfilled duty, a cause of mockery, an empty rather than a full sign on the landscape and in time.

The events narrated were dramatic, the plot of brutal clarity: intense political competition between men of power leading to murder and a vow of revenge. The killing was presented as if it had been inevitable once agreement between the rivals had proved impossible to achieve; the opponent demonstrated his capacity to be the author and prime mover of the story.[7] There was no expression of moral outrage or of breaking commonly accepted norms. The Minister had faced 'a particular kind of pattern of harms and dangers, a pattern in which individual lives find their place and which such lives in turn exemplify'.[8] He had died. A paradigm of political relations between men of power had been, was still being, realized.

The sense and social experience of form, rules, moves and master narratives was established in the telling. The event on the steps of the Presidential Palace was specific, but it occurred within a wider, encapsulating narrative time as if it were only one further moment in the pattern of repeated confrontations by powerful men of a ruling class in 'their' public space. Both Minister and challenger are immortal and immortalized in the story. The narrative takes place in the wider order of 'aristocratic time' and it establishes and secures their identities as persons of power and reputation.[9]

The young men engaged me in a narrative remembering of a past on a site intrinsic to the story; in the rehearsal of a present in which that past was a presence, as coffin and name; and in the anticipation of potential future sequences which, like the coffin itself, were held in social suspension. The speakers' own engagement was itself a narrative element. Not only did their agha fathers play their various parts in the story as companions, attendants, dependents; the sons were all inexorably cast as characters in the present as in some future episode of revenge, or of the equally important failure to enact that socially sanctified task. The narrators, like the site of that particular narrative occasion, were intrinsic to what they told and to the realization of the active anticipations that were socially present in narrations.

I, too, as the structuring and motivation of this book witnesses, was and am drawn into, situated and situate myself within, the animating play of narrative.[10] But I am also in certain respects outside local narratives which constructed 'Akkar' for me, framing and shaping them. My own narrative is also framed and shaped, in turn, by anthropological constructions and discourses, changing theoretical preoccupations, the passing of time, shifts in my apprehensions of Lebanese history.[11] Distinctions between those frames, as this book will show, are sometimes highly permeable and ambiguous.

I have chosen to begin this book, written twenty years after my fieldwork and thirty-eight years after the death of Muhammad al Abboud, with a representation of the landscape of Berqayl and Akkar *as if* through his eyes and in his experience – to see and read the landscape from the unique viewpoint of the powerful. The Minister's domain lies beneath his gaze and he is the focus of men's regard; he is the centre of a landscape formed and given meaning by the controlling force of his possession. This visual/spatial perspective is crucial both to the fantasy and to the actualities of power, to the fantasy as part of the actualities of power.

My reason for this choice is that local discourses of domination constructed men such as the Minister and his father as the creative points from which hierarchy and social order derived. Men such as he were represented as being able to look into, as well as over, the subordinated. Their will, pleasure and command were given as explanations for the unfolding of specific events and, at the most general level, for the world being as it was. This 'myth of the will' is fundamental to the idea of agency and hierarchy.[12]

'The Minister' is a synecdoche, a part standing for a whole; and, located in the empty mansion, a metaphor of a political order in the widest sense. The rhetorical stress is upon the impressive organization, coherence and enduring nature of this particular narrative of power. The Minister is apart and distinguished because of his relations with so many vital other elements which play their singular and collective roles – his father, the companion, the coffee-maker, the crowd waiting below in attendance, those who glance up at the balcony from the mosque area below, the house itself, visible from afar and which men cannot help but see above them, the opponent and the President. The narrative admits of, demands, those competing for power with the Minister: that contest is essential to the content of the story. A permanent vigilance and readiness is essential in maintaining that position on the balcony, smoking the nargileh at one's ease.[13]

This chapter begins the interrogation of the construct of 'the Minister', both locally and in my own initial apprehension of it.[14] Two further questions can then be raised concerning, first, the conditions of existence of seemingly self-evident and self-explanatory power; and secondly, whether there were changes in the overall historical patterns of domination.

The disruption to the figure of the Minister is only the first of a series of different kinds of disjuncture, incongruity and instability which run through this book and set its overall tone.[15] The point must immediately be made that they are not of the same order and that such metaphors also imply juncture, congruity and stability. Thus the assassination of Muhammad al Abboud effectively put an end to a local dynastic project and changed the political state of play in ways affecting many people. At the same time it was the type of act whose possibility was a permanent, coherent part of the narrative and the discourse of domination. Powerful men might perish, lose influence, wealth, property, followings and social place. The coffin was locally an unusual phenomenon, an aesthetic, rhetorical flourish, but there was no difficulty in seeing it as an intensification of an existing imperative of revenge and the uncertain processes of purification after the pollution of bloodshed. Astonishment was for strangers.

The villa had become part of the mundane frameworks of everyday life. What was so startling and almost melodramatic to me in the first experience was unproblematically comprehensible to my companions, and it was to become so to me too as time went by. The building was both extraordinary, beyond tradition, law and expectation in ostentatious ways, and also absorbed into the ordinary, the material and moral landscape everyone knew and moved through in their daily lives. Yet of course landscapes are never simply 'there'; they are culturally and politically formed perspectives and assumptions, ways of imaging and talking of the world. Both palace and coffin were figures of power, and of time past, present and future condensed into the name 'Muhammad al Abboud'. They were representational constructions, which is what I mean by 'figure' in writing of the Minister. That figure and that name were ways of framing history, giving a specific significance to time, and of configuring 'truth' around the cultural axis of the man of power and his capacity to be extraordinary.

That truth depended on a double violation: the villa, already in its architecture a unique form of residence, was transformed against all usage into a habitation for the dead; and the coffin likewise was transformed by being located out of its proper place (and I should add that the closed coffin in itself was an infringement on custom, as Islamic practice in the village and elsewhere requires that the shrouded corpse be taken out of its bier to be laid in the grave). The agent of these transformations sought to impose his narrative of history upon others. Abboud Abd ar-Razzaq, in decreeing the continued, anomalous presence of his son's body there in the building which had represented his social status, constructed a composite, material image of domination and violence suffered and intended. The way in which he did so was unique, beyond what anyone else had anticipated or imagined. In doing so Abboud fulfilled the 'character' of the 'great bey', of the 'one who goes to excess' and becomes the supreme figure of order in negating the order through which others imagine existence. Figure, name, narrative, agent were all part of the discourses of power within which the landscape of the village and the world of the great estates 'made sense'.

House and coffin represented in one dimension an apparent end of a family's authority and of a period in which the village was the centre of Akkari politics. But that coffin was also as if in suspension, a sign of possibilities yet to come, of potential for the reciprocal act of bloodshed and another change in the relations of power. Who might execute it? Abboud had had this other son, but no one thought him the likely agent who would cleanse the shame of Muhammad al Abboud's murder. The boy in Switzerland had essentially been sent into a safe exile and was discounted as an instrument of vengeance. But there were the old lord's nephews on his sister's side who intended, it was said, to fulfil their duty one day by killing the still living and still powerful rival. So the villa was not merely inert space with a macabre, closed room. It was a gauge for a possible future, a constant reminder and summons. If people strolled past without giving it a second glance, there was nonetheless a sense in which the Minister remained an active sign and a real presence, still a figure in the landscape over which he had once gazed on summer evenings.

His father, Abboud, had made him so. As in life, so in death Muhammad al Abboud had essentially become a character in his father's narrative of the House of Muhammad Pasha. Men indicated the palace and the closed room to say that that was what Abboud had done. The old man's will was memorialized and made an active part of the physical environment of the village, just as it was in his ostentatious mosque and his own, uniquely elaborate tomb that was itself a shrine of power. Abboud determined the representations and the signs of power, even after his death.

Yet he could not determine their meaning. The great bey might seek to impose himself upon the world, but he could not guarantee that others would participate in his fantasy and way of imagining power and time. He could not guarantee that the unburied would continue to weigh like a nightmare on the brains of the living until the moment of vengeance. Abboud had done everything possible: remarriage, another son, the handing on of vast estates. But the coffin might still come to seem 'empty', empty of significance in the day-to-day world of villagers and national politicians alike. The story of Muhammad al Abboud's murder might not form and structure men's actions or anticipations of what might happen. It might cease to be in the active memory of beys who saw in the Minister's disappearance and in the later death of his father nothing particularly extraordinary but rather an opportunity to create a political space for themselves where previously they had been excluded.

Now, in 1971, eighteen years later, Muhammad al Abboud had been transformed by murder into a figure in an unfinished dramatic narrative. 'Eighteen years' might be a phrase making sense to the visiting anthropologist, but it is essentially an inappropriate way of structuring interpretation. People did not reckon time and action by such one-dimensional and calendrical simplicities. Some people judged the lapse of time as being 'too long', but others urged the avengers-presumptive on and defended the delay. They were waiting for the right moment. Enemies said sardonically that they were merely putting on the appearances of intending something to act but in fact did not dare to play the sacred role of restoring desecrated identity. Was the sign of the coffin heavy or light, strong or weak? Did Muhammad al Abboud still impose himself on the village from his high place or was his closed room only the mark of an exhausted melodrama?

And – to pose the wider analytical questions once more – what were the conditions which made possible and persuasive such narratives of coercion, violence and social order produced by the will, pleasure and acts of the great lords? Had those conditions and the forms of domination changed over time?

CHAPTER THREE

Contexts and Contests

Akkar as 'Other': Planning and Revolt
on the Plain

To understand the conditions of existence of narratives of power we need a greater sense of the regional and national positioning of Akkar at the period of my work. This northernmost part of the governorate of North Lebanon had already achieved a reputation as a contested and threatening space, identified with coercive domination, collective violation. Akkar was represented both as exceptional and as typifying the contradictions of contemporary Lebanon.

> There are no villages properly speaking but here and there agglomerations (about 30) of 15 to 20 hovels made of fragile materials (corrugated iron, dry stone, reeds) sheltering an agricultural sub-proletariat which is essentially nomadic, for it is rooted nowhere: nothing attaches it to this soil on which it is not born since nothing belongs to it (neither land, nor house, nor even regular work).[1]

The Lebanese Ministry of Planning IRFED report of 1959–60 divided the whole country into different zones based on a combination of geographical and sociological criteria. The plain of Akkar was Zone 1 of the Ministry's divisions of North Lebanon. The report went on to demarcate two sub-zones, the plain proper (128 sq. km. out of a total of 176) and the hills above in which Berqayl lies.

Ministry planners concur that the coastal plain is the most deprived region in all of Lebanon.[2] The planners selected the settlement of Mas'oudiya as representative. Four hundred inhabitants live there, two-thirds of them Syrian, all labourers or sharecroppers, and 'their insecurity is total'. Annual income is estimated on the basis of 125 days of work a year at 1,500 to 2,000LL, exactly the same as the agricultural labourers in the village in the foothills a few kilometres south-east in which I worked a decade later.[3] At every level of measurement of the report's chosen factors – health, sanitation, economic and technical, social, educational, leisure and psychological - its rating is miserable, 'the lowest in the country'. Trachoma, malaria, dysentery, worms, high infant mortality are all present; without electricity, sanitary installations, not even a mattress for furniture, the cultivators lived in 'a total promiscuity of persons and animals'.[4] As for the cultural level, 'it is absolutely bad everywhere (zero rating) because of the total illiteracy even among the young'.[5]

The powerful stereotype of a 'peasant character' intrudes, despite the overwhelming evidence adduced by the planners themselves of the real nature of the social situation. 'The peasant seems careless, lazy', they say, citing different reasons for this 'temperament'. But they go on immediately to point to the great difficulties of the cultivator. The climate is unpredictable. Rainfall, on average 1,000 to 1,100 mm. a year, is irregular and falls heavily at a time when crops have least need of it. There are important river resources, yet water management is very limited. Drainage is poor, flooding frequent. Winter frosts and periods of high winds pose major problems.[6] Society creates another, no less serious, problem. The sharecropper and his family have no legal status protecting them, as their contract with the landowners can be revoked each year.[7]

The IRFED report had many readers among the governing strata who saw in it a blueprint for modernization and for the formation of a 'modern' state. Other readers of a different kind also found in its discourse of change an inspiration for a rather different movement. The town of Tripoli, to the south of the plain and its main urban market, had its impoverished quarters, especially those on the northern side of the city on the road leading out to Akkar through the markets and taxi stands of Bab Tebbane. From those quarters, partly populated by impoverished Akkari cultivators who had left their rural lives for the city, came a 'hero of the poor', one Ali Akkawi, who rallied the shebab or young men of his quarter.[8]

Of Palestinian origin, he had read the report of the IRFED mission which gave a scientific, modernizing, statistical basis to his language of oppression and uprising. In the late 1960s and up until 1972, he was a key figure in challenging the authority of the state and the notables of country and city in language that was part IRFED, part revolutionary leftist.

There was not one school, he claimed, not one hospital for a population he estimated at some 60,000 people in the quarter. The parties of the left had failed as much as the bourgeoisie. One must fight for the people, for electricity, sanitation, health services. One must organize demonstrations, attack banks, loot shops, and give to the poor. And one must organize the peasants of Akkar against the 'feudal lords', supported by the state. His group, *Al Fellahin*, The Peasants, were 'to develop class struggle in the countryside' and establish a 'popular armed base' in Akkar on a Guevarist model.[9]

By the end of the decade following the IRFED report, Akkar and the north had become known to newspaper readers as politically unstable and socially agitated in both urban and rural settings.[10] The *Daily Star* issued its twenty-third supplement on Monday, 4 October 1971 under the cover title: 'THE RAPE THAT LAUNCHED A REVOLUTION. THE PLAIN OF AKKAR. WHEN WILL THE MIDDLE AGES END?' The paper identifies Akkar with individual and collective public violation of women and the family in the archetypal act of coercive desecration. The reported rape of the thirteen-year-old peasant girl by a landlord's son before the helpless eyes of her parents, who are compelled to watch by the rapist's armed bodyguards, becomes a metaphor of rule. Rape stands not only for a whole 'backward' agrarian set of relations constructed on violence, but, by extension, for relations of power and property within the modern state.

Victim-participants are compelled to attend helplessly upon their own public degradation. The story is known and told by others in narratives of fear and power. A national newspaper makes it a media event, and a symptom of an oppressive social order. The *spectacular* character of the reported rape in a small rural settlement, like the murder of the Minister on the steps of the Presidential Palace in the centre of the capital, is of its essence. Power is to be personally demonstrated upon subjected bodies.

'Relations between peasants and landlords in North Lebanon combine all the ingredients of an explosion which could shake the nation socially and economically.' Lebanese society itself is at issue, says The *Daily Star*.[11] Though the article does not say so, the centre of the revolt was Mas'oudiya, that same village chosen by the IRFED experts as the representative example of exploitation and poverty.

The photographs used in the text have dramatic captions that appeal to a universal imagery of oppression and resistance: 'While cattle eat, people go hungry in Akkar, where even animals are better off'; 'REVOLUTION: Peasants assemble in a village square with revolt running through their veins'.[12] In the context of a Beiruti readership enjoying the explosion of services and luxury consumerism that marked the capital at this period, the Akkar plain is the 'Other', the contrast term *par excellence* to the world of the Lebanese middle classes. Beyond and outside modern time and space – for it is perceived as medieval, feudal and primitive – the plain is at the same time a symptom of an internal, contemporary, 'Otherness' of life-threatening corruption.

The paper uses an urban intellectual to speak for the labourers. Dr Khalid Saghiyeh was a lawyer living in Tripoli who himself came from an immensely prosperous Greek Orthodox village of Akkar. Head of the union of peasants and workers identified as mobilizing the resistance by the villagers, he was known for his Syrian Baathist sympathies.[13] His survey showed that '3% of the proprietors own 73% of the plain of Akkar, and 97% of the proprietors own 27%', the plain being 25,000 hectares (p. 5).[14] Revenue is divided in yearly (verbal) sharecropping contracts on a mean ratio of 58:42 (landlord: peasant), though it can be as much as 67:33 in the landlords' favour.[15] The average holding is five to six hectares, as it had been at the time of the IRFED survey twelve years earlier. In addition, the weight of costs is often 100 per cent upon the cultivator, though the landlord sometimes pays 50 per cent of the water and fertilizer.[16]

These claims were broadly supported by Stickley and Sadr, American University of Beirut agronomists, in their study on land tenure. They found that 90 per cent of sharecropping contracts, both seasonal and annual, were verbal (Stickley and Sadr, 1972, p. 6), which accords with my own research. They comment on the 'highly inequitable lease contracts' in the Akkar plain, meaning by inequitable: (a) that the amount of rent they (cultivators) paid was more than the rental value (opportunity cost) of the farm; and (b) that the landlord's share of the total revenue was more than his share of the total cost. They reinforce, with better analysis, the IRFED conclusion that tenants had no incentives to increase investment and production.

Saghiyeh's one-year survey of the sixteen small, scattered settlements of the plain with a population of 3,548 out of a total of 180,000 for the 183 villages of the whole of Akkar, suggests three important recent trends:[17] First, half the peasants had migrated to the city over the previous ten years (and to precisely those quarters in which Ali Akkawi had his influence. There was also increasing overseas migration, for example, to Australia); secondly, land was being rented out or sold by the beys to investors from Jordan, Palestine and Zahle (a market town in the Beqa'a valley); thirdly, renting of land by peasants from the landlords was increasing as sharecropping arrangements declined.

The landlords, asked by The *Daily Star* for their views, accused Syria, and by clear implication Saghiyeh, as a person of Syrian Baathist political persuasion, of fomenting the troubles. The beys were not all wealthy men of property. 'Less than a handful' owned more than 100 hectares, while many 'are debt-ridden, and they have large families to provide for' (p. 10). One powerful owner particularly opposed by the revolt, said that the landlords were no longer rich as they had creditors to satisfy and agriculture gave poor yields. Another bey, one of the biggest landlords, expressed a paternalist bitterness at the violence: 'We feel the peasant's happy and sad moments. We share our land with him, to live and let live. This is what we get in the end' (pp. 10–11).

My own research led me quickly to see that 'the landlords' did not share a single, homogeneous class position. A few were both economically and politically very significant at national and local level. The material position and influence of these men came not only, or even primarily, from rural holdings but from urban investments, property, marriages into the families of other notables or 'new money', and positions in key national and local political alliances. The greater number had sold all or part of their lands over the years as competition with rivals, division through inheritance to individuals leading to smaller unviable holdings, and the cost of maintaining appropriate lifestyles of high status consumption, took their toll. The *déclassés* landlords spent much time manoeuvering to place their children in middle or lower range white-collar occupations, or the police and army through the mediation services of more powerful kin or patrons – a familiar enough pattern in Lebanon. Most had moved to houses and apartments in Tripoli or Beirut, and few of the landlords lived in what had once been their home villages, though they kept their houses for visits and might celebrate weddings or funerals 'in the village'. Low returns on poorly managed estates with insufficient investment, debt, electoral failure, and ill-judged marriage and property strategies added to the pressures.

Successful reproduction of status demanded that everything be done to make sons doctors, lawyers, engineers and businessmen by fathers who realized that landed property had decreased in importance as a basis of membership in the political élite. Some had taken advantage of a marked rise in land prices, where the property was close to new state-funded irrigation works, to sell to 'outsiders' who saw in Akkar a good place for investment in capital-intensive and highly profitable crops such as citrus or winter vegetables grown under plastic.[18]

The *Daily Star* spoke of 'vast areas' owned by investors in Beirut or Tripoli, who had been accumulating land as beys sold from the late nineteenth century on.[19] Local people frequently knew nothing of this, not even the names of the more recent outsiders, referring only to 'one from Tripoli', 'a Jordanian', 'a Beiruti'. All other larger plots of land, by contrast, were identified with owners whose biographies and kinship relations were, to one degree or another, known. Landownership, therefore, was to a degree becoming a more abstract, impersonal, market-related set of constraints identified with capitalist, agricultural enterprise.

These 'absent' forces were quite as significant on the plain as the 'present' figures of beys. Too intense a focus on the 'transparent', and almost mythic, coercion of the acts of desecration and violation might actually conceal the power of these different, yet no less violent forms of relations of production for the cultivators.

The beys' chief claim to a shared status lay in the genealogical trees which took them all back to a single ancestor in the seventeenth century, but they did not occupy the same place in terms of relations of production, or what Max Weber called life chances and position in the market. Yet those claims to a collective, historic status honour had their weight. 'Genealogy' ordered time, space and narratives. Fellahs and aghas knew, and had good social, political and economic reasons for knowing, the names of the different beys of different families, narratives of their histories and of how they were related through kinship, sometimes in more detail than beys did themselves; who owned, had sold, had bought exactly which named olive grove, citrus garden, or plot of land; who had married whom, who was winning, who losing in political manoeuvres; who had risen over time, who fallen. For many reasons, therefore, men would refer to 'the beys' collectively as a dominant stratum with whom they had always, in many forms, to deal. 'The landlords' were still the frame and context of the cultural and material discourse of everyday life.

Between Plain and Mountain: the Village of Berqayl

The significance of 'the village' in the histories, life experiences and culture of different strata varied greatly. It is that diversity I want to sketch briefly at this point to give the reader the necessary elements of context for what will follow in the rest of this study.

Berqayl is situated in the second line of foothills up from the coast at the foot of the mountain, looking down over the plain. People spoke of it as part of a region called the *Qayta'*, which extends up to the major mountain settlements of Fneidek and Michmich above and is almost entirely Sunni Muslim in terms of religion.[20] Before the village lies a mini-plateau area, planted in olive trees which are the main local cash crop. Controlling the road leading up to the Jurd or mountain, and with easy access to the coast and the Tripoli–Homs line of communication, it is not difficult to grasp the military and strategic values of its position and attraction for the three descent groups of beys who had based themselves there since the eighteenth century. The plain, the sahel, had been well known as a place where 'the beys used to ride their horses', a phrase often used in reference to a not distant past before Cadillacs and Buicks replaced the horse as necessary marks of aristocracy and display.[21]

Official figures in 1967 for those holding identity cards with Berqayl as their place of origin, but *not* necessarily resident, give a total population of 3,210 (1,757 males and 1,453 females), all Sunni.[22] But there were those who had moved down to Tripoli, or were away in the army and came back irregularly on leave, or those fellahin who once lived in the village but were now permanently on the plain. The population changed markedly by agricultural season and work opportunities. In the summer the tractor and harvester drivers, nearly all from agha families, would go off for three to four months as far as the Gezira of northern Syria and the Beqa'a valley in eastern Lebanon to bring in the harvests. The same men might look for construction work in Tripoli or Beirut, using their much sought after skills in a booming sector of the Lebanese economy.

Poorer cultivators worked some 120–150 days a year on the plain (June to October), or on one or another of the beys' nearer landholdings. Some stayed in shelters where they were cultivating. They might plant summer (root crops, sometimes tobacco, carrots and tomatoes) and winter crops (winter wheat), leaving a son on the plain all year and, if they were desperate for cash, getting daughters to work for the family or as day labourers for others at 3LL a day, half the wage of men. If the crops were bad or the market prices went down (for example, because Syria stopped importing tomatoes from Lebanon, as happened while I was there), they would borrow money from Tripoli brokers at rates of up to 25 per cent. In the winter months they returned to the village and 'sat', the word men used for times of inactivity and increasingly for 'unemployment', the shameful state of being workless.

Those who were styled aghas, especially the older men, had their own intermittent relations to the material space of the village. The senior men had spent their whole lives associated with beys' families whose properties had stretched well into Syria. Land nationalizations there of 1958 and 1961 had effectively ended the landlords' power and made them rely on their holdings in Lebanon proper. But until those nationalizations aghas had been accustomed to living and owning land themselves 'in Syria' (as well as near Berqayl or on the plain), sometimes bringing up their children there, over-seeing sharecropper production, controlling the cultivators, and engaging in land disputes that were more often dealt with by staff, knife and gun than with lawsuits. At the time of my fieldwork in 1971, such men had only been more permanently 'in the village' for thirteen out of their fifty- to seventy-year lifespans. They had gone back and forth with their beys to Beirut or Damascus, attended on them as honoured companions in their reception rooms, and defended their own reputations as men capable of facing and issuing challenges. Their sons had frequently followed in service to the same beys and now worked as bodyguards and drivers according to need. The beys and the aghas had more to do with Berqayl as changing sets of property and political links of conflict and alliance than with the village narrowly defined as constructed space.

The beys themselves had their main residences in Beirut or Tripoli, though they still recruited their apparatuses from Berqayl. The younger men among them would return from time to time for funerals, marriages, or election campaigns. The olive harvest attracted them too, for management purposes and the settling of speculative deals which had been made in the winter months on olive production when they needed to sell olives ahead for ready cash (not infrequently without their father's knowledge). But they participated, or wished to participate, in the glittering consumer society of the capital. Politics and property might demand their personal presence occasionally, but few any longer showed or felt they needed to acquire that intimate knowledge of persons and histories which marked the rule of their ancestors. The village, marked by its keen hierarchical and social honour divisions between strata, had no leisure facilities: no café, no bar needless to say (being a Sunni Muslim settlement), no club, and indeed no concept of 'leisure' in the capitalist/Western sense. Summer evenings in the reception room of the old *dar* might be pleasant for a day or two, joking, playing cards, gossiping with servants or companions, but not too much more. The beys were in and of the cities. The village was boring.

'Berqayl' was thus a fluctuating set of relations and histories of power of considerable spatial and personal variation.[23] My own sense of mapping the village in 1971 drew on men's talk. I found that it was easy to find aghas or fellahin (though not beys) who could tell me who lived in every house in the engineer's diagram, how many children they had, and make an estimate of income which was very seldom disputed by others. Aghas tended to have a more precise awareness of, and interest in, each other's economic position than the fellahin might have of their superiors' internal affairs. Furthermore, agha and fellah alike knew who had been with which bey in the past, where, and with which cultivators. Such knowledge was motivated by practical interest and by the need to place persons in terms of social ties and positions.

There were around 520 buildings that were classified as making up the material construction of the village at the time. However, residence clusters of brothers adding on a room to their father's dwelling at marriage were the norm, particularly among the aghawat. So that what might be mapped as 'one house' would sometimes be a small complex of rooms or, increasingly, separate two-room houses belonging to male siblings who were either unmarried or had wives and often children. In 1971, sixty-two of the buildings, mostly fellahin, were 'empty': that is, the owners had either 'gone down to Tripoli' (23), were on the sahel (9), or had for other reasons of absence left the property vacant.[24] Three new machine-driven olive presses had been built in the early 1960s, two belonging to aghas and one to a member of a fellah family who had acquired property while working for a bey and shown an aptitude for opportunistic and longer-term dealings. There were thirty-four 'shops', selling a very limited range of goods and five of them were defined as permanently closed down; some were only open a few months in the year, some opened irregularly, most were part of residential units.[25] Twenty-three dwellings were single rooms, and fifteen houses were lived in by women without a male head of household, nine of them being widows, two of whom had small children.

I have adapted Maps 4 and 5 to indicate how far the status honour hierarchy was mapped out in terms of village residence. Areas called the *Hara* (the quarter), *Marouche*, and upper and lower *Bustan* (garden) were entirely inhabited by aghawat families. Differences were immediately visible in the form of the buildings and the overall nature of the residential 'quarter'. In the Hara the buildings were all in the older Lebanese style, constructed in large stone blocks with the entry to the rear off the path having an elegant pointed arch. They fronted in straight lines on to paths or what had become poorly surfaced roads. The beys' older fortress homes, built in heavy stone and with a large open reception area outside, and the newer 'palaces' such as Abboud's château, sat close together up on the hill, serviced by their own paved road. Scattered on the slopes just to the north were clusters of fellahin dwellings on very narrow dirt paths that were usually no more than spaces between the walls. Their homes were either built in rough stone and mud, or, increasingly, in breeze blocks.

The main area of fellahin habitation, the *Zawiya* (Map 6), was on the steep hill opposite Muhammad al Abboud's empty villa. Zawiya, a term most often used for a lodge of a religious brotherhood, derives from the presence of the tomb of a holy man just at the corner of the upper cemetery. This was thought to be the site of the original foundation of the village. Significantly, however, there was no collective celebration of the holy man's identity. The *Jneine* (garden), further along the line of the hill and a continuation of the Zawiya, was also entirely fellahin, as was the *Krum* down in the valley below the aghas of the Marouche. Other areas simply had no particular name and people referred to 'near beit so-and-so'. Building was beginning to follow the line of the road up the mountain, and increasingly down the road leading to Tripoli where construction was easier and some of the fellahin families had acquired their own small plots.

The two cemeteries showed the hierarchical division quite clearly. The beys' tombs with their elaborate grave posts marked by turbans and inscriptions detailing rank were set apart from those of fellahin further down the slope. Aghas were interred in modestly marked graves with a small stone on the hill leading up from the old mosque and in a different area from the fellahin also buried there.

Around the old mosque, the plane tree and the spring was the zone people referred to as *qalb ad-dai'a*, the heart of the village, and its major entry point from the roads coming in from the coast. A person in the Marouche, for example, or the Jneine, might say they were 'going to the dai'a', meaning this mid-point of village space. The open bier in which all, bey, agha or fellah, were carried to their graves was propped up against an outside wall of the mosque (see Plate 3). The washing table on which corpses were ritually cleansed stood to one side under the colonnade at the doorway. Most men came here for the Friday prayers. There was no reserved area for women who thus did not attend but prayed at home. If men were involved in a quarrel or dispute in which blood was involved with another family, they went to the upper mosque or avoided such spaces altogether.

That upper mosque, with its grand chandeliered and carpeted interior and high walls, had been built by Abboud Bey. Its tall minaret was the only village landmark that could be seen for miles and the whole building was obviously as much a demonstration of his wealth and dominance as had been the construction of his château which faced it on the opposite hill. His elaborate tomb behind its ornamental iron grill was a square, shrine-like construction within the mosque enclosure.

Hierarchy and social classification seemed to be cast in stone.[26] Spaces were never neutral, but were part of the social universe of the particular group living there. Everyone would be assumed to have a purpose if they came to a particular zone of the village. Networks of paths and tracks, however, meant that it was easy to avoid using roads or to find an alternative route from A to B if one needed to or if there was any reason for not wishing to be seen in a given social zone. Such paths also gave women ways around the village that were defined as less public than the roads and tracks. Men who sometimes came to sit outside a small shop built very near the old mosque where the main road entered the village and owned by an impoverished agha, would nearly always be aghas themselves.

If the young men of school age wanted to 'go for a stroll', a *kazzura*, and get away from the high definition of social space, they ambled off in small groups, or alone and reading a book on a hill track or down the narrow road leading to Tripoli, for that space was treated as 'outside' the village.[27] The school which had been established less than ten years before allowed for boys of the same generation to mix if they felt so inclined. Some agha and fellahin adolescents would do so since they were not yet encumbered with the mature social identities which might make such camaraderie almost impossible. Yet attempts to found a social club or *nadi* for 'the youth' had foundered several times because of disputes over who, agha or fellah lads, should control the finances and make decisions. So it was rare to find a teenager who would describe one from the other stratum as 'my friend'. That status tended to be reserved for young men he might meet working in Beirut or Tripoli. 'Friends', *asdiqa'*, came from outside.

Everyone knew where others would be at a given time of day or night, and what they would be doing. Patterns and places of activity through the seasons were familiar. Word spread quickly about who was engaged for what task by whom, who was 'sitting', who had just got a job in Tripoli, who was planting or harvesting or marketing what and with whom. People knew pretty accurately where everyone would be at a given moment. When men said that they 'knew everyone in the village' they meant this comprehensive knowledge of practices, places and times.

Many, whatever their social position, spoke in 1971 of Berqayl 'now' as 'poor' and 'backward'. They made comparisons with other villages in Akkar which showed what 'progress' could mean in the new houses and consumption goods. People would say that 'the Christians' were so much more knowledgeable, learned, forward-looking than 'we' were. You only had to look at their lives to see the differences. 'They' had emigrated, been educated and benefited. They had a 'future'. 'We' did not. 'Here' in Berqayl there was nothing. It was not that there was any inherent quality in Christianity or Islam which produced such a situation. Rather, 'Christians' were locally assimilated to higher class and status position in Akkar and were credited with having exploited the advantages of privileged access to French educational institutions as well as to their success as émigrés.

I have already said that histories, like space, were framed in terms of the lives and property of the beys. Aghas, too, claimed the honourable genealogy and collective history to which their attachment to the lords and their own position as men of violence and landholding in their view entitled them. Where fellahin were not held to 'have' descent, ancestors and genealogy, the aghas asserted their glorious family and past.

The aghas spoke of their foreign origin. They were 'Circassians', though there was no repertory at all of tales of life before they arrived in Lebanon in the later nineteenth century (some said earlier). The older men had differing versions of their arrival in Berqayl. One said that they had been in the village 'two hundred years'. Their ancestor, named as Kasr by one man but nameless in other accounts and absent altogether in yet others, was said to have fled from the Caucasus 'because he had struck another man in the eye'. People called him 'Jurakis'.[28]

Violence thus plays the motivating role – as in so many Lebanese narratives of origin – whether as physical confrontation, blood debt, vengeance, 'anger' or state oppression which one must escape. His son, Marze, came to Berqayl, while two other sons went respectively to Homs and Mount Lebanon, another quite typical trope of the dispersion of brothers who are fleeing pursuers. Others said they had come from the city of Homs where they had fled from Jebel Druze in Syria after making a revolt. Marze changed his name to Khalid so that his pursuers would not know him (a reason other versions ignore). He married a woman from Berqayl, or perhaps brought her with him from the south. Some said he had a son called Muhammad who had two sons, Muhammad and Abd as-Salam from which the two branches sprang; others said that it was Marze who had the two sons.[29] The origin story was unstable and inconsistent.

The branch springing from Muhammad was called Beit Khalid, and it was subdivided in turn into three, Beits Ahmad, Muhammad and Mustafa from the names of Muhammad's sons. Most of Beit Khalid were down in Tripoli and had been for two generations. At the time of my research they were small landowners, traders, white-collar employees in government service such as education, artisans in carpentry or repair work, owned shops (a pharmacy and a general trading store), or had joined the police. They married endogamously, or with Tripoli families, and only a few married into the other agha branch which had stayed up in the village. One of those who remained in Berqayl, a man in his seventies at least, was the *mukhtar* of the village, responsible for religious endowment land and property (of which there was hardly any), the issuing of identity cards and relations with the governorate. He had been a murafiq (companion) of Abboud and was still responsible for the state of the château and Muhammad al Abboud's villa, and the trees on the slopes behind. People said he was 'rich', with 'a lot' saved, several hectares of land and '100,000LL'. When men wanted to give an example of how an agha could become wealthy and a landowner through years of service with the beys, the mukhtar was one of the two prime examples.

That other branch of the aghas, said to be from Marze's son Abd as-Salam, was referred to collectively as Beit Abd as-Salam. They were divided into four main beits to which constant reference was made in everyday life, Ibrahim, Abd al Latif, Abd ar-Rahim and Abd ar-Rahman (Figures 1–4). The four beits, which were not corporate groups with joint holdings, would not necessarily act together on given issues. Attachment to competing beys with competing interests had, over the years, produced sometimes bitter quarrels, even killings.

Nevertheless, the beits were spoken of in contexts of general discussions of 'the village' and of marriage and descent as if each had its own collective identity. Some held that persons of different beits had different 'natures'.[30] There was some geographical concentration of men in the same beit, particularly in the Marouche area (Beit Ibrahim) and the Hara (Beit Abd al Latif).

Genealogies or genealogical references were made to males only. Aghas would not normally refer to women in any discussion of descent, though they were willing to do so when specifically asked in a one-to-one conversation with someone I knew well. Status etiquette and respect demanded avoidance of women's names or of public reference. Fellahin informants, on the other hand, would often spontaneously give details of sisters and daughters in a genealogy, including their names. Clearly this distinction marked crucial differences in women's positions in the two strata, as fellahin women had often been servants and worked in agriculture and were thus 'known' in a pejorative sense. Women of the beys' families not seldom had their own status as persons of influence and were known to control property, make key decisions and participate in election campaigns in visiting houses. Such a public identity marked a superior class position.

Discussions of marriages involved much cross-referencing to women as sister, maternal cousin, and so on to so-and-so, and paternal or maternal aunts featured quite as much in tracing out links between men as did more narrowly defined patrilineal links. The patriline was a series of statements about honour, status and claims to social position. Where such elements were not relevant, the strong patrilineal emphasis yielded to a much more complex set of cross-reference through women.

Allowing for those who had emigrated or lived elsewhere, there were around eighty-seven males who might, in principle, answer a call to arms.[31] When people spoke of 'respecting' Beit Abd as-Salam this was part of their meaning. And it was one of the reasons why the beys acted with caution, politeness and guile in their regard.

Yet the days when the aghas owned land, rode their horses, and attended on the beys had changed. No less than thirty-four classified themselves as 'chauffeurs', as drivers of cars, tractors or other machinery, or as owning their own taxis; fourteen had joined the army or police, mostly the former; eleven were labourers taking seasonal or daily employment wherever they could find it; six were *wakils*, or deputies in charge of managing land holdings for beys, five counted as cultivators of their own property, four owned shops, and only three were referred to as landowners, while three more worked in public companies such as electricity; two were students in teacher training, one was permanently out of work; another was in jail for an accidental killing, while one 'did nothing and never had'. Most men had done a little of everything, ploughing, gun carrying or attending on a lord, working as a mechanic, selling, general agricultural labour, and many had spent a period in prison following some dispute.

Incomes were thus highly varied. The more well-to-do were those who had their own olive presses (two men with perhaps 13,000–15,000LL yearly from that source, and who knows what from other enterprises, including the rumoured illicit appropriation of parts of the crop on a bey's estate); taxi ownership (seven men with 8,000–10,000LL), or land and agricultural machinery for hire provided a good living (variable depending on property, but between 5,000 and 15,000LL). Then came regular army positions (3,000–5,000LL), government employ (one man was reckoned as having an annual income of up to 20,000LL, allowing for fiddles and activities on the side), and the 34 chauffeurs who often doubled as bodyguards or attendants (3,000–5,000LL). Better-off cultivators with small holdings of their own land or leasing from beys might make 5,000LL plus. Labourers who worked on roads, buildings, terraces or as cow herders might perform other tasks such as olive pruning or harvesting, or take anything they could get on a daily wage basis (1,000–2,500LL). Two men were formally defined as 'wanted'; one slept outside the village but got 1,500LL or so from the bey on whose behalf he had carried out the act for which he had been found guilty *in absentia*; the other lived by robbery, extortion of money from beys, and usually left the village by the early afternoon in case the police or military should come for him.

The majority of the fellahin were in fact still engaged in cultivation, though the word fellah itself was a pejorative term indicating the lowest stratum in hierarchical position rather than a simple signification of occupation.[32] And, very importantly, men of this stratum used the word for self-reference just as they also represented the local order as one of beys and aghas over fellahin.

Of the 334 male fellahin household heads (using Map 5 numbering of each 'house' as the unit), 132 were classified by informants as workers/labourers (*fa'il/shaghghil*) in agriculture earning between 1,000LL and 2,000LL a year on a daily labour basis. Men said of such a person *haltu da'ifa*, literally, 'his condition is weak'. Another sixty-eight were cultivators (*muzara'*) working on small plots with short leases for the most part, with annual incomes estimated between 1,500LL and 2,500LL. Agriculture thus occupied 200 out of the total of 334. Thirty-seven were shopkeepers or traders (a mixed category which includes three barbers, four butchers and slaughterers, two donkey peddlars, two selling from a pickup, and three classified as 'merchants' who set up deals in olives and grains). The majority of these incomes were very low, around 1,500LL.[33]

Now this is all a rather crude snapshot at one point in time. Men moved from one job to another, raising one or two animals on their own or another's account, combining different kinds of agricultural work from hoeing to pruning, labouring on the roads or ditch clearing, running a shop and giving up to lease a small plot or doing both, emigrating for a year to Australia in one case and coming back 'because of loneliness' and 'doing nothing'. The categories men are put into for my purposes here are thus not fixed, though they reflect locals' own self-classifications and the more general terms did characterize men's lives and biographies. Furthermore, households depended very much on joint incomes from different members as and if available. Working sons would be expected to pool incomes with their fathers, at least prior to marriage and they might continue to make a contribution afterwards as well. Thus one fellah had six sons, one in the army, one in the police, one a carpenter, one working in Libya, one raising animals and one in school. Through their help he had given up his previous work as an olive pruner and barber to open a shop in Tripoli and he was probably making 3,000LL. Others had young children only at that time; and if they had girls but no boys they might be obliged to let them work as labourers too.

One last figure. Forty-nine men of fellahin background were credited, on their own account and without allowing for the contributions of others, with 3,000LL plus per year. Seven reputedly had over 10,000LL a year. These were men who had been able to acquire land through army incomes, money from emigration (though this was rare), service with beys that had led to opportunities for skimming, getting cheaper leases, or a job such as inspector of water sources, the capital from which would be enough to invest in six or seven hectares on the plain and to consider planting oranges. Money that had gone into acquiring a garage in Tripoli, or in leasing olive groves with money gained by what others enviously hinted was informing the security services and smuggling, was well spent. But it did not necessarily translate into social prestige or influence.

People differed slightly over how many fellahin beits there were – eleven or twelve was the consensus, though some gave a single household as being one beit on its own. Fellah beit origins were either said to be indigenous, in which case the beit was held to have been displaced from its lands by the beys, or from another area, in which case the founders were said to have 'fled'. Whereas bey and agha narratives of origin were premised on what might be called 'noble flight', following armed confrontation or personal combat and the assertion of power upon arrival in the region, fellah accounts centred upon the displacement of the weak and dispossessed.[34]

Though there were fellah men who were able to give genealogies of their own beit, this was not common knowledge and interest in tracing the beit back was seen as somewhat idiosyncratic. Histories, regarded as structured by subordination and almost servile labour, were little discussed as far as I could tell. 'History', in the local sense of the word *ta'rikh*, related to status honour and was not a word I ever heard used by men of fellah descent of themselves.

The older men had spent nearly all their lives working under aghas and beys on the estates and landholdings. One fellah in his early sixties, whom I met very early on in fieldwork, spoke with enthusiastic pride of Khalid Bey Abd al Qadir, a very important political figure who had been one of Abboud's most significant rivals in the Mandate period and after. 'He frightened (*khawwaf*) even Abboud', he said to me, as if challenging my imagination at such an impossible but true fact. He had ploughed and cultivated some of Abboud's land in Syria *b'il quwa*, 'by force', a typical phrase used of land seizure, and Abboud could do nothing about it. He was 'very generous'. There were no less than thirteen iron rings in the walls of his palace where horses could be tied. Thirteen! My informant almost seemed to dance up and down in his enthusiasm. If Khalid Bey came to his small home village of Amyoun just south of Berqayl, then 'the whole of Akkar would gather at his house'. Abboud used *zulm*, tyranny, while Khalid would never take anything from anyone by force (save, as he had just told me a moment before, from Abboud himself).

This idealization of the generous, fear-inducing and fearless lord to whose palace everyone comes was typical of the hagiography of property and force. The figure of 'the good, just bey', part of whose virtue lies in his being capable of overcoming 'the evil, unjust bey' in violent contest inducing 'fear' in his opponent, recurred in many accounts. The same lord might be characterized in both ways depending on a speaker's social perspective. The capacity to instil fear being a central trope of power discourse and practice it is not surprising that the frightening figure who imposes awe upon others through his transcendant potencies is also 'adored'. Bathing in his light lights up one's own social darkness. The social being of the humblest is felt to be illuminated and given value by that same power at which the fellah trembles.

The same informant, who had eagerly volunteered this story to me on our first meeting, had had experience of both good and bad. Born in about 1909, he became a *khudri* or organizer of sharecroppers with Abdullah Bey al Muhammad when he was twenty-five, a job which he described as looking after cultivation, riding a horse and watching for theft. Under the overall control of a wakil or overseer, the bey had had about four khudris in the vicinity of Berqayl and Amyoun and three on the plain, but the informant was the only one actually from Berqayl. He had actually been in control, *mistillim*, of the village of Semeiya on the plain near the Syrian border. 'Before that I stayed in the village and did nothing.'

Using his position to do the sharecroppers and cultivators small but absolutely crucial favours, such as fixing a better lease agreement or getting a lowering of rent, he was able to buy land of his own. His father, he said, had had fifteen shunbul of land of which two or so were olives, but lost it by force and fraud (*tazwir*) to Abboud. He was able, thanks to his service with 'the good bey', to recover land in his generation. He had begun to prosper, and after what he defined as a 'row' with 'his' bey, he had gone off to work in the Electric Company at the Nahr al Bared river works just north of Tripoli.

My informant thus had, and made great play with having, a superior position to those he had controlled. Certain beys, to this petty landowner, had been a means to rise from 'doing nothing' as the son of a dispossessed fellah, to a position where sharecroppers were under his gaze from the saddle of his horse, the beast so identified with hierarchy. Well, it was not *his* horse exactly, but the horse which the lord allowed him to ride. And for a fellah to ride was a social transformation. He gave me an abbreviated genealogy of Khalid Bey, including details of sixteen marriages and precisely who the women were, and the number of children. The bey's ta'rikh was firmly in the fellah's memory.

Adolescents were going to school, but they were the first generation and only one or two older men seemed to have a book at home – a copy of the Quran perhaps. Many were functionally illiterate. Men in their twenties and thirties had often had no education whatsoever, 'not even going to the sheikh for the Quran', as Abu Walid, a thirty-three-year-old fellah who became a close friend, said to me. 'We don't know how to read and write. How would we?'

Abu Walid had worked from the age of ten, ploughing for Abboud Bey, as his father had done before him. His three elder brothers had all worked as labourers, as did the three remaining younger ones. Two others died in their teens or before and the eldest brother had also died relatively young, murdered in his shop after a quarrel with the aghas (see Chapter 10). This eldest brother, Ali, had had seven children, three boys and four girls, who all now lived with their mother in the house just above that of Abu Walid. The latter 'and Allah', as he put it, looked after them after the brother's killing.

At the age of thirteen Abu Walid had become a *khawli* or supervisor with five men under him, all from other fellahin families and much older than he was. This was a matter of pride to him, and he saw himself as having real capacities as an organizer and worker in agriculture. After a row with Abboud over the amount of hay he was entitled to, my friend had spent a couple of years with no work at all as a result of the lord's excluding him from any job. Finally he had become a watchman over an olive grove for another bey, and by 1971 when we first met he had spent nine years working as a general overseer for the widow of Muhammad al Abboud.[35]

Abu Ali, the father, was in his early seventies and was still living in the single space stone and mud house next door to Abu Walid. His wife was now dead. The house contained stable space for the donkey and chickens in one corner, plastered mud storage containers for grain, meal and straw in another, a corner for cooking, and a fourth with quilts and a mattress. He had started working in the decade after 1910, originally as a donkey boy transporting stones, sand and water to the village, hoeing and raking, road digging or working to clear the paths and roads. He had worked a *feddan* of land (roughly seven hectares) for Abboud for about thirteen years for fourteen *shunbul* of grain a year (something around 1,400–2,000 kilos).[36] The bey owned the tools, draught animals and animal products.

Abu Ali told me that when Abu Walid was small they had lived off a couple of flat loaves of bread, cracked wheat, cabbage, and the occasional rabbit. If he did well he brought in four or five lira a day. The old man said: 'In those times we ate like birds.'

As I became more familiar with narratives of this kind, and to reflect on the implications for an understanding of the society in past and present, the idea of narrative itself began to assume greater and greater importance. The links between the Minister on the balcony and fellahin eating like birds were constructed in telling, and telling was as integral to practical life as share-cropping contracts and the multiple forms of violence that were so constantly expressed and experienced. It is to a general consideration of narrative, therefore, that I now turn.

PART TWO

State and Local Narratives

CHAPTER FOUR

Narratives, Powers, Persons

Every particular view of the virtues is linked to some particular notion of the narrative structure or structures of human life. Alasdair MacIntyre, *After Virtue: A Study in Moral Theory*, (2nd edn), 1985, p. 174.

So (in heroic society) to understand courage as a virtue is not just to understand how it may be exhibited in character, but also what place it can have in a certain kind of enacted story. *Ibid.*, p. 125.

Narratives as Social Practice

This book focuses on narrative structures of social life and enacted stories in a changing society.[1] Alasdair MacIntyre uses the ideas of narrative and story enactment to explore the nature of virtue in an ideal-typical 'heroic society', that of the Homeric texts, in which narrating or singing the deeds of heroes was as integral to the nature of social action as the deeds themselves. In a society in which morality and social structure were one, as he puts it, the telling of stories was not simply a mode of representations set in a context of social relations. It was a key constitutive element in those relations and in the creation of contexts in which name, reputation, authority and a man's *due* were established.[2] Enacted stories motivate and animate the social processes of which they are an integral part. 'It is not just that poems and sagas narrate what happens to men and women, but that in their narrative form poems and sagas capture a form that was already present in the lives which they relate.'[3]

After Virtue derives from a treatment of literary texts. My own writing, in contrast, is concerned with the social practices of narratives-in-use in the everyday life and history of a Lebanese region in the early 1970s. This book is thus based on anthropological fieldwork in a contemporary and rapidly shifting society in which men constantly told stories about, and gave accounts of, themselves in terms of contest, status and domination. Narratives centred on men's due and worth, seeking to establish that deeds were commensurate with claims, actions congruent with words, appearances matching with reality. 'A man has his value', as the Lebanese phrase has it, and that value had constantly to be demonstrated and defended in the unending work of creating and sustaining identities.[4]

These scenes, disputes, conversations, re-enactments and enactments had to be caught 'on the wing' in a multiplicity of situations and only written down by myself after the event. That writing itself was the product of my own translations, framing, editing, interpreting, partial understanding and misunderstanding within the terms of my own anthropological narrative structures.

There were no contemporary written texts, no poems or sagas, no specialized role of poet or singer, even though one service of the lords' companions was to evoke their bey's and their own greatness and valour on collective occasions; and their fellahin were equally expected to 'speak for' the bey.[5] A man claiming status hymned his own and his descent group's praises according to the conventionally expected terms, language, gesture, tone of voice and with the anticipated vocabulary of motives and structures of interests others, though not all, knew so well how to read.[6] He ridiculed, parodied and mocked competing claims. Some were regarded as having a gift for such performances. They had the style and skill in spontaneous challenge and riposte that were so much prized. Others – and they might be of any stratum – were judged culturally incompetent.

Though narratives were fundamental in male social life, rhetorics or performance in trying to give *force* to an argument were not all.[7] The force that was stressed as extraordinary derived in part, of course, from contrast with the unstressed ordinary. People tried, as they do everywhere, to fashion and routinely negotiate accounts of different aspects of the everyday world: of chance meetings, social occasions, minor disputes, political manoeuvrings, family affairs, work, illnesses, births, marriages and deaths. Often it was these mundane narratives, lying as it were in the shadow of the more obviously dramatic stories with which they might indeed interlink, that led me to interrogate the extraordinary and seemingly exemplary more closely.[8]

Questioning Narrative Structures

Men made critical judgements about others', and sometimes their own, narratives. They heatedly debated what constituted honourable conduct in different situations, from the murder of a relative to the suspected theft of a gun, or a fight in a city street. Was it inappropriate, to take one argument in which I was politely asked my opinion, to take vengeance against any save the offender? Or might one choose any man within five degrees of kinship? Or was it permitted to pick on the one judged the most socially valuable to his family?

They frequently disagreed. It was taken for granted that narratives were contested and potentially multiple. Versions of narratives and what accounts were taken to be 'true' emerged out of social negotiations where very unequal resources might be in play between participants.

Narrative coherence might be far easier for one side to assert than for another. Perspective, the place in the social field from which one spoke and the resources one commanded, was critical in the making of such social claims.[9] There were always, at least potentially, multiple and opposing voices which were shadow presences in the most apparently unchallenged narratives. That men should have different accounts was recognized in social life, for narratives were central to the negotiation of the realities of power and authority. The account of 'what happened', whether or not an 'event' had occurred and, if so, what was its nature, always had a rhetorical purpose, however veiled: it sought to persuade or impose upon others, 'the truth' of a situation and a social order. And every narrative of a present event tacitly or explicitly drew on claims and assumptions about the value of different genealogies, pasts and biographies. That the reproduction of social honour and the avoidance of social dishonour were problematic was a given of local discourse.

Men talked about how they talked. They spoke about how they and others told their lives, as they had no doubt always done; and demonstrated, as again they had no doubt always done, an acute awareness of irony, ambiguity and contradiction in social life.

Yet a more fundamental questioning had emerged, for they perceived that awareness to possess a 'new' quality deriving from 'changing times'. 'Then', in their common representation, the virtues and narratives of hierarchy were not in doubt, whatever the flux and shifts of power and property. 'Now' the very ground and validity of those ways of acting, speaking and being was at issue.

What kinds of narrative structure and enacted story were possible in the contemporary world? Just how 'heroic' and 'honourable' could men be in a burgeoning *laissez-faire* Lebanon of which they were not autonomous, whatever the fantasies of self-sufficiency in status might be? Were men condemned to be perceived as presenting false appearances whatever they did? Were their much-vaunted virtues merely an amusing sign of the 'backwardness' of the periphery to those at the centre? In any case, was there, had there, ever existed the homogeneous and coherent 'narrative structure of human life' posited by certain narratives of power and violence? Had the apparent certainties of hierarchy 'then' in fact contained the seeds of the ambiguities of life 'now'? Irony, springing from a perceived and unbridgeable gap between seeming and being, threatened to become the dominant mode, animating narrative and historical consciousness as a whole.

These are my formulations of historical problems being experienced in one degree or another by everyone, but particularly by those who had claims in terms of being bey or agha. Such questionings had their particular contexts too. Men of these strata frequently acted 'as if' things were unproblematically as they had always been: under their control. Not infrequently, things still were. Balances of social force remained unequal. Nevertheless, the fact that such questions did arise in local discourses was part of complex processes which had also made imaginable the public contesting of dominant forms and structures by the dominated.

Histories and Interrogations

'The practice of recounting events in ordinary discourse comes to mediate the emplotment of larger historical events in the world.'[10] The practices of local narrative gave shape and form to far wider processes of social change within the region as a whole.

Narratives may appear to be reiterations of what has been told before and of how it has been told. For enacted stories, to be accepted as persuasive and true, must strike observers and participants (the distinction is often unclear) as just that – performances of scripts, moves, gestures, expressions, intonations and dramatic structures which are both original and conform to practical aesthetic expectation of how such things simply are. Their social weight, their narrative coherence in any given context, depends upon demonstrating that the act is commensurate and congruent with 'the virtues'.

An anthropologist might say with Edward Bruner that 'culture changes as it is enacted, in practice'.[11] The actor, speaker, performer and audience member, on the other hand, recognize a fit with the unchanging schema of storytelling and of what is appropriate. Or they claim to recognize such a fit between person, act, narrative, aesthetic and morality. The particular act or event is held to demand to be told in the way it is proclaimed self-evidently to have 'really' happened. Equally, persons may not recognize the narrative performance as authoritative or plausible.

Given stories are variations on, and framed within, master narratives of history, of the nature of the community in space and time, of hierarchy, identity and place in the world. Master narratives shift too, especially if they are no longer experienced as providing a complete and transcendent context. They may come to seem inadequate in the emplotment of larger historical events, fatally incongruent.

The bases for the contextualizing, framing, forming and interpretation of relations and actions may become visible rather than hidden in the routines of natural conduct. And that visibility, which has arisen in the conjunction of many historical processes, makes the assumptions of cultural work and truth in the day-to-day themselves questionable. To put it another way, repetition of cultural conventions is revealed to be a social fiction rather than a taken-for-granted. Incongruity and incoherence may come to be regarded as central to social identity and to the social world in general.

Repetitions and Re-enactments

'Muhammad al Abboud' was told to me. And retold. My first instruction in the discourse of power and violence through the figures of the Minister and his father, Abboud Abd ar-Razzaq, was often repeated in those early days of fieldwork. Men of both bey and agha strata glossed the names of the major characters, interpreting their purposes and intentions in great or little detail;

they evoked previous events, particularly around the name of Abboud Bey, more or less fully; and they situated his son's death as a critical moment in regional as well as village history, in the '*now*' of the present as much as the '*then*' of the killing, with many or few nuances. Then and now were distinguished, but they were also narratively co-present rather than simply sequential, and each telling re-created that co-presence.

Distinction in chronology and sequence might, however, be critical in different ways for different persons. Speakers used the event of the murder to mark a key point in a much longer history and a much wider space of political relations and structures. Berqayl had been a 'capital' of power and glory, said the aghas. The killing changed all that, since it effectively destroyed the dominant family power of Abboud. Today the village was nothing but a poor place, a place both socially blocked and sinking back into a kind of ahistorical obscurity. No one would hear of Berqayl 'now'. And in the yet-to-come? 'There is no future' they would say, in a much-repeated phrase and an almost incantatory tone, with a characteristic negative tilt up of the head, pursing of the lips, and quick raise of the eyebrows.

Men of the fellahin stratum, at our first meetings, seemed to contextualize and speak of the social world in the same ways. The discourse was of lords who dominated through exploitation and force and against whom men were helpless. But after a few months I became aware that, for some of them at least, the killings of son and father were part of a period of slow, small increments in social and economic standing. Their 'now' was freer, fellahin said; things were no longer as they had been 'then' in the 1950s, which stood for the largely undifferentiated past ages of fellah subordination. Now it was possible for some at least to experience a present in which they had access to small landed property and work other than that of a poor sharecropper. It was possible, too, to imagine 'a future', however vague, inconceivable only some fifteen or so years before; or at least to use the word 'future', *al mustaqbil*, with however precarious a sense of meaning and evocation that did not necessarily have any precision but was not an invitation to ridicule and accusations of pretension.

Younger beys, by contrast, sons of an aged but still influential father who had been a local rival of Abboud but without his political importance, asserted that their father would win a parliamentary seat at the next election, due in 1972, and gain a new source of power.[12] Thick photograph albums produced on my first evening courtesy call to their old-style residence up on the hill where all the beys had built in heavy stone since the late eighteenth century, showed groups of affluent men in two-tone shoes and 1930s' suits at the horse races in Beirut, or at some social function surrounded by notables and attendants. They pointed to this and that figure of national power or influence who was allied with their father, sketching histories in the names of powerful 'friends' and men of influence.

No one else in Berqayl had photographs or cameras; that mode of recording and representing family and past was another monopoly of the beys. For the young beys, theirs was the memory, theirs the narratives and the ways of representing past and identity which a man like myself, an educated foreigner, would understand. It was self-evident to them that if I were interested in histories they would naturally be my privileged interlocuters. For only the beys had, and were, 'history'. Only they could speak and be 'spoken of' as significant and signifying. Only they could be written: one inscribes the families whose power inscribes itself on the landscape and persons of others. I could not, surely, 'write about' anything else. It was a statement, not a question. Their power alone, personal and genealogical, motivated narrative.

Narrative repetition was a powerful element in my own, as well as local people's, socialization. I learnt to recognize typical ways of narrating, plots and storylines as well as styles of delivery. Without quite realizing what was happening, I, too, began to anticipate how a telling of particular events in the lives of beys, aghas and fellahin would unfold. Reiteration and recollection gradually emerged as patterning experience, as patterned elements in experience, and as part of the routines of everyday social life.[13]

I thus heard many other narratives in different genres, some richly comic or ironic, that became part of the increasingly familiar repertoire. Memories were performed: the narrator or narrators frequently imitated the tone of voice, posture, gesture or movement of the protagonists, including dramatic renderings of their own declamations and challenges where they had been personally involved. Listeners were also participant, cueing speakers verbally or by facial and bodily expression responding to, urging on, or anticipating the next phrase. The audience helped to create an ambience, dramatizing particular moments, criticizing the phrasing of the account, interrupting with remarks intended to draw attention to the speaker's way with words or to score a point at the expense of someone else present or of a character in the story, controlling the rhythm and timing of the emergent narrative occasion.

Narratives emerged in different settings and frames: at weddings, the Quran readings and gatherings of the forty-day mourning period, celebrations of the Prophet, when sitting outside a shop, standing around in the road, on formal or informal visits to others' houses, or strolling along a path.[14] Speakers used them rhetorically in argument, didactically, to demonstrate what was exemplary behaviour by a real man (or its opposite), to illustrate the ways of the world, make claims, show off, mislead and deceive. And men used them, too, for the sheer pleasure of it; for the affective charge that could be created by the skilfully timed, shaped and pointed evocation of particular events figured and transfigured in narrative performance.

The cast of characters became familiar to me. Abboud was a major figure, but there were many others – Khalid Bey Abd al Qadir, Ibrahim Pasha, Osman Pasha. All three had been major landowners of Akkar whose villages of origin, respectively Ayyoun, Berqayl and Bebnine were within a few kilometres of each other. And all three had sons active in national politics, competing among themselves as had their dead fathers. Talal al Mir'abi, the younger son of Khalid Bey (who would emerge as one of the two Sunni Muslim deputies in the parliamentary elections of 1972); Jud Ibrahim was in his seventies but preparing to stand in those elections (though he would die a short time before they were held); Bashir al Osman, was a parliamentary deputy, as he had been for many years (but was finally to lose his seat in 1972). Names of well-known agha companions or 'men of honour', the *qabaday*s, recurred in association with those of the beys and in accounts of challenge and response. Comic stories featured men whose pretensions to valour were ludicrously exposed when danger in fact presented itself, or turned on some botched ambush, or on misinterpreted acts which had led to the complete confusion of one or another party. But all the narratives spoke of persons who had played, or still played, a part in local life. I waited in vain for myths or jokes or tales of the distant past: 'real' characters and events were always the armature of the tale.[15]

Other narratives, histories and memories were present and informed men's practices, constituting their social world without being repeated in the performance, dramatized style. People would explain to me, for example, how the olive grove of the orange had acquired its peculiar name, so that I would understand its condensed significance (see Chapter 8). But that account was not part of the narrative performances and I never heard it so evoked. Nor were the accounts of the genealogy of each named plot of land which had passed from one owner to another through inheritance, force or sale. These significant histories of the landscape and of power were discussed and sometimes disputed. They were part of the stock of knowledge at hand. Only if there was a dramatic event associated with a particular acquisition did it become part of the more overtly aestheticized repertoire of performances.

Different kinds of narratives existed that could not be, or were not, told but which 'everyone knew'. Of such narratives I only learned much later when it became clear that in my ignorance I might unwittingly cause serious social embarrassment (as indeed I did). Some were unspoken because of the silence required about acts of polluting bloodshed in which the group's standing and internal relations were compromised.[16] After some months, agha men began privately to mention the death of someone at the hands of his first paternal cousin and the consequent patterns of social avoidance, avoidance which I had not noticed; or how another man had become unpredictable, asocial and a danger to the group and no one now spoke of his once heroic act or responded to any of his brusque, sometimes insulting behaviour. Men would discreetly check on what I did or did not know. I had to learn not to mention certain names or to make certain references in front of certain other persons involved in such cases. Speech might precipitate action by shaming through the articulation of a carefully unspoken narrative of injury into whose silencing prodigious social energies might be invested.

Another, and even more significant, form of silence existed. Women were very seldom mentioned in men's narratives. It was considered quite inappropriate to speak of them. The exceptions to this avoidance involved those at either end of the social scale. The mothers, wives and daughters of men in powerful positions nationally or locally might be spoken of in accounts of political processes in which they had played a part. These accounts showed marked respect and practical evaluation of such women's importance in the ways in which family affairs were run in the furtherance of their aims and ambitions. The very poor women of the lowest social levels, on the other hand, might be mentioned in scabrous stories by the aghas to show how they or the beys used the fellahin. But in general women were not spoken of. I only very occasionally heard sexual gossip and then found it quite impossible to judge how far it was common knowledge or how widespread such gossip might be.[17]

My own field experience increasingly led me to focus on disjunctions which were part of the more routine practices of social life. These were great or small breaks and fissures between and within narratives or rhetorical practices, as my companion's dismay at the roadblock showed. Narrative interpretations routinely pointed to alleged gaps between false appearance and real intention, contradictions of view and opposed perspectives. As I became somewhat more familiar with the patternings of life, upon which I received constant explicit instruction, I realized that these disjunctions were both the product of deliberate purpose and the subject of exegesis by those around me. Men delighted in taking the narrative another had produced of his acts or place in the world, present or past, and retelling it so as to render it comic, or to demonstrate the reverse of the significance claimed by its subject. Narratives were reworked, reauthored, retold to different audiences in different ways, taking control away from their 'author'.

The rhetoric that life was a tissue of calculated performance, aesthetic elaboration of form, artifice, and downright lies behind which one had to look for the true interests and aims of others was common to all. In this sense a violence that was not physical coercion but was of a more diffuse kind and integral to accounts of human relations permeated those relations.

There might be an ideal, often stated, of the transparent hero who is exactly what he seems to be. I was told soon after my arrival of such a man, dead some years before. There was the much repeated tale of how he had seized property documents from the hands of one of Abboud's rivals from another village in the rival's own reception room, in front of all his attendants. With magnificent calm he had issued the formulaic challenge: 'I shall be sitting out there beneath the plane tree smoking my nargileh if any of you is man enough.' He had done so, 'at his ease'. No one had moved against him. His violence was represented as having achieved a kind of epic, narrative purity.

Transparency of that kind was, by definition, extremely rare. The opacity of ordinary social life was represented as reaching its extreme in those to whom the hero was attached. The great men of power excelled in quite different ways. If the name Abboud Abd ar-Razzaq created fear, it was only in part because such heroic figures and other 'men of honour' were associated with him. Abboud and those of his kind were spoken of as paragons of cunning, possessing often malignant and always dangerous insight into others' goals and real intentions; not unusually they went beyond any moral constraint, violating every value of ordinary men. They were feared, not only because they controlled through their ownership of property and labour the life chances of so many, but also because they were capable of 'anything'. Narratives of power played constantly on these themes of concealment, insight and ruthless transgression of the integrity of others.[18]

What I shall call the 'generation of the fathers' among the beys and the aghas often championed the values of 'the true man', who was as he seemed. They attacked the sons as useless wasters of the accumulated patrimony of status. The 'generation of the sons' felt they were caught in a social order where, even if they wished to and were capable of it, acting as characters in their fathers' stories was impossible. They spoke as if they could not but know that this 'as if' involved a collective pretence in which performance had become divorced from social realities.

The sense that 'our' universe of hierarchy and excellence was being transformed by wider processes which could not be represented in our repertoire of description and interpretation was often conveyed to me as if life were structured as a joke rather than the high seriousness of challenge and response. Beys and aghas might represent themselves as victims of their self-deception and of the transformations of a world shifting in economic, cultural and social terms which transcended their own.

Seen from the perspective of those of 'fellah' origin these world shifts represented rather the beginnings, however uncertain, of an access to property and social capital that had only a few years before been unthinkable. Their commentaries on the narratives of hierarchy, as may easily be imagined, often took a sardonic form pointing to the 'lie' at the heart of the stories.

As the months went by after that first day in the village I came to pay far more attention to the passing, ephemeral encounters. One man might take another on in a contest of mockery, or, through some cunning manoeuvre, spoil another's show of dignity, or out-talk and out-insult a peer before an audience. Such incidents were no less significant than the narratives of great events for the practical world of everyday life. Moments like these, punctuating ordinary routines, might be eagerly retold for a day or two by those who championed the winner and then slip out of explicit reference, sedimenting into the reputation of individuals formed over their lives. I could easily miss the importance of such micro-encounters by paying too restricted an attention to the more generally repeated narratives that had been stamped on people's memory and representations of themselves and others.

Different people told different stories, or 'the same' story in a different way, or denied that there was a story to tell. The partiality of the view in social time and space from the top of Muhammad al Abboud's palace is crucial. For there were other views, voices, histories which complemented or contested what the name 'Muhammad al Abboud' represented. 'The high balcony' enables me to emphasize how much that view was available only to a certain kind of participant observer – the powerful. We shall see how much more complex relations of power were as the book progresses.

CHAPTER FIVE

Fathomless Ocean

Ottoman, French and Lebanese officials also looked out over Akkar from high places. These men, servants of an old Empire, a League of Nations Mandate and an independent Republic successively, represented the landscape beneath their gaze through a series of written texts. They surveyed the region, shifting its political, economic and social boundaries as the administrative organization and concerns of the period varied. Through reports, monographs and proposals, they made Akkar known to rulers as a set of resources and relations and attempted to facilitate its utilization and control by state authorities. For in all three cases, as we shall see, the region was regarded as virtually autonomous and beyond, not only central power, but civilization and the modern order.

Written texts were part of a set of representations, political practices and institutions, part, that is, of the realities and facts which they 'objectively' recorded. Through these accounts, the idea of systematic observation as a tool of government and power and as an instrument of truth was realized. Akkar became an object to be observed, measured and, if possible, administered and transformed.

Intervention and development of one kind or another were always the *raison d'être*. Each text in each period shows a conception of 'reform and progress' and of likely obstacles to their achievement. Resistance by indigenous forces, whether political, social, economic or psychological, was found to be multiple. Indeed, in many of these writings, Akkar is constructed as the very type-case of all that frustrates or blocks the state, enlightenment and modernity.

Those for whom or in whose name such observation and reporting was carried out – the Ottoman governor during the First World War, the Mandate High Commissioner of the 1920s and 1930s, and the Lebanese President of the late 1950s – confronted Akkar as part of a set of technical and social problems to be resolved. Officials wanted, within the shifting discourse of modernity and the state, to know how to achieve greater efficiency in agriculture: better methods to harness the water supplies, to change crop types and rotation systems, to introduce new fertilizers or machinery. Inevitably, other concerns impinged upon the purely technical. How did the system of property holdings really work? Should it be rationalized?

But there was an overriding *political* question: what was to be done about the absolute power of the great landlords?

Each of these states itself confronted its own fundamental political problems: of legitimacy, of contesting communal and political loyalties, of unstable regional relations with other states, and of the inadequacy of civil and military apparatuses. None of them – Ottoman, French or Lebanese – was secure or established in stable discourses of power and functioning institutions which constituted a strong centre of government. The officials all struggled towards a way of articulating and regulating the role of the great lords of Akkar. Could they be part of a state narrative of modernity, or did their power completely contradict such a project?

The successful pashas and beys of Akkar, despite the changing central authority, remained the principal political representatives of the state at the regional level. Appointed to their functions and ranks by the Ottomans, they also held formal office and position in National Assemblies under the French, and retained their powers under the independent Lebanese governments of post 1943. Beyond Akkar, they were members of a national class of dominant landowners with a very high degree of autonomy from, and influence over, state institutions. Theirs was the effective writ that ran in Akkar for most of the period.

'The state' was therefore far from a fixed element taken for granted by any of the writers I shall examine. The Ottoman provincial government of the First World War period, the French Mandate Commission of the inter-war years, and the Lebanese Presidency of the late 1950s were all problematic institutions to both rulers and subjects alike. The Ottoman Empire contended with European determination to push for territorial acquisition and economic domination. Its Arab officials, even as they wrote their account of the province of Beirut within which Akkar was included, were aware of tensions occasioned by current Arab nationalist opinion. The Mandate, bedevilled by an inadequate administration, budgetary problems, an authority disputed by Arab nationalists, and rivalry with the British, assigned to its military officers, agronomists and geographers the task of assessing the political and economic regime of Akkar, a newly incorporated border region within a Greater Lebanon created by the French. Finally, in 1959, the Lebanese Presidency, having survived the constitutional crisis and civil war of the previous year, was represented by an incumbent seeking a new basis for the legitimacy of the state at a moment of great regional political turbulence.

'Modernization' was a weapon in the transformation of political authority. The authors of official texts might all adopt unquestioningly the narratives of progress, science and historical evolution from backwardness to modernity; however, as we shall see, their certainties were challenged and contradicted not only in 'Akkar' but in their own political practices at the widest level.

The texts thus yield a great deal of information about Akkar at different periods. They examine taxation, land tenure, landlord–peasant relations, agriculture and so on, often in great detail. But reading them and deciding how to interpret them requires of course an awareness of their unexamined assumptions about modernity and order rather than absorbing the perspective of their own self-perception as the disinterested experts.

Akkar as Absence, Silence and Disorder

Two government officials of the Ottoman Empire ready themselves for a journey into Akkar in 1916:

> One day my companion emerged from wearying reflection and said: Must we prepare ourselves?
> Yes: We must prepare ourselves to plunge into that sea whose depth we do not know and of whose breadth and expanse we are ignorant ...
> If only there were a guide to show us the way ...![1]

Rafiq Bey al-Tamimi, deputy director of the Sultaniya school,[2] and Muhammad Baghat Bey, director of the School of Commerce, travelled throughout the *wilayat* or province of Beirut in 1916.[3] Their journey took them from the south of this 355 kilometre coastal strip of Syria to the northern boundaries – from the administrative districts of Nablus and Akka to those of Trablus ash-Sham (Tripoli) and Ladhqiya (Lattakia). 'Azmi Bey Effendi, governor of this province of the Ottoman Empire, had charged them to write a report which would be 'useful for the study of the general conditions of our country' and 'reveal the truth of our sacred land'.[4]

Their commission had come at a very difficult time. The course of the First World War, in which the Ottoman Empire was allied to Germany, was uncertain and its final outcome known to no one. Ottoman reformers had sought to change the operations and structures of the state in line with their perceptions of modernity and bureaucratic rationality. Other states, Russia, Britain and France, had for some time posed political and economic problems to the Empire. Throughout most of the nineteenth century Britain and France had sought to strengthen their often rival influence in Mount Lebanon, Palestine and even Syria as a whole.[5] Arab nationalism, a relatively new phenomenon, was beginning to threaten Ottoman domination. A recent Arab revolt in the Hijaz, led by the Sherif Hussein with British encouragement, created another significant danger.

Wilayat Beirut, published in Beirut in 1916 at a moment of acute crisis for the Empire, attempted a comprehensive enquiry into 'general conditions' in the province.[6] Their book would provide an administrator with the kind of knowledge and scientific ways of knowing which appeared to permit the European imperial powers to master the world and menace the Empire.

On the title page of Part Two of *Wilayat Beirut*, the authors proclaim their intentions:

... geographical, historical, spiritual, moral, social and health inquiries; the study of antiquities, of social groups' particular characteristics, of categories of land-holding; and researches into religion and language, literature and fine arts, education and agriculture and commerce and public works; and the condition and description of these two districts.[7]

The exhaustive list was meant to convince the state's representative that they had recorded 'everything'. Rigorous observation, measurement and completeness were now becoming necessary to political rule, at least to reformers. Compendium, social encyclopedia, government information manual for the formation of policy, record of a voyage – this book fulfilled an enlightened nineteenth-century purpose by transmitting a welter of 'facts' to a literate and official class. The bibliographical sources show the same intent and support claims to (European) scientific thoroughness. They include writings in Turkish, the official language of the Empire (7 entries); Arabic, the language of the book itself (33); French (75); English (22); and German (15).

The different genres combined in the text are instrumentally articulated by the recurrent tables of statistics, guarantors of accuracy and verifiable truth. Wherever possible the authors provide numbers: to measure distances and areas in square kilometres or to place villages by latitude and longitude. Figures enumerate populations and religious groups, the major prevalent disease cases and the sick entering hospital. There are tallies of arrests for criminal offences and figures for port traffic, for the extent of different types of soil, for crop yields, and much else. What constitutes information for the state requires the magic of numbers, and those same numbers claim a precise, modern authority for the text.

Scientific method guides their steps. The province presents no obstacles to Tamimi and Bahgat's measured progress. Approaching the last stage, they arrive in Tripoli, the major city of the region. Enquiries there accomplished, the travellers head north.

Suddenly, Tamimi and Bahgat are directionless and baffled. A 'fathomless sea' lies before them: Akkar. Here was no point of reference, no authority to lead them. Instead, there was a blank, an emptiness of unknown dimensions. Yet they had to prepare – with what rhetorical reluctance and flowery literary hyperbole – to set forth. By what route might they travel? 'Were there only a guide ...!'

Vain hope: 'Then we knew that the pen of investigation and research would be our staff, and with it we would measure the position of our blind steps in this unknown land.'[8] The move into such metaphors and heightening of style set the classic frame for intrepid travellers heading into the wild. The pen that places their blind steps establishes that difference with all that has gone before which will constitute the region for the reader. Akkar had heretofore been beyond the horizon of literati. It was a place deemed largely unworthy of written record in the biographical dictionaries and chronicles that were the dominant genres of historical writing which preceded Tamimi and Bahgat's new form of observation. The deeds of princes, notables and jurists of the city or of Mount Lebanon formed the substance of such texts and were given appropriate traditional form and language.

A chronicler such as the well-known Emir Haidar Shehab would record the Kurdish origins of the House of the eponymous ancestor Mir'ab, whose name was given to the whole descent group of the beys of Akkar: 'The Mir'abis are a people of noble rank and horsemen of excellence'.[9] He relates that Nasir, Mir'ab's son, settled in the regions of Akkar and that the reputation of Nasir's son, Shadid, spread far and wide for courage and horsemanship, those two great virtues of military rulers. He notes the occasions on which they gave refuge in their northern marches to other notables who were defeated in some struggle and fled from their enemies. Ali Bey al Asad, a grandson of Shadid who was at one time governor in Tripoli in the early nineteenth century, earns several references. The author notes dealings of the Akkari beys with the Emir Bashir, ruler of Mount Lebanon. But Akkar had only a marginal and intermittent place in his and other chronicles. Writing concerned the social significance of persons of status, learning, honourable descent and power. The beys of Akkar, in their distant province, were as much on the edges of this kind of historical text as they were of the spheres of interest of the rulers of Mount Lebanon and Damascus.

Tamimi and Bahgat were creating a new kind of subject and a new kind of text, one in which even the most miserable and un-writable of regions and groups could be sited. It is a text organized, neither around the deeds of emirs and learned men, nor the horsemanship and military prowess of the Mir'abis, but by the self-consciously 'modern' programme of scientific classification and description.

The travellers finally decide to take a carriage to the little centre of the *qada'* or sub-district of Akkar, Halba, and thence to strike out for the interior. At first all goes well. From al Badawi, a blessed place for it is the shrine of a much venerated holy man just north of the city, they move into the eye of the storm. The contrast is total. A violent wind sweeps over them with a 'sea of swirling dust whose waves crash down upon the length of the road'. The 'scorching heat' of the July day causes them the 'acutest torture'.[10] Their carriage lurches along a road, which disintegrates into a mass of broken stones, following the line of the Tripoli–Homs railway constructed only five years before.

Tamimi and Bahgat meticulously name each village they see to right and left and each mountain to their right as they go north. They pass over the first of many bridges across rivers and streams and leave reed huts behind them. Men and women squat at the entrances to gardens 'consumed by time' selling fruits piled up in the dust: lemons, pears, apples, water melons and peaches. Crossing the river called 'the Cold' (*Nahr al Bared*), they come to the 'Abde station on the railway line, but it is only a hut near a small jetty and two *khan*s or storehouses. Nothing disturbs the silence but passing cameleers and donkey drivers. In the distant harvested fields they see camels standing in the burning heat, a villager stretched out alone on the earth in the shade of the animals or another who stands leaning his shoulder on his staff. These inert and isolated silhouettes are the only figures in the empty landscape.[11]

It is time for the rigour of numbers. First, they delineate the boundaries of the qada', which is seven and a half hours in length and nearly nine across (by horse). The level of precision increases. The total area is 376,841 *dunums*, 285,163 of which are fields and only 9,028 planted in mulberry and olive trees with 2,562 in groves and gardens, and the rest (30,082) for animal husbandry. They list the dunums cultivated and the amount of production of wheat, barley, maize, millet, chickpeas, beans, lentils, green peas, onions and sesame.

After the boundaries, the population. For the Muslim year 1332 (from November 1913 to mid-November 1914) they record a total of 42,363 persons: 21,467 males and 20,897 females, in categories ranging from the largest, that of the Muslims, in descending order through the Greek Orthodox, the Maronites, the Catholics and finally the Protestants. They note that the census population total of AH1323 (1905) is 11,451 less than the later AH1332 figure and tell the reader that it is useless to seek causes for this level of increase over ten years. The reason is all too simple (p. 234). The official procedures of registering and recording are unreliable. For the population scattered in the mountain villages, they say, the numbers owe everything to 'whim and conjecture' and nothing to accuracy. The census itself is no sure guide to truth about Akkar.[12] It states that 13,790 persons work in agriculture, 13 in commerce, 1,857 'live without work or occupation'; there are estimated to be 6,876 landowners; and finally, 7,151 have been taken for the army during the present war (p. 250).[13]

There are three main geographical divisions of the region. First is the coastal zone, the Sahel: six and a half hours in length and only three across; soils are alluvial, there are no obvious marks of ownership, and one finds on each of the chain of low hills rising from the plain the remains of a ruined fortress. The second division is the Wasat, the central area which varies between 300 and 600 metres in altitude and where one sees mulberries grown for the silk industry and olive trees for oil. And the third is the Jurd which reaches between 1,000 and 1,500 metres and was until recently covered by thick woodland (that is, the construction of the railway and the war have decimated the forests).

The qada' is not officially divided into sub-districts, but the inhabitants and even the state itself consider the Qayta' area, which includes the villages of Berqayl and Fneidek, and the Jumeh with its largely Christian settlements of Minyara, Rahbe and Baino, as if they were sub-districts.[14] Of the 168 villages of the qada' one-third are inhabited by Christians, most of whom work as cultivators.

Even in this marginal region they find the impact of European capitalism on taste and production. There is little manufacturing or industry, but there are six small silk workshops in Maronite villages in the Wasat. Christians have taken over carpet production from Turks and established workshops in four places. Measurements have been changed.[15] Not only that. The import of the cheaper, light European carpets has done great harm to the industry. Locals now use mostly a pale red on the European model which is not fast and fades quickly.

The figures for education are baldly stated. Five per cent of Muslims and 50 per cent of Christians know how to read and write. The Muslims will not let their girls go to school. Only six out of the 168 villages have schools at all. Before the war there had been foreign schools.[16] The English language, they report, is spread among the (Christian) inhabitants because of their wish to emigrate.

Tamimi and Bahgat represent the social world as a kind of violation of linguistic convention. In Halba wretched shelters are made of stone cut out of the west side of the hill where stands the insignificant little town of barely 1,000 people. The interior sections of these dwellings 'cannot reasonably be called rooms', and only the proudest in Halba are painted or washed with lime. The floors are of dirt. 'The people of Halba live in these stoney nests side by side with their agricultural implements ...' (the expressive dots are theirs) (p. 241). The narrative continues:

> and one finds amidst this rocky shabbiness a few brick buildings which look like houses. Then the Government Office and the municipality, and the house of the *qaimaqam* ... and would that I knew whether these are houses? or what on earth I should call them? (pp. 241–2)

Nevertheless, the people of Halba, these unfortunates who live at the extreme of misery in this shapeless, undifferentiated agglomeration, actually divide their village into five named quarters (*mahallat*) and use, astonishingly, such urban terms as house, road and quarter (p. 242).

Their final observation on the construction of Halba is the important one, illustrating the absence of culture and the defining marks of community. There is no church, even though the majority of the inhabitants are Christians, and worshippers have to go to a neighbouring village called, curiously enough, 'Sheikh Muhammad'. And the single mosque is 'truncated' – that is, it has no minaret (an observation which they place in an explanatory bracket).

Tamimi and Bahgat are particularly incredulous that Halba should be the designated centre of the qada'. Thirty years ago, they note, the centre was transferred to Halba from the village called al Burg, only because Muhammad Pasha, father of Ali Pasha and an influential man of Halba as *qaimaqam*, the government representative at this level, wanted the site of government representation in his village. Other villages are larger, Berqayl is one of several with more inhabitants, but the Pasha's will prevailed.

The people of this wretched village are like small children, without qualities of spiritual perception, bereft of all light and civilization, mere corporeal beings. One looks at their faces and sees emptiness devoid of all meaning, learning, and experience (p. 250). Rarely, add the authors, resorting to occidental rhetoric and stereotype of 'the East', does one find this degree of 'unadulterated oriental rusticity' (p. 251).

They add a practical official's note: this obedient and submissive character is ready for direction and administration more than others, if unfortunately lacking in energy (p. 251). Geography, 'spirit', and political subordination or rebelliousness are invoked in a manner typical of observations on many Mediterranean societies. Tamimi and Bahgat inform their readers that the people of the plain are more deficient in spirit than the inhabitants of the mountain. The former are obedient and peaceable, while the people of the Jurd are known for their roughness, willfulness and obduracy. Recently, gangs of robbers from the mountains have terrorized the coastal areas, attacking the villagers whom they consider cowardly.[17]

The Christians, observe the authors, do not fit this picture. They are ahead of the Muslims in intellectual advance, work and social life. But emigration draws their eyes abroad, away from the homeland. Money from America has renewed building and order in their villages and increases all the time. People say that half the Christians of Akkar live off remittances. Unfortunately, when they return, they bring no worthy characteristics but rather idleness and laziness, using their money to guarantee that they do not have to work. They have suffered greatly in the war which has cut off their links with the world of their migrant relatives (p. 249).

Tamimi and Bahgat give a political explanation for both the submissiveness of the Muslims and their low social condition: this wretchedness stems from the oppression of the tyrannical 'princes of Akkar'. The villagers are excluded from civilization and progress, not because of some psychological quality or immemorial tradition, but by the arbitrary power of the rulers for whom they labour.

Convinced that the ruin of the spiritual and social landscape is not 'natural' but is indeed the consequence of the domination of 'the princes of Akkar', Tamimi and Bahgat mix the history and genealogical descent of the beys, a census of their numbers, characteristics of the most important beys, and accounts of ways in which they exploit their absolute power:

> They [the beys] assert that they came to this region from the direction of Hikara [in Kurdish eastern Anatolia MG] 200 or 250 years ago and that they were Kurds, but today are arabized ... There are about 1,000 men and women ... and all say that they are from the dynasty 'Mir'ab' which divided and increased in branches over time. Men of the 'Akakara have the title of bek and this is the mark of nobility of descent. ... Among these haughty souls are 15 principle figures, they are at the very highest degree of power and domination ...
>
> Those who hold sway in the region of Akkar ... set up centres of their

influence in the villages of Berqayl, Majdala, Bebnine, Biri, Habshit, and 'Ayyad.' (p. 246)

Some of the beys are enormously rich, and 'the wealthiest of them dwell in Berqayl' (p. 246).

The rhetorical figure of the anonymous 'any villager you ask' is employed to denounce the princes. This collective voice, as if in direct speech, tells of anarchic violence and unbridled destruction:

Each of these men of power – and there are around five hundred of them – has men and bodyguards fully equipped with weapons and dependent on their every sign and command. Some agree with others to join their forces and violent fighting breaks out between them. And they destroy the olive trees; they kill some, suborn their bodyguards, steal their wealth and seize any occasion and reason to cause harm, even if their victims are relatives close to them this does not restrain some of them. (p. 247)

The mechanisms of exploitation are detailed by the authors who carefully list the different taxes taken from the villagers: one-third of the harvest; a tenth of the whole yield from the share of the cultivators alone; a sum appointed for the year and known as the '*dukhaniyya*'; the *shakara*, a shunbul of produce from every feddan cultivated; further, the lords regularly charge three times the value of the seed advanced to the fellah for planting when the harvest comes in (p. 247).[18]

The unconstrained, limitless power of the local ruling élite is the ruin of Akkar. Tamimi and Bahgat present a caustic analysis of their useless extravagance and unbridled excess. The organization of the beys' houses is a deficient as their families are full of every vice.[19]

Political, tyrannical excess (*zulm*) arises from excess of luxury consumption and indulgence, a favourite Enlightenment and Orientalist theme opposing the old order to modernity. In Tamimi and Bahgat's view, the beys rule with tyranny and exploitation because they live in a style of unthinking and improvident extravagance. Force is necessary to maintain opulence. The massed bodyguards are the instruments guaranteeing the luxury of the princes' visits to Tripoli and Beirut. The social order is no true order at all, for it violates every obligation and all propriety.

This particular form of power has its own psychology. The princes have violent and coarse spirits which incline towards 'legendary nobility', fine horses and possessions, and, above all, the longed-for title of bek and pasha.[20] (In attributing this power of 'desires' rather than reason to the lords, Tamimi and Bahgat place them in that category of persons who are not socially mature; in this respect they are like women and children.) Recently, however, there has been a clear awakening, at least by some of the lords, though only half of them have any proficiency in reading and writing. There must be swift reflection on the means to enlighten this group. For if they were to achieve such a happy condition, these rich persons would be the most useful for Akkar (pp. 251-2).[21]

In this world of polar extremes, with no past and no memory beyond that of the lords with their need for 'legendary nobility', the princes of Akkar are the antithesis of proper government. Their domain, the fathomless sea upon which only the pen can navigate, is a universe unto itself. Akkar, its landscape and its inhabitants are the contradiction of known civilization.

Reform and Arbitrary Power

Tamimi and Bahgat clearly support a reformist view of the needs of the Empire. 'The princes of Akkar' are figures standing for a more general way of practising power, found perhaps even at the capital itself, that must be eliminated by more rational, modern authority. More specifically, the imperial centre must bring these quasi-autonomous provincial rulers under control in administrative and fiscal terms if reform is to be successful. Both are major themes in nineteenth-century Ottoman political history.

The same Empire had used the beys and pashas of Akkar for many years for fiscal and military purposes. And the lords had used the Empire in what was, in effect, a constantly renegotiated interplay between local and state forces.

The fiscal system depended upon tax farming or *iltizam* of a given unit, a *muqata'a*. This right was auctioned, annually or often for longer periods and the holder, the *multazim*, was charged with collecting for the state the taxes due as well as an annual fee, usually in coin and paid in instalments. He could then gather for himself, most often in kind, such profits and exactions as he might and speculate on changes in market prices or monetary fluctuations. It was not uncommon for the tax farmer to pay a negotiated rent to the state for his rights to farm the muqata'a for life (the *malikane* system).[22] Mir'abi beys held such tax farms, certainly from the early eighteenth century. Provided that they ensured the return of the taxes to Istanbul there seems to have been relatively little attempt at state supervision.[23] Once they had effectively been entrusted with military and security duties as well, leading houses were positioned to assume effective local dominance. Their gradually consolidating powers made exactions from the cultivators on trees, flocks, new livestock, transport, milling and others still easier.

Hublos has detailed the developments in Akkar during that century in respect of changes in taxation practices. In a situation of competition between the lords for the tax farms the governors could exploit their competition to raise the value of the iltizam to the state. As leading beys came to assume what were *de facto* rights, not only for life but which could be passed on to their sons, the authorities in Tripoli had rather less freedom for manoeuvre. On the other hand, the state itself might increase tax demands, as it did by stages in the last three decades of the century.

Despite the dominance of the beys, there were challenges. Records exist in the Islamic court archives of official complaints against the multazims by cultivators, particularly in the second half of the nineteenth century when the Ottomans attempted some degree of reform.[24] There are indications also of government worries about the ruin of the regional economy because of the burden of exactions on the cultivators. Hublos suggests that towards the end of the Ottoman period there was a new tendency towards a strengthening of fellah rights in cultivation, witnessed by the spread of written work contracts between owner and fellah spelling out the conditions incumbent upon each.[25] And in any case, the flight of labour was not in the beys' interests, particularly in periods of acute scarcity. They needed to tie fellahin, not only by taxes and debt, but by 'protection' and a degree of paternalist 'forgiveness' of debt, the gracious giving of seed or clothing or food, attendance at a funeral or wedding, being a 'good bey'.

At the same time, certain houses of beys became economically and socially weaker as they were displaced by others in the competition for land, revenues and followings. The decline of these weaker houses enabled the strengthening of their competitors, such as the wealthiest noted by Tamimi and Bahgat as living in Berqayl. Consumption patterns of the upper strata changed rapidly in the later nineteenth century on the model of the tastes of the European bourgeoisie, and increased costs took their toll.[26] Here Tamimi and Bahgat's strictures on the beys 'desires' become relevant, though not in the same idiom of domination by the passions. The modes and exigencies of claiming and transmitting social distinction and rank became more elaborated and demanding. Display in house structure, furnishing, dress, food, sumptuary expenditure according to the standards established in Tripoli and, more significantly, Beirut, could be extremely costly. For beys competing in local politics and for influence with the state it became imperative to have residences in Tripoli or Beirut as well as in their home villages. Not only that. The city offered new investment opportunities in manufacturing and different services. One leading bey had a share in setting up a cotton weaving factory and flour mill in Damascus in 1884, and was involved in the company established to set up a tramway between Tripoli and Minya.[27]

The other side of this was the gain of greater influence in Akkar by the merchants and leading families of Tripoli. They took the opportunity to acquire greater control of lands on the plain as the impoverished Mir'abis were forced out.[28] The merchants had considerable powers of price setting for Akkar's agricultural produce. In bad times it was from them that the beys raised loans, loans which they could not always repay. Fellahin livelihoods depended on such Tripoli families.

Urban notables penetrated Akkar in other ways. Members of the Naufal and Khalat families formed a company to make the Tripoli–Homs road, opened in 1879 by the governor of Damascus, passable for traffic of vehicles. The beys had an economic interest in keeping this road open and in trying to maintain security of trade for their own purposes as much as for those of the state.[29] The road, so complained of by the Ottoman officials, was a symbol of the links between lords and merchants, links in which the city was predominant.

Akkar was thus not the 'fathomless ocean' of Tamimi and Bahgat's rhetoric. If the 'unbridled passions of the beys' were a source of oppression, there was a system of iltizams and taxes that had been part of standard state administrative practices and which reforms had largely failed to touch in the region. The beys were active in their support for, or opposition to, the Committee of Union and Progress which had deposed the sultan in 1909.[30] A local Society of Arab Ottoman Brotherhood had been established in 1908 with much celebration and reciting of poetry in Halba itself by Osman Pasha Muhammad. Others opposed him on personal or political grounds and favoured the entry of French authority, the most prominent among them being Abboud Abd ar-Razzaq. Abboud was also a candidate against the bey supporting the Committee of Union and Progress in local elections called in 1912.[31]

If the Akkari landscape was 'empty', that was in part due to the relatively enormous proportion of men taken for military service in the war by the Ottoman government; to the swarms of locusts of 1915; to state appropriation of grain and the terrible famine of 1916 and 1917 which left a mark on the memories of those I spoke to many decades later (see Chapters 8 and 9). If villages were so desolate that 'a fox would come in and there was no one to drive it out', as a local man told me in a vivid image of the wild invading the settled, Bahgat and Tamimi knew the reasons why.

CHAPTER SIX

Precarious Archaism

Latifundia and Mandate rationality

In the current situation, the plain of Akkar is one of the most prosperous areas of central Syria. Possessing fertile soil, sufficiently abundantly supplied with water, having a fairly well developed network of communication, controlled by a class of large landowners whose progressive tendencies are clear, one can calculate that, given modern agricultural materials, improved cultivation methods and a properly set up irrigation network, the plain of Akkar will become an agricultural centre of the first importance.[1]

The authorities of the French League of Nations Mandate that displaced the defeated Ottoman Empire in 1919 had hopes of Akkar as a material resource. They saw the 'current situation' in the former Ottoman Syria, with some degree of self-legitimation, as chaotic: an insecure citizenry shut up in the largest towns and plagued by cholera and typhus, impassable roads, constant pillage and massacre, nothing to eat, total economic and social stagnation.[2] On 24 July 1923 High Commissioner Weygand soberly assessed the realities. Syria suffered from an enormous imbalance of trade with imports about four times the size of exports. The silk trade had not yet recovered from the wartime cutting of many mulberry trees. Agriculture was crippled by insufficient irrigation, non-existent credit and flaws in the cadastre. Out of a possible four million hectares, only one million and fifty thousand were under cultivation.[3]

Luquet noted that Syria was the tributary of Europe for almost all manufacturing products.[4] Syria, he says, needs industrial agriculture such as cotton with higher profits 'to serve more easily as capital for exchange in the purchase of European goods'.[5] In turn, it could produce a large part of the cotton needed by the French cotton mills.[6] Unfortunately, such new agriculture is capital intensive and unattractive to French investors. Moreover, mechanization will work only after a 'veritable revolution in agricultural technology', which demands currently non-existent support structures, men trained as mechanics and even more money.[7] And there is no money.

The High Commission staff had to determine the boundaries of *Le Grand Liban* and decide how to govern Syria and Lebanon.[8] They turned to the technical specialist, that supreme figure of modern rationality and planning. The Commission needed to know, in the title of Professor Paul Huvelin's

well-known report of December 1921, *Que Vaut la Syrie?* (*What is Syria Worth?*).
In regions such as Akkar, where they could not rely on the historic links that
bound them to the predominantly Maronite Mount Lebanon, French officials
were very dependent upon scarce documentary information. They desperately
appealed to their small cadre of officers, technical specialists and *conseillers*
for material on the size, topography, physical and chemical constituents,
hydrography, population, property forms, and crop patterns of the region.[9]

The technical survey or monograph, based on field studies and any
statistics available, became the primary representation of Syria and Lebanon.
These texts were intended as instruments enabling interventions in what
were identified as existing problems.[10] The region became one more resource
to be inventoried and utilized by French scientific agriculture under the
control of a single official, the *conseiller administratif* of the *caza* (French
transliteration of the Arabic qada'), the first of whom was a certain Captain
Mieg, a cavalry officer.[11]

Officials like Mieg confronted many problems. Not least was the fundamental issue of comprehending and reconciling all the local units of weights,
measures, distances and areas. Detailed notes in books and surveys explained
that the Mandate had to deal with diverse forms for reckoning property and
produce. Writing in 1936, the agronomist André Latron began his book on
rural life in Syria and Lebanon with the very anthropological insight that
different logics were at work and had to be studied *in their own terms* in order
to be understood:

> At first sight the customary measures seem disordered and without any logical
> foundation. Under the same title one often finds units varying from one region
> to the other, while units of the same category may be given very different names.
> In fact, in Syria as elsewhere, metrology shows a large sum of human experience.
> Agrarian measures are in a close relation with labour power or with transport
> by man or animal; they vary according to the forms of property; they are adapted
> to the nature of the produce, to the economic and social necessities of the
> place.[12]

Power and property relations required a similar grasp of the terms of local
socio-logics. Efforts to map and measure the social and economic landscape
of Syria began with attempts to place the owners of what the French experts
called the 'latifundia'. Achard, like others, quickly realized how much property was concentrated in the hands of a small number of landowners. The
four great families of the city of Hama owned a hundred villages in that caza
alone.[13] Such villages were usually possessed in their totality and often contig-
uous. Jacques Weulersse, a noted scholar, drew attention to the numerous
medium and small domains comprising the ownership of one or two villages.[14]

The latifundia presented the Mandate with major problems. Jean Donon
regarded the large estates as the 'chronic illness' of rural Syria (as of the
whole Ottoman Empire) and their proprietors as 'insatiable parasites devour-

Berqayl in Spring. From the road to the Jurd. Almond blossom on the hillsides. Abboud's mosque and grave (small dome below minaret). Zawiya quarter left, Hara right. Large building centre is the supplementary school. Olive groves cut by north road to the coast over the foothills.

Old mosque, plane tree and open coffin in which all were carried to their graves. The washing table for

Probably of Abboud as a young man in an Ottoman academy uniform, late nineteenth century. Marked as 'Cabinet Portrait' and taken at G. Amirayan, Photographe, 29 Rue Okdjoular-Bachi, Constantinople

Young bey and his murafiq, same period as 3. Note murafiq's formal waistcoat and the adoption of the overcoat.

A gathering of major beys and landlords in the Mandate period. Abboud is standing in the centre, Osman Pasha seated to his left,

A mechanic's day off. The dismantled engine is being worked on at the back of his house on the pathway. In bad weather it would be moved indoors. No one except myself was present and he was, I think, unaware of being photographed.

An old man's occupation: the Hajj at cards. An agha small landowner and one-time qabaday, he always put on his formal jacket, waistcoat and embroidered shirwal trousers, together with his headdress, for the game.

Celebrating a return from hospital, young men dancing the *dabke*. Only the man with the white handkerchief and the teenager in the centre of the line

ing it (Syria)'.[15] The landowners expressed no interest in techniques of agriculture and had no figures for crop production. Even more peculiar, 'most of them do not know the extent of their domains'. This generalization is closely followed, however, by an observation concerning two measures of property that are significant to the landowners themselves. The first is one of time: 'One of them replied to us: "To cross my property is a six-hour ride in one direction and seven hours in the other."' The observer arrived at his own acceptable measurement, 'a pretty parcel of land of 100,000 hectares'. Though convinced that the owners were incapable of measuring their own holdings, the same investigator recorded a second, and even more revealing measure: 'When one asks the extent of his fields, the proprietor immediately gives the number of villages on their surface.'[16]

Labour was the key unit of measurement. 'The number of villages on their surface' meant the villages which belonged to the latifundist. The landed proprietors lived from the labourers. In the most exploitative sharecropping arrangements they advanced the cultivators funds, tools, draught animals and seeds, all to be repaid at usurious rates of up to 400 per cent at harvest time. Not only that. Landlords collected a tax on the harvest, the *dime*, stipulated at 12 per cent, but often in fact increased by an owner. Each sharecropper contributed his labour to an endless renewal of an endebting process for which the word 'serfdom' was commonly used in reports. Sharecroppers were tied to their latifundist in multiple and coercive ways, including 'customary offerings' at festivals and obligations for labour on public works, practices the French deplored but did not abolish.

An immediate question arose: Could domains so vast and indeterminate really be the property of those who claimed to possess them?

> Knowing how easy it is to manipulate the registers of the Turkish cadastral service, the uncertainty of the boundaries fixed such as those currently in existence which are represented by a rock, a tree, a ravine, a construction ...[17]

A discrepant discourse of property and possession reinforced the official tendency to perceive agrarian Syrian society, perhaps 'oriental society' *in toto*, as vague, undefined, malleable. What and where are the boundaries? Revision of the cadastre was therefore deemed necessary.

Officials considered the latifundia the key to a structure of rural–urban relations in which the parasitic towns kept the countryside in strict dependence. Wealthy, absentee landowners tied up peasants in credits and debts. Latron represents these two worlds, so intimately connected through exploitation, as socially and culturally alien to one another. For, he says, the townsmen travel little in the countryside fearing either robbery or being cheated, while the peasant is scared of the towns.[18]

French experts deplored the 'irrational' failure of the absentee urban landowners to obey capitalist economic imperatives: 'the landowning class is as indolent and outmoded as the class of sharecroppers is wretched'.[19] Owner and producer should be one and the same. The fact of the undivided estates was for a time the established explanation as to why 'the individual (landowner) has no concern to establish a rational improvement by his own work or money ... technical ignorance and the spirit of routine oppose all effort at economic renovation'.[20] Was it for such latifundists that the Mandate should establish an Agricultural Bank? Yet the same specialists who lamented the retention of undivided estates by the great landowners criticized the extreme and 'inefficient' fractionalizing of land which resulted when the peasants used the Islamic mode of inheritance.

The retention of large undivided estates might have seemed inefficient, but of course it made local political and social sense. The great families were collectivities with hegemony over the society at large. Latron, quick to see the implications of dividing or not dividing the lands, explained that families of notables need to preserve their social rank. While a family is strong, its head will direct its own *société d'indivision*, organize cultivation and share out the revenues between those holding rights in the property. When members of the family emigrate to neighbouring towns or abroad, estate management is left to the most competent or to the one who wishes to take on the task, and may even go to one who is not a relative.[21] Certain of the beys and landowners, moreover, were quick to appreciate the opportunities for rationalization, and expansion offered by the circumstances of the Mandate. They might combine acquisition of lands, registration of personal landownership under the new cadastral survey, intensification of investment, changes in crops and production, and local political alliances with officials to create a 'modern' power greater than that they had held before.

Contradiction and impasse seemed to be everywhere. The *dime*, the tax on produce, had 'disastrous consequences'. But Luquet conceded that, in the current circumstances, the income from the dime was too advantageous to the public purse to be foregone.[22]

French policy thus led to the support of those notables whose ruinous practices and unproductivity Mandate reports so severely criticized. No independent class of small proprietors on the great plains existed which could be used as an element in agricultural change or for political support. The experts were troubled by a general problem of labour shortage in the country as a whole for current needs, let alone for any large-scale, capitalist development projects; and labour was difficult to control. There was only one powerful class and there was no alternative but to work with it.

Other reasons for collaboration were pressing. Constantly restricted by shortages of funds and personnel, both civil and military, the Mandate enterprise also faced general Arab nationalist opposition. Agronomists and officers came to realize that the High Commission was, in fact, dependent upon the powerful 'feudal latifundists' in its efforts to control the unstable countryside. Moreover, a majority of the great landowners were also urban notables effectively in charge of finance and the gendarmerie in the towns.

Military control of the regions was necessary to put down the occasional large-scale revolt and to counter the persistent 'troubles' and 'armed bands'.[23] In 1927, the administration had to dispatch Senegalese troops to clean up the Halba-Syr region 'where bandits have been noticed on several occasions for some time'. Elements of the 3/17th unit occupied the Berqayl area where they were joined by the eleventh company which stayed overnight on 27 April. It was reported that 'the troops were well received everywhere by the villages, especially in Berkail [sic] and Syr where the notables had the honour of receiving the officers to dine'.[24]

Other reports expressed reservation about the real nature of the support of the beys and notables and their actual role in the manipulation of violence and disruption. Even pro-French beys might secretly stir up violence in order to gain credit for restoring order and to show their importance to the Mandate. After one 'rebellion' in 1926, Abboud Bey and others accused the troops of pillage and profanation. The assassin of a French sergeant in Berqayl appeared to be under the protection of the same Abboud Bey. In any case, the report concluded rather perfunctorily but with a hint of a very different appreciation of the root problem, only the provision of a proper road, a dispensary and a stable prosperity would achieve pacification.[25]

With regional control a matter of such vexed interest, it is scarely surprising to find a Lieutenant Vertier dispatched in October 1927 to make a study of the beys of Akkar and of the region in general. The young officer's 'notice sur l'Akkar' says that the power of money and family are 'unlimited'. His military eye perceives a military geography: that the beys have chosen their village sites usually on the slopes of the last hills bordering the plain, in order to overlook and control their cultivators, count the caravans and the flocks at pasture. He singles out Berqayl, village of Abboud Abd ar-Razzaq, Ibrahim Bey and Muhammad Bey al Mustafa, Asad al Omar, Mahmud Bey al Ali and his brother Abd al Kerim Bey. Others live in the last foothills of the high mountain and a final group at Khraibe.[26]

Violence of different though related kinds is therefore prominent in the French accounts of a region they called 'archaic'. Weulersse may have spoken of 'the oriental peasant' in essentialist terms, but he also saw owner–labourer relations as a kind of permanent class conflict which led to no new articulation of forces: 'between him (the fellah) and his masters there is an unspoken and continuous struggle in which his only weapon under normal circumstances is theft: ... the brutalities of the bailiffs are the natural response'.[27]

The violence of the Mandate itself, however, is represented as no more than a necessary policing action against 'brigands'. Such violence was endemic to French–local relations and labelled 'troubles'. But to the population the French seemed to act in no way differently from others seeking to achieve dominance through force.

Weulersse and other specialists often employed characterizations like 'rural proletariat' and 'typical oriental' with no apparent sense of contradiction.

They also used the term 'feudal', which evoked a society frozen in time and irredeemably backward. The discourse employed categories from different worlds and historical frames as if they were part of an utterly coherent whole. Now, however, this archaic world was compelled to enter 'the current of civilization'.[28] The writer-expert becomes an agent of the forces leading to that extinction of the archaic, for he is, to himself, an emblem of the coming of time, memory and observation.[29] Yet he might also be, in practice, the agent of a reproduction, intensification and development of exactly those 'archaic' relations of power and property whose dissolution was being proclaimed as inevitable.

The Captain and the Bey

The name of a French captain called 'Mieg' became very familiar to me within days of my arrival in the village in 1971. 'Abboud and Mieg were together', was frequently repeated by both agha and fellah speakers. Each was represented as demonstrating in his actions that flair for the unexpected, 'needing no one', seizing the moment, imposing his will often against heavy odds, and the capacity for arbitrary as well as systematic violence that fitted the type of respected political leader. Their relationship, as well as similar links in accounts of other landowners and administrators, was perceived in the early 1970s as a model and foundation of later relations with the political centre.

The discourse was centred upon coercion and fear imposing 'respect'. Mieg was alone, just him and his dog, but he had imposed his authority on everyone 'by force' (b'il quwa); Abboud shot a boy just to try out a rifle; Mieg inflicted penalties and exactions on a whole village (or villages) as he wished and no one dared defy him; Abboud smashed a man's head against a wall in anger 'for nothing'.

Arbitrary acts of personal pleasure complemented systematic practices of power. The two names also recurred in conversations about land agreements, property accumulation or loss, competition for the control of resources, and the operations of political leaders in relation to the government. The frequent reference and vividness of narrative accounts of their collaboration created such a sense of presence that I found it very difficult to think of Mieg and Abboud as anything but contemporary. Though the narratives concerned events which, in terms of linear chronology, had taken place forty to fifty years earlier, the figures of Mieg and Abboud *were* contemporary. They were a primary narrative coupling in men's discursive positionings of themselves in space, time and social life. The French captain and the Akkari bey encapsulated and transcended far more than 'a period' in the narrow historical sense. They stood for the totality of what was spoken of and experienced as the foundations of power that made Akkar what it was. Changes were measured against the benchmarks of their rule, itself seen as changing the landscape; accounts of archetypal confrontations and acts of true manhood were placed under their sign; powerful sheikhs were represented as showing their capacities in miracles against both of them; other important beys took on their narrative delineation as allies or, more often, as opponents of these two icons of domination. And each of the above elements in turn reproduced the significance of the two paragons of violence and order. They possessed, still, presence in the narrative landscape formed, still, by their names. In short, their aura and glamour remained intact.

That a leading Sunni bey should have so closely allied himself with the French, against the currents of Arab nationalist feeling and the majority of his peers, was taken to be a mark of Abboud's cunning and political intuition. It was never spoken of in terms of a betrayal of Arab nationalism or as in any way compromising Abboud's reputation.[30] Mieg, that is, the French administration, desperately needed local backing against pro-Syrian sentiment on the part of the notables of Tripoli and Akkar as much as for military control. The French needed credible local figures with land, strong men and dependent cultivators at their command to back them and to lead opposition to those beys who sided with the nationalists supporting Akkar's incorporation into Syria rather than into the new Greater Lebanon. They needed influential Sunni members of new electoral bodies and commissions.

In return Abboud had privileged access to the benefits of the administration and legal indulgence for his men who were, according to several informants, given *de facto* rights to carry weapons and supplies of cartridges and revolvers at a time when others were forbidden them. They also had lenient treatment when caught infringing the law or when a complaint was made against them. Abboud and the aghas associated with him effectively had *carte blanche* on his domains and in his relations with other rival landowners. Moreover, at a time when attempts were made to extend land registration and the French had at their disposal the state lands of the Ottoman sultan which were to be leased out for later sale, the alliance offered rewards in the increase of landownership and power over local villages.

Abboud's own local base, Berqayl, with its two other bey 'houses', was made the *markaz* or centre of the Qayta', one of the five administrative areas (*mudiriya*s) of the caza of Akkar, in 1923.[31] Equally indicative of Abboud's influence, the *baladiya* (village council), which had been established in Berqayl as one of five in the region in 1918, was abolished in 1926 at his urging.[32] The power to exclude populations from services and infrastructure continued to be an important attribute of a bey. These relatively small adminstrative changes have their importance. They point to the way in which the new state, whose structures and practices were only emerging, was localized and personalized. Whatever the rationalities of agronomy, planning and French political ambitions in the region, the coming of direct European rule and its 'new' political institutions on the ground meant the consecration of a more systematically applied domination by those beys who could exploit the developing circumstances.

Land, Labour and Conflict

Conflict between beys or between beys and aghas over land and labour ran through the majority of the narratives concerning social hierarchy.[33] A dramatic confrontation might be represented on its own as if self-contained, with no further contextualizing necessary. Yet it would usually emerge on some other occasion that the fuller significance of the moment actually related to property and control of territory.

When, either in response to my specific questioning or to an appropriate conversational conjuncture, older aghas launched into accounts of their lives as companions/bailiffs, they characteristically interspersed stories of specific confrontations often involving physical violence, with explications of types of sharecropping and tenancy arrangements in that area, and details of ownership. The latter entailed histories of named villages, families, groves or plots, sales or inheritance, shifts in crops, though dates seldom played a part in the telling. Men knew which agha and fellah had been with which bey, where, and for how long.

Narratives thus demonstrated a shared common stock of knowledge held by the aghas of the senior generation who had been landholders and bailiffs themselves at the period of the Mandate and continued to be so. They knew the history of the landholdings of all the major local beys, histories which entailed assessment of the social space occupied by the landowner's 'house', its transformations and their causes. The present landscape of power and property was read in these dimensions which constituted locally an exhaustive historical description and practical analysis.

Disputes between beys seemed to frame many agha biographies. Abu Ali recalled going at the age of about fourteen (c. 1931) with older relatives of his family to expel a bey and aghas who had a share agreement on land in Syria. Abboud claimed the property as a result of an unpaid debt. He had lent them money at high interest. When grain prices fell they could not pay, so he got a legal judgement against the owners and enforced it through seizure. 'The Alawis [the labourers] went mad', said Abu Ali. 'They shouted: "Beit Abd as-Salam have come!"' Around the same time the boy had gone with his mother's brother and another relative to occupy a village and take over control from aghas based in Majdala.[34] By such acts the names of Abboud and of Beit Abd as-Salam became *names*, sufficient in themselves to cause fear, obedience, and careful calculation of the odds among opponents.

Abu Ali's biography as a wakil began and continued around the themes of contest over property in which the instruments of coercion might be debt and armed force combined with legal support. If the tithe or *'ushr* was to be collected or the share of the harvest, it might require a display of force at collection point, even if the agha went on his own with only a (illegal but winked at) revolver. The government, in the person of an officer supposed to control weapons, would send cartridges. Mieg made allowances for an agha without a permit, especially if he worked for Abboud Bey. When a *mukhtar* was recalcitrant and disputed his right to act as he wished in a matter, Abu Ali went and kicked him out. Legally he had no such powers, but he still took the seal of office and told the man's superior to appoint someone else.

Land disputes might involve what were routine matters of encroachment in which fellahin would typically be obliged by their bey to cultivate another bey's land 'by force' as a trial of strength. Abu Ali spoke of the occasion when a Tripoli leader's fellahin took the cows of the bey he was working for and corralled them on their property. The owner ordered Abu Ali and another wakil to seize the opponent's herd. They began by tying up the Tripoli bey's own wakil and then released the cattle. A law case followed between the bey's and Abu Ali was sentenced to six months. Sure of his bey's support he did not surrender to the authorities because he 'had no one to take his place'. Eventually he went to Beirut and the bey's lawyer got him 15 days suspended sentence. 'For revenge' he took a revolver and a rifle (of which he said there were only two in the village) and let his herd loose on the crops of the Tripoli bey. When two men came up to challenge him he fired between their horses legs and off they galloped.[35]

This narrative was typical of many and showed the interplay of violence, law and government during the period. It was accepted that a murafiq might be jailed for acts committed on behalf of his bey; and if the bey had influence he would be swiftly released and well looked after during his imprisonment. State and uncultivated lands were being competed for as private property, beys were jockeying for influence and the control of dependents, the French were only one party in complex negotiations over politics at local, national and regional levels.

Narratives such as that of Abu Ali show the constant negotiations, often conducted in agonistic form, which delimited social, political and economic space. The murafiq and bailiff played a crucial, and easily dramatized role, in such personal confrontations. If behind the qabaday was an influential bey and a powerful beit of aghas that too inhibited would-be challengers, save those of an equivalent level. An individual name usually had a collective significance.

There were those who could quell a rebellious village just 'by speech', such was the force of their 'word' and prestige. The hero did not need even to speak or threaten because his presence, or his mere name, sufficed to deter others from any challenge. His olive grove, uniquely, required no watchman. Everyone would know a series of accounts of his acts, a biography of incidents of contest, each one held to demonstrate the same qualities of being which were both exceptional and stood for the glory of the whole agha beit.

Bey–Agha Tensions

One narrative gives a clear idea of the tensions that arose between beys and aghas and shows the role of the leading and most reputed of the qabadays of the time, Abboud's agha murafiq Abd ar-Rahman Said.

> Abboud coveted some land here in the daiʻa, just down there beyond the Hajj's house, and wanted to join it to his. So he sent fellahin to plough it. The owner, Yusef (an agha of Beit Abd as-Salam), kicked them out. Then he stormed up to Abboud's palace, insulted and struck him. Abboud's chauffeur, a Beiruti called Osman, grabbed Yusef and Abboud struck him with a staff and knocked him down. (In another version the chauffeur punched him in the face.) Yusef came down to the Hara quarter and mobilized the whole agha group to go up the hill against Abboud. Abd ar-Rahman Said found Abboud sitting on the steps of his palace with a rifle, not afraid of what might happen. He took the rifle from Abboud who said: 'Will you take the gun and leave me without anything?' 'I'll deal with it', was the reply. (In the other version, Abd ar-Rahman Said saw Abboud drawing a gun and said to him: 'If you shoot any of the family I'll throw you out of the window'.) The murafiq defended Abboud against his own family and said that they would have to answer to him for any harm to the bey. The next day a bey from the neighbouring village of Ayyoun came and formally made peace between the two sides.[36]

The key alliance of Abboud and Beit Abd as-Salam was only preserved, in this narrative, by the intervention of an exceptional figure linked to both. Both keep their honour because of his acknowledged stature. He disarms bey and agha family alike, guaranteeing each against the other.

If aghas were regularly involved in inter-bey disputes and might oppose each other when associated with rival landowners, they might also have to confront beys directly or indirectly. Agha narratives showed an acute consciousness of the ways in which they too had been forced to sell because of debt, market conditions, rising living costs allied to low yields, and other factors. They also stressed the 'cunning' of the beys, who sought to displace not only rival beys while building up their estates, but also constantly tried to tilt the balance of power *vis-à-vis* the aghas more to the beys' side. (We shall see this theme developed in Chapter 8.)

The lords were aware that collective action by the agha group might pose at least local dangers; that the force harnessed in the murafiqs and wakils was conditional on calculations of interest and readings of variations in power; and that undercutting the independent material base of the aghas would tie them more effectively as dependents. They knew of cases where beys had been killed by aghas, and that in the later nineteenth century (the date was vague) a whole 'house' had been driven out of the village after directly challenging the aghas.

These considerations led to at least two attempts by the beys to use fellahin as wakils – one in the late 1920s and the other at the end of the

Second World War – and to displace aghas from this crucial articulating postion in the social and economic order. Both plans were defeated as the agha group rallied against a collective threat. In the second case, agha teenagers and young men beat up (or in one instance, knifed) the fellahin concerned, destroyed crops and threatened the beys they took to be responsible. They did not hesitate to demand money, even from Muhammad al Abboud, or to plan to shoot up the bey's car as he drove by, to the exasperation of their agha elders who felt that such uncontrolled acts menaced the relationship just as much as any design of the beys. A formal meeting between the beys of the village and Beit Abd as-Salam was finally held at which the landowners blamed the whole beit and not just the young men. An uneasy peace was established.

Agha–Fellah Disputes

The sense of growing tension between the fellahin and the aghas of the village was much spoken of by both sides as a present reality intimately related to historical events. Collective violence between one fellahin beit and the aghas broke out exactly at the time of the beys' second clash with Beit Abd as-Salam. I shall give the two agha accounts of the same incident one after the other direct from my notes taken at the time of speaking.

Speaker A: (Participant, in his early twenties at the time of the events. He was then engaged in smuggling grain in wartime and acting as wakil for a bey's house. At the time of our conversation he was a wealthy farmer with political connections in Tripoli and was regarded by some of Beit Abd as-Salam as 'the head of the family'.)

At that time my brother and Said Ahmad of Beit Abd al Hamid from the Zawiya [i.e. fellah] were on the plain. Said was with Beit Abboud and my brother was with Beit Mustafa Bey. There were bad relations between them. I struck Said in the face with a stone. People wanted to make peace between us. My brother was sitting in a shop in the Zawiya. Mustafa Muhammad of Beit Abd al Hamid was also involved in all this. My brother said: 'We'll make peace with Beit Awad [who were trying to restore good relations] because they are sheikhs and we kiss their hands. But Beit Abd al Hamid are dogs.'[37] Mustafa heard him and started a fight. My brother beat him and knocked him down and Said came up and struck my brother with a staff and knocked him down. Beit Abd as-Salam went up to the Zawiya – me and Bashir, the others, all of us, and clouted everyone with staffs. One of us was struck with a knife. Bedr [the agha involved in confronting Abboud over land] knocked down Mustafa Muhammad. They were using knives. I tried to kill Mustafa, but Said Ahmad knocked me flat. Bedr was wounded with a knife and went to get a revolver to shoot them, but he couldn't make it and died.

Next day early – this was in 1940 – I went up to the Zawiya with a shotgun and Hajj Abu Hassan [independent landowner and wakil with a reputation for courage] and Jamil Asad [speaker B below] and started shooting up the area where Beit Abd al Hamid lived because Mustafa had killed Bedr. I fired sixteen shots and the entire Zawiya fled. Quite a few got hit. I came back down.

After Mustafa got out of jail we made a general peace. Abd ar-Rahman Said [the most noted agha qabaday and murafiq] had great honour and integrity. 'I will not go to the Zawiya until either Mustafa or I die', he said. He never did go up there until he died and Mustafa never dared face him. Two years later Darwish [one of the teenagers who threatened the beys and beat up the fellahin] wounded Said.[38]

Speaker B: (Then a teenager; the Jamil Asad of the account above. At the time of our conversation he was an impoverished outlaw who lived 'on the mountain' and only came to the village in the morning.)

Abd al Latif [speaker A] was at Kerke on the plain with Muhammad Bey al Umar. Said Abd al Hamid was with Asad Bey al Umar in the same village in Syria. The two of them had bad relations. Both came here to the village. Said was riding a horse here and Abd al Latif struck him and knocked him off. A month or so later Abd al Latif's brother found one of Beit Abd al Hamid at the mosque and said: 'Would you dare muster your lot against Abd al Latif?' Then he struck him.

Beit Abd al Hamid got together and wanted to attack Beit Abd as-Salam. One day Abd al Latif's brother and Mustafa met on the path from the Zawiya and Mustafa struck him with a staff. A fight started. Abd al Latif went up with a revolver and shot the place up and they fled.

Both sides gathered and there was a lot of fighting up in the open space at the top. Bedr got hold of one fellow who was very strong and a brute in a fight – this was in 1944. One of our men grabbed a knife from Mustafa but stabbed Bedr by mistake. On the next day Bedr died. Me and Darwish – we were 16 or so – got involved. Darwish shot Said, who had struck another of our fellows with a knife, and I shot Mustafa.

The next day the whole Beit went up from here and shot up the entire village. The sister of a man from Beit Abd al Hamid was among those hit. Then our beit sent me and Darwish to harrass them and cause them trouble. One day Darwish's father was slaughtering a camel. Along came Said Abd al Hamid, and the father's hand started shaking with fear. Darwish shot Said three times. The fellahin got the whole Zawiya together. So Abd al Latif and another agha who also had a shop up there moved down to this quarter, the Hara. Darwish was caught in Syria and did three months jail there and three years and seven months here. It was 1944.

The two narratives were told to me in response to a direct question to each speaker with no other person present in the first case and speaker B's two young sons and a nephew in the second. The qualification is important because such accounts of the shedding of blood were restricted to specific, limited audiences. No one would refer to the events at an evening talk or re-enact the words or gestures of the moment. Where blood remained an issue between houses, whatever formal peace might have been made, talk about it was suppressed.[39] Bedr's only son was alive and thus under the duty and burden of at least being taken to be ready at some time to revenge his father's death in these somewhat ambiguous circumstances: just who had killed his father, and was it the deliberate act of a fellah or, potentially equally complicated, by mistake but by one of the agha beit? Since this narrative focused very directly upon open conflict between fellahin and aghas there was an additional reason for silence. Neither man had any problem telling me 'in private'. 'Everyone knew', and it was vital that they did because what the narratives spoke of still structured relations in significant degrees. But 'no one spoke'.[40]

Both accounts anchor the affair in relations between the beys, and in the collective nature of relations between strata. The original dispute was to do with competing land claims of the landlords, and the fact that one of the landowners' agents was an agha and one a fellah exacerbated the matter. The respective houses were mobilized in a sequence of confrontations, verbal and physical, and peace was refused, it seems by both parties.

Readers will have noted the obvious discrepancies between the narratives in terms of sequencing, and not least in the crucial matter of the killing of Bedr. As the topic was never publicly broached in evening gatherings or general conversations, there was no pressure to a standardization of narrative or to privileging one rather than the other.[41]

Speaker A, a family notable and important in the wider social prestige of Beit Abd as-Salam, did not mention that he and his brother, noted aghas, had been obliged by the affair to move from their shop that was situated at the top of the hill where the space of the Zawiya began. The outlaw mentioned this move, however, signalling more clearly that the aghas had by no means been able simply to triumph over the fellahin. True, they had chased all the cultivators from their houses and committed other acts of violence. But one of the aghas was dead, one stabbed and others struck. In terms of their own sense of relations between the strata, this represented a very unstable and destabilizing moment in the continuous shared history.

Despite such a confrontation, relations with the fellahin throughout the Ottoman and Mandate periods were frequently represented by fellahin and agha alike as a simple pattern of repression and coercion. Both commonly described the fellahin until the 1940s as *meyyitin*, 'dead'. 'We screwed their women and beat them', as a low-status agha friend said, with some amused nostalgia. 'Yes indeed', an old fellah with some reputation for giving talismen and healing chimed in: 'You were very hard to us.' The agha went on: 'If Abboud was angry with them he would send Abu Adnan up to the Zawiya to throw them and all their belongings out of the house.' A fellah with a new shirt had it ripped from his back. 'They (naming two agha murafiqs who confirmed it) used to grab a man and throw him to the ground and the bey would stamp on him', said one fellah.[42] In the holy fasting month of Ramadan, Abboud never let cultivators have the all-important first meal breaking the fast, the *iftar*. He thus denied them even the proper form of religious practice and turned fasting into starvation. Worse, the starving had to feed those with plenty. A fellah told me that the wakil or the bey would shout from his house top: "'Tomorrow bring chickens, or a sheep, or flour, or cooking oil'", whatever they wanted.'

The coercive structuring of relations might be modified. Just as an agha might well serve the bey's house served by his father, or stay as wakil for a landowner over fifteen years or more, so he might work with the same fellahin for long periods. That family of cultivators might also have been with the same lord's house over two generations, occasionally even more. It was not unusual for a cultivator to remain with one agha for his working life, which would begin from around the age of ten. All kinds of practical day-to-day negotiations would necessarily take place. 'Theft' was spoken of as something constantly engaged in by fellahin. But some said that the poorer wakil also had to *dabbar halu*, 'look out for himself' as the common phrase had it, in conditions where he was not necessarily able to make ends meet. No doubt blind eyes were turned, unspoken understandings reached, and mutual knowledge built up through the life-cycle and rituals of marriage and death moderated the harshness of material life. In one or two cases fellahin had become well known as qabadays, as individually feared as a reputed agha but without the collective force the agha could mobilize.[43]

Sharecropping agreements varied: 40–42 per cent to the owner and 60–58 per cent to the cultivator was common, with all the expenses being on the latter, who would often be in debt for money or grain to the owner. Proportions might vary a little from year to year. Some share agreements were 50–50 if the fellah provided labour, plough, animal fertilizer and animals. One agha of Beit Abd as-Salam, on the other hand, had four local Alawis working his land in Syria who only got a quarter of the harvest and 'you could kick them out when you wanted to'. Where there was an acute labour shortage for the size of the holdings then fellahin from the village might effectively act as wakils and take a larger share.[44] Such cultivators tended to own their own shelters or houses, and sometimes draught animals, sheep and a cow. Their level of life might thus not be obviously distinguishable from some of the wakils and they might have their own sharecroppers or labourers. Cowherds bore the feeding costs of the animals bought by the owner but took a quarter of the harvest of the land they worked and had a right to the calves. These men, the *murabi'in*, were for hire. Simple seasonal labourers, nearly always Alawites, 'had nothing at all'.

Cultivators were thus by no means in the same economic and social position. And there were enough accounts of an agha confronting this or that settlement and forcibly taking his or the bey's harvest share, or beating up recalcitrant fellahin or 'rebels', or catching someone stealing crops to show that active resistance of different kinds was a constant element of these relations. If the aghas existed, as one said to me, for 'praising, manly deeds and putting on a show', the fact that so many narratives dwelt on tensions with the beys pointed to some of the real complexities of the links between lords and their murafiqin.

Lands were being registered as private property. Large estates were taking on a fully legal form. Labour was relatively scarce and frequently tied by physical coercion to the landowners as much as by economic dependency. Debt might socially cripple anyone at any level. Beys were competing for economic and political predominance in an increasingly monetarized economy. The style of life and consumption patterns were changing: 'They started eating different food from us', as one old agha put it. Great landowners built great houses, required apartments in Tripoli or Beirut, sometimes educated their sons abroad, ran cars and frequented the racetrack. Above all, the successful ones developed their economic and social base through modernizing agricultural methods and investing in urban property.

The place of Abboud in the discourse of power is defined as much in reference to these factors as to the face-to-face confrontations in which he personally participated, unlike many other landowners. The land inherited from his own father had not been considered to be particularly valuable in production terms, but Abboud drained it and made it more profitable. He took advantage of cheap land prices in Syria to buy large tracts with money borrowed from a paternal uncle, Ali Pasha, money he was able to pay back. He exploited to the full his privileged relations with Mieg and his institutional positions to build up the largest estate holdings in the region. His son was groomed to succeed him, not least by studying law in Paris, entering into politics, and continuing his father's vigorously pro-French policy.[45]

Abboud Bey could convert the position inherited through the house of his father Muhammad Pasha Muhammad and Ottoman tax farming into the status of a 'modern' landowner and regional political leader. Enabled by the Mandate to build up his estate on both sides of the Lebanese–Syrian border (an area dominated by the latifundists from the coast inland as far as Homs and Hama) he could increase the breadth of his economic and political opportunities. The marriage of his only son to a daughter of a leading Hama landowning family, the Barazis, indicates his social strategy. To the élite of Beirut, Akkar might be a distant and socially marginal region with which they historically had few links; its representative, however, was no mere local chieftain. In a period when landowners were the preponderant class in the National Assemblies, Abboud Bey typified a dominant social force: a man who could exploit both old and new powers expertly and ruthlessly.[46]

Such a man had rivals. He was opposed within Berqayl itself by the house of Mustapha Bey, but also from neighbouring settlements, by Khalid Bey Abd al Qadir, whose family came from Ayyoun only a short distance due south, and by Osman Pasha in Bebnine on the low hills leading down to the coast on the way to Abde and Tripoli. In the fierce rivalry and competition for the new power available through the Mandate, weaker families who could not sustain their own interests became clients or sold lands to the greater lords. Rivalry altered through each shifting alliance with the French, with Arab nationalists or with Christian members of the financial and professional bourgeoisie in Beirut.

Agha and fellah narratives about Abboud stressed the fact that he was pre-eminent in switching from cereals to olives wherever feasible. Trees were planted in neat rows, 250 per shunbul of seedlings and 100 to 120 mature trees in the same area. Land planted in olives increased in value from 1,000–2,000LL to 10,000LL. The last mulberry trees for silk production were cut down. He brought the first caterpillar tractor in before the Second World War, and the first tractors after it. Chemical fertilizer and new strains of crops followed later. And – a matter referred to again and again – he kept immaculate accounts. 'He would go mad if a single olive was missing', one of his murafiq's said. 'You could never just turn up and say that an animal had died of illness. You had to produce the skin.' 'He knew every sheep and goat he owned.' The level of superhuman surveillance, revealed in the common view that 'you couldn't steal from Abboud', set him apart from his competitors. This preternatural power of knowing and reckoning, of innovating and rationalizing, of entering every aspect of the operations of his estates in his account books, was as extraordinary as any act of violence, gratuitous or otherwise. Wakils were given *written* instructions and made to write down transactions. If they did not carry out the orders quickly enough they were sent terse reminders.[47] This accounting was treated as being of the greatest significance in marking changes in agricultural practice in Akkar. It represented a new ordering of the landscape, part of a move to establish a more total domination.

The rationalizing innovator, investor in Beirut property, and champion of the French Mandate was also the bey who personally confronted fellahin and aghas face to face, killed to test a rifle, built roads with forced labour, and constructed a Franco-Italian château in the village with blue stucco walls and interiors full of luxury furniture covered in brocades and velvets. The landowner who so eagerly embraced a more obviously capitalist agriculture with conspicuous economic success was also the bey most reputed for his direct physical intervention in the control of subject populations, and as the most ruthless opponent of other landowners in struggles over the control of political space.

It is easy to see why, as a narrative construct as much as a specific historical person, 'Abboud' should be such a complex, dominant figure. He does indeed seem to embody crucial processes of social life for a whole region and set of histories. The sheer rhetorical and narrative force of 'Abboud' made it locally very difficult to imagine other ways of constituting history, social identity and the operations of power. What 'Abboud' represented in an intensely personalized discourse of power, was thus lived and remembered realities, past in present and present in past.

CHAPTER SEVEN

Underdeveloped Periphery

Mediocre, Deficient and Deprived

We find in North Lebanon the most striking deficiencies in the country.[1]

Between 1959 and 1961, under the auspices of President Fuad Chehab and the Ministry of Planning, the IRFED Mission and the Lebanese research teams, a total of around forty persons, conducted a full-scale study of the resources and potentialities of Lebanon. More than four decades after the travels of Tamimi and Bahgat, these specialists applied the full panoply of modern techniques and methodologies to zones and sub-zones of the country. As the discourse of planning and of modernization was at its apogee in the West and in the Eastern blocs, Lebanon too would now prepare its first Five-Year Plan.

Lebanese readers knew the economic and political background to the IRFED Mission very well. In Iraq a revolution in 1958 had displaced the monarchy installed by the British and produced a military regime under Qasim. In Syria prolonged governmental instability had led in 1958 to a new regime unified with Egypt in a United Arab Republic which had passed a land reform act and shown some 'socialist' intentions. Egypt itself, under President Nasser, was a major force in Third World as well as Arab politics. The new Lebanese President, Chehab, had shown an understanding of that fact and an acknowledgement of Lebanon's 'Arab identity', an understanding not appreciated by his opponents. As the oil states generated ever-greater revenues, Lebanon was benefiting enormously from the flow of funds, attracted to Lebanese financial expertise and the relatively safe refuge, attractive also to Arab capital frightened by talk of socialism elsewhere.

The instability and disequilibrium of the region involved Lebanon inextricably in a set of fast-moving and confusing processes, often to the enormous profit of certain social groups, particularly in the financial and service sectors.[2] Some, however, questioned whether its political institutions would be able to survive.[3] The previous President, Camille Chamoun, had precipitated the 1958 civil war by wishing to stand for a Second Mandate which the constitution did not allow him.[4] Chehab was the Army commander who had succeeded him. He wanted to reverse the *capitalisme sauvage* of his predecessors and to diminish the rapidly increasing divide between capital and regions. 'Change' was therefore seen by the new presidential administration as both necessary and intensely problematic. The Plan would manage change, partially through the provision of a unified language to be imposed upon a non-unified society.

President Chehab aimed to establish a 'modern' state and society which would transcend the limitations of Lebanese political and social practice as the Chehabists saw them and would lead ultimately to a qualitative shift in the political economy of the country. The whole of national space was to be subjected to scientific observation prior to, and during, its planification by the state. In a country celebrated for its *laissez-faire*, liberal economic policies, the very idea of such a Plan, with all its étatist and interventionist implications, was indeed part of a new language that was bound to be opposed by powerful interests.

Using the Plan as one of its key instruments, the state would take to itself controls and functions over the economy, investment, and certain political spheres and relations. In short, national space would not only be surveyed, it would be reshaped. The IRFED report was part of a struggle over the nature and powers of the state itself.

'Considered in its totality, Lebanon appears as a society in transition dominated by a very intense individualism and by a communitarianism of religious origin.'[5] The introduction diagnoses, in language that makes a moral as well as political appeal, a basic inequality between social groups. National cohesion and a *sens civique* can only exist, it says, if everyone feels that he benefits from 'national economic solidarity'. Privileged groups should try to narrow the differences between their conditions of life and those of less favoured groups (p. 17). They should show 'fiscal loyalty' and accept a costly and great effort for the development of what are called '*des zones en souffrance*'. Thus will oppositions always latent between groups be diminished (p. 18).

The report designates Beirut as the image, the symptom, and even a cause of disorder. The city is a representation of that individualist rationality against which modernity must struggle. For Beirut is not only a cosmopolitan city, the pole where all the innovations of comfort and science are united and distinguished one from the other, it is a place of international commerce and finance whose *hommes d'affaires* maintain a vast intercontinental network of personal relations. Here, the profits of the oil states are spent and invested. Every buyer finds a seller, every seller a buyer. 'Everything is constructed on personal intuition and on the secret' (p. 18). The only rationality is personal. Every operation is short-term. The Plan is long-term.

Here are not one, but two paradoxes. The very reason for the success of 'Beirut' as a regional and even a world pole of economic affairs, its total liberalism and untrammelled financial activity, is the obstacle to further, qualitative development into another kind of progress. And secondly, precisely those elements identified as the characteristics of 'being Lebanese', namely intense individualism and religious communalism, are also identified as the sources of potential breakdown. What others see as prosperity and the vindication of *laissez-faire* policies, the introduction to the IRFED report represents as the mark of accelerating entropy.

Lebanon, says the Mission, has become two societies, distinct yet at the same time inter-penetrating. Beirut – all flux, turbulence, disorder, and unbridled finance capitalism – is one society, an ever-growing expansion which swallows up land and migrants alike, influencing the whole country. The other is composed of a growing sub-proletariat, a belt of poor and sometimes wretched villages and rural areas suffering from penury and sometimes from insecurity as well. The riches of Greater Beirut and the misery of the sub-proletariat are the products of the same social forces. Peasants who come from the world of villages with their 'millennial traditions' are swallowed up into the dynamic confusion of the transformed and transforming city, a complex process which deeply affected both the north and the south of the country.[6]

The rhetoric of the introduction links a vision of modernity to an acute political danger and a critique of the social and economic order symbolized by the capital. Little by little, warn the writers, the conditions of a 'popular reaction' are coming into being, mitigated to a certain extent by community membership, but the reaction itself may become the reason for conflict (p. 19). Although the report designates Lebanon an 'individualist' society, it also speaks in terms which have a collective and quasi-class character. Its writers favour a bi-polar scheme of 'rich and poor' and refer ominously to a growing gap between them. A transformation must be effected, or there will be untold consequences.

'The expert' is the hero of the development narrative, and like all heroes, he, and the state for which he metonymously stands, encounter enemies. He is obstructed by what are rather coyly termed 'current structures', that is, different sections of the dominant classes. His concepts, theories and methods appear unjust to a society which is radically liberal and individualist. For the expert unavoidably promotes intervention by the state, 'in order that a greater rationality introduce itself in the totality of the structures' (p. 20).

The sword of technocratic objectivity is rigorous, statistically based enquiry of a global kind. The enquiry displays all aspects of Lebanese society on a scale of one to ten measuring different 'levels of life': cultural situation, leisure, psychological factors, education, domestic situation, sanitation, economy and technology, residential, habitat, sanitary amenities, domestic amenities, education equipment, family, social, and cultural situations. This positivist vision is represented as everything that short-term, personal, secret Lebanese individualism is not: for it is long-term, impersonal, public, universal and general.

Whom is the expert to save? The underdeveloped – the 'margins' of Lebanon, the north, the north-east and the south which enter into the category of underdevelopment (p. 26).[7] These regions illustrate what the report discreetly calls 'certain anomalies' in Lebanese society. As we have already seen, the experts saw Akkar as the type-case of undevelopment: 'The whole of the zone is afflicted with such multiple deficiencies that we must limit ourselves here to stressing only the most serious' (II–5–6).

In the hills, the sub-zone where Berqayl is situated, the specialists observe little improvement. Nonetheless, there are 'real villages' where the peasants, agricultural workers and sharecroppers of the large properties of the plain own some dry lands planted in cereals, vines and olives, 'and, often, their houses'(II–5–4). Two or three of the roughly twenty villages are reasonably important, but none has either running water or electricity. Some proprietors live at a higher standard, but they are a minority.

Here and there the experts find exceptions to the general pauperization, for example, the regions of Qubayat and Andaqat in the middle plateau area, though everywhere else in that sub-zone is of a *médiocrité générale* (II–5–7). Akkar is not an economically or socially homogeneous space. The Jumeh sub-zone, residence of big proprietors and of people who have made money by emigration, is richer (II–5–8). People aspire to improved comfort and housing, to emigration and work in towns which create opportunities 'useful for their evolution' (C–11). Baino is exceptional, its great prosperity born of emigration (II–5–21).

Like Tamimi and Baghat before them, the planners find that the mountains have been little studied 'because access is very difficult' (C–13). The four 'real villages' and multitude of little hamlets have no tarred roads, drinking water, or electricity. Where there are schools they are primitive. In Michmich, the selected 'type village', the levels of life are all very low though it is true, that two families formerly owned all the land *'whereas now the peasants have 60 per cent of irrigated lands and properties are becoming smaller'* (II–5–9, my emphasis). The fellahin have started to cultivate apple trees, but only very hesitantly (C–13).[8] The prognosis remains sombre.

Improvement will be difficult to achieve, in the experts' eyes, because the inhabitants of the mountain show such limited concern for progress; 'the receptivity of the adults is completely passive and borders on indifference'. The cultural level is 'completely devoid of positive elements' and barely preserves the traces of 'a traditional culture' in the course of disappearing.[9] There are other 'traces': the level of the family shows 'vestiges of a tribal life where the women's place is reduced by polygamy and the preference for boys'. The column of Negative Factors in one table lists 'very marked autarky' and 'tribal régime; illiteracy; stubbornly resistant population'.[10] Among a few indicators of evolution, the acquisition of land remains predominant. Some houses now contain a bed and a radio, but there are few external signs of changes in consumption or of technical innovations (II–5–10).

Of Halba the experts express views very close to those of Tamimi and Bahgat. The paths are in a bad state. There is a minimal degree of urbanization; no water or electricity; no bank, no cinema, no secondary schooling. With improved communications to Tripoli, the little centre of some 3,600 residents has lost its former importance: 'in the current circumstances there is no possibility of growth for Halba' (II–5–B–3–2). Tripoli, the real social and economic pole, onesidedly dominates all the diverse zones which are linked to it *but not to each other* (my emphasis).

Emigration is the only 'indigenous factor' of change in Akkar. There is no other internal dynamic. The region has, however, an external dynamic. 'Outsiders' have entered Akkar, buying land and introducing new market-oriented crops and technologically up-to-date methods in the use of machinery or chemical fertilizers. The experts instance an entrepreneur from Saida in south Lebanon who has purchased property, planted windbreaks of trees, sunk wells and made a plantation (for oranges). People from the town of Zahle in the Beqa'a valley have come over and grown important cashcrops such as potatoes, carrots, tomatoes, peanuts and vegetables using sophisticated methods. Machinery is in more general use. Every year citrus cultivation increases; tobacco, a rich and intensive crop, gives good returns (II–5–C–33).

Elsewhere, however, the Mission shows that agriculture has declined considerably in the period 1950–57 compared to industry, transport, commerce, property, public administration and other services. Its annual rate of growth is very low and it represents a declining economic sector.[11] Many rural families, in general peasants, small or waged cultivators, have low income levels: nearly 56 per cent have an annual family revenue lower than 2,500LL, that is about 200LL per month. 2,500LL is the level below which people are classified as 'poor', a category into which fell around 40 per cent of the population, or 49 per cent if one includes the 9 per cent of *miséreux* with less than 1,200LL per year.[12] The prosperity of the present clearly owes little if anything to the rural areas.

What is to be done? The experts recommend that an infrastructure be put in place. Populations should be stabilized by improving facilities and establishing a socio-economic framework profitable to all population groups (II–5–B–3–6). 'The development of this zone is constrained by *the poverty of the peasant cultivators* and the absenteeism of the large proprietors. Change requires *a property and agrarian reform*' (II–5–C–7, emphasis in the original). The state should intervene, technically and legally.

At precisely this point, silence falls on the subject of the reform of land and power relations. There is no further development of the subject. The experts resume their survey, leaving only this trace, this bare utterance on the system of property. At the very moment of intrusion in the text, politics vanishes.[13]

Akkar demonstrates that a sub-proletariat exists whose needs the state must first identify and then answer in order to avoid the fundamental conflict that threatens 'Lebanon'. However, nothing very individualist or communitarian is identified in an Akkar represented as composed chiefly of groups who are socially and psychologically unprepared for change or indifferent to progress.[14]

The report tells us a great deal about the economic and material conditions of the region. Yet the 'deficiencies' of Akkar are without a history. Though the specialists quantify data with relentless thoroughness, they describe no processes at work. Akkar is without dynamic, save that of movement out by emigrants or movement in by investors. The social forms and relations constituting 'Akkar', reduced to indices of exclusion in a timeless world of numbers, remain unseen beneath their all-seeing gaze.[15]

Diary of a Landholding, 1953–72

The notable of Beit Abd as-Salam who had both the largest landholding and the greatest influence with the governorate in Tripoli was, by the time of my fieldwork, an established man of means. His villa, the only one in the agha area of the village, was surrounded by a balcony on which he would sometimes sit on summer evenings looking down over the Hara and the valley beyond. It was no accident that he thus adopted the practice of power for which Muhammad al Abboud was remembered. He was the only villager who had constructed such a balcony and built his house with a 'front door', which was approached through elaborate wrought-iron gates up a short tiled path overhung with vines. Houses traditionally did not have front doors. Entrances were 'at the back' facing on to a small yard and away from the path or street, shielding the inner world of the domestic unit from the outer, public world. Like the Minister before him, the notable had adopted an urban model of the house. In so doing he asserted his distinction from, and superiority to, others. The chandelier-hung dining room furnished in plush and gilt, equally distinct, expressed the same claims to worldly station.[16]

Gaining that distinction had been a struggle. He was the younger of two boys and his older brother, still living, was Muhammad al Abboud's doughty murafiq and a noted hunter, held to exemplify the 'old ways' celebrated in many narratives of violent confrontation with his lord's opponents. The father had married again upon his first wife's death, and came to favour the two sons his second wife bore him over the two boys of the first marriage. The half-brothers had, as half-brothers were expected to do, difficult relations. Moreover, the father sold off most of his landholdings to fund consumption expenditures during his last years of life in what was universally interpreted as a gesture of 'spite' against the sons, who were left with nothing. The father was thus represented as acting to render extremely difficult the reproduction of status in the next generation. He threw away the property so vital to the transmission of social position.[17]

The future landed notable had started life poor, as a small cultivator leasing land and occasionally acting as a strong-arm man for a bey. Members of his descent group asserted that he had been able to acquire the capital that made land purchase possible by 'smuggling' during the Second World War, and various deals after it. His influence with the governorate in Tripoli was held to have started with his brokering of a marriage for a leading official with whom he had become close during the 1950s. Whatever the case, he had begun modestly in the 1940s, leasing two or three hectares on the plain. By the time I met him he ran an estate of some fifty hectares, owned and leased, on which he employed fellahin families. They were totally dependent upon him and supported him in any dispute as well as following his instructions in elections. He also operated in different ways in Tripoli, and had good connections with the governor's office, which enabled him to intervene in situations of legal dispute involving villagers, or at points where *wasta*, brokerage and influence peddling, was needed. He was known as a supporter of the Chehabist governments of the 1960s, and of the long-serving Deputy in the National Assembly who was from the neighbouring village of Bebnine. Suleiman Franjieh's succession to the Presidency in 1970 did not seem to have had any deleterious effect on his position.

The Hajj, so titled because he had made the pilgrimage a few years previously, was thus a man of some clout. Members of his fraction of the agha descent group, Beit Abd al Latif, spoke of him as *ra'is al 'ailat*, head of the family. Men of the other sections might not accord him that title, and the mayor's family of Beit Hassan, the other major section, were inclined to belittle his status when speaking before an audience of their own. But everyone acknowledged that he had the best external links and was the only one who could operate 'outside'.

The Hajj spent much of his time in the summer months down in his house in the midst of his fields on the plain and playing an active part in the administration of his holdings. The farm manager was the eldest of his senior brother's two sons. The Hajj himself had no children by his marriage but his nephew, Muhammad, was effectively treated as the Hajj's son and the landholder was formally addressed as 'Abu Muhammad', 'father of Muhammad'.[18]

Muhammad had worked with his uncle for most of his adolescent and adult life. He prided himself on his efficiency and knowledge of his job, and on running an enterprise on carefully planned lines. In our conversations he stressed his 'modernity', rationality and concern purely for farm management rather than all the 'empty talk' of status and honour. When I showed interest in the way in which the Hajj had built up his landholdings, Muhammad volunteered to give me an account of the entire history based on a series of notebooks which he had kept since 1953 on the precise evolution of his uncle's estate. 'I have written down everything', he said with great pride, 'every year'. And though he prepared a summary rather than reading out the entire contents of the notebooks, he was keen to stress to me that what he would tell me was 'recorded in writing'.[19]

Both Muhammad and I saw this document as unique in its context. No one else had prepared such a written narrative of productive activity over the years. Others might well recall the same details of costs and practices and how they changed, but not with the attention to chronological sequence and comprehensiveness of detail, let alone written down. They would have no practical reason to do so. Muhammad clearly felt that he had. His life was constructed, or rather charted through and written down in the notebooks with their distinctive mode of recording, ordering and privileging of technical knowledge over 'status'. We shall see that he divides the phases of development of the estate by changes in crops, methods of cultivation and technology, and land prices.

At the same time as Muhammad's account helped me to understand the rise of a local agha notable, it also made clear the wider processes of change within the agricultural sector as a whole in the region during the 1950s and 1960s. He shows us something of the costs, calculations and strategies that a consciously 'modernizing' estate went through in those decades as the markets and range of crops cultivated changed.[20] At the same time, we should recall his interest in demonstrating a rational policy of agricultural innovation and management and, through that demonstration, the *difference* of his life from that of others. Muhammad establishes that 'life' through work and organization, not through status. This is his claim to uniqueness.

The following is a condensed version of seven pages of notes taken in English during a single long discussion [all bracketed comments are mine]:

In 1953 the Hajj owned two to three hectares on the coastal plain. He directed operations himself, there was no one from the family with him. He leased 35 shunbuls of land from Muhammad Bey al Mahmud, Jud Bey and the other beys. Leasing was cheap then, 250–300LL a year for growing pistachio and maize; for wheat it was 100–150. We didn't plant tomatoes or vegetables because they needed too much capital. Pistachio and maize were low cost – labour was cheap, the best worker only got three to three and a half lira a day and if one got that he was a king. Labourers usually got one and a half lira, or two if they were good. There was a market for pistachios, but it wouldn't make the kind of profit it does now and you had to wait five months in which you had nothing between planting in April and harvest in September. A hectare would make 50–60 *shwal* [shwal, a dialect word for sack, my informant glossed as 35 kilos]. A shunbul would take ten people to dig and hoe. We didn't use fertilizer, didn't know how to. Each hectare would yield 300LL or so profit.

Maize was planted with the pistachio but we didn't consider it much for harvesting, so if you made anything that was 'from heaven'. It didn't cost much and fed the cows. We kept one cow ourselves for milk. [Animals regularly crop the plain after harvest, fertilizing it as they move.]

After the wheat harvest we would bring in a heavy duty tractor for turning over the soil [the soil being too dry at the end of summer for ordinary machinery]. That cost 30LL each hectare. We'd leave the land through six or seven months of the winter and then plough it with an ordinary tractor at 15LL per hectare. We had to hire the tractors from outside at that time. Some soils were very light, and in those cases we used oxen for working, not tractors which made the soil impossible to work, though others did not agree.

We waited for winter rains and if they didn't come we brought in the man
responsible for water supply in the area to water the land at ten lira a turn. ...
Then we'd use a pair of oxen at ten lira a six-hour day, four pairs of oxen for
each hectare, with two girls sowing behind them earning three lira daily. The 17
shunbul planted in pistachio took seventy or so turns of oxen at 700LL with
50LL for labour, and the rest of the land we planted in wheat.

When the pistachio gets larger after two months we water it once and each
hectare requires four waterings, one each 20 days. After the last one, we leave it
for a month without water. ... Pistachio needs drying in the sun. If you take it
green and put it in sacks it turns black and rots.

Muhammad went on to explain that wheat did not get very good results at
that time, though people began to use chemical fertilizer, and the cultivator
might make a loss. They would only lease for wheat on two-year agreements,
alternating with pistachio. From the entire holding of 35 shunbul he estimated
annual profit during the years 1953–63 at 7,000LL a year.

Profits were invested in land. The Hajj bought twenty-five of the shunbul
he had previously leased from the beys, paying 2,000LL for the best land and
1,000LL for the less good. Muhammad gave the name of each bey who had
sold, not least because that formed part of the commonly cited local history
of how the beys had begun to lose their lands. 'Now the Hajj could sell for
half a million if he wanted to', because of the increase in land prices on the
plain by 1971.[21]

The beys had started to sell, Muhammad said, 'because the fellahin would
steal and profits were low'. The significance of theft in his account, as in the
accounts of others, was critical:

The manager (wakil) only got 400LL worth of grain and couldn't live on that so
both he and the peasants used to steal. The bey would end up with just over a
third of the harvest (instead of a half or two-thirds). If the bey was a qabaday
he could only go to the landholding during the day, and the stealing was at
night, by wakil and peasants. Both sides hated each other. That's why the beys
thought it easier to sell up. In any case, rents were low.

As happened in many of the narratives I heard, changes tended to be
credited to a shift in a kind of endemic class warfare, usually exemplified by
the tale of a particular bey and 'his' fellah. Only figures such as Abboud Bey,
whose capacity for creating 'fear' was credited with the near-miraculous power
of preventing anyone from 'stealing', were said to have been able to stop the
impoverished fellahin from taking what they could. Muhammad's account
shows us a little more, however, because it indicates the kind of tacit
understandings, even solidarities, between wakils and fellahin that no doubt
operated over long periods of time. And, also no doubt, the beys were aware
of the levels and kinds of unauthorized appropriation of produce that their
subordinates practised.

What Muhammad did not say was that a bey's sons might secretly sell olives ahead of the harvest to relatives or aghas with some cash in order to fund the sons' entertainments in the city.[22] They stole too, unless their father was very careful. Nor did he add that beys were furious with agricultural watchmen drawn from Beit Abd as-Salam, accusing them of stealing more olives than the thieves against whom the watchmen were supposed to be protecting the groves at night. One or two beys tried to exclude Beit Abd as-Salam men from guarding altogether, but the unfortunate fellah replacements were beaten up, and the aghas regained their places by force. The beys' tempers were not improved by their knowledge that groves managed by senior agha men were free of such predations.[23]

Within the discourse of production and costs, the language of personal capacities to enforce one's will and right again still characterizes Muhammad's representation of rural relations. That 'rents were low' emerges only as a brief secondary observation, and he made no comment on wider changes in the beys' positions that might lead to land sale.[24]

Muhammad marked out 1963 as a key year of transition. He began to grow carrots on a hectare or two, the first time the soon-to-be high profit vegetables appeared locally, making 1,500LL per hectare. Fine judgement was required, he stressed. The crop needed a lot of labour in winter and those with family labour did better, since they had lower costs, than those hiring on the market, as he was. Predicting supply and prices could be tricky, 'and I didn't want to send 20 tons to market because the prices would go down'. He explained carefully the costs and methods he used for growing this crop whose coming pinpointed a shift in the economies of farming.

From 1963, too, the leasing of land rose steeply to 500–700LL a shunbul because there started to be good agricultural gains as the Beirut market for vegetables expanded rapidly with economic growth; though he noted that tomatoes, a high-profit crop while I was there, were not yet being tried. In 1966 the Hajj began to plant broad beans, four or five shunbul with green peas. Both crops were low cost:

> If you succeed with broad beans you make 2,000LL profit and if you lose you only lose the 235LL you paid for cultivation, and so what? You make that up on the pistachio which grows very well with beans. Peas are the same and are like fertilizer for pistachios. And you get two or three crops of each.

Success with broad beans and peas was followed in 1966–67 by a relative failure with okra which only made money for those with family labour. In 1968 he grew the first tomatoes on two hectares. High winds, much lamented scourge of Akkar agriculture, destroyed the first crops. Tomatoes were relatively capital intensive – 1,000LL for cultivation and 600 as rent, and one could not plant pistachios afterwards but only carrots – so the loss was serious. A hectare takes 9,000 plants for a total cost of 450LL. Add in labour at 150LL, 70LL for fertilizer, 300–400LL for hoeing, another 125LL for a second fertilizer, and a lot of watering and you are looking at a high potential loss. With good luck, on the other hand, you make 4,000–5,000LL a hectare. That in turn depends on how much has come on to the market and if you want to market it in Syria, on whether the border is open. ... Zucchini and beans were also good. Depending on the market, 'zucchini buys the land its planted on' at 6,000–7,000LL a hectare; beans would make 1,500–2,000.

> The Hajj had done well to buy when he did. And he's just purchased two hectares on the plain from a bey's son for 16,000LL, in an area where prices could reach 20,000LL if it was both near the road and in proximity to the river or irrigation works. The Hajj had both. But he has high expenses, with everyone making demands on him for favours, the wider family using him, the costs of the needy whose wants he looked after. But he only spent on necessities. He avoids anything forbidden, like wine or women. He only spent on necessities. And he would not cultivate with anyone on a share basis. The Hajj only worked on his own, even if in some ways it would be better to have at least some joint enterprises.

Not only the Hajj benefited from proximity to the road or the irrigation projects. Beys who had sold much of their holdings but had been able to keep such sections found themselves with lands which, in strictly market terms, were worth more than their whole estates would have been ten years before. Thus it was publicly said of one leading bey's family that they had lost the lands that had once stretched 'from the snow to the sea', but were still financially better off than before. Speakers would lament or rejoice in the disappearance of the estate and reputation of the house of Ibrahim Pasha. When they did so, they referred, not to the money, but to the social value of the widely distributed holdings in the mountain and on the plain, holdings around which had been articulated a now vanishing complex of relations of power and production.

Muhammad incorporated the characteristic style of 'defending' his uncle into his narrative of modernization, as any subordinate did of his superior. He lauded the landowner's virtues both moral and economic – his frugality, independence (even if it contradicted Muhammad's own sense of what might be advantageous), and avoidance of the forbidden (while others jealous of his influence asserted the contrary). He stressed the collective demands made on his uncle, both by aghas and by fellahin, and the costs of being a man of substance. The estate could not simply be run according to economic calculations, there were other factors that constrained a notable cultivating a position as broker with the powerful. He did not mention, though others did, that the Hajj was said to lend money to needy beys at interest rates which gave a good profit.

The Hajj himself had his own very public views of the worth of 'people here'. On his evenings at home in the village house he would mock their 'ignorance'. After piously describing himself as one to whom God had been good, he gave a wildly caricatured imitation of the Sufi zikr, parodying the

repetitive chants of the Names of God and pantomiming exaggerated movements back and forth, which made the company roar with laughter. 'Look at
these young men', he said to me with dismissive contempt. 'How can a
father let his children grow up in front of his own eyes as jackasses?'

He would have to pay 12,000LL wasta to get one into the police force.
Why? They were all useless bastards, a much-repeated refrain. 'Why did I
bother to acquire an estate', he exclaimed, waving his hand at his young male
relatives, 'when this lot of idiots will simply sell it off and won't work it.
That's one reason why I don't plant lemon trees. They take time and effort
and no one will keep it going. I'd prefer commerce to farming if I could
start again, but it lacks the satisfaction of working and seeing things change
and grow.'[25] If there was no future in Berqayl it was because the shebab were
rubbish and nothing would come of them.

The Wealthy Few

The Hajj was one of four men of agha descent who were spoken of locally
as wealthy. The second and oldest of these, a man in his seventies, lived in
a large and imposing house perched on top of the hill above his olive groves
on the other side of the shallow valley below the village. Abu Faiz had been
another of Abboud's chief companions. His money, gained through 'gifts of
respect' from the bey, a shrewd sense of the opportunities his position gave
him to extract his own share of surpluses from cultivators, and a rumoured
closeness to a bey's sister, had enabled him to consolidate a medium-sized
estate. Some of his holdings came from buying out other aghas who were
forced to sell their lands. He 'ate' them. One son was doing business in West
Africa, another being educated in Spain. The old man, who had no education
himself, had followed the pattern of investment of human family resources
he had seen among the high-status groups.

The third agha who had made money, but who had no pretensions or
interest in influence or wasta, came from a family with no property. He had
begun as a barefoot labourer, men said, nothing more. In time he had become
a manager of labour groups for a bey. Finally, after Abboud's death in 1958,
he was put in charge of a large landholding belonging to one of the heirs
and officially took a third of the profits. People said the fraction might be
much higher and that he privately owned five hectares of olives as well as
leasing more. He was held to be ignorant of the ways to use money to create
social obligations and services or simply indifferent to such a position, apart
from employing young agha men in his new olive press at harvest time at
rates which were regarded as far from generous for very onerous work over
long hours.

The fourth of the wealthy was in his thirties and a younger brother of the
mayor. He had got into the Chehabist *Deuxième Bureau*, a powerful parallel
government organization under Chehab and his successor, and had used the

local power that gave him to establish his own material position. By the time the Bureau lost its power under Franjieh he had made his pile and got out. He, too, owned one of the new olive presses, from which he made 'a lot'. There were other, more obscure interests elsewhere about which men speculated, but with little concrete information to go on. He lived in Tripoli, had married from the city, and had little to do with Berqayl save at the time of the olive harvest.

In conversation he was cynical, and seemed proud of a reputation for being calculating and apart. 'Laziness was bred into them', he said of the village. 'People were used to receiving fourteen sacks of grain and two cans of oil under Abboud, and that was fine for them.' An olive grove watchman got 500LL or so during the season plus what he stole, so he was content. The aghas thought work was beneath them. He'd started with little and grown big so that now, he told me, he got jobs for young aghas in the army and teacher training. He had worked hard for sixteen years, 'in the office until midnight'.

In his first year with his new olive press he had lost 20,500LL; in the second he had made 7,000–8,000LL and this year (1972) he estimated that his profit would be around 40,000-50,000LL. In addition, he had bought olives ahead from Jud's sons the previous winter at 35LL a container when they needed cash and the price now was 95LL, so he would make a tidy sum.[26] But you had to be careful. Arguments often arose over who would press how many olives with whom, and about payments. Threats of force and/or legal action were common.

The 'rich men' of the agha stratum in this period thus came from three different generations. The oldest had established himself in the Mandate period through the old route: the murafiq who begins by using his link with a powerful lord to build up his own position and then sends his sons in new directions with the assets of the newer dominant classes. The others had started later with little or nothing in material terms, but by opportunistic exploitation of particular conjunctures of events had made themselves financially secure. The Hajj exploited a wartime emergency and a personal connection in the city; the ex-labourer took advantage of the situation after Abboud's death; the youngest, the *Deuxième Bureau* man, grabbed the chance to use his government post to make the maximum profit in cash and contacts.

A Bodyguard's Job

The same period which saw so much change in agriculture was not marked by major shifts in relations of force and alliance between the landowners. Economic losses meant that the number who could sustain a life of status and influence diminished further, especially as those costs escalated in the 1960s. Low returns on 'traditionally' run estates where capital was insufficient to finance modernization and sharecropping returns were relatively poor led owners either to sell, to rent out more and more land, or, in some cases such as Masoudiya, to try by increased coercion to tie labourers to estates. The successful invested in urban property and businesses, diversifying as the economy expanded.

Competition for political power between the major notables was acute. Elections had become critical in this competition and for obtaining access to the booty of the state. Stakes were getting higher and higher. Resources for the disbursement of benefits necessary in the maintenance of dependable followings were tied to politics as well as to individual wealth. And in politics, as the story of Muhammad al Abboud makes clear, violence might still play a central role. The position of murafiq, bodyguard and hired gun thus retained great significance for the local population.

Narratives covering the years from 1945 to the early 1960s told by the many aghas who worked for the beys showed no diminution in violence. In the management of lands and labourers, or in relations between major landlords, overt coercion continued to be a major theme.

The following is a condensed version of one such narrative which refers to events of the middle 1950s.[27] The speaker was my own attendant who had then worked for Abboud. He said that the bey paid him and another agha 1,000LL to shoot two men: an important rival Berqayli landlord, Hussein Bey (a pseudonym), and a leading fellah supporter of Suleiman al Ali, Abboud's rival, after Muhammad al Abboud's death. The commission worried him, though he portrayed his companion as being very gung-ho about the killing. But the attendant expressed some scruples about cold-bloodedly shooting down the victims. What could they do?

> I told my friend we should start an argument with Hussein Bey, deal out a punch or two, and if anything more happened, well, it happened, but we couldn't just kill them. 'But Abboud will be angry', he said. 'We'll just have to make up a story to tell him', I answered. So one day we found the fellah down at the mosque praising Suleiman al Ali for this and that and generally making propaganda and we didn't challenge him. But on his way home we stopped him and insulted al Ali and al Ali's father and family. My friend went to pull out his gun, and the fellah dragged me to one side and said: 'Look, I get 200LL a month from al Ali and a blank cheque for whatever I spend here on hospitality for getting support for him. I have to live too. I'd prefer to be with Abboud, but he won't have it, so what can I do? Abboud pays you 100LL a month.' Stuff like that.
>
> I said to myself, 'He's right', and stopped my companion shooting him. We made him promise not to come down to the mosque and make speeches for al Ali. He agreed, and off he went. Now we had the problem of what to do about Hussein. My friend wanted to wait at night by the bend in the road and kill him as he walked by. I wasn't having any of this. I told him: 'What's the point of having to flee the government and maybe get shot and have to run away from the village? It's much better to shoot up his house, walls and windows, and make a huge row about it.'
>
> So we did that one night. A few days later we went to see Abboud in Beirut

and when we entered his reception room he glared at us and told us to sit far away from him. He spoke to all the others very courteously as 'agha' and 'pasha'. When everyone else had left Abboud said we were liars who'd conspired together and not done anything at all. I protested that it wasn't fair. We'd shot them and the fellah wasn't seen in the village. 'Rubbish', said Abboud. 'You're lying.' He was furious.

Then Abboud hired another young agha to shoot Hussein and paid him 3,000LL. When the lad came to the village and went to his house he got in an almighty row with his father, who was in Hussein's pay as murafiq. His father clouted him and told him to get out, emigrate. So the son went back to Abboud and said: 'I've been kicked out of the village, but on such-and-such a day you'll see, I'll shoot Hussein.' He got another 2,000LL from Abboud and the same from his family. The day he was supposed to do the shooting he emigrated to Brazil and hasn't been heard of since.[28]

The narrative shows very well the pragmatics of violence, 'lying', and the kinds of negotiations that might occur around a specific act. My companion represents himself as preoccupied with calculations of self-interest and with working out the balance between following Abboud's commission and the likely dangerous outcome for himself. He is willing to risk the bey's formidable anger rather than the consequences of murder (whatever his appetite for the deed might have been). The uncertainties of the law, and perhaps Abboud's diminished influence under the Chamoun regime, make him hesitate. Flight, classification as an outlaw, or some years in prison with Hussein Bey's family doing everything to block his release – weighed against these possibilities the aged bey's wrath seemed worth earning.

The friend is portrayed as headstrong and ready for action, whereas he is swayed by the fellah's appeal to the similarities in their situation and the practical interests of every man. Forcing the fellah out of the heart of the dai'a and shooting up Hussein's house are the public acts of hostility that are both 'a show', but also demonstrate a controlled level of violence and intimidate Abboud's opponents. The other young agha, caught between contradictory forces of father and Abboud can only escape them by following the father's order to emigrate.[29] And he does so, tricking the bey out of a considerable sum of money in the process. He is lost to his family.

With Abboud's death and the changes in landholdings such narratives become rarer. Berqayl was no longer identified with the power of the once-dominant old bey. Agha men spoke of the period of the 1960s as one in which 'work' became more and more significant.[30] Violence continued to be integral to relations of power. All leaders needed gunmen, managers and drivers who acted as bodyguards. But the period of the *Deuxième Bureau*, which was very powerful in the region as elsewhere, constrained the powers of any bey or notable who did not support the state. Moreover, the ever-increasing significance of Beirut and other forms of investment for the beys, land sales to outsiders cultivating for agro-export, the changes in methods of production and organization of labour, the shift from sharecropping to leasing, and the factors which Muhammad's account illustrates, all tended to reshape the space of overt coercion and physical violence in politics and in the practices of everyday life.

Cultivators on the Plain

What Muhammad did not mention when discussing the beys' land sales was the position of the small cultivators during this period of agricultural modernization. A couple had also opportunistically exploited relations with beys or intelligence services to acquire land of their own. One family had built the only two-storey house in the Zawiya from the proceeds, so everyone swore, of a brother's banditry. 'No one goes there', men said dismissively, when I reported on their enthusiastic showing off of the house to me. Others used salaries from government work, the army, or years in utility companies to invest in land. A windfall inheritance from a wife's brother who died in Brazil gave one man of the very poorest families the chance to buy his own land and make about 5–6,000LL a year. Many were lucky if they averaged the IRFED poverty level of 1,500LL.

The cultivators did badly, being in just as precarious a position with the movement in of outsider investors and changes in agricultural methods as they had been under the beys.[31] The 'freedom' of market relations proved a heavy burden. They could often only afford poor, heavy land that was badly drained and difficult to work. As the yearly leases went up, it was difficult to find the money to work as much land as they had done under sharecropping arrangements.[32] There were fewer opportunities to be a *khawli* – labour supervisors over five other men – as some had been for Abboud, often for periods as long as twenty years. They looked back nostalgically to a time when a khawli 'had his prestige'. Still, by cultivating crops such as onions, carrots, and tomatoes and root crops for the Tripoli market, fellahin could sometimes make enough to live on, though seldom more. Working with family labour, as nearly all did, a man might have several years of loss because of fluctuations in the market or a sudden suspension of imports of tomatoes to Syria. So instead of making around 3,500LL from leasing four shunbul of land, you might lose 1,500LL.

Fellahin were frequently in debt to brokers for loans. There were only limited strategies available to the poor fellah: casual labour, girls and women of the family doing seasonal agricultural work for three lira a day, perhaps selling from a barrow in Tripoli, running a small shop stocking a little sugar, rice and cooking oil, perhaps just 'sitting' during the winter months. As one said to me: 'I can't emigrate. I've no work, no post, no factory job. Our conditions of life here are miserable.'

'Chehabism' had only a very limited success. The infrastructure was expanded in some areas of Akkar and utilities were brought to more villages, along with limited developments in education and medicine. But by the time of my fieldwork, Berqayl itself showed only limited signs of such policies, having no clinic or post office and many houses without electricity or piped water. Fellahin who got into construction or metalwork began to profit from the improvements some could now afford on their houses, as they moved from stone and earth to breeze blocks and reinforced concrete. For many, however, life remained 'miserable'.

PART THREE

The Weight of the Ancestors

CHAPTER EIGHT

Famine and Memory

The Olive Grove of the Orange

Karm al Leimun, 'the olive grove of the orange'. Of the *orange*? The incongruity puzzled me.[1]

Moreover, the title contradicted local practice by which each olive grove, indeed most landed property, is known by a single proper noun with the current owner's name attached when appropriate. The landscape is divided and given form by nominal inscriptions; each grove, each field, each garden has its title and a commonly known genealogy of owners past and present. When discussing property, men speak always in terms of such names of places and persons which encapsulate histories of the movement of land, wealth and power. Here the usual form changed.

To add a third dimension to its anomalous character, the grove was sometimes called by another name altogether: *Karm al Adami*, 'the grove of the decent man'. No other holding had two titles, each seeming to point to some event or metaphor that I could not grasp but which made the link between olive grove and orange, or grove and 'decent man', meaningful. Yet each name seemed to point to a narrative, a 'just so' story of how the grove came to bear its title(s).

The *ra'is al baladiya* (the mayor) told me his story of how 'the grove of the orange' was so curiously inscribed on the landscape:

His paternal grandfather, a noted agha, had been riding on the plain with one of the the most powerful lords. It was the time of severe famine during the First World War and people were starving.[2]

> The lord was eating an orange and the agha said: 'I would give anything for that orange.'
>
> The lord asked: 'Would you give your olive grove over there?', pointing to the trees on the foothills above them.
>
> 'Yes I would.'
>
> The bey handed him the fruit.
>
> Later the agha was in the lord's reception room when he was surprised to be publicly challenged by the bey in front of the many men who were gathered there: 'What, Abu Ali? Aren't you a man of your word?'
>
> Puzzled, because he did not remember the brief incident on the plain, he answered: 'Of course I am.'

'Well, didn't you say that you would give me that grove in exchange for an orange?'

The response came at once: 'Take it.'[3]

The mayor, grandson of the agha, glossed the story with a rueful smile. That was how we aghas lost our lands over the years, he said. We were prodigal, did not think, would do anything for honour and *murajul* (manly display). The lords were *mal'un* (cunning) and outwitted us, and that was why we no longer had our social position and our lands. 'That's how we are', preferring glory (*majd*) to material substance, name to reason, and the grand gesture to personal interest.

The account was clearly framed as the 'telling of a tale' and was represented as both symptom and condensed symbol of 'our' historical self-subversion and self-delusion. But unlike so many of the narrative performances I have discussed, the story of how the grove got its name was not being repeated at evening gatherings or for an agha audience's pleasure on some social occasion. It had become a story that was known but not narrated in any public setting, though it was told to the foreigner living in the village.

How was I to understand 'the grove of the orange'? The mayor represented the incident as an exemplary episode of a longer-term history – as an explanatory narrative account of the loss of status and land over time. 'Take it', the fatal phrase surrendering patrimony for glory, seemed to him transparently and self-evidently illustrative of the fatal flaw in agha identity. The words, in his reported speech, were made into a key instance of a general agha vulnerability to the rhetoric of challenge and response, a vulnerability which had vital historical implications. He used the moment of the giving away of the grove to illuminate the whole process of social decline from the 'then' of the famine to the generalized 'now': that is how we have come to our present social position of lack of property.

My informant constructed the material decline of Beit Abd as-Salam as the result of a whole sequence of such moments of loss with which the surrender of the grove for the orange was metonymically linked. He appealed to my awareness of the diminution of his own and the whole group's status. The ra'is also presented the story as the demonstration of a collective state of being, 'how we are': a group that could not distinguish between reality and gesture; a group that was prisoner of its own language of honour confrontation, trapped in narratives of autonomous, individual action that paid no attention to material constraints. At the same time, he represented the exchange of lord and agha as by synecdoche characterizing the whole nature of the relationship between them, between the men of cunning and their victims, the masters of history and the dupes.

The ra'is al baladiya appeared to go beyond the confines of the discourse of honour to comment upon that discourse, a rhetorical shift accomplished by what I interpret as his use of *irony*. I say 'his use', but the irony I heard in his tone and which distanced him from his ancestor was conveyed to me as if it were simply the impersonal product of, or inherent in, the unfolding of a history and social changes between 'then and now' rather than the ra'is's own rhetorical mode. The change of context and meaning were created, in his telling, by the passing of time in which the proud phrase 'Take it', meant to demonstrate and guarantee the honour of the champion answering the lord's challenge, came to demonstrate its opposite, honour's precariousness and loss.

The perspective of the figure who appeared in the narration as 'my grandfather' now seemed purely self-delusory. The hero no longer filled out all narrative space, making impossible any response but the awed acceptance of his overarching claims. He was, rather, viewed with detachment. 'We' too, the aghas, can be viewed with detachment in 'our' attachment to gesture and grand word. But now we see that characteristic for what it is and can make it a subject of talk, something that would be unthinkable for the grandfather.

Though the act of answering to the challenge was represented as disabling the descendants through loss of land, the ironic turn was also an enabling one for the narrator. A narrative control was created out of restraint and detachment, even as control of resources was lost.

The mayor established a relationship of contrast rather than of resemblance between orange and grove, act and consequence. He represented the orange and the grove as manifestly incommensurable and their arbitrary equivalence in this exchange ridiculous, not sublime. As he told it, the act was fundamentally contradictory. The words 'Take it' did not enhance and reproduce group honour, but performed precisely the opposite function: they diminished it and contributed to the impossibility of its reproduction. So the restraint and sobriety of expression of the grandfather with the superb economy of his two-word response were not intepreted as marks of his great social value and station. They were rather a false economy of speech; the terse performative utterance was a simulacrum of a hero's style which, instead of reproducing status, wastefully squandered the patrimony necessary for a hero's existence over time and into another generation.

The ra'is thus denies that the social honour at stake in challenge and response establishes its own transcendent frame of meaning. Honour does not guarantee its own eternal values, as in the heroic tales it should. The grandson ironically reverses the significance of the grandfather's act. He inflects the narrative, bending it to show that if it is indeed an illustration of a narrative life and form which demonstrates the major characteristics of personal and social life, what it in truth captures is the aghas' central characteristic of being duped by their own illusions: they have acted as unwitting agents of their own loss of excellence by behaving in ways they took to demonstrate that excellence.

The tale of the hero, creating and controlling an event and its meaning, turned into the tale of the 'fool' mastered both by the machinations of another and by his own misguided sense of what was truly at stake. Epic gesture was transmuted into absurdity, the grandfather into the victim of his 'particular notion of the narrative structures of human life', to use Macintyre's phrase again. Not only that, he had made his descendants victims too. In the narrative of loss, the grandsons were forever denied the possibility of inheriting the ancestor's identity and status because of that ancestor's own meaningless sacrifice for the honour of his name. They paid the price of the sacrifice, because they had been deprived of the property without which status honour could not exist precisely because of the grandfather's vulnerability to appeals to 'his word'. That vulnerability demonstrated all too obviously a general characteristic of the social being of the aghas.

The effect of this turn in the meaning of 'Karm al Leimun' is to interrogate the very nature of status honour narratives as ways of telling the world, validating status and demonstrating excellence. The implication of the ra'is's narration, as I interpret it, is that narratives of the glorious past can be told only in terms of irony and contrast. Whereas honour denies any distinction or break in meaning between act and the meaning of the act, irony establishes a distinction between act and significance. There can be no icons in the ironic mode, for in that mode there is always a gap between what seems and what is. This perspective thus has a close affinity with the sardonic motto *ad-dunya kizb*, 'the world is a lie', rather than with a timeless truth.

Yet this interrogation is not as complete as it initially seems to be. We should not miss the fact that the ra'is's narrative stress on the *personal* agency of his two main characters still reproduces the language of the agent and of 'how we are' which is so central to the honour narratives. Though he reverses the significance of the story, making something very close to a buffoon out of a hero (and out of the agha group as a whole), he remains partly within the conventions governing the shifting of heroic to comic mode rather than going completely outside them. His own discourse strives to hold together both irony and the ideals of personal agency, and is not as transparent as it appears.

Was there not still present, too, an aura of the glamour, the charm of the word and the name that had not yet lost quite all its magic?[4] Imagine having an ancestor like *that*! The element of distinction, played out in a drama before the audience gathered in the great lord's manzul (reception room), is not entirely negated by the ironic turn.[5] The grandfather stands out from everyone else, even if the grandson's rueful smile and shake of the head position him in a historical sequence leading to an unglamorous present.

The ra'is's very mode of telling me about Karm al Leimun preserves a relationship to the conventions of honour stories. Dialogue and drama between men of rank for whom 'word' and performance are supposed to be one are central to his presentation. The contrast between the 'private' conversation of the two men riding on the plain and the public evocation of 'keeping one's word' in the arena of the manzul is most important. For the key moment upon which the story turns is the lord's transforming of the 'promise' on the plain into a public giving of his word as a challenge before an audience. Their presence, though unspeaking, is crucial. The promise is now not so much spoken as rehearsed before their eyes, and the encounter is made subject to their judgement. Finally, the ra'is represents the words of the protagonists as performative actions: the agha promises, or is made to seem to have promised. Confronted with his words before the audience now witness to the terms of the exchange he does not hesitate: 'Take it.' The deed is accomplished in the utterance. The mayor thus makes a narrative of the episode, 'feigning to make the world speak itself as a story'.[6] In these respects his narrative reproduces certain of the conventions of honour narratives that he in other ways subverts. History and memory are still constituted in the extraordinary words and deeds of outstanding figures in dramatic scenes. Challenge and response remain the dynamic of social life.

To point out this aspect of the narrative is not to deny the degree to which the ra'is inverts the values of the 'traditional' honour tale. Most significantly, he gives property priority as the foundation of status honour. This is an important reversal of the basic presuppositions of status. In heroic narratives, exchanges of property (and money) between bey and agha are either represented as a function of virtue and excellence, usually offered by the lord 'out of respect' and as an acknowledgement of the inherent quality of the agha, or they are accomplished by violence and seizure. They are never a payment for services rendered and never a means of acquiring honour through mere material possession, for that can never be honour's equivalent.

The grandson's telling, by contrast, makes land the *sine qua non* of status and of that personal autonomy, that freedom from need of any other person or material possession so vital to the image of the man of integrity (*karama*) and 'place'. Once given away under the compulsion of his own word manipulated by another, the grandfather and his descendants are lost. The ra'is demystifies his ancestor's gesture and the magical power of 'the name' and makes visible what was previously occulted by the imaginary power of 'a man is what he is'.

The ra'is's narrative perspective asserts that the exchange demonstrates a double deception: the lord tricks the agha into handing over the grove by challenging him in public by his name and with an invocation of his word; and the agha deceives himself by acting as if his name and word could make an orange worth an olive grove. Honour, says the mayor, does not produce its own universe of significance. If the aghas are now living in a world where it is ever more difficult to defend their status position, where they see their own position in many ways as marked by weakness and backwardness, the presence of the name Karm al Leimun on the landscape is the permanent reminder of the cause of that degradation. It is a remembrance of historical loss, and of the subjection of even the most heroic narrative to time and interpretation.

The Grove of the Decent Man

Concerning the second name of the olive grove – Karm al Adami, 'the grove of the decent man' – a story without irony could be told to the stranger.[7]

The informant who first mentioned this additional (not alternative) name was also a member of the aghas, though from a different branch than the mayor. He was a man in his forties and described himself as a murafiq and supervisor for the house of Jud Bey Ibrahim; others said he was just a khadim, a servant who worked for a very low wage. He also arranged water sales and dealt in olive oil and cereals on the side whenever he could. His father, a leading descent group elder of Beit Abd as-Salam, had for many years been a murafiq and estate manager of a powerful bey who was a rival of Abboud. The old man was famously irascible and obdurate, claiming to 'have nothing to do with anybody'. Although my informant's own life showed a significant personal loss of status since he was no more than a dependent of a family of beys, the family of five sons and the prestigious father still had a certain social weight as 'Beit Mustafa Qasim', the old man's name. They lived in a tight cluster of houses built around the original rooms of their grandfather. Two of the brothers, who worked as mechanic and tractor driver respectively, had reputations as qabadiyat who knew how to handle a gun and would not draw back from any challenge; another kept political and other connections gained through attachment to the *Deuxième Bureau* in the 1960s and spent much of his time in Beirut, affecting disdain for the crudity of the village; of the remaining two, one had emigrated to Brazil some fifteen or more years before and had not been heard of since (see story, p. 109), while the youngest was regarded as a poor sort of fellow who got labouring jobs from time to time.

This man, Muhammad, enjoyed telling me about how the estates used to be organized, the terminology used for different kinds of labour agreements, the ranking of the retainers and so forth, and he would introduce accounts of economic and social arrangments in the region when he thought it appropriate. Other members of this stratum spoke of him as having an interest in, and knowledge of, 'the past', something shared by few of the younger generation, and they directed me to him. To meet a questioner on these subjects, someone who addressed him as a man to be spoken to and sometimes wrote down his words as we talked, clearly gave Muhammad pleasure. I, in turn, was glad to find someone who would think it worthwhile to detail how agriculture had been organized.

The mayor's story of Karm al Leimun prompted me to ask about the time of the terrible conditions during the First World War. I had been speaking to an old, celebrated horseman and murafiq from Beit Abd as-Salam, who would have been somewhere between fourteen and eighteen years old at the outbreak of the war, who said to me of the famine:

We grew and ate wild plants. The Turks made heavy taxes on the people in grain and seed. You had to steal from yourself in order to exist. Turkish officers used to come here poor and leave rich by taking money. Out of a thousand soldiers there would be two hundred Turks with the rest from here; the Turks would be wealthy and the rest wretched.[8]

Another senior man of the immediately junior generation spoke of the Turks 'taking all the food they needed and burning the rest and all the people starved'. I wanted to know how Muhammad would recount the conditions of those days.

He made it clear that the famine was not a 'natural' disaster. It was due to a situation of dearth, produced by conditions of war and the beys holding grain back to sell at a high price. He told me how the Turks requisitioned supplies; the cultivators had to pay punitive dues in kind and production suffered, not least because of the loss of labour brought about by conscription into the Ottoman army; the beys had done everything possible to exploit the situation by hoarding and virtual debt enslavement. Conditions were appalling, people were dying, the Turks were oppressive. 'One man with a lot of land sold it for 36 kilos of wheat', he said, to show me just how extraordinary conditions had become as a result of state and landlord policies. Thus began the process by which the aghas had come to sell so much of their land to the lords.

It was in that awful time that Karm al Adami got its name.

The mayor's grandfather – or was it perhaps his father? Muhammad couldn't remember – was riding with one of the beys on the plain and the lord was eating an orange. The agha said: 'Be good enough to give me a piece.'[9]
'No, I won't', the bey replied.
'Give it to me and take that grove over there.'
The bey, surprised, asked incredulously: 'Do you mean it?'
'Yes', declared the agha.
He took the piece of orange from the bey and went and wrote him the land, the whole three-quarters of a hectare. ('Write the land' means making a formal legal transfer of the grove.)

The narrative of Karm al Adami is clearly very different from that of the mayor. The speaker presents the necessity imposed by critical historical and man-made conditions as a sufficient explanation for exchanges which would otherwise be non-equivalent. Value was transformed because the circumstances were so utterly transformed. Even men who were *mallakun*, landowners, were reduced to struggling to satisfy their basic appetite for food. 'A lot of land', the ultimate resource of social and material life and prestige, might be given for 36 kilos of wheat, the most common but now the most valued of crops. Disproportion and incommensurability ruled and there were those who would take advantage, for they had created and exploited these abnormal conditions of exchange.

The offer of the grove for the orange, which the bey could not initially believe was meant seriously, was represented as a dramatic, and dramatizing, sign of the despair to which men were driven, giving up their most precious resource for a moment's relief from hunger and thirst. The story of the 'grove of the orange'/'grove of the decent man' became, in the mouth of this informant, a story of *need* which drove the agha into the most asymmetrical and otherwise unimaginable exchange.

The name Karm al Adami therefore also constructs a metaphor of a disordered world in which the identification of olive and orange becomes possible. In contrast to Karm al Leimun, however, it memorializes the desperation and impoverishment of the companion who is subject to the imperatives of his time and expresses his extremity in extreme form. With this name as its shadow, Karm al Leimun takes on a different connotation and tone. It points to the general derangement of the social order during the famine rather than to the purely personal answering to a name.

Both narratives, that of the mayor and that of the servant, were given as in some sense materialist, realist accounts which explained a process of social decline. Both were told from the perspective of property owners, the speakers sharing the sense that there was something extraordinary and dramatic in the event, whatever their contrasting views. (I think that all the aghas knew both accounts, though Karm al Leimun was the more commonly referred to if it was thought that I did not know the reason for the name.) And both largely excluded fellahin from their accounts. An agha did not give accounts of fellahin unless they featured as objects of domination in some way in his own narrative purposes. Land ownership is the measure of gain and loss here. But while the mayor produced the figure of a world in which individual ruse and self-deception created the anomalous exchange with its fateful and ironic consequences, the servant of the beys presented the very different picture of a world where coherence, congruence and commensurability *could* not rule. The first placed the famine in the background as 'the time when'. The second brought the famine to the fore as determining context and cause.

Name and word lose their role at the narrative centre of 'how that karm got its name' in the adami version. They have no explanatory or determining power: the encounter is between a bey and an agha, two property owners in a hierarchical order, but that is all. The servant constructs a different kind of history from that of the ra'is. By the same token, on the other hand, it could be argued that status honour is preserved from historical critique. Honour remains 'in brackets', and there is no specific affinity between this narrative and the notion that 'the world is just a lie'. The story is depersonalized, and the loss of property of the aghas has nothing to do with self-delusion, acts of miscalculated personal bravado or over-sensitivity to a challenge. His history allows for the discursive practices of honour to be maintained 'as if' unaffected by time, something the mayor's account does not permit.

Muhammad's narrative, though it too used dialogue as did that of the ra'is, subordinated the telling of direct speech to a wider setting of action and event signified by 'the famine'. The Karm al Adami version makes personal helplessness rather than personal performance the central organizing function and eliminates the whole idea of challenge and response. Starvation, not the word of the hero, is the issue; the bey's brutal refusal rather than his cunning drives the action. Weakness and vulnerability in the face of deprivation determine the outcome. The acknowledgement of need, always denied in accounts of status and personal integrity, becomes the narrative's principal motivation. 'We' had no choice. His final detail, 'and he went and wrote him the land' corresponded to the very different strategy of the telling in which the action of actually transferring the land was only accomplished by the formal writing of a document, and not by the magnificent performative utterance of the mayor's story.

'Writing' might be interpreted as standing for an important historical change in the overall nature of property relations and of relations between beys and aghas in general. Formal legal recording was becoming necessary for the transfer of land, though it by no means excluded the use of *force majeure*. A different kind of claim and authority for possession was made in which the performative utterance was no longer central.

Luxury and Need

There is a further, related change which lies within both narratives, but which takes its greater significance in the historicizing trends of the Karm al Adami. We are told that the famine was a time when 'a lot of land was given up for 36 kilos of grain' – grain to make bread, the basis of subsistence. That which makes it possible to produce had to be surrendered for the one essential product. Now to give up land for bread makes sense in the reversed logic of famine. That seems a 'natural' image. But for an *orange*?

We can grasp a more specific quality of the narrative if we ask what sort of food 'an orange' represented. Orange groves (and citrus in general) were spoken of as having been at the beginning of this century a completely new form of cultivation, coming in when cereals, more specifically wheat, were by far the most widely cultivated crop on the plain and olives the most important cash crop in the hills.[10] The sahel (the plain) had become the economic centre of gravity of Akkar, displacing the mountain.[11] Men pointed out to me the groves of olive trees that were systematically planted in rows on the shallow terraces of the foothills previously given over to wheat by beys such as Abboud Abd ar-Razzaq, beys who were striving to increase the economic value as well as the extent of their holdings in the first two decades of the century.[12] Production was rationalized in new ways. The landscape was slowly made subject to a modern and systematizing order of investment and control.

Muhammad and others also spoke to me of the cutting down of the mulberry trees (of which only one remained in the village) as silk production collapsed in the early part of this century. They spoke of a growing, if limited, investment in oranges by the few landowners who had the entrepreneurial instinct, sufficient capital for the initial heavy costs, including those of constructing proper drainage and irrigation, and access to the required technical advice.[13] An orange was therefore not merely 'something to eat in a time of dearth'. It stood for a new, capital-intensive, high-profit and relatively high-risk pattern of cultivation on the plain.

The rationalities of such practice had much more to do with modern capitalist farming and marketing than with status honour and the giving of one's word. Oranges as a crop and a grove of orange trees as land had the highest value (they were at the time of my fieldwork what attracted external capital to the Akkar plain, together with the cultivation of winter vegetables under plastic). In local terms they would have been a mark of real luxury in the first decades of the century. Even in 1971 there were relatively few orange 'gardens' on the plain where they were grown.[14] In 'the time of the famine' their exotic nature would be even more pronounced. Oranges thus had had nothing to do with everyday necessity. They were outside the ordinary lives of everyone save the very well-to-do and represented new wealth, new methods, and new tastes.[15]

In this light we might see the stories of Karm al Leimun/Karm al Adami having an allegorical dimension relating to power, exchange and historical transformation. The orange is 'shown off' by the lord who demonstrates that he is not subject to need by his feeding on luxury. Famine does not touch him. It is desired by the companion, subjected to a need of which the lord is the agent. Want compels him. The price of tasting the new order, for those who can hope to do so but do not have the means, is the offering up of the most precious part of the old. The fruit is a sign of capital and the capacity to change the productive landscape. More specifically, the piece of orange can only be truly exchanged with the men of wealth and modern investment for the sacrifice of what previously had had by far the greatest value, the olive grove; and in making that sacrifice, the participant risks losing his whole place in the social world. That world is not stable and guaranteed by heroic virtue or the assertion of word and name. Rather it is a place in which men who possess luxury and what makes luxury possible increase their resources and power by playing on the appetites of others in a game in which resources are unequally divided from the beginning.

The Voice of the Ancestor

So far I have given these two narratives as if they were the only ways of recounting how an olive grove acquired its peculiar names and such an anomalous, illuminating, status. And indeed they were the established accounts which seemed to exhaust the significance of the history the name of the grove contained. Certainly I accepted them then as 'all there is to say' on the topic. But it is important for the interpretation of narrative to question such seeming completeness and to examine the possibility of other, suppressed narrators telling a different story. It is also important to ask how the shift in audience over time affects potential interpretive practices.

A 'shadow' interpretation is cast behind the highly defined and well-lit figures and events the mayor presented: there is another narrator and another audience. I suggest that we should imagine a third narrative voice that has been both present and absent, that of the agha hero himself as he is figured in the account of Karm al Leimun. He seems to be unproblematically situated; we think we 'hear' him quite clearly, from his request on the plain to his 'Take it!' in the reception room. Yet perhaps his words are not as transparent as they appear in the versions and glosses I have given. What if his words, particularly his response to the lord's challenge, hit his audience and his bey with a rhetorical force lost in the mayor's telling? What was that force? What if the agha was not the figure of self-deception so many of a later generation made him? What significance might the act of giving his grove for the orange have had for him? Having answered those questions, we should go on to consider the nature of the change in audience. For in both accounts and in my own writing so far, that first audience in the manzul has remained merely anonymous and silent, despite the importance of its role. What is that importance, and in what ways is it different from that of the mayor and his peers or juniors who 'know the story'?

Viewed from his own position the hero is *not* 'exchanging his grove for an orange'. That is the modern narrator's definition of 'what happened'. But it is not self-evidently the truth the mayor takes it to be. What the companion is doing in 'his' perspective is answering to his name and making it good in an ideal-typical performance of challenge and response.[16] He chooses to accept the lord's challenge and demonstrates that he could turn even his joking word not given before an audience into something weighty and serious. His word is so powerful that he can make the incongruent congruent, an orange commensurable with an olive grove, *if he so wished*. And before the assembled throng in the public arena of the lord's reception room that is exactly what he does. He wins his story by doing something extraordinary and defying the everyday logic of material calculation.

How does he do it? In what *form*? The agha answers to his name, 'Abu Khalid', uttered in challenge by the lord and makes the grand gesture with superb, and characteristically heroic terseness: 'Take it.' This utterance, which eschews all elaboration for a bare, ordinary phrase that the context makes extraordinary, focuses the values of the whole discourse of status honour in its instantaneous response to his name.[17] In the most condensed way he achieves the sublime. As Gérard Genette puts it:

'Sublime feelings are *always* rendered by the simplest expression' (Domairon).

Old Horace says, quite simply: 'Would that he had died!' Medée says: 'I!' Genesis says: 'And there was light.' Nothing is more *marked* than this simplicity: it is the very figure, indeed the perfect obligatory figure, of the sublime. Obligatory and reserved: to use it to express less elevated sentiments or situations would show a lack of taste.[18]

The agha thus turns Karm al Leimun, named after his astonishing act, into a metaphor of true honour, seamlessly combining act and being.[19] If the lord sought to play with him, the agha would triumph, *not* by denying the challenge, but by going beyond the ruse and superbly *choosing to do what no one else could even imagine doing* – to give up the grove because it pleased him to do so.[20] Desire, pleasure and the demonstration of transcendence, here are the ingredients of a narrative miracle.

The logic of honour in this voice goes beyond all others. The loss of a most valued possession is transmuted into riches in prestige and symbolic capital by the public and conspicuous display of surrendering prized material resources. For what are they when a man's name is at stake? Here is autonomy indeed. What a superb moment! Prestige and name are integral to the capacity to exercise authority; to being sought out by powerful men as a proper ally; to being shown the marks of status honour, honourable address, deference and those gifts of other material resources, including land and gold, which beys would offer out of 'respect'; above all, to being spoken about, told of, and represented in narrative occasions in tribute to a man's *qima* (value) and *markaz* (social standing). This was how the reputation, *sum'a*, integral to personal identity and authority as an agha, was achieved.

Was there anything such a man might not do? A man capable of such exceeding of others' standards of conduct, such going beyond the everyday expectations of exchange, is a man to be feared. And to be cultivated.

If, at that moment on the plain, his desire was for the orange, then his ability to state and act upon that desire opens the way to a realization of what, for others, would be socially inconceivable. The hero refuses to define history through acts of politics and exchange. He demonstrates, rather, that it is the act of desire, which is also the act of pride and of will, which can define the space and time of history. He wishes to slake his thirst; he does so, whatever other men reckon the cost. The orange has a greater value because it is what he *wants* at the moment of the promise, not because he suffers want. A descendant may later narrativize this instant as the moment of the fall from status, but it may also be apprehended as an assertion of the sensual over the political. Men would be compelled to acknowledge the immense rhetorical weight such a performance bears, whether or not they approved or lamented the hero's superb gesture.[21]

Is not the narrative of Karm al Leimun also the narrative of another kind of irresistible desire and gratification? The hero cannot resist the appeal to the beauty of his own 'face'. He wishes, he needs to see himself in others' eyes as he imagines himself to be in all his dramatic style. And he imagines himself as the subject of a narrative, told eternally as the exemplar of an extraordinary master of form and act. Status honour seems the narcissistic quality of gazing at the self in the pool of reputation in which an idealized, dazzling figure is perceived. For that no price is too great.

Looked at from this point of view the public sacrifice would have been seen and experienced as self-sustaining rather than self-deceiving, and as bringing its reward in an enhancement of that aura so central to repute. Far from there being an ironic sign over the action, the agha achieves the classical embodiment of word, name and person in complete coherence and intelligibility. Self-constancy is demonstrated through the keeping of the word in circumstances in which the control of property might so easily have been taken to be imperative. Abu Khalid does not vary. He makes himself appear in word as in deed the image of social integrity in its fullest sense, the icon of honour, in spite of all contrary pressure. His selfhood is reproduced through this dramatic fulfillment of a promise: 'Take it.'

Such a reading suggests at least how the narrative might once have been told and remembered as 'a heroic story' in which elements that might support other, and later, readings were suppressed or invisible. This version would certainly be for public narrative performance and re-enactment over time; it would apparently guarantee temporal continuity of the name of the hero, and, with him, of the aghas for whom he stood as an exemplar of their difference from others.

Here the audience plays its crucial role. To that audience the famine is a lived reality (not a reported event in the distant past as it had become by the 1970s). It feels the need and want in the body, in the unsatisfied appetite. Hunger, migration and the taking of men for the Ottoman army are all immediately part of people's experience of the time. That is the framing for the lord's challenge and the agha's response. Silent during the drama (as later related to me) the audience is the public whose talk must be earned, who must, as it were, be *forced* to go away and tell others of what it has just witnessed. Miracles have to be disseminated by men lost in amazement, men who feel they have no choice but to acknowledge the 'perfection-in-itself' of the act. The hero gains his reputation 'in their eyes', but also through their mouths.

The agha audience repeats, rehearses, makes vividly present the original, extraordinary moment to those who were not in the manzul. They become present and actively participant in the community of shared narrative, in the act of remembering and reconstituting a moment which stands for their own historical identity and excellence. The servant audience watches. Unimaginably distant from participation in the challenge and response, part of its function is silent tribute; there are murmured or loudly articulated formulaic phrases of wonder, and later retellings of how 'they' are, these higher beings. Each telling reproduces the glamour of the lords and aghas, and confirms the exclusion of the cultivators from the spheres of status and property. Perhaps some, in their own domestic space and away from the manzul, mock such prodigality? A private and safe laughter can be imagined that in its very restriction to privacy pays tribute to fear and subordination.

Later 'audiences' are audiences only in a very different sense. No one repeats the narratives at social evenings or on public occasions. People know the stories of how the grove got its name – they have not been 'forgotten'. But some are not sure whether it was the ra'is's grandfather or father who was involved, or whether the scene in the manzul ever really happened. The mayor takes an ironic tone and tells a stranger of the weakness of the aghas for great gestures and challenges. The epic certainty and closure admitting of only one interpretation in what I have constructed as 'the grandfather's version', has been replaced by a plurality of voices.

Grandfathers, Fathers and Sons

Let us examine this grandfather, and his grandsons, more deeply. For the way in which the ra'is al baladiya spoke to me when he was talking about his own life and relation to his father and grandfather throws a different narrative light on the ironical history of loss of Karm al Leimun.[22]

A man of around forty years old in 1971 – he was not sure of his exact age – the ra'is was the oldest member of what was referred to as 'Beit Khalid Ali', the name of his father. (For reasons I shall explain, there was no reference to Beit Ali after his grandfather.) The wider unit was called Beit Ibrahim after the apical ancestor (see Figure 1); Khalid Ali is no. 9 on the genealogy and the mayor no. 38. The social focus by the time of my fieldwork was thus on the restricted father–sons cluster, rather than on the grandfather–sons–grandsons line. The mayor's four paternal uncles and two first cousins on the same side, all of them deceased by 1971, were simply spoken of as part of the wider unit to which they all ultimately belonged: they were members of Beit Ibrahim which, with Beit Abd al Latif (Figure 2), was one of the two numerically largest descent fractions of Beit Abd as-Salam. Only one of his father's paternal uncles, Abd al Qadir (no. 6 on the genealogy) had given his name to a beit, Beit Qadur (or ad-Dur), and their numbers were somewhat smaller (we shall see below why only these two families were known as beits).

Khalid Ali had married three times. His first wife was a Christian woman from the village of Qureyat. She had 'about ten' sons, all of whom died, and a daughter who survived and was married into Beit Abd ar-Rahim, one of the four main fractions of Beit Abd as-Salam (to Khalid's FFBSS). On his wife's death he remarried. His second, and much younger, wife was his daughter's husband's older sister. She bore him eight sons, of whom the mayor was the second. When she too died, Khalid Ali married a daughter of a famous sheikh from the village of Haizouq (she was still living during my time in the village). This wife in turn had five sons, the youngest of whom had died when quite small and was buried 'with the sheikhs' in Haizouq, his mother's natal village.[23] A baby daughter had also died.

Two sets of half-brothers thus made up the total of eleven living males between the ages of forty and nineteen. Three of the four youngest (nos 45, 47 and 48 on the chart) were as yet unmarried and lived in their mother's house just next to that of the ra'is (no. 46 married while I was in the village); of the others, all married, one was in the army but visited regularly, two were in Kuwait (nos 42 and 43) and were neither heard from with any regularity nor were said to be sending any remittances (though one did return for a rare visit during my fieldwork. See Plate 17 for a photograph taken on that occasion); another, who lived in Tripoli, had made a good career for himself out of being in the military intelligence services during the 1960s and he now owned a machine-driven olive press in Berqayl and had other investments elsewhere, though he was not thought to share them with his siblings. The two brothers immediately following the mayor in birth both worked with him on their landholdings, though one of them did very little and played no real part in public village life. In the ra'is's generation there were already twenty sons from seven marriages, including his own three boys, and all were teenagers and younger.

The cluster of siblings who were permanently resident in the village lived in a set of five households of small one- or two-room houses. These were built on to or adjoining Khalid Ali's original house which served both as the common family meeting point and contained the sparsely furnished reception room when visitors came on business concerning the baladiya. The other fifteen households of Beit Ibrahim lived in five smaller but separate clusters of dwellings within a radius of about 200 metres of the mayor's group in a quarter called the Marouche. Since this area was some way north along the line of the hill from the centre of the village and the other groups of Beit Abd as-Salam, the Marouche was spatially quite distinct (see Maps 4 and 5 of the village and quarter).

Ali (no. 2), Khalid Ali's father and the mayor's grandfather, was much the oldest of the five sons of Ibrahim Abd as-Salam (no. 1).[24] He had been a landowner with lands in three villages in Syria, about 100 hectares, in a joint arrangement with 'one of his brothers'. (I should note that others ridiculed this figure.) He died before the mayor was born. Ali had married his paternal cousin Ahmad Abd al Latif's daughter, but she died; then 'he took one from the Jurd' who bore him two sons, Ahmed and Muhammed (nos 7 and 8) and three daughters (two of whom married paternal first cousins and one into another fraction of Beit Abd as-Salam). Finally, he married from the *fellah* house of Beit al Misri, the mother of Khalid himself, Ibrahim and Mustafa (nos 9, 9a and 10).[25]

On his father's death, Ali's eldest son, Nabil (no. 7), had sold the 100 hectares before his younger half-brother Khalid Ali grew up and had gone off to America 'about 60 years ago' (that is, around or before the beginning of the First World War, a time of relatively high emigration from Lebanon). Nabil left one son (no. 22) with nothing to inherit. Nabil was much older than Khalid and there was nothing anyone could do to stop the transaction, which had enormous implications for their position as landholders. There were other losses of property. The grandfather, Ali himself, had sold off about twenty hectares or so near the village of Tall Hayat to the beys.[26] One shunbul (now owned by one of the fellahin who acquired some landed property in the previous ten years) had been bought by the father of Adham Bey; three shunbuls of cereal land went 'to the beys' and three more planted in olive trees to Beit Jud Bey. Now what was left was one shunbul of olives, and another five on the hill above their houses, but only eight *keila* of that was planted in almonds and olives.

The grandfather's brothers had poor reputations. The mayor bluntly described three of them, Said, Mustafa and Abd al Qadir (nos 3, 5 and 6), as 'thugs' (*mugrimin*, 'criminals', men who know no code of honour and will do anything since they have no moral sense at all). They had been with Muhammad Pasha and done his dirty work for him.[27] Mustafa (no. 5) had been killed in a fight over beys' property by a paternal first cousin, As'ad al Ali. The two men were companions to different lords and had become enemies defending their masters' competing claims to a parcel of land. The murderer was himself killed by Mustafa's brother Abd al Qadir (no. 6) and his son had fled to America (I imagine in fear that Abd al Qadir planned to kill him too and also to avoid being involved in the duty of taking revenge against a numerically more powerful group).

Other killings had occurred in Beit Ibrahim Abd as-Salam. The dead Mustafa's wife had then been married to his brother Umar (no. 4) and had born him a son (no. 17). This young man was killed by his half-brother, Hassan ibn Mustafa (no. 18), in a quarrel. Worse was to come. A paternal uncle of the ra'is who was 'mad' (no. 9a) shot another of Umar's sons, Qasim (no. 15a).[28] This left the descendants of Umar as an impoverished and shattered group: two sons (nos 17 and 15a) had been shot dead; one (no. 16) was 'mad' and never married; one (no. 14a) emigrated to America; one (no. 15) went to a village on the plain (to leave village space and avoid a continuance of a feud where the odds were heavily against ,him) and married a 'beduin' woman. Their two sons stayed on the plain, married their mother's brother's daughters and had nothing to do with the village. Only one of Umar's six sons (no. 14) had remained in the village, and his two sons were both pauperized agricultural workers.

There was thus no reference to 'Beit Umar al Hassan'. Similarly, the descendants of Said (no. 3) were, by 1971, limited to one man (no. 24) who was the only son of his father. He was married and had two small boys. His two paternal uncles (nos 11 and 13) died without children. Number 11 had 'owned land' in Syria and sold it, but had kept 'some land' here in the village. He died young of 'fever'. Number 13 had opened a shop in the village and 'didn't sell anything'. Hassan ibn Mustafa (no. 18), too, had died without sons. Of his two daughters, one had married no. 12, a famous qabaday who had no children with his other three wives, who all shared the same house; she bore him a son (no. 24, the joker figure to whom I refer in Chapter 10). The other married out into a fellah house, a group the mayor described as having been 'brought from Egypt as slaves by Muhammad Pasha' (Beit Selim, whose story we shall see below, pp. 141–7). This was the only marriage between a fellah family (in this particular case very low status) and a woman from the agha groups. The marriage was never discussed by the aghas and the marriage relation led to no social ties as far as I was aware. I could never discover whether this alliance occurred because the aghas did not wish her to be married within the beit lest any male children eventually pursue or became embroiled in blood debts in a second generation, but it is the only explanation which I can put forward. If my suggestion is correct it adds an intriguing dimension to the complexity of the incidents which involved the aghas of Beit Ibrahim in killings, emigration, forced displacement, accounts of 'madness' and complicity in 'forgetting'.[29]

Only the offspring of Abd al Qadir Ibrahim remained in any numbers. So the whole of Beit Ibrahim by 1971 was spoken of as effectively comprising just two sub-beits, Beit Qadur (referring to those descended from Abd al Qadir Ibrahim) and Beit Khalid Ali.

Khalid Ali had three other brothers, the mayor's paternal uncles, apart from the one who had sold off the land in Syria: Muhammad (no. 8) had died before the ra'is was born; Mustafa (no. 10) had died childless when the mayor was three or four years old; the last of them, Ibrahim (no. 9a), also childless, was the 'madman' referred to above.[30] From the early 1930s only Khalid remained of the five sons of Ali al Ibrahim.

Khalid had acquired property: he purchased three shunbuls in Merliya from a man in the other agha beit, Beit Khalid; eight *keila* came as an inheritance from his maternal grandfather of Beit Misri; he bought another feddan 'from someone else', and a garden of some fruit trees from a paternal first cousin (the son of the murdered Mustafa) who had married Ali's sister; he also had a dunum from another Beit Abd as-Salam owner from Beit Abd ar-Rahim. Then he bought a shunbul from another paternal cousin which he planted in olives himself. On top of these holdings, he used to lease fifty to sixty shunbuls in Merliya (on the basis of giving two shunbuls of grain, 300 kilos, per shunbul of land), and made a large profit during the Second World War when grain prices rose dramatically.

Throughout his adult life, Khalid Ali had been closely linked with different beys, unlike his father who had been an independent landowner. He was the wakil or general administrator of Asad Bey from the mountains of the Jurd to Hamidiya on the Syrian coast, 'from the snow to the sea' in the classic phrase. He had acted for the bey's children after their father's death. They were all part of Beit Muhammad Pasha. Then he was the guardian (*wasi*) of

Muhammad al Abboud, who was the great grandson of Muhammad Pasha. The mayor himself was a manager for the two young beys from the same house upon whom lay the duty of taking revenge for the killing of their uncle, the Minister, nearly twenty years before. The link with Beit Muhammad Pasha had continued.

Relations with fellahin labourers were also spoken of as having been stable. Ali had his own two cameleers from one of the fellah houses for thirty years or more, and people stayed to work with him for long periods of time. This was a not unusual account of labour relations sustained over two generations between agha and cultivator sharecropper families which the aghas represented as part of the 'order', the *nizam*, which had once prevailed and now been lost. Such a representation, of course, made the aghas themselves the pivotal and articulating point of the entire system of land and labour.

'My father', said the ra'is, 'was head of the family (ra'is al 'ailat). He was the one who 'had made the man they call the head of the family now; that one had just been a servant', he remarked dismissively, speaking of a notable who now dominated relations with powerful political figures. 'And in any case', the mayor added, 'I myself was the one who brought this other man into politics in 1958, introducing him to the governor. I used to be always on the go to Merliya and everywhere.' Khalid Ali was *the* notable (*wajih*) of Beit Ibrahim, 'he held the reins (*zimam*)'.

'A man who was in control was more harsh (*asharr*) than anyone else', because in those days only the ones who were most brutal and vicious could get anywhere. 'Only two or three of the whole of Beit Abd as-Salam knew how to eat', he went on, using a key expression in the language of power, an expression employed to indicate taking advantage of things and people in the world and devouring all that one could. A real man was possessed of a huge appetite, for food, sexual activity, and forms of violence in the acquisition of prestige and material advantage. 'The beys destroyed the village completely', the ra'is added, reflecting that had more of the aghas possessed the necessary ruthlessness they would have been able to resist the beys, the masters of guile and 'eating'. As it was they had been eaten. 'Now it's all politics, and seniority is important too.'

The ra'is al baladiya ended his narrative with the appropriate praise formulae used of men of social standing, incorporating himself fully into the line of noble ancestors: 'My grandfather opened a manzul (reception room). My father Ali opened a manzul. I took it over and as its foundation was good, it came to me.'[31] This was his genealogy of social standing, from which he competitively excluded the rival, more recent 'head of the family' who had eclipsed him in public prestige.

Violence, Loss and Gain

The unpredictable patterns of fertility, mortality, resource distribution, individual action and violence within three generations are very strikingly highlighted in this narrative history of the mayor's descent line. A large number of sons, a basic kinship strategy and hope, was no guarantee of survival, as the fate of Umar's children showed; accumulated land might be stolen or sold; property and relations with the beys made relatives into enemies, with dire consequence. The need to be 'harsh' was an imperative for a social order conceived of as articulated by intensely agonistic relations of unrelenting competition.

In the light of this second narrative about his ancestors the ra'is's version of how Karm al Leimun acquired its name looks rather different. The processes of property loss and gain now appear much more to do with mundane though crucial issues of patterns of family relations, economic need and the capacities of some to seize opportunities to exploit the situation better than others, than with grand gestures and ironic commentaries. The story of the ride on the plain and the dramatic moment in the bey's manzul represents a loss of status honour in a powerful performative utterance that denies need: 'Take it.' In doing so, ironically enough, it masks or distracts the eye from competition in a market for land, a valued resource that was increasingly becoming a commodity as much as a source of honour.

The account condenses many of the themes around property, hierarchy and violence that run through the local memory of all strata. We can see the importance of the developing market in land and the way in which an independent agha landowner, Ali al Ibrahim, having first built up his property and later sold some of it, had reduced the status and wealth of his own family (and I note that part of one property sold to the beys was in the hands of a man of fellah origin at the time of my stay). Then, in the next generation, the narrative creates the figure of Khalid Ali, one who 'knew how to eat', just like the beys. He pursues a double strategy, for he becomes a companion and land manager to a house of beys, and at the same time reconstitutes a petty landowner's position by buying land from relatives who needed the money and were obliged to sell. (I say obliged, the assumption being that no one sold unless driven to it by want.) Moreover, he seizes the chance for wartime profiteering on wheat, and thus exploits famine just as the bey had exploited the situation in the Karm al Leimun tale.

Violence against, and exploitation of, kin runs through the narrative. A half-brother treacherously sells off joint resources. Uncles are 'criminals'. Khalid Ali 'eats' others and is 'more brutal', for that is the way to become the patron of a manzul and 'head of the family'. Groups belonging to Beit Abd as-Salam are divided by association with different beys, a division leading here to the extreme of killings by paternal first cousins because of lords' conflicts over property. A son runs away to escape further killing after the death of his father; half-brother murders half-brother; 'madmen' shoot others dead; men flee to the plain and to America.[32] A powerful sense of centrifugal pressures is created in which men lose property or life, not because of grand gestures and inherent weakness for the rhetoric of challenge and response, but because of conflict over land. 'The 'ailat' becomes a figure of division and mutual devouring rather than of solidarity and cooperation. Agnation is as much a source of instability as of stability, of destruction as of reproduction.

This double-sided quality of patriliny is mirrored in terms of the intensely ambivalent relations with the beys. On the one hand, there are long associations over time – guardianship, companionship, violence in support of claims, estate administration. On the other hand, there is a representation of the aghas being tricked, played on, killing each other because of their masters' quarrels, and selling their precious land to the same lords. The figures of power created in the narratives give and take away, protect and sacrifice, support and undermine, make and break, are sources of continuity and discontinuity. That is how they are defined and given narrative form in relation to 'us', the aghas.

The mayor's father and grandfather are unmistakeably the central figures of his story, heads of the whole descent group and men of prestige indicated in maintaining a reception room to which 'everyone came'. This was not the view of men from different agha sections. Others from within his own group, as well as from other fractions of Beit Abd as-Salam, never spoke of Khalid Ali as having been 'head of the family' during the period of the 1930s and 1940s. Indeed, the general consensus was that the leading notable had been Khalid Sheikh Othman from the Beit Abd ar-Rahim branch of Beit Abd as-Salam (see Figure 3). Nor were 'my grandfather' and 'my father' stable narrative figures. Muhammad, the servant of Jud Bey, was not sure whether it was Ali or Khalid who had ridden on the plain and made his fateful request for the piece of orange. Others said that it was the fathers, not the grandfathers, who had sold the land on the plain. Such versions located the blame firmly on the more proximate generation and historicized the account, rather than appealing to the general rhetorical expression of 'that's how we are'. Interpretations of the role of the generations were strongly at variance within the aghas themselves.

The ra'is's own reputation, furthermore, was contrary to that of his forebears. Men spoke of him as 'humble', or 'a good man', the opposite of the epithets he himself applied to the older generations for whom such words were indications of weakness and incapacity to respond to the exchanges of challenge and violence. Indeed his 'humility' was in part the reason that he had been able to head the winning coalition list in the baladiya elections. Had he been 'harsh' it might have been very difficult to constitute a list at all, let alone carry it to victory. The other groups of Beit Abd as-Salam would never have voted for anyone who looked like an aggressive champion of one fraction over the others, or who had a reputation for seeking to assert his name and authority in competition. Nor would such a man have been able to garner votes within the different fellah groups and to get a list of candidates from among them who would take their 'houses' with them in sufficient numbers. The ra'is's 'weakness' in terms of agonistic pride was a strength in terms of the collaborative consultation at least ideally required in the council. His remark that 'now it is all politics' pointed to a different mode of operation and a different personal identity from that of his ancestors. In his very ambivalence towards his ancestors – the grandfather who gives land away with the grand gesture and makes status for the mayor's generation impossible and the father whose 'brutality' and capacity to devour others he so praises – the ra'is shows the oscillating pattern within agha memory and narratives.

His own narrative presents a continuity in the signs of social authority from his ancestors – the vaunted manzul – but his position as ra'is depended on his *not* truly 'being their son' in his own persona and in the judgements men made of him. This narrative represents a different past in which irony plays no part, save for the irony of the mayor's own social role.

The Narrative of Beit Qadur

The instability of narrative figures has yet another dimension. The oldest living member of Beit Qadur, Abu Ahmad (no. 27), insisted that the story of how Karm al Leimun got its name concerned neither the ra'is's grandfather, nor his father, nor anyone in Beit Ibrahim at all: rather, it was Mahmud Abd al Latif (no. 2, Figure 2), the oldest son of the founder of Beit Abd al Latif Abd as-Salam, *not* Ali al Ibrahim, who gave the grove away to Umar Pasha.

In Abu Ahmad's narrative the 'gift' stood for a whole process of 'giving away' which characterized bey–agha relationships. The beys used to gather together fifteen or so of the men of Beit Abd as-Salam, men of his own grandfather's generation, and flatter them. They would send horses as presents, entrust them with important missions to different villages, call them 'agha' and treat them with all the signs of honour. So the men of Beit Abd as-Salam felt 'what do I want from five shunbuls of land', and they would let it go in exchange for status and respect – 'for nothing'(*bi-balash*), Abu Ahmad said with a wintery smile.

The beys used 'politics' too. They got the aghas out of the area of Rumul near Berqayl by offering them land in Syria in exchange, or by taking land in return for interceding with the Turkish government in any dispute, or for 'favours'. 'You could buy fifteen shunbuls in Syria for the price of one here, and before the First World War the beit had had 100 shunbuls there.' Abu Ahmad remembered that his own family had spent 'about twenty years' in Syria altogether.

Abu Ahmad's father had got into trouble with the government and became an outlaw 'in the days before the French'. He was eventually taken by force into the Turkish army in about 1916 and never returned. The Turkish government said of those who refused to go 'we'll take their wives', and the father had two wives and felt he had to obey. One of Abu Ahmad's paternal uncles (no. 20, Figure 1) had been the father's administrator for the lands on the plain and had not gone to Syria. He had possessed about five shunbuls of land in the village region. But he was impoverished after the war and had to sell them: part was bought by Abboud Bey, and part was 'eaten' by his cousins, Khalid Ali and Abd ar-Rahman Said (no. 12). The uncle became a supervisor of a few sharecroppers (a khawli) with Beit Mustafa Bey and stayed with them, working for a share himself. A second uncle (no. 21) had gone to America in 1912 and spent ten years or so there. On his return he had leased land from the beys and had become a cultivator who worked the land with them (a *sheddad*). He had no land of his own because everything had been sold to the beys, but took 50 per cent of the crop and paid all the costs of cultivation himself. He died 'and left what his father had left him: nothing.' As for the youngest of the uncles (no. 21a), he had been taken for the army by the French and 'he died in Syria, they said'. This uncle, too, had sold the land he had inherited to the beys.

Abu Ahmad's grandfather was described by the ra'is as a 'criminal', but to Abu Ahmad he was a 'prince', an *emir* who possessed ten to fifteen shunbuls here in the village. This grandfather in this narrative represents a vanished golden age of stability, property and status, all of it lost in the succeeding generation. He is the touchstone of status honour. The father and uncles are destroyed and destroy themselves step by step: beys' flattery and aghas' susceptibility, conscription and death, impoverishment and land sale, inheriting and leaving nothing, all play their part. But the basic cause is seduction by the powerful. The men of Beit Abd as-Salam are seduced, charmed from their real status and possessions by the dazzling play of the signs of status, respect and honour; by gifts of that great symbol of chivalry, the horse; and by fine words and the trust that being charged with important commissions indicated to the world. The magic worked, and as a result a genealogy lost its meaning, for if nothing is inherited and nothing left, neither land nor name, what is descent? In this narrative, the father's generation betrays both their father, the emir figure, and their sons by falling under the spell of the Beys. The enchanted aghas have given up the reality for the show.

Abu Ahmad had spent most of his life since the age of ten with the beys. He had begun as the boy who served the nargileh pipe and coffee in Abboud Bey's manzul, a similar beginning to that of Abu Juwad's narrative which I discuss below (p. 150). He had been jailed during the French Mandate for badly beating up some cultivators on Abboud's orders and Abboud had got him out of prison 'by buying a pardon from France'. A year or two later he had gone to Jud Bey Ibrahim and been a wakil for him in the village of al Qibbe on the plain for ten years. He began to take land on lease on his own account. Half of it was worked by fellahin on a fifty-fifty sharecropping agreement and the rest by *murabi'in*, cultivators who shared a quarter of the produce between the five or six of them. Each of them had a pair of cows or oxen, and 'they were like servants for us'. As wakil he made a bit of money with cattle dealing and took some of the grain. After the Second World War he came up to the village from the plain and began to work for himself, growing crops in the olive groves, though he did not have any olives himself.

Jud Bey, for whom Abu Ahmad had worked, described the grandfather, Abd al Qadir, as indeed a qabaday. One of the sons had been 'just about alright', the bey said to me, but Abu Ahmad's father he contemptuously called 'a horseman and a chicken thief', an ironical blending of two contradictory status figures. As for Abu Ahmad, he was a 'dog' and would die one, and 'nothing would ever come from him'. One of Jud's attendants (no. 24) said that Abu Ahmad's failure to 'do anything' after his son was shot dead by accident by the ra'is's maternal uncle's son showed weakness: 'he has no idea either how to be someone's enemy or their friend', said the attendant with derision.[33] In this informant's view, Abu Ahmad should have taken vengeance, or at least insisted that the father of the killer never again visit the Marouche quarter where Beit al Ibrahim lived, even if he was the mayor's maternal uncle. Beit Qadur's social identity was 'nothing, zero'.

The Past in the Present

I have already said that the narrative of Karm al Leimun had been changed into a story that was simply *known* rather than endlessly *related* as part of the repertoire of status performance, a performance which, by the mayor's time, the narrative was seen to undermine rather than to reproduce. This transformation showed at least a partial freeing from the power and ideological glamour of the fathers. In rendering the exchange ironical, the descendants take control of their ancestors whose 'face value' they no longer accept. They become the authors of the story and reinterpret the meaning of the characters' actions.

That narrative authority, however, is of a particular kind. For the aghas also represent themselves in their contemporary loss of status and their position of ambiguity as the products of the story and as figures determined by its unfolding. That, in my view, is the meaning of the mayor's ironic awareness of the continuing power of the fathers which has put the sons in a permanently false position as 'liars': whatever the latter do, as they attempt to maintain the appearances of and claims to the status honour which distinguishes them socially, is fatally undercut by all that the ancestor's 'Take it' is made to represent; their material resources have been 'given away'. Moreover, to defend their own distinction is necessarily to defend that of their fathers. Claims to being agha depend on descent, genealogy and a shared history of status honour deriving from those fathers. Yet how can one make those claims in the light of Karm al Leimun?

The mayor's irony articulates the dilemma of a group represented as caught in a historical double bind: they must advance the social claims of men commanding the resources of status honour and social significance, but it has become impossible for them to act in that manner. There are other, complementary, tensions. They must stay with the beys, yet the beys 'eat' them; they must be a solidary group, yet they 'eat' each other. At the same time, consciousness of that double bind and of the impossibility of resolving a dilemma structured in such terms gives the creative potentiality for the elaboration of multiple accounts and interpretations of 'the past' and of 'what we are'.

So the story of Karm al Leimun in its different versions remains known *because it is a reading of the present*; it is perceived as relevant to a grasp of the intrinsic ambiguities of the aghas' social position and their sense of their own collective identity. It is indeed the expression of essential aspects of their group historical situation.

The narratives had become part of a discourse of 'how we have lost so much of our social base and become liars', rather than a claim to respect and station. The servant located the famine as a key moment, and situated the bey's companion within social processes over which he had little control. The mayor's version projected back in time a contemporary rationality of property, resources and social position and re-read the past in its light. In that light, of course, the ancestor was shown as a deeply ambivalent figure. Karm al Leimun in both tellings is inscribed on the landscape as an ever-present sign of contradiction.

The four voices — that of the ra'is, Muhammad the servant, the grandfather, and Abu Ahmad — tell stories with very different meanings. The ra'is al baladiya re-imagines history: he (and those who remember the narrative in this way) transforms into social farce the exchange of the olive grove for the orange, an exchange which had once been heroic. The servant speaks of Karm al Adami and makes it a metaphor of need and power. The grandfather's voice, in my interpretation, demonstrates his capacity to rise above the ruse *precisely by choosing not to avoid it*, thus gaining the status crucial in a cultural universe in which honourable response and prestige giving is vital to the continued exchanges of status honour and the group. Abu Ahmad claims the princely status of his grandfather, and shows how only those who know 'how to eat' can prosper; others 'give it all away' for the show of respect.

Karm al Leimun, which is also Karm al Adami, shows us the dialectical tensions between and within possible emplotments and narratives. It illuminates the strains within the discourse of power, property and status honour and the ambivalence at the heart of the lord–agha relation. Beys accumulate, take advantage, possess, calculate. Aghas disperse, sacrifice, obey the dictates of 'name', act as if with a fine disregard for strategies, or under the bitter rules of that term denied by honour: necessity.

All four versions are narrated by aghas. It is their memory and their sense of communal identity which is being constituted by the four voices, though in different ways. The grandfather's voice which I have re-created is in the timeless, epic mode, distant from ordinary life and from what ordinary men might imagine as a possible exchange. Yet it is close to, indeed the emblem of, that virtue and excellence which are ideologically central to anyone claiming an agha's place in the world. The grandfather speaks within the universe of the charismatic and transcending power of the name, the charm which transcends men's merely routine imagination of what could happen. His descendants weave together accounts of a specific, historically located moment with their present experience of decline, though they do so in contrasted ways. The narratives of the karm become narratives situated in, and constructive of, a 'real' and not an heroic time, with vital consequences for the emplotment of wider historical events and processes in the world.

'Fathers' emerge as unstable and destabilizing figures. Patriliny and patriarchy are constantly questioned in narrative, memory and historical practice. Sons are abandoned. Half-brothers betray half-brothers, first cousins kill each other, men are 'crazy' or 'criminal', they devour the substance of others or leave nothing to their children, destroying their own master narrative of status honour by giving away what is vital to ensure the continuance and coherence of the story. Intermittency becomes a structuring force. Men struggle to reproduce, memorialize and guarantee narratives of being and place in the world against the ruptures, absences, and arbitrariness that continuously subvert them. Epic becomes farce. The ancestors do indeed, in Marx's famous phrase, weigh like a nightmare on the brains of the living.

CHAPTER NINE

Fellahin and Famine

The fellahin are absent from the narratives of the olive grove and the famine. The voice of the cultivators is unheard. Their distance from the grove of the orange is the distance of those excluded by definition from property and excellence. Yet of course they too 'knew' versions of how the name arose and in recounting the changes in the status order over time they adopted the ironic mode of the Karm al Leimun narrative. It became a comment on the historical self-undermining of the aghas who still sought to present themselves as a superior order of social being, despite the contradictions of their position.

Fellahin used to say, echoing the mayor's remark, 'that's how they are' as a derisive aspersion on the aghas vaunted karama, integrity and social status. For them, too, this version of how Karm al Leimun got its odd appellation was part of a critique of the aghas' historical role. But this was a critique by members of a stratum the aghas still represented as subordinate and outside the realms of status honour altogether. Fellahin might therefore sardonically refer among themselves to the 'olive tree of the orange' as an example of the historical stupidity of those who had dominated them.

Fellahin irony was not the same as that of the ra'is, by definition, for the cultivators spoke of a 'they' and not a 'we'. Their exclusion from the narrative might be turned, in this instance, to their advantage. For it enabled them when speaking 'as fellahin' to laugh at their supposed superiors' illusions and ignorance of the realities of power; to claim the kind of 'real' insight demonstrated by those who can observe the follies of the ways in which others destroy themselves without realizing it until too late. They could adopt the place of the amused commentators on the historical self-destruction of men such as the grandfather. In my terminology, the aghas thought themselves privileged tellers of the narratives of distinction, giving themselves over to the fetish of the person and the apparent glory achieved by the grand gesture, without ever realizing its truly contradictory and ambiguous nature.

Did the story of the karm not show, as one fellah friend said to me, how the aghas lived in a world of deception, of kizb? He could have the pleasure of telling the agha tale as an unambiguous proof of the way in which the latter were trapped in their own show of status. In this sense a fellah could appropriate Karm al Leimun as a bitterly amusing demonstration of the self-deceptive nature of the aghas' whole show of status.

Yet that laughter did not negate the subordination to which the cultivators had been subjected, nor deny its force. In one dimension, indeed, it made that subordination more bitter. For in ridiculing the aghas who had ruled them, the cultivators' own past, too, might be turned into a kind of mockery. To have been the virtual slaves of men like that! Yet narrative points of view were no more homogeneous among the fellahin than among the aghas, as I shall try to show in this chapter.

What was 'the famine' to fellahin? A concentrated image of the condition of poverty and want, of vulnerability and subordination that had characterized their everyday lives, its significance was still not entirely of a distant 'then'. Their accounts of that past placed 'the famine' in a historical landscape in which it was a particularly striking but not exceptional condition; it represented the worst of a continuing experience of hierarchy and violence. 'The famine' was one of the references for older men to use as an image of 'how bad things had been'; it was evoked as one of the exemplary moments when suffering and tyranny were at their most intense. There was no one to give an olive grove for an orange, or 'a lot of land for wheat' among the labourers and cultivators. They themselves might be given in exchange.

Four Fellah Narratives

1. The Captain's narrative

'My grandfather was bought for a pail of milk in the time of the First World War hunger.'

Here is a direct fellah voice, telling in one single line a different yet complementary story of famine and incommensurate exchange. The speaker was an officer in the Lebanese army, Muhammad Selim. He was a man who had risen to a position no other person in the entire village had ever achieved, and he came from perhaps the poorest and least esteemed fellah family. People said of them, 'they were slaves', the only group of which that was held to be true. Muhammad Selim's biography represented one of the greatest transformations of an individual imaginable in a universe where only a few years before the idea of even an agha – let alone a despised fellah – becoming an officer, would have been taken by everyone as a ludicrous fantasy.

The Captain's small descent group, Beit Selim (see Figure 5), still lived in the row of stable-like, one-room houses in which they were said first to have been lodged in a status barely higher than the animals. There were only four households. One man was an unemployed building labourer who kept his family in Tripoli on a monthly remittance of 100LL from his son in Australia. Another was a general day labourer who raised calves for their owners for a small extra income. A third was employed by a powerful bey's widow as a watchman and agricultural worker. The Captain himself seldom came to the village, and supported his younger brother who lived in Tripoli. Their collective presence in the village was therefore as marginal as their status as beit.

The officer's own career seemed in every way a social contradiction, a peculiar aberration of hierarchy and a source of envy in others. In public he was treated with the greatest respect, but he never received visitors in his small house and very seldom visited others, preserving a conscious social distance from fellahin and aghas alike. He assured me that several hundred letters had been sent to the Commander of the Lebanese army by villagers, mostly those of his own fellah stratum of social origin, to inform on him for being 'political' or 'Nasserist'. These were charges guaranteed to hurt the chances of a Sunni Muslim officer in an officer corps that was predominantly Christian. 'That's how they are,' he used to say to me with considerable feeling when speaking about 'the people here': 'Everything is envy and malice.' The only thing to do was to avoid them.

Villagers always gave a stock account of the Captain's rise in the world in terms of the particular favour of a senior officer, a typical patronage narrative of personal favour, rather than by any reference to the Captain's abilities. Both agha and fellah informants seemed to regard his rank as a personal violation of social position rather than a mark of any collective break in the patterns of status. Telling his story in the language of patronage normalized his position in local conventions of biography, rather as if he were one of the fellahin young men who had been chosen by the beys as bodyguards and made a life as instruments of a powerful man's will and violence. Perhaps the letters followed the same logic of personal favour by trying to induce personal disfavour as the way of reasserting collective control over his disturbing individual social ascent. The Captain certainly referred to this 'venom' as a block to any further advancement and a manifestation of 'the village' trying to destroy one of its own.

The officer's story is one of origin, the founding moment of a beit's presence in the place. The famine is the beginning and limit of their collective memory. The narrative establishes 'in one line' their social identity as slaves, creatures who could be bought and sold. The beys' power makes this grandfather commensurate with the pail of milk. The exchange is represented as the routine practice of such a time. The ancestor's own person is the property to be exchanged between lords, and that person is valued at no more than a few litres of milk.

The story is not one of anomaly or irony, or even an illustration of a point that food was in so great demand that one might go to the extreme of exchanging a man for it. Rather it was a recording of 'how it was then for us'. The lords could make a reality and a metaphor of identity of man and milk, a metaphor of the power to make equivalent and commensurable what they wished. The extraordinary element of the story lay in the beys' absolute authority which established its own measure expressed in the simple terseness of: 'My grandfather was bought for a pail of milk at the time of the First World War hunger.'

A relation of identity is established between the domination of the beys and the famine; the time of starvation and need becomes a metaphor of power. The great hunger is a figure for the lords' arbitrary imposition of their own terms of exchange, the terms of life itself.

The style of the utterance seems to me to have a double aspect. On the one hand, what is striking is its very prosaic quality, the matter-of-factness heightened by the flat, economical reporting of an event. And at the same time, in the context of its present telling, the image poetically separates itself from that same everyday as a shock, a violation of an implicitly claimed human, moral and natural order of things.

There was no other detail, no direct or reported speech, setting of a scene, characterization of the participants or framing in extraordinary circumstance. The person 'possessing' the grandfather and willing to exchange him for the milk has no narrative role. Moreover, the Captain said he knew nothing of the grandfather or where he was from, though the darkness of the skin of family members inclined him to think they were from 'India' or 'somewhere in the east', outsiders even to Arab society. What men knew was 'that they came to be in the village', and the rest had no significance for memory or public telling. Everyone I spoke to was familiar with the story of the pail of milk and assured me it was 'true', I think both as fact and as a demonstration of the nature of fellahin subordination in that social order.

'The pail of milk for the grandfather' was also a story of contrast, of how things were 'then'. It is the fellah equivalent of the ra'is's 'now it is all politics'. Those days had gone. Muhammad Selim's own life strikingly contradicted the image of slavery. For he had become a man of some importance in the military hierarchy. He was a man of significance of whom one might speak, enviously or otherwise, though his origin lay in the extreme case of anonymous insignificance of which, by definition, nothing could be said. The person of the teller was now extraordinary in the light of his account, an extraordinariness which he was convinced others sought to limit and reduce by their jealous attacks. The number of treacherous letters he said had been sent to the army Commander were indeed an index of his success, a tribute and witness to his rank and social distinction.

If the narratives of Karm al Leimun/Karm al Adami were given as historically recording a key moment in the loss of property and social decline, the 'pail of milk' now witnessed to the possibilities of an exceptional, personal, historical rise that would once have been unimaginable. It testified to the realization of a personal identity in a situation in which such a realization was socially held to be excluded. The unequal exchange demonstrated the extremes of the logic of the *general* order of slavery and genealogical hierarchy, but the career of the narrator had come to show how that logic might yet be defied by an *individual* fellah. Muhammad Selim might thus frame his life – paradoxically, given the constraints of cultural form – with a story that was the absolute opposite of the honour narrative principles, pointing to himself as transcending the given forms and insisting on his difference from his anonymous grandfather.

2. *Abu Marwan's narrative*

The Captain's much older paternal cousin, Abu Marwan (no. 16 in Figure 5, for the details of which he was the informant, a man probably in his later sixties or more), gave a different and more elaborated version of the story of 'slavery' and exchange. He told me that the family came from Pakistan, 'some say we were Pashas there, but who knows?'. The father of the original Selim, Abu Marwan's grandfather, was called Abdullah; he and his wife died on the road to Mecca to make the pilgrimage. They had two boys who somehow came into the care of 'a Pasha in Syria' who 'gave' one to a bey in Danniye (a village in the mountains to the south) and the other, Selim, to a bey in Berqayl 'for a pail of milk'. Selim brought up Abboud Bey, he told me. 'We are not interested in making a big display about our descent', said Abu Marwan, 'or talking about being Circassian and aghas and that kind of stuff.'

Abu Marwan's narrative situates the 'grandfather for a pail of milk' in a quite different time frame than does Captain Selim's account. Abboud was a boy in the later 1870s and 1880s, not during the time of the famine in the First World War. Abu Marwan thus places the exchange for the pail of milk simply during the time of the Turks and the childhood of Abboud, and not specifically in a period of famine and need. The moment of 'giving' the young brothers who have mysteriously appeared in Syria in the hands of 'a Pasha' is thus generalized into a condition of being rather than tied to a particularized moment of hunger. (The ra'is al baladiya commented that Beit Selim were 'brought as slaves from Egypt' by Muhammad Pasha in another variant of the family's past.)

Abu Marwan had lost his own father for a key period of his life because of a bey's power. The father was 'very strong and agile' and was of the same generation as Abboud, with whom, as I would put it, he anomalously shared a 'father' in the person of Selim. He had had a confrontation with the lord 'in the days of Turkey' and had fled to Brazil where he stayed for eighteen years. Abu Marwan was only two or three years old when this happened – another abandoned child – and he was brought up by one of his paternal uncles. When the father eventually returned, he was supported financially by his offspring and he was thus incapable of playing the role a father should assume.

There had been eight male and four female children in the father's generation. Ahmad (no. 3), had been a real qabaday, Abu Marwan said: 'an outlaw, crazy and living crazily, always against the beys and extremely strong natured'. He shot and killed a man from Beit Haddara 'like that, in a row'.[1] This man's brother (no. 8), a young man 'who was the tallest and toughest in Berqayl', was shot dead by Turkish soldiers who mistook him for his older outlaw sibling (the death of a brother or cousin because of the violence against the powers that be is also a theme of narratives and experience – see Chapter 14 and the story of Tewfiq and Walid).[2] A third male (no. 4) had gone to Brazil just before the First World War and never returned and all contact had ceased, though they knew he had five children. A fourth (no. 10), the uncle who had brought up Abu Marwan had started as a spice seller but then got ill and went to work as a khawli (agricultural organizer overseeing three or four sharecroppers) in the mountains of the Jurd for Muhammad Bey al Umar. He was twenty-five years with the bey, who was the worst man in the world.[3] The lord was infuriated when the uncle's boy (Captain), Muhammad Selim, did well in school and the bey's son only passed a certificate. So the uncle went 'fantasia to America', as Abu Marwan put it, to stay with another brother (no. 7a, a man who lived abroad for fifty years before returning to the village where he died after two years in about 1963). Three years after the uncle came back from his fantasia 'he started a little buying and selling olives ahead of the harvest and hunting, things like that'. Of the other two males in that generation, one (no. 7) married here and had one daughter, and the other (no. 12) had 'some sort of odd sickness or something' and died quite young and unmarried. Of the eight males in the father's generation, four of whom had migration histories and one of whom had been shot, only nos. 2 and 10 had male children themselves.

Abu Marwan's eldest brother (no. 13) was still living. He had been the watchman of the house of Ali Muhammad al Umar, one of the beys. According to Abu Marwan he was very changeable, 'one hour like this, another like that, no position in life and no reason'. He had married four times, three being women from other fellah houses and all childless; the first wife died, the second he repudiated, the third died. The fourth, however, was the only woman of the agha Beit Abd as-Salam ever to have married into a fellah beit and it was she who bore his two children, a boy and a girl.

The whole narrative is a counter genealogy and counter history. Abu Marwan asserts the value of the most disprivileged of houses against the discourse of status honour from which it is excluded. In key respects he reverses the account of Beit Selim told by aghas or beys. The ancestral pair of the slave house come from a distant land which is here given a particular value, for they are perhaps from a family of pashas. The genitor, Abdullah, bears one of the classical Muslim names, 'servant of God' (and not slave of man). The couple die on the pilgrimage to Mecca, a blessed fate that adds sanctification and an elect place in Paradise as martyrs to their possible aristocratic origin.[4] The two orphaned boys then appear abruptly 'in Syria' in the hands of a powerful pasha who 'gives them away'. 'Slavery' is thus framed in a quasi-mythical tale of transformations of identity that is founded in distant origins, lost rank, holy death and the sudden and unaccounted for reappearance of the parentless brothers, given by a powerful prince to the lords of Danniye and Akkar. One vanishes from the narrative, the other becomes 'our grandfather'.

Servitude transmutes into a relationship of a particular closeness: Selim – the perfect, the whole, the secure as his Arabic name indicates – cares for the child Abboud, whose own father, Abd ar-Razzaq Bey, had died when he was very small. Selim 'nurses' the young fatherless bey, a symbolic equivalent of the milk for which he, the nurturing attendant, has been so non-commensurately exchanged. Or rather, more than an equivalent. For Selim gives in abundance to the child Abboud though he has himself been exchanged 'for nothing', only a pail of milk by which no human should be valued. He gives far more than that for which he is given, and far more than the vulnerable boy, who will grow up into the icon of power, gives in return. The slave becomes a substitute father, a father characterized not by power and authority but by a maternal role of protecting and raising the child. He performs both the roles of his martyred parents, combining male and female in one figure.

The theme of the absent, lost, departed or inadequate father takes on another dimension in a poignant juxtaposition with the career of Abboud Bey; for we know that this fatherless man, who became the most powerful of patriarchal figures, lost his own son unnaturally by murder. The theme is present, too, when Abu Marwan's own father abandons him and flees Abboud's wrath. And the motif recurs when the uncle who cared for him also vanishes for a time 'on a fantasia', but after the lord who brought such misfortune had become jealous at the success of the slave's grandson, Muhammad Selim.

Yet, at the same time, maleness and the physical power of the male, different complementary aspects of the fathers, are present in ideal form as if in overvaluing compensation for those same fathers' absence and flight before the beys' wrath: one uncle, cut down in his youth, is 'taller and stronger than anyone else in the village'; Abu Marwan's own father is 'very strong and agile'; a third is of an 'extremely powerful nature' and he kills. 'Strength', in this narrative, is as much the attribute of the fellahin as it is of the beys and aghas. Abu Marwan's narrative is thus absorbed into the master narrative of masculinity, physical force and 'nature' by the use of these expressions typical in descriptions of heroic figures. Furthermore, in a different idiom of distinction and hierarchy, Beit Selim show a different kind of strength, for they also literally out-wit the lords. Muhammad Selim succeeds in school, out-shining the bey's son and provoking the jealous anger which prompts a 'fantasia' exile, represented as a kind of whim and fancy which takes his father away for three years.

The narrative is intensely oppositional and contestatory, asserting the virtue and excellence of the despised beit in the language of agonism and of rupture: men have major disputes with beys and flee to Brazil; or they are 'crazy' outlaws and oppose the beys all the time, their 'madness' an apt figure for such isolated and anomalous behaviour; or they die by mistake at the hands of the state; or they go off to America and are never heard of again. Violence runs through every aspect of the account as coercive anger forces men into exile and flight. Arriving arbitrarily in the village from a distant land in exchange for a pail of milk, some of them are forced no less arbitrarily to flee it for a distant land. Others go down to Tripoli, away from direct relations with the lords. Yet others seem to represent in their own conduct the 'unreasonable' quality of a life in which social continuity has been constantly disrupted; they become figures of changeability, 'one hour like this and one hour like that', 'without any reason'.

Arbitrariness of origin is once again a sign of how a house comes to be in Berqayl and Beit Selim presents the most extreme, but by no means untypical, fellah account of arrival in the village: wandering, death, and the power of a pasha dictate their presence. But the same power that brings them to the village can drive them away. Arbitrariness of power is represented as permanently dictating life chances and the very condition of existence. There is a pattern to its operations, but it is a pattern constituted by irregularity, intermittancy and unpredictability arising from the asymmetries of social relations between fellah and bey. Only the 'crazy', those who live outside in the mountains as outlaws and who kill 'for no particular reason', can resist and remain.

'Anger', provoked and expressed, is a metaphor for a relationship of domination and subordination. Moreover, a lord's wrath is represented as recurrently precipitating events; or rather, it is the narrative key to the events which give form and structure to the memory of a fellah beit and to their apprehension of their place in the world. 'Anger', the rupturing violence of *za'al*, powerfully moulds collective biography and experience.

Opposition is shadowed by dependency and continuous relations of subordination. For the bey–fellah links serve as the nodal points of the story, joining the entire history together. Seen in this light, the pasha who 'gives the boys away' is the real founder of Beit Selim. He places them, as his gifts, where he wishes. The narrative thus pays its own tribute to that will and power of the lords which, in other dimensions, it appears to contest. Yet by claiming personhood through contest and insisting that the men of Beit Selim cannot simply be 'given away', for they are capable of being outlaws and resisting the lords though they may have to flee as a result, Abu Marwan refutes the servility attached to the name. The men of Beit Selim, in his narrative, do not realize their being and function simply as instruments of the dominant. They assert themselves as persons, and resist depersonalizing power.[5]

3. The old hajj's narrative

The old man's small, stone two-room house was just on the other side of the boundary wall of the bey's house which I had rented and we could therefore be described as 'neighbours'. 'Could be', because men of power and poor cultivators are not 'neighbours', whatever the physical proximity of their dwellings might be, and to use the term would, in most situations, be regarded as anomalous by both. Since I was already an anomalous figure, however, there was at least the possibility of invoking the social piety of a relationship which would normally be excluded. It was still difficult to establish conditions under which the hajj and I could 'talk', for the distinctions of status between us were so great that it was not easy to find what would be accepted as an appropriate mode of interchange, and a person of standing was not expected to show an abstract 'interest' in what a person of low standing might have to say about his life and world. I made the proper ceremonial visits on occasions of mourning or celebration, but even that courtesy was subject to a certain comment by aghas as social obligations I 'did not need to perform': 'how could the ustaz Mikhail have social duties to camel drivers?' one demanded scathingly. 'No, they are neighbours', others said, praising my punctiliousness, protecting me against attack and thus showing that they were well disposed towards me while providing at the same time an account of my actions which cleared me of a breach of status practice.

So the old man and I were able to address each other on formal occasions, though neither of us found it easy to establish a manner of 'talk' between two persons so unequal in social position. It was very difficult to find any ground upon which my wish to discuss 'the past' with him in a way that might make social and cultural sense could be constructed. An appeal to his age and memory as part of my project to study the history of the region furnished us with just enough of a shared basis of interchange for him to find my coming to his house on such occasions a reasonable act.

My neighbour, who said he was eighty-eight years old, was no longer working and the family was obviously extremely poor. But he had made the pilgrimage to Mecca, paid for by his sons, something only one or two fellahin had done, and was therefore known by the respectful appellation of 'hajj'. He told me that he had been a cultivator before the First World War and had worked 'in Berqayl', which referred to the lands around the village. 'No one had anything. My grandfather [meaning here 'an ancestor'] came and built here.[6] The houses were ours.' The village was very small in the days of the Turks, 'all stones and mud'. He had cultivated on a half-share of the produce, he said, or a third or a quarter to the owner, and all the expenses had been on the fellah. The beys lived in the village then – Umar Pasha and Ali Pasha, who died in 1924. (This was an unusual precision of chronological marking, perhaps for my benefit and to indicate to me that he recalled exactly the date of this momentous event, a key one in his story of the passing of glory from the village.) 'He had a fine manzul. They had power over many people.' Then he added: 'As they weakened, the village grew greater.'

In those days a fellah had to give a feddan of labour and a calf and 500 Turkish *qirsh* to the bey if he wanted to marry. His own sister was to be betrothed to one of the fellah armed guards of the lords, and the latter would not permit it. Ibrahim Pasha and his son, Jud Bey, as well as the celebrated Sheikh Ahmad Shakir (the mayor's maternal grandfather), had come and stopped his father writing the document of marriage because they did not wish it.

'My father', the old hajj said, 'used to work six shunbuls of *ba'l* [non-irrigated] land for the beys, and four of ba'l belonging to Ahmad Abd al Latif Abd as-Salam' (the same Ahmad Abd al Latif whose daughter had married Ali al Ibrahim, the mayor's grandfather).[7] All the land belonged to the aghas then. They were stronger than the beys when it came to land in the village. His father had worked twenty-five or thirty years with Ahmad Abd al Latif. He had two pairs of oxen. Cows were cheap then, only two and a half or three gold lira. They grew wheat and barley on the land of Beit Abd al Latif Abd as-Salam. The women worked too; everyone worked in the wheat fields. A labourer used to get a quarter of a lira per day and eat from what he grew. A 100 kilos of wheat cost two silver riyals, and the same measure of barley cost one riyal.

'We worked barefoot. We were poor, wretched. I went to Argentina, to Buenos Aires in 1913. We knew people there who had migrated before. I worked with the German Electric Company. We were forty-six or so from Berqayl. Two of my brothers were taken for the Turkish army and died, and my father and mother were both old. We emigrated and came back in 1920.'[8] Others in the hajj's descent group were cameleers, the same men who the ra'is told me had worked over many years with Khalid Ali.

This narrative circles around 'having nothing', death, migration and labour. Barefoot people live in earth and stone houses. Their sons are taken for the army and never return (let us recall Tamimi and Bahgat's figure of 7,151 taken into the army from Akkar out of what the official census gave as a total population of 21,467 males).[9] 'The famine' is a metaphor for the condition of the wretched fellahin. Yet even here there are distinctions and differentiations based on possession and property to be made: 'the houses were ours'; the father owned two pairs of oxen, others had camels. For there were wage labourers who did not own their houses, who had no draught animals and who depended upon the quarter of a lira per day. Money is represented as already playing an important part in the value of labour, animals and subsistence goods.

Both rupture and continuity play their part. The hajj leaves his country, his brothers are arbitrarily taken, they disappear for ever, a man is prevented from marrying. At the same time, the rupture in his biography is not a narrative rupture, for such events are represented as typically constitutive of fellah experience and seamlessly incorporated into the collective and personal account. The hajj, unlike his brothers taken away for the army, returns from a distant place, and establishes a continuous relationship of labourer and owner with Beit Abd al Latif Abd as-Salam (a kind of continuity which the mayor also mentioned in his account). As bey and murafiq might be together for many years, so cultivators and landowners or administrators might have links that formed a joint history of beits articulated through the labour process and through the narratives.

The hajj's theme is work, and the extraction of dues and costs from the fellahin: what they had to pay; the offerings in money and kind necessary to secure a marriage which the will of the beys and sheikhs could thwart; the involvement of everyone, including the women, in the labour process. Work is the burden of his tale; its compulsions and 'duties', rather than the overt violence of Abu Marwan's narrative, are what preoccupy him. The narrative tells of a world where agha and fellah might remain bound by labour relations for many years. In that world a great lord exercised his power from 'a fine manzul', for such a man held power over many. The force of the lords is acknowledged, their definition of who and what men like the hajj were, is acknowledged in the recognition of the centre of power in the reception room, the stage on which the most public scenes of authority were collectively enacted.

The historical movement of the account reverses and complements that of 'the grove of the orange': reverses, because it is a narrative of gain, small but real, rather than of loss; complements, because the hajj also witnesses a decline in the personal presence and dominance of the men of power. In this narrative the houses of the beys who kept the fine reception rooms and ruled over many people grow weaker, and as they decline so the village expands.

The great lord's manzul in all its show and galvanizing force is no longer the stage of power. The hajj speaks of 'the time when', with a hint of nostalgia in his evocation of those who 'ruled many' and lived as great men should live. But their disappearance renders possible his own appearance, their decrease is the increase of 'the village'.

4. The qabaday's narrative

The form and type of identity established in the preceding narrative contrasted strongly with an account from a different generation and social level of the fellah stratum. The hajj had a relative by marriage, a vigorous man of sixty when I first met him in 1972, who belonged to Beit al Umari. This man, Walid Abu Jawad, was keen to talk to me and had no hesitation in suggesting that we meet so that he could tell me about 'those days and how the village had been'. He had spent most of his life in the beys' service as a labour supervisor and strong-arm man and felt no inhibitions about our discussion. Indeed, he wanted to use it to establish his version of fellah history that would challenge the one he knew I was given by the aghas.

Walid had lost his own father in the First World War conscription.[10] 'The Turks took many from the village,' he said. 'There was no one in the place at all – a fox would come in the afternoon and there was nobody to drive it out. Many died of sickness and hunger. There was no medicine.' There were 'not ten houses' built in concrete when he was young, and 'not more than a 100' houses made of wood and stone in the village.

At the age of fourteen, in 1926, he had been living in a shelter on the plain. One day he went hunting for game and met Muhammad Bey Abboud who said to him: 'Come into my service.' So he went to the bey's house in the village and sat in his manzul, making the coffee and handing it round to guests as his lord's qahwaji or coffee-maker. When Muhammad Bey wintered in Beirut he was one of those who looked after his local interests. He became a wakil for some of the land in the Berqayl region, responsible for its management and labour organization. Walid had had five men working under him, each one with a pair of cows, 'for there were no tractors in those days', he said, 'just a primitive harvester and no threshing machines'. The share-croppers took a quarter of the produce, but they had to do the cultivation 'for nothing', as he put it, and had no rights to any of the olives. 'They used to take their share of wheat and store it in their houses to make flour and bread.'

The French wanted to count everything and know about everything. How many people? How many cows? Were the cattle for milking or ploughing? How many donkeys, chickens, goats, sheep? What were the yields of fruit, olives, cereals? You had to give a certain amount – very low – to the government in those days.[11]

Walid stayed with Muhammad Bey until the outbreak of the Second World War when he linked up with a French army officer. The officer had asked for two qabadays from each bey in each village. Muhammad Bey had got 500 qabadays altogether from the Jurd and the whole area, and assembled them in front of his palace. 'The bey sent me off on an errand, but the Frenchman said: "Give me the one who served me the lemonade. Give him to me and I'll take four men from you, two from Halba, one from Ayyoun, and one from Haddara." He liked me and I became his bodyguard and general organizer.' The officer made Walid report on everything they saw on their journeys around the region. Then they had a row. 'I disagreed with him, and drew a gun.' So he had fled to Abboud Bey's protection.

After a period with the English, gathering information and working in some shady business that involved the black market in grain 'with a young guy I knew', he made 'a lot of money on smuggling and a big profit in the market in Tripoli. I could have bought land for 46,000LL, but I didn't. No brains.' Walid joined up with another French officer, this time reporting back on what the English were doing: 'their camp, the officers, their names, what guns they had, that sort of thing. Then I spilt the beans to the English and told them I'd work with them for nothing.' They gave him 2,500LL but 'didn't trust me'.

He had a lot of charges against him for arms smuggling during the period of the war and Khalid Bey Abd al Qadir, a powerful man and rival of Abboud Bey, promised to get them lifted if Walid joined him. So he did, and the charges duly melted away because the bey was close to the French and had a lot of influence. Khalid Bey's men shot and wounded Abboud in Halba in a political quarrel in 1943 or so.

Khalid Bey had a large village in Syria that was not paying anything to him and was defying his authority: 'He sent me off there and I brought in the whole harvest, everything, all the grain and produce of the summer months, the lot', he said to me with great emphasis, stressing that he had brought the place to heel entirely alone and by his own authority. The bey had large sections of many villages – Arida, Tall Bibi, Sheikh Zenad, Khreibe, Shass. 'I was in charge of all of it and operated out of Arida where I became mukhtar. I appointed deputies in each place. We tried growing rice and cotton but they failed after only a few years.'

There was a row in the early 1950s between Khalid Bey and Abboud Bey over Khalid's lands in Khraibe. Walid had been busy smuggling tobacco at the time and Khalid Bey's wife complained to him that Abboud had taken the land and ploughed it with machines. 'We went to the Qaimaqam (district head) in Tartous to make a complaint, and then we went and kicked out Abboud's tractors and ploughed it ourselves with oxen. But Khalid Bey's brother-in-law was a no-good who caused me a lot of difficulties and I would not let him interfere on the land. He made problems for me, so I left them in 1952 or 1953.' Another bey made a complaint because Walid and his men had shot up his people in Tall Bibi and Arida in a land dispute over property which Khalid Bey had on lease from a local family. 'We wanted to occupy the whole village, but found about 100 soldiers there. Suleiman Franjieh had to settle it.'[12]

In 1953, the year Muhammad al Abboud was killed, Walid joined him as his murafiq to protect him against a murder attempt. But not long before the Minister was assassinated Walid had a row with his chauffeur, a man from Beit Abd as-Salam, and shot and wounded him, 'so I left Abboud's service'.[13]

Walid worked for a time with the Electricity Company, then Bashir Bey al Osman took him up to the large mountain village of Fneidek on an invitation to a reception there. He was locally well known by this time and the beys were always on the lookout for men with his experience. A rival bey, Ali Bey Abd al Karim, cut the road at the village of Michmich, just before Fneidek, because the two lords were electoral opponents at that time.[14] There was shooting and one of the rival's men was killed. Bashir Bey told Walid that now he had better stay with him as a murafiq in case Ali Abd al Karim tried to take revenge. So he stayed with Bashir, and when there were elections in which the two beys were again opposed 'we shot Ahmad ash-Shunbur (a fellah of Berqayl allied with the opposition) here in the village and I was sentenced to two years. I went to jail and got a pardon after a year and a month and got out at the time of the revolution in 1958.' He returned

to Bashir Bey and was still with him as a murafiq when we had our conversations. 'Now I gamble as well', he said.

He added his own narrative of village settlement. 'The village was an old
Christian monastery, Deir 'Aqil.[15] Bi'r 'Aqil was the name of the mosque
spring, hence Berqayl.[16] We were the first in the dai'a, we of Beit al Umari.
One person from Beit Sharaf ad-Din came to the village, he was a Shi'a, and
he married a girl from our family and gave us some land measured out with
the rope of the headdress. Sheikh Awadh, the founder of Beit Awadh, was
originally from Sfeina and he was thrown out of his settlement and was
fleeing to Wadi Jamous. He stayed instead with us of Beit al Umari and
began to educate the children. He married a daughter of our founder and
ran the mosque and its endowments.'

The names of the fellahin houses themselves in Walid's account of local
common-sense etymology have a particular signifying power. 'Awadh means
'place of refuge' or 'sanctuary'. So the name contains the explanation of the
origin of the fleeing sheikh as one coming to a sanctuary. My informant's
own beit name, which derives from the root 'a-m-r, comes from the root
meaning 'to inhabit; build; people, or establish a settlement'. Thus it, too, is
identified with the founding act claimed for his ancestor. Sharaf ad-Din
means 'the honour of religion', here associated with a Shi'a, not a Sunni
Muslim. The marriage with the daughter of Beit al Umari thus unites the two
sides of the Islamic religious tradition. The vanished monastery both establishes Christianity as having been at the foundation of the site and succeeds
it historically by the two Muslim branches of the faith. A dense composite
history is encapsulated in these few, brief phrases.

'There was no Beit Abd as-Salam or Khalid,' he continued. The Mir'abi
beys gave land to the aghas who came often to the village. The lords took
all or three-quarters of it by force. They would encroach on other people's
land by ploughing it, build a fence around it and give you a shunbul of wheat
and send you on your way. They took the olive grove of al Dendashliya and
al Bishkhaniya, which was five shunbuls of cereals from Hajj Abd al Majid
al Awadh. They seized the grove called az-Zeitoun (the olive) from Said
Rashid al 'Umari. 'All this was not less than fifty years ago.'(that is, the
period during or just after the First World War). Bishkhaniya Sheikh Osman
belonged to Sheikh Osman and Abboud Bey took it from him by forced
purchase.[17] On another occasion Abboud had taken ten or twelve men from
Berqayl, ridden over an area he had his eye on for his own landholdings, and
driven off cultivators who were working government land. 'Then he registered
the land in his name and paid some money for it.'

Walid Abu Juwad's narrative is that of a man known as a qabaday, a
companion of powerful lords and a dangerous opponent. He tells of an
individual rise in the world as remarkable as that of the Captain, though of
a quite different order. He had not only been a young servant, then murafiq
as well as a labour supervisor for the beys since the age of fourteen, but had

done very well as a smuggler during the Second World War profiteering on wheat, and as a gunman. In terms of his personal life history, from the disappearance of his father on Turkish conscription when he himself was only two years old to his current place as a murafiq and gambler, he had experience on every level of local power relations and violence, and was old enough to have seen all but the earliest years of the Abboud period.

Walid's autobiographical narrative begins in a double absence of significance – he too is a fatherless boy and from an impoverished fellah beit. He makes himself significant, valued, spoken of, and speaking, in two registers. The first is that of family: 'We were the founding family' is his boast, giving a past to the ignoble and dispossessed. He does not claim 'a genealogy', but he does assert an originary role, a moral and temporal precedence, for a family displaced by the later usurpers. Walid himself thus narratologically comes from nowhere *and* from the founding house of the village. The second register is that of his own agency and capacity for violence. For him, unlike his old relative the hajj, a fellah could assert value and excellence in terms of the agonistic discourse of status. From the desolate image of the fox in the village and the orphaned child he moves to the assertion of his own story and biography (*sira*). He is autonomous. He alone brings in all the harvest from a rebellious village. He makes money smuggling guns and grains. He is picked out by the men of power when only a fourteen-year-old boy and a pattern of his life is established. Each of them – Muhammad al Abboud, Abboud himself, Khalid Abd al Qadir, Bashir al Osman, a litany of the great political names of Akkar – wanted him close to them for their protection and to run their estates. He has been a part of their apparatus of fear and respect. (I should note that Beit Abd as-Salam respected him too, and I heard aghas refer to him as a real qabaday and as a dangerous man to cross. His wounding of the agha chauffeur had never been avenged. They said they would have tried to eliminate him if he had stayed in the village during the period of feud detailed in Chapter 10, and Walid had prudently moved down to Tripoli, indicating that he was 'outside' the affair.) Like Abu Marwan's 'crazy' outlaw uncle who always opposed the beys, Walid's disputes with an individual lord are always within a framework which preserves unchallenged the order of the beys' power. They needed him, and he depended on them: to get him off legal charges and to cover his deeds with their power and connections to Mandate or Lebanese authorities.

Walid's narrative represents him moving from bey to bey as it pleases him, shooting and challenging as he goes, and he portrays himself as using English and French officers who also pick him out from the crowd (of five hundred others in the case of the Frenchman) and think they are using him. He plays his cards, as he wishes. But when the opportunity comes to purchase land, he turns it down: 'No brains,' he says. The refusal of the bargain is surely as grand a gesture in its way as the giving of the olive grove for the orange. The fellah qabaday carelessly brushes aside the possibility of acquiring land as if it had no power at all to attract him. Just like that. 'No brains', he says with a smile, a phrase which seems ironic but in this context is transformed into a boast of magnificent and extraordinary disregard for conventions of value to which others cling. He speaks as if he were both mayor *and* grandfather, in ironic lament *and* proud demonstration of autonomy. Such an image seems to me to be at one with the self-representation of the man who refuses to be tied down, but who moves constantly through a highly individualized universe of power and reputation. Walid refuses to be 'a landowner', to invest, produce, accumulate through organized cultivation. He will bring in a harvest for the bey despite the opposition of an entire village and do it 'on his own', that is an act of formidable nerve, violence and fear-inspiring reputation. He does it because it pleases him to demonstrate his ability to confront others, not because he is the lord's man. But he turns down the opportunity to buy land. Walid is a gambler, he takes risks and acts 'as he wishes' and 'alone'. He is the author of his life.

The life narrative frames the famine and destitution in a history of seizure of land from the first inhabitants, people who themselves had come from elsewhere. The first settlement had been Christian; the ancestor of his own beit simply appeared from no known place of origin; the second comer was a Shi'a Muslim; the third was a man fleeing from his own village. Into this mix of identities and displaced figures came the beys and the aghas, who 'had not been here before'; a different kind of history and social order commenced, and a different kind of displacement. The beys' descent group name, Mir'abi, is from the verb *ra''ba*, he insisted, to terrify or cause fear.[18] That name in all its signifying power is the ground of the social order and marks a social and moral rupture with the past. His etymology – a commonly cited one – powerfully represents the universe of signification and power in which he claims his place.

That he himself was an instrument of the powers oppressing the fellahin illustrates the realities of power and is the other element that structures his narrative. One of Abboud's most celebrated agha murafiqs had said to me: 'We were cunning. If we saw a promising lad among the fellahin we would take him for the beys';[19] Walid's story of Muhammad al Abboud, and later the French officer, spotting him and taking him into personal service, is the type-case of such recruitment from the fellahin. Most of his life had been spent as the instrument of the rule of the beys, which for him seemed to hold no irony or contradiction at all, no more than did his profiteering at a time of extreme need in the Second World War set beside his image of the destitution of the famine in the days of the Turks. Nor could it seem contradictory. For the fiction of autonomy attained against all the social odds depended for its self-persuasive rhetorical force upon 'not seeing' anything but his own capacities as the key to his biography.

He himself embodied on an individual level the violence used by beys to seize land from others. The capacity for force, deception and 'eating' by the exploitation of any situation was what had enabled him, a man of a fellah beit, to establish a quite different status position from his peers by those criteria which compelled respect, violence and property. Walid was a qabaday, a man others feared. That is what makes his biography possible.

Fellahin do not have social identity in the world of status honour and landed hierarchy: Walid achieves identity. Where the ra'is begins his narrative with autonomy and land and laments the loss of both, Walid reverses the narrative direction. He begins with nothing: he has no father or grandfather, and makes an identity through his own actions. The ra'is laments the loss of signifying power because of the deeds of the ancestors; Walid designates himself as a subject with a history which he has made through his own agency. The ra'is remembers his grandfather in an act which sacrifices the future; Walid creates himself as a figure to be remembered in the future. Both serve the beys.

PART FOUR

Marvellous Stories, Dirty Deeds

CHAPTER TEN

Gallous Story or Dirty Deed

Blood between Agha and Fellah

Contested histories were not only matters of rhetoric and daily negotiation of position in the world. Specific acts of personal coercion and violence were a constant in the practices and narratives of bey, agha and fellah relations. Such acts had acquired an even greater significance in the context of post-Second World War developments in Akkar. Divisions and distinctions between agha families had grown, in attachment to different lords and interests and in material position as well as personal reputation. The position of certain fellahin beits in terms at least of numbers and standards of living had come to equal that of many of their supposed superiors by social honour and descent. Tensions between the two might flare into violence, and that violence generated sequences of events and histories that might have unintended consequences for all concerned. Confrontations between them touched the heart of local social hierarchy, and at the same time prevented the emergence of wider relations which might serve to diminish the power of the landlords, something of which the beys were acutely conscious. Men might spend much time in trying to read and predict possible outcomes, aware of different paths actions and narratives might take, or be constructed as having taken. And a hero figure might end as a social threat to the very group whose champion he had once been.

Synopsis: *Ali, a fellah, and his companion Ahmad, an agha, squabble over a prostitute they have picked up in Tripoli and taken in Ahmad's car to the plain. Ali strikes Ahmad with a knife, wounding him though not severely. The aghas, furious at this injury from a member of what they consider an inferior social stratum, plan vengeance. They commission one of their young men to kill Ali. He does so, shooting his victim in the latter's shop. He is jailed. The fellahin threaten to murder a leading agha but do not do so. Mediators arrange the payment of bloodmoney. On his return to the village some years later the killer becomes gradually marginalized and his social identity loses its heroic cast. Fellahin and aghas sustain a peace in which they each have a different interest. The narrative becomes a story that should not be publicly told.*

Episode 1. Where the Quarrel Begins

Ali, a member of one of the larger fellah beits, was a crony of Ahmad, who was from one of the agha family sections. Both men worked on the estates of the widow of Abboud Bey – Ali organizing production on part of the land and Ahmad, who had been the old man's chauffeur the day he was shot in Beirut in 1958, as a driver of tractors and harvesters. One evening they picked up a prostitute in Tripoli and took her off in a car to the coastal plain just north of the city, an area of isolated and unfrequented places. Once arrived, down near the shore but still in the car, they had a row about the woman. Ali pulled a knife and stabbed his companion, who managed to get away and return to the village. The wound was not major, but blood had been shed. Moreover, it was blood *between* rather than *within* social honour strata.

When one or two of the men of the agha groups discreetly reported these events to me during my fieldwork some twelve years later, they said that as soon as news of the incident reached them they had immediately started to excoriate and insult (*sabb wa shatima*) the name of the offender in public. They spoke of themselves as having, from the start, acted in the classic response style with its initial phase of ritual abusing and defiling through words. Those who were reported as showing the greatest fervour (*ashadd al hamasa*) had wanted to rush off and immediately 'slaughter' the man who had violated their karama, and they were only held back with the greatest difficulty by other, more senior men. Two of the leading shebab grew their beards as a sign of intention to carry out their revenge.

Commentary

The rhetorically strong term *dabah* (slaughter, used of the sacrifice of animals as well as the killing of humans) frequently features in narratives of violence. Its metaphoric power moves the event into a sacred mode, differentiating it from the everyday. The word gives a far stronger sense of ritualized and ritualizing action than does the ordinary term *qatal*, which is as often employed for striking the opponent as for actually killing him.[1]

The 'slaughter' trope is used to sanctify the act of revenge and to stress its purificatory and meritorious quality as well as its obligatory nature. The speaker makes the gesture of cutting an animal's throat, the edge of his right hand being drawn hard down across the back of his left wrist as if using a knife. This gesture refers to the Islamic mode of slaughtering animals which prescribes verbal formulae as the beast's throat is cut. A further effect of the word dabah is thus to animalize the victim in a very particular way and with a very particular referent, and to image him as totally vulnerable to the act and power of the sacrificer who uses him for his own cleansing.

Fervour, or hamasa, is the quality of fierce readiness to defend person and 'house' that every real man should have. To say of someone '*indu hamasa*, he has hamasa, is to pay tribute to a vital element of honour. We might say that it is that element or force which will produce events in the world of confrontation. In the socially mature, this quality becomes part of their identity if they have shown the capacity to rise to the defence of the beit in the face of any threat. The important thing about such men is that they combine powerful feeling with self-control and a will to revenge in its proper form. 'Young' men, on the other hand, though they may demonstrate an instant outrage upon any slight and immediate readiness to retaliate on behalf of themselves or their beits, lack self-mastery. Their hamasa, though admirable, is incomplete. They have to be restrained from mere formless violence. Typically, others will counsel a period of calculation, of reckoning the odds, the choice of the right moment, as they hold back the eager champions. Righteous feeling yields to the discourse of weighty decision.

The intense emotion shown by the young men is eventually made subject to seniority and reason, but only after a struggle that also has a ritualized and dramatic dimension. For even though revenge killing in white heat – and this is a pre-eminently 'hot' moment – establishes an immediate riposte and has a 'heroic' character, it is none the less tacitly devalued. The shebab must show a readiness to act at once in a public display of the passions which any injury to honour invokes: they become 'wild', unbridled with rage, shout angry curses and dramatically lose their self-control; they will kill at once, *fauran*. They show what fearful forces will be unleashed on the enemy. This phase of very visible and audible loss of self-control is crucial. With its eventual mastery in the following phase by the older men is realized the ideal relationship between emotion and reason.

Untrammelled violence of the junior yields to the controlled form of the senior. The act of vengeance itself should be weighed for its exact appropriateness. It must be carried out with a pondered deliberation that requires time to emerge, unlike the spontaneous but less fully intentional expression achieved in the demands for unmeditated dabah. A proper sacrifice to cleanse the house of the pollution of blood requires due form and a proper, public setting for its full accomplishment.

The story of *agon* works its way out in narrative sequences of fully intended exchange, seldom in an instant riposte. Men seek to fit their acts and to shape their memory of past events of bloodshed into the accepted aesthetics of representation. In versions of their own performance they edit out, or try to edit out, anomalous behaviour and ambiguous meanings as if they had not arisen.

The hot violence of polluting abuse and desecrating insult in the highly formulaic sabb wa shatima associated with the shebab, was therefore represented to me as being cooled, after the greatest effort, by the mature experience of the senior men. They were imaged as the masters of the narrative, the determiners of events to come. They divined the full meaning of the outrage, tested its implications, argued the rules and imperatives of their honour, selected consensually the victim approved for the 'slaughter'. And the slaughterer. Abuse yielded to debate, passion to reason, junior to senior. Choice led inexorably to act. The narrative was perceived and created as having perfect, paradigmatic form.

When my agha informants told me the tale of the wounding, they followed very much this general, and ideal-typical, pattern of plotting. Ahmad was wounded. The shebab reacted furiously. Older heads had prevailed. The young men were reined in. Time for strategic reflection was gained. Yet although the young champions were restrained, narratives always included the fact that two of them, the only full brother of the wounded man and the senior of his paternal first cousins, grew their beards. They marked themselves with the most important male sign of a state of pollution, mourning and a vow that the wearer will not shave until his honour has been restored. The growing of the beard constituted a sacralizing act and a powerful statement of intent. Two leading members of the shebab, publicly and irreversibly, were engaging their own personal honour, making it unlikely for any but the most serious consequences to follow, and relatively soon.

My interpetation of this important moment is that the sacred nature of the sign of growing the beard was meant to pre-empt any cautious suggestion of a settlement and to commit men, whether they truly wished it or not, to vengeance. This public act made it almost certain that no one would be able to define the issue as a relatively slight 'wounding', rather than 'bloodshed'; nor could one imply that compensation might perhaps be sufficient once emotions had cooled.[2] The 'face' of these two important men was now also at stake. Senior family members were not ceded full mastery over the way in which events would unfold. They had to reckon with a powerful constraint upon their own freedom to determine the right course of action. Their strategic choices and ability to manoeuvre were being limited by the shebab rather than following directly from seniority.

The quarrel over a whore and the blow of a knife was turning into a narrative of status honour, blood and violent revenge. A dirty deed was on its way to becoming a gallous story.

But where exactly did the narrative, as distinct from the story, begin? Clearly there were parts of the story which could not be told and on whose suppression the narrative occasions depended. Thus, the same informants who told me of the circumstances of the wounding made it clear that public repetition of this narrative of an agha response to insult always used to begin at the wounding alone without any preliminary framing of the key event. The founding act appeared as if it had no setting but had simply 'happened': Ali stabbed Ahmad. This terse opening moved virtually without elaboration into the reactions of the shebab.

Reasons for this narrative curtailment are not far to seek. The setting and motive were suppressed in public reference, because the squabble over the prostitute was an event culturally loaded with negative value and no setting for serious confrontation between men of honour. The incident did not belong to the repertoire of 'self-evidently' heroic competition. Quite the reverse. It really was a dirty deed and nothing to do with virtue and excellence. The two men were doing what could not and must not be publicly talked

about, since it was a matter of illicit sex. That they were also cronies out to
share a prostitute put them doubly on the wrong kind of equal footing. Ali
and Ahmad were not merely participating together in a shameful activity;
they were also 'friends', a fact which blurred the distinction of agha and
fellah which suddenly became so relevant to the aghas as a result of the
bloodshed.

This narrative had therefore to begin with a censorship of the 'real'
beginning of the story which could only be referred to on occasions defined
as private. It was thus present but as a shadow form, a whisper in the
background. Collective agha interest necessitated censoring the dishonourable
and giving voice to the honourable. 'Everyone knew'; no one spoke aloud.
And for reasons which will become clear later, the fellahin did not constitute
the story as narrative at all, but covered it in silence.

The opening episode thus masks its problematic nature through censorship
of the context of the wounding, substituting its own context of honour. It
commences abruptly, with the crucial moment of the shedding of blood;
insult and threats, the demonstration of hamasa, the restraint urged by wiser
counsels, and the growing of beards swiftly follow. Anything else is irrelevant.
The narrative also mutes the detailed implications of pressure exerted by the
shebab and any idea of negotiation with the seniors.

Time is initially telescoped, and the action is represented as moving at
great speed from bloodshed to reaction. The blow of the knife contains in
itself a whole range of possible futures. So the dramatic momentary event of
the wounding is narratively grasped as structuring the *durée* to come. The
inevitability of retaliation, however, is represented as established, as an 'always
going to happen', though the precise means and moment are as yet in
suspense. Intentionality is established as the motive force inexorably pushing
the narrative forward. Those who have hamasa will see to that.

Here we need to pause to consider the different perspectives in which this
narrative was constituted. In such circumstances, of course, no one quite
knows what will happen, or when, or at what tempo. In the unfolding of the
narrative, on the other hand, the listener waits for what, in most cases, he
does already know will be the next episode, experiencing a different kind of
tension and temporality.

To understand that unfolding, I then (and the reader now) needed more
interpretive capacity and the resources to exercise it. In the normal course
of events the wider social context of the narrative could be taken for granted
as part of a shared understanding of what was typically at issue in such cases.
To those taken to be in one degree or another outsiders, and especially to
a stranger in the anthropologist's peculiar status, parts of it had to be explained
if they were to grasp the relations between the different characters.

My informants knew that they could not assume adequate knowledge on
my part and had to assess my level of interpretive capacity. Everyone else in
the village, and not a few surrounding ones, could automatically supply some

version with a greater or lesser sense of social nuance, interest and political awareness. The events would, after all, have been *akhbar*, news, over the whole region. An incident such as this, involving men of an important village, always was. This raw material already shaped in transmission as akhbar had to be worked out, sifted and glossed in talk and might be heard in many forms depending on the participants' social positions. Narratives are always the product of debate, revision and reflexive interaction conditioned by time, the evolution of events, the number of repetitions of the narrative and the character of various tellers and audiences. Which narratives became privileged – and there might well be competing versions which gave very different significance to what was at stake – would be a matter of shifting political and social conjunctures at a given time, and might change as new events occurred.

The incident constituted a challenge from a fellah to an agha. The aghas were bound to see in the situation a threat to the hierarchy of status honour. Their private evaluations of the sordid nature of the original incident were irrelevant. Collective status had been challenged by an 'inferior'. Yet in what did that lower position in the hierarchy of status consist? Times were changing. That same 'inferior', Ali Bashir, was a friend of the wounded man; they worked on the same estates; and though Ahmad, the driver, had a marginally better position, they were in material terms on an equal level as wage earners with the lord's widow. Some fellahin were acquiring a few small lots of land of their own here and there, nothing much and sometimes leased rather than owned, but it marked a change of great symbolic significance. Some aghas had lost or were losing their land, not least those who had been dispossessed by Syrian legislation of 1958.

These shifts in the boundaries, practices and social meaning of 'agha' and 'fellah' made it all the more important for the aghas to insist on difference. The absolute clarity of the discourse of blood and vengeance veiled the ambiguities to which the wounding directed men's attentions. The language of contest, of a pure 'we' against a pure 'they', suppressed life's other realities. An element of punitive assertion of domination was therefore present, made all the more acute by the evolution of social relations.

'There was blood in it', and people would be able to construct different possible plots which might unfold and to dispute, with more or less sophistication, the relative likelihood of different potentialities, whose varied consequences might possibly extend far into the future. They could imagine narratives flowing from the wound as conventionally and ineluctably as fairy stories follow 'once upon a time', because in this universe the shedding of blood is a powerfully generative and transformative event. Moreover, 'everyone' knew about it. The incident would be a topic of intense debate, with debate itself influencing the actions of the parties whose interests were specifically engaged, since they would quickly learn how people in the region as a whole defined what was truly at stake. Men in other villages would be an attentive audience of events in Berqayl. Some would be well informed, or might persuade others that they were, and would form judgements affecting the reputation of the agha descent group in the wider social sphere. Such judgements might affect local political and economic relations.

The beys would be watching. Closely. Abboud's house was implicated. Rival houses might find some advantage in calculated intervention. Always attentive spectators of disputes which might test the reactions of the aghas, the lords would be talking too and making their assessments known. Their reading of the aghas' conduct might have implications for assessing relative strengths for future policy or action. They might be quick to take advantage of any perceived feebleness of purpose. The lords had already begun to use one or two of the fellahin as administrators of small areas, as well as having attempted, unsuccessfully, to employ them as bodyguards. The aghas had foiled that scheme. But they had to be vigilant and show no sign of weakness.

There were fellah groupings who saw themselves as having no solidarity with the offender's beit with which they had no specific kin or other links. They had got themselves into major trouble, they would have to get themselves out of it, was how one or two phrased it to me years later when tactlessly pressed on the subject. The aghas had been brutal before, and would be again. Their association with the beys was still very important. 'What could we do? They were tyrants and liars,' said a friend.

Disparate audiences, therefore, were observing events with keen eyes. Within Berqayl itself there were no homogeneous social blocks. Different groups of beys and fellahin had ties, of employment or clientage for example, with different aghas, and they might well wish to avoid any disruption to those links. A lord whose family depended for bodyguards or agricultural management on an agha family would not want them to lose prestige since that would reflect on his position. A fellah who regularly was allowed to gather firewood and was recruited to work in the olive or wheat harvest on a landholding controlled by an agha would want to support his precious access to a livelihood with talk defending his patron's account in any manzul where he might have a voice. He would be all the more keen to do so since failure to *dafa' 'anhu*, stand up for him, would probably get back to the agha, with inevitable results. And there were always those from any group who felt they had a reason to wish one side or the other good or ill and would offer interpretations of events accordingly. Peoples' interests and readings were certainly not uniform within each grouping.

Nor should we forget that narrative occasions were always a source of pleasure and potential contest. One or another man might seek to show that he could put a fuller and truer interpretive gloss upon events, on what had really happened, what participants really intended. To be able to dominate a gathering by offering a narrative construction of events which others might accept or be rhetorically forced to accept by superior capacities in telling was an important achievement in social identity.

An unambiguous and violent reaction from the aghas was construed as imperative. The growing of beards was not the only powerful sanction against anything less. More generally significant was the fact that compensation, not uncommon in cases of wounding, was almost automatically ruled out by the inter-strata nature of the offence. It would have been taken as an acknowledgement of equality of exchange between the two sides, something which the aggrieved agha party was compelled to deny if it wished to maintain its position.

What the aghas chose to do was to establish an asymmetric exchange of a greater violation for a lesser, a killing for a wounding. They seem to have been determined to demonstrate that they could set the terms in the agonistic exchange, that they could define it and transcend any sense at all of mere equivalence. Fellahin had to be shown unequivocally that they could not violate their betters without the most extreme sanction.

Time was of the essence, as always. The passing of months without action might be read as infirmity of purpose. The aghas wanted to be the masters of time, to be seen to strike when they thought the moment ripe, and meanwhile to leave their opponents in an agony of anticipation. A suspiciously long lapse of time would occasion comment, analysis and interpretation, forms of social pressure that would constrain freedom of action. Just how long that 'suspiciously' might be is itself a matter of the opinion of key publics. The period before the response therefore always requires a nice sense of social judgement. Everyone is asking the question: 'Will anything come from them (*yitla' minhum*) or not?'

Episode 2. The Moment of Decision

Who would be chosen to do what, and to whom? Where, how, and when? This was a time of suspense. But a suspense full of speculation, discussion, anticipation; full, also, of the risk of some unexpected encounter between opponents that would provoke a sudden act with unlooked for consequences.

The identity of the potential victim in this case was clear to everyone: the author of the insult himself. In certain circumstances some men hold, against considerable opposition, that it is perfectly honourable to kill a close relative of the offender rather than the offender himself if that relative is a more prestigious or valued member of the family and his loss would do them the greatest harm and shame.[3] Not here. Ali himself was the eldest of the brothers in his family, all cultivators, sons of an extremely poor day-labourer father who lived in a stone and mud house on the hill in the middle of the Zawiya. Ali had made it into the relative security of a position with Abboud's widow. He was the proper target.

The narrative moves into a second phase when, some three months after the wounding, the aghas found the right instrument of revenge, quite as important as defining the right victim. One day a young man from a small agha family group who was harvesting down on the plain was visited by senior men with an important commission. They instructed him, as I was told, to 'go and look for Ali Bashir [the offender], take a revolver and get him'.

This episode then comes to dramatic conclusion in a third and final phase. Only a few days afterwards the chosen young man walked, alone and in broad daylight, up the steep hill separating the quarters of the fellahin and the aghas. Totally exposed to view, the road cuts through the barren space of the cemetery lying on either side. Everyone could see him, a fact much insisted upon in accounts. At the top of the hill, he approached the small, ill-provisioned shop owned by Ali Bashir who was standing at the entrance looking on to the saha (public space) before it. The boy simply said to him: 'Do you want it here in the shop or outside?' Ali ran back inside, grabbed his gun and was shot in the wrist, his weapon falling to the ground. The killer then emptied his revolver into Ali's chest. He died instantly.

Turning his back on those fellahin who had witnessed his deed, the killer – and now hero – walked back down the hill. Some say he returned to pick up one of his sandals that had come off in the fracas, others that he was barefoot. All agree that he presented his back to his enemies in a grand disregard for his own safety. No one dared retaliate.

This archetypal *geste* of agonistic indifference fulfilled every requirement of the heroic act. He was as superb in exit as he had been upon entry. The aesthetics of violence were in all respects harmoniously achieved.

My informants all remembered that a senior of their number, a renowned hunter, companion of the lords, and also a paternal half-brother of the wounded man, hailed the young hero when he came down to the lower mosque at the entrance to the village exclaiming: '*Ya 'aish! Reja'it shabb!*' ('Long may you live! You have returned a man!'). He saluted one who had gone up the hill a boy and come down a true, arms-bearing young man.

Commentary

Why was the young tractor driver an appropriate agent of revenge? There were three main reasons. The wounded man was his mother's brother, his *khal*. Since his father was dead and he had no paternal uncles, the maternal uncle's authority was most important.[4] The relationship is regarded in ideal terms as a close and affectionate one, less formal and constrained by authority than links on the paternal side. Secondly, the wounded man's brother, his other khal, was the head of a family with a little property, land and agricultural machinery to protect. Though this maternal uncle had grown his beard – his brother was, after all, the victim and it was therefore appropriate for him to do so – it was probably tacitly understood that such a man usually avoids the direct act of retaliation. He had a lot to lose. And thirdly, the killer was but seventeen years old at the time and unmarried. His older brother already had a wife, and the younger one was still a child. Absence of immediate dependants might restrict attempted retaliation to a relatively dispensable figure, though that would probably also, of course, entail a new cycle of killing. If Abdallah went to jail, which would almost certainly happen if he survived his mission, no dependants would be left to be provided for. He would be given money each month by his uncles, a regular arrangement in such cases, until such time as a powerful intercession by a political figure could be obtained.

Such boy-man figures, in transition between social states and identified with imperfectly controlled force and feelings, are often utilized when revenge is to be carried out. They are in a condition of incomplete and precarious socialization, at an age when a single act of collectively endorsed violence can mark their dramatic, ritual entry into the deeply valued manhood of the true qabaday. It makes their name known. They become feared and respected. Suddenly they earn a place in a story, perhaps even in their very own story.

The choice of an adolescent, moreover, is shadowed by a closely connected though unspoken knowledge. One who is not yet a full member of the adult male community may, should circumstances change, be construed to have acted 'wildly'. He is not mature, not a fully responsible adult. His ambiguous status may be used as a mitigating factor in any later negotiation if, for whatever reason of *realpolitik*, his side come to feel that their better interest has shifted to require a settlement. The hero may undergo subtle redefinition to reappear as an individual, immature in action and deficient in the full weight of manhood. There is room for at least some degree of dissociation from his bloodshed, should the need arise.

The senior men knew what they were doing when they made their annunciatory visit to the seventeen-year-old. They offered him the possibility of transformation. They could endow him as an individual, as the sacred instrument of collective family duty. He would become the agent of a central event in the narrative. The nephew was in all senses a proper executioner of the family's revenge, appropriate through family position as well as through what was described to me as his known readiness for violence. Judgements about his nerve and character also played their part. He did not disappoint.

The choice of setting for the deed was socially and aesthetically perfect. This, too, is a subject much discussed. Men favour the public place, the light of day, an audience, an appropriate theatre for the playing out of the drama. The courtroom is often cited in debate as an ideal setting: the man accused of murder can be killed before the very judges who are there to dispense the law of the state and with the maximum attention to the glorious revenge guaranteed. The figure of Muhammad al Abboud at the foot of the stairway of the President's palace offered another paradigm of setting and frame. Abdallah's long walk up the hill to the open space before the shop therefore fulfilled a powerful narrative demand. The hero advanced, alone, into the heart of the space of the enemy. He challenged the offender coolly, with grim certainty and few words. He killed him before the eyes of all his kinsmen, and, turning his back on them, walked away. They dared do nothing.

The killer knew, as all men do, that *how* vengeance is taken is as crucial as that it is taken. The spectators play a vital role. The act must be seen, there must be public witness to the incontrovertible fulfilment of the duties of blood. If that public is the kin of the victim, and the place their social centre, so much more satisfying the performance, so much more telling the narrative. The hero is seen and heard of.

The narrative made it seem to me as if the boy had been prepared and trained for that moment. And of course he had. This is how heroic narratives image their central figure – alone, confronting dangerous odds, reducing opponents to public impotence by penetrating their intimate space and humiliating them in their own eyes as well as the eyes of all the world. He is told as having perfectly identified himself with the ideal model of excellence, as having become an icon of sacred violence.

This exaltation of the salute when Abdallah came down the hill, an authoritative benediction by an elder fully endowed as a master and arbiter of the forms of violence, marked the triumphant fulfilment of the conditions of manhood at their most testing and extreme. It acknowledged the transformation of an individual identity and the beginning of a 'biography', a sira. In addition, it celebrated the rejuvenating power of blood, cleansing the collectivity from stain. The house was reconsecrated. Purity had been restored. The champions shaved their beards. The second narrative episode closes.

Episode 3. Avoidance and Collusion

Now the aghas had to anticipate possible retaliatory action. Word reached them that the fellahin were saying they were going to kill the richest and most politically active of their descent group, then living with his wife in Tripoli and not in the far greater safety of his own village quarter. This man was himself half-brother to the boy's mother through a common father. He was not only very prominent, therefore, but also close kin to the killer. In the city he was more vulnerable, but he could not be seen to flee to Berqayl.

Very publicly, three of the aghas left for the city to protect their senior man and lived with his family in his apartment for a month. Beit Abd as-Salam had to be seen to be able to defend its own wherever they were. Nor was that the only move down to Tripoli. The murdered man was the maternal nephew of the formidable qabaday from Beit al-Umari, Walid Abu Jawad, whose history closed the previous chapter. Beit Abd as-Salam had a healthy respect for him and they had to be prepared to kill him as well, because he was now too dangerous to them in the village. He left for the city, tacitly acknowledging the weight of the odds. This symbolic withdrawal from the village arena was taken as a distancing, at least for the time being, from the whole affair.

Warrants came for the arrest of the killer and four of his relatives who were held to be accomplices. One fled to Kuwait for a time, and eventually the family notable was able to arrange release from the warrant for all of them, save the killer himself, through connections in the security services.

He could thus mediate the processes at the level of the legal apparatus. Meanwhile the other beits in the village sent two or three members to make *sulh*, a truce, between the parties.[5] Four leading figures from these groups went in to the man acknowledged as ra'is of the peasant beit concerned and asked what his demands were, since to him was due the bloodmoney.[6]

Negotiations followed. After some initial disagreement and demonstrations of reluctance a sum of money was fixed, 8,000LL, exactly half that first demanded by the dead man's family. The next day the entire agha descent group held a meeting where contributions were decided, roughly according to ability to pay. In solidarity, members of the other major agha family, mostly based in Tripoli, made a contribution, even though they were not directly implicated in the cycle of violence. The contribution marked a public alliance 'of one blood and co-responsible', demonstrating status alliance against the fellahin.

At a later meeting in the house of the senior *muslih*, the money was paid in one lump sum. A truce, sulh, had been arranged.

Commentary

The family of the dead man must have known that Ali had been singled out for attack precisely because no direct threats seem to have been made against him by his opponents. It is just such an *absence* of furious talk, bloodcurdling oaths and promises of dire retribution that is alarming: 'silence frightens', as the local phrase has it. If, after the initial insulting and rage expressed by the young men, a group 'says nothing', one knows that they plan to act. This kind of 'silence' is a powerful sign of intent. Moreover, to give such a sign and then to do nothing is to invite a real loss of face and reputation. The time scale is shortened, too, since this unspoken declaration of purpose raises expectations of swift, not long-delayed revenge. It puts pressure on the group maintaining it to perform the act to which the sign points.

The fellah family thus faced a major problem in judging their own level of retaliation, and their own real capacities. Their strength and their problem was that Ali Bashir had six brothers, a large violence group, one whose manifest human resources made it more difficult for them not to act. Had there been one or two only, the practical difficulties would at least have mitigated local judgements as to whether they could 'do something' or not. But with six people expected something. And the size of the group also showed that Beit Abd as-Salam were not afraid to take on serious opponents and publicly humiliate them.

Letting it be known that they intended to kill the agha notable in Tripoli, the fellahin asserted the imposition of their terms on the exchange, precisely as their opponents had done earlier. They too would go one better and raise the stakes, to the life of the acknowledged ra'is al 'ailat, the head of the agha family. At the same time, the very fact that they 'talked' about what they were planning to do indicated at least the possibility that they were 'really' intending nothing. The fellahin were not 'silent'.

Whether serious plan or only rhetorical insistence by the victim's family that they too could escalate the level of violence, the significance of this narrative development remains. Their opponents took the threat seriously; and though the attack was never carried out, the very acknowledgement shown in sending men down to Tripoli to protect their notable forfeited a rhetorical point against the discourse of status honour hierarchy. The fellahin, whether or not they had actually intended to carry out another killing, forced their enemies for a time to recognize the threat as real. Agonistic exchange was not on different terms after all, or so the fellahin could claim in their version. Aghas would claim, of course, that Ali's family did not dare to take them on, six brothers or no six brothers, and that the fellahin had lost face by not daring to attempt their supposed design. It was all *haki*, just 'words'.

In fact, the threat was the prelude to the truce. The intervention of the other village beits quite soon afterwards enabled the victim's group to yield grudgingly to collective pressure after their gesture of revenge. Since the aghas were happy with peace, too, they were not about to make public denunciations of the others' 'cowardice' or lack of manliness. What was said among themselves might be a different matter; they had shown they were the masters.

Both sides were now caught up in modifications of social practice from which there was no escape. From the very moment when blood was shed in the car down near the beach, space and time took on new, dangerous significances for those who were party to the dispute. The establishment of the truce made no difference to the imperatives of avoidance; enemies must stay out of each other's sight, however 'sight' is defined. To 'avoid' others in a vengeance relationship requires an intuitive grasp of typical, conceivable patterns in such cases and also demands sophisticated apprehension of dynamic social geography.[7]

The whole arena of combat, of course, may extend beyond 'the village' in its immediate, physical, sense. People have to make a whole series of spatial adjustments. They have to think of just how they can get from A to C without passing through B. The latter may be the quarter of the opponents, a field where one of them habitually works at a given time of day in certain seasons but not in others, the terrain socially defined as within sight of the house owned by a relative of the victim or killer. At what time of day may one of 'them' walk down that path, harvest in that grove, or chat idly outside that house? In summer, many cultivators go down to the plain and one needs to know where they have their holdings, and what paths they take. The public spaces of Tripoli – the area of the market, the place where the taxis for Akkar wait, certain cafés – become potential arenas for sought or unsought dangers. Men have to know the range of a rifle shot. The *savoir faire* needed is complex.

Managing unexpected situations requires great skill and the quickest of reactions. How *not* to have a confrontation is quite as demanding a social art as is staging a challenge. At certain moments people who wish to avoid violence must collude in 'not seeing' or 'not knowing' the manifestly seen and known. Capacities for instant judgement and reaction are acutely tested. Moreover, there is always the risk that tacit understandings of avoidance will be disrupted by someone unwilling to accept these actions as honourable, someone who is in fact out looking for trouble or to embarrass the parties involved.

For the workings of fate only the most general provision can be made – the chance encounter in Tripoli, for instance, or getting into a taxi or on to a bus where one of 'them' is present and cannot easily be ignored – these moments test nerve, swiftness of assessment, and decision to the utmost. Many lack these abilities; then 'anything may happen'. In more predictable situations – funerals, marriages, mulids and other customary social occasions where attendance is requisite – one has to discover just who else will or will not be present. One can never determine, when time and space have become so strategically loaded, whether avoidance will not yield to sudden confrontation, even if neither party actually seeks it.

The all too familiar questions arise. Does silence mean a deep, vengeful seriousness of intention (*niya*), or is it even more of a bluff than the insult and fury proclaimed by the other?

'Avoidance' is thus a complex set of practices. It is not making certain references, or telling of certain events before certain people. The space of talk has to be redefined too.[8] Avoidance is a kind of silent dialogue in which interpretation and judgement are as crucial as in any verbal exchange. Men are aware here too of the views of others and of how their own behaviour is being discussed, judgements which may influence a group's sense of itself and how it must act if it is to retain 'respect'.

The whole meaning of sulh in such cases is bound up with avoidance. The payment of money in itself might be a formal closure to the exchange of violence, but that closure is never secure and the social separation that has marked relations since the bloodshed continues.

What sort of sulh did men anticipate? The manner of payment affords one clue. The immediate, once-for-all handing over of the diya in full indicated a disinterest in any further relationship as much as it offered an end to the sequence of violence let loose by the original wounding down on the plain. There was no marriage between the two parties, and no pattern of joint economic venture. The aghas were insisting on their social separateness and distinction from these 'lower orders'. In my view it rhetorically signalled a rejection of any continuous process of non-violent exchange over time with the fellahin family.[9] Moreover, payment in cash and/or land after a killing, though fairly common, leaves the recipients vulnerable to the damaging charge that their blood can be 'bought'. For the truly honourable, opponents will say, *al akh ma biyinbi'a*, a brother is not purchased. No mere coin can recompense for murder. Those who accept such a proposal may be presented as accepting the incommensurable of money and blood as if it were proper and honourable. This may be a difficult accusation to counter.

Aftermath

An accuser stepped forth. Publicly, he denounced the elder brother of the murdered man in front of the former's own house. My informant, a young agha, told how the denouncer had called the elder brother of Ali Bashir a woman (*mar'a*) and a coward (*jaban*) for the shame of taking money for a killing. At one level the insult was obviously serious, but it was an insult with only one satisfactory reply: action against the aghas. To respond with a blow, for example, would not only leave the charge unanswered, it would provoke yet further violence, this time with one who, crucially, presented himself as a supporter urging the fellah house to proper action. At another level, therefore, the speaker was engaging not in insult but in an evocation of the rules of proper honour behaviour.

The denouncer was a village man from a fellah house that was internally divided and of little influence. But he himself had achieved some weight in regional politics and indeed a wide, analytical grasp of its operations. For years he had been a close collaborator with, and agent of, the bey who was held responsible for the murder of Muhammad al Abboud. He had stayed loyal through the long years of his patron's exclusion from power. Once a communist (he had been at a conference in East Germany in the early 1950s as he once told me), he had identified himself with Nasserism and Arab nationalism during the civil war of 1958 and had been an important local organizer of opposition to the forces loyal to President Chamoun. He was thought of as astute, 'political', intelligent and persuasive in his rhetoric, and an opponent of the aghas at every turn. Though his own beit was not united behind him, he had a wide network of relations throughout Akkar and was a skilful negotiator. Disputes of this kind were familiar to him, and he must have seen a good moment to work on hostility to the aghas, the bitterest opponents of the lord with whom he was so closely associated. Here was a chance to embroil them in a continuing struggle. His gifts as a peacemaker were thought to be equalled only by a complementary genius for stirring up problems. He was *mal'un*, a cunning devil – even his bitterest opponent granted him that title – and he had picked his moment.

What, I asked, had the denounced brother replied to this affront, labelling him by two of the classic terms of dishonour – woman and coward? '*Abu 'Id ma biyihki. Adami.*' My companion replied, tersely: 'Abu 'Id doesn't say anything. He's a decent man.' And he was correct not to respond, went on my informant. The public appeal to the due account of blood was 'in reality' a strategem to keep the reciprocal violence going so that the aghas would remain embroiled with a peasant family, thus giving the denouncer room to stir the pot of opposition more vigorously for his own political gain. The young agha added that this denunciation in the name of the true virtue of the honour code was in fact an attempt to disturb the peace relations (*yushawwish*, he is confusing or complicating things, in contrast to the apparent clarity of the rules of honour the denouncer asserted). The high rhetoric of honour was being used for evil or mischief, *sharr*, not truly for the professedly disinterested defence of a transcending value. 'In any case', he went on, with a great expression of contemptuous dismissal, '*ma biyitla' minnu shi*', he doesn't get any results, nothing comes of it. 'He's just a liar.' The fact that very often something *did* come of the denouncer's manoeuvres made it all the more important to denigrate him.

My informant had a further gloss on the whole affair. The family of Ali, the murdered man, were secretly glad to be rid of him. He had been one of those types who went around acting the qabaday, beating people up and treating them with contempt (*yahinuhum*). He was one of those men who menace the futures of their whole beit by disruptive and irregular behaviour. They are a risk to everyone, as indeed he had proved to be. They have no judgement, you never know where you are with them. People in the village viewed such men as agents, not of the coherence of honour, but of social disjunction into which they drag others.

The young agha's rhetorical strategy was clear: praise the character of the dead man's elder brother; discredit the author of the denunciation by 'revealing his true motive' and by alleging that he would use an appeal to disinterested honour for base interests of his own; and, finally, devalue the victim, categorizing him primarily as asocial and beyond the bounds of honour obligation rather than in kinship terms as 'the brother' for whom the sacred duty of revenge was unavoidable and represent him as a source of danger and disruption to the whole village, his own beit included. Thus devalued, the acceptance of money could be more easily justified.

There is a rhetorical problem here: devaluation of the dead man also devalues the killing. How appropriate can such a person be as the opponent in a tale of honour? If he is described as tough, dangerous and quick to respond to any challenge, in short not a man to mix with, does not his death honour the taker of his life? But if description, answering to another set of social and rhetorical needs, shifts to my friend's dismissive terms, then the story takes on a different resonance. The significance of the narrative itself is changed.

This raised an intriguing question: why should my young agha informant bother to defend the murdered man's brother against denunciation? Undoubtedly, there was a charge to answer. Yet at first sight it seems to concern only the fellahin. The peasant beit were the injured party (*majruh*, also called *musabin* or *jarhin*). It was they who had apparently abandoned blood vengeance for cash, they who appeared unwilling to take on the greater power of their opponents, especially since the allied agha group, based chiefly in Tripoli, showed conspicuous solidarity with their 'kin'. Surely the aghas could enjoy unalloyed satisfaction in all this?

Yet the aghas had their own powerful interest in establishing the brother accused of cowardice as 'adami', the denouncer as a liar, and the mediation as successful. More than happy to settle matters so favourably to themselves without the continuous risks posed by a blood feud, they wanted a closure to the narrative, or as much of a closure as one can ever have. Emphatically they did not wish for an extension of violence with all its attendant uncertainties and costs. Thus at this stage good reason motivated the aghas themselves to defend the murdered man's family against the charge of 'acting like women', rather than publicly revelling in their opponents' failure of nerve as they might in other circumstances have done. Aghas who spoke discreetly to me about the issue stoutly argued that a proper course of action had been followed and that no dishonour was involved in the acceptance of money. How might the denunciation, with its dangerous appeal to the rules of vengeance and violent exchange, be answered, if not by the rhetorical strategems employed by my young informant?

The collusion of the two sides in maintaining the conditions of the peace rested on other important material considerations. My fellah friend, the dead man's brother, worked as one of two overseers who organized local labour, olive harvesting and general supervision of the estate, for the widow of Abboud Bey. He thus had little time for anyone like his denouncer, who was so linked to the death of Muhammad al Abboud. The other overseer was her agha employee who had brought me to the village. The fellah had cordial working relations with his agha colleague, also a poor man of low status within his group who was, fortunately, not identified by close kinship to the killer. Those relations were necessary to efficient management of the widow's property. Her landholdings were large, the ramifications of any dispute correspondingly wide. It was useful for her to have one man from the fellahin and another from the agha groups; it kept open relevant economic and social links to the village as a whole which were important for votes in elections and keeping local support against other beys' houses. The incomes of many families were involved. No one had an interest in upsetting this understanding, unless it was the denouncer who had his own good reasons.

The landowner would not have failed to notice that the government had become involved through the arrest warrants and the deal with the security services. Law, vengeance and local mediation were always in an intricate balance, but Abboud Bey's widow would also realize that state involvement created another arena in which powerful opponents might find a way to advance themselves at the expense of those attached to her.

Furthermore, it was true that the agha 'head of the family' who had 'arranged' things through his contacts thereby reinforced his social prestige as one who could fix problems with the security services. But he might not wish future and dangerously open-ended obligation to draw on his credit with powerful figures should more arrests follow any further violence. No one among the aghas wanted a warrant hanging over his head, nor the inconvenience of a quick trip abroad for an indefinite period if it could be avoided.

A whole tangle of motives therefore gave both parties to the dispute good cause to pursue complementary rhetorical courses. In the period closely following the mediation, the offended family of the murdered man 'talked' while the offenders 'kept silent', as it was put to me by my agha informants. In other words, the fellahin initially continued to use the verbal violence of insult on their own territory and within their own stratum, though never outside that space as far as I could discover. Such 'talk' masked the settlement of the dispute and the acceptance of money in a show of rhetorical violence. At this point in the sequence of events violent words were not the prelude to some new attack, but rather part of 'cooling out' the dispute and maintaining face by those whom everyone knew to be defeated. Men would have interpreted this ritualized verbal abusing as part of the process of making closure acceptable to those who had effectively been worsted. Since the 'talk' was never outside the fellahin quarters, the aghas could act as if nothing was happening, thus playing their part in the conventions of the situation and tacitly assisting the peasants' face-saving performance. They could endorse the stance of the victim's brother whom they classified as 'a decent man' and whom they exempted from ridicule both publicly and privately among themselves. The aghas thus 'said nothing', a silence which they would present as betokening self-mastery, not to be mistaken at this point either for the silence of intended revenge or for that of weakness.

The 'talk' as threat or insult seems to have quickly faded away. For the peasant beit the wounding of Ahmad had turned into a series of events and accounts that could not be consecrated in narrative occasions at all. No one spoke about it (which meant, among other things, that the name of the killer was never mentioned before anyone of Ahmad's beit, since naming would have constituted a sacrilege).[10] This self-censorship, which was also a muting compelled by the outworking of events, resulted in a different kind of silence from that of the aghas. The latter could also suppress public comment about the dispute. But among themselves, and no doubt before allied groups, the wounding of Ahmad had become a narrative of insult wiped out, manhood enacted, heroism attained. Given the outcome, outsiders could safely be left to endorse the agha version of their actions in the path of honour.

Exchanges continued through a delicate reciprocity. People recalled a time when there was hardly any verbal communication at all between members of the opposing groups. But judgement could be exercised over boundaries to be drawn between those who were or were not directly implicated. There are always zones of ambiguity and room for the play of definitions. We have already seen how the practical interests of work on the estates of Abboud's widow maintained important links. Over a time period never clearly defined, several of the killer's less immediate kin and men with no real social position or reputation to defend had indicated a willingness to treat the matter 'as if' resolved or themselves as not engaged in any way, avoiding any reference to it as assiduously as each side avoided the social space of the other. Teenage boys at the school began to socialize, treating events as something in 'the past' and before their time, something for the mature adults to ponder but of no direct interest to them. As mere 'boys' they were freer than their fathers, not responsible for events. In the long term they proved a useful bridge between the two camps. Indeed, the young agha who spoke against the denouncer was one of those who frequently accompanied me to card-playing evenings in the manzul of the adami brother, who had become my friend before I learned his history.

He had his own rhetorical performance. Identified as adami, he was 'a good man' who engaged in no public insulting or disruptive behaviour. He was to be commended, but not in terms of honour where his failure to act by breaking the peace and taking vengeance for the dead brother inevitably recalled the absence of qualities requisite to the man of honour. At best he was adami, unable to compete in the demanding world of agonistic exchange, 'poor fellow'. Events had pulled him into an inescapable situation. He was involved. Yet he could not, or did not, act on the public imperatives of the remorseless code. His situation was recognized by everyone.

Counterbalancing the ambivalent adami characterization, he asserted a determined public persona. He kept open a manzul, in this case quite a small reception room, receiving cronies and visitors with tea, coffee and cigarettes, an expensive matter for a man with only his own wages to sustain the family. He strode round his quarter of the village in a quasi-military khaki uniform, a revolver very conspicuous at his side. His way of walking seemed to speak of determination and a goal to be reached, denying the unfulfilled task which shadowed him. His voice was gruff and loud, the classic style of the hard man; and though he treated others with respect and correct form, he did not hesitate to berate people for practical flaws in their work or for some unarguable failure in, say, judgement over agricultural matters. My friend acted out the everyday signs of *rujula*, masculinity, in conditions which did not in fact allow for its full realization. He embodied a contradiction of which his performance was both a product and a constitutive element, an unstable resolution which always depended on others for its very existence.

The Changing Shape of Heroism

The crucial other was Abdallah, the killer. What role was to be played by the young hero who had gone up the hill a boy and returned utterly changed?

After seven years in jail he had come back to the village amidst all the traditional scenes of rejoicing at his restoration. He remained at the centre of the story in a double sense, because the killing that placed him there also made of him a potential victim. Revenge might yet be taken. Next, it would be his turn. No one could predict when another adolescent, this time from the fellah beit, impatient with his elders' silences and rhetorical self-justifications, might seek a name for himself by avenging his murdered relative. Abdallah's own life, after all, was an example of transfiguring drama.

That transfiguration had its cost as well as its glory. Abdallah should have been the most unambiguously restricted by the practices of avoidance and the restructurings of village space and time. His family wanted the customary discretion expected of a man in his position. Seven years had passed while he was in jail and his beit had evolved its own collusion with the family of his victim, a collusion which particularly required that his presence above all should be regulated. Far more was at stake than his personal identity, and the beit now hoped to constrain him for its wider purposes. The day should not find him 'visible', socially defined as 'within the sight' of those he had desecrated. Presence itself would be a challenge and a threat to peace.

Abdallah challenged those conventions. Though he lived in the Marouche quarter surrounded by other agha houses right at the opposite end of the village to the Zawiya up on the hill, he would frequently leave the safety of his home area to amble nonchalantly into the public space below the old mosque, where the road came into Berqayl. He would stroll into the yard in front of my house just above the mosque, for example, within sight and range of any fellah in the cemetery above who might pick him off with a rifle, as a friend said in some alarm. Others spoke of him going off alone to Beirut to the cinema, right on Hamra street amidst its crowds, fashionable cafés, and potential for unexpected meetings. Abdallah did not obey the rules his own beit (and that of the fellahin) most wished to him to follow. He denied restriction and his kinsmens' authority, making himself very publicly, and dangerously visible.

Moreover, he was prepared to cross another, moral, boundary. He became, as it was put to me, 'a fannas about women', boasting of conquests in Tripoli and Beirut in a way that defied the conventions hedging the perilous world of sexuality. He acted as if he could assert standards of his own choosing. This created consequent tensions and dangers. To be known as a *niswanji*, a womanizer, was bad enough; to brag about it was far worse. That tacitly threatened every man's sharaf and violated all the standards of male propriety.

To cap it all, Abdallah involved himself in some way or other with Fatah, the Palestinian resistance movement which had a local base in the large refugee camp of the Nahr al Bared river only a few kilometres away. He liked to hint at mysterious but powerful connections and to throw the name of Fatah around a little too casually. This might drag a powerful force into village affairs with who could know what results?

The hero's whole position was problematic. He had carried out a sacred duty, and, as a result, had made his own death more easily imagined by the community. In these circumstances, how would Abdallah find a family ready to give him one of their daughters in marriage, especially since he boasted of his sexual adventures? Had he been from a major house of the descent group, owned property, or already established a respected position, things would have been different. But he was from a poor family branch without land, neither of his two brothers had any standing, his father was dead, and only his mother's two full brothers provided help to their nephew on an intermittent basis. He did a bit of tractoring here and there, but it was risky; he was not able to go to certain fields, and in any case no one thought he was reliable.

Making his name by the gun had not translated into a secure life once he was released from prison. Far from it. No lord seemed to wish to take on someone with his biography. Abdallah was a risk with too many complications. The avenue of bodyguard or bey's qabaday, often thought suitable for someone who had a violent reputation, was closed too.

Besides, time was passing. Nobody wanted publicly to remember the great founding event of his biography or to identify him as the man who restored the honour and integrity of the group. For many aghas and fellahin alike had an interest in 'forgetting' his moment of glory. They had come to their tacit understanding that the matter was resolved and wanted no reminding. Silence, not speech, was required. There were even those of the younger agha men who said among themselves that the cry of triumph with which he had been hailed as he came down the hill after the killing, 'you have come back a true man!' was a shameful piece of outdated, empty talk. They were at school with fellahin peers and saw themselves as a very different generation than the old hunter and companion who had consecrated Abdallah those years before. The once exemplary act was becoming a different kind of event, known but in the shadows, familiar but not by this stage re-enacted or narrated at an evening's gathering when stories were told. What price honour now?

I could not, and still cannot, be sure whether the one-time champion was unable to apprehend the dynamic processes of honour, or had grasped them only too well. To me it has sometimes seemed as though he mistook the single heroic act for a sufficient and permanent guarantee of a timeless and unchanging identity; as if he could be the measure of all things and no other criteria, no consequent events, were relevant. He appeared to be carried along by the force of the narratives of insult and revenge in which he had been steeped and whose central character he had assumed in the act of killing. At the same time, did he not play on his transcendance, going beyond the expected codes of behaviour of one in his place, flouting the constraints those whose honour he had restored now placed upon him? He made his kinsmen pay for removing him from the shared, publicly rehearsed memory of the group, in unease and concern that the delicate balance of relations they had achieved with the murdered man's family might be shattered. Was he looking for another death, and was it his own?

His own relatives in Beit Abd as-Salam spoke of him as unpredictable, sudden and irrational. Too ready to see offence or a possible challenge, he appeared to be searching for some replication of the originating moment of his public biography. In this he shared the fate of many who take on the role of killer and who figure in the discourses of both purity and pollution, heroes and sources of danger. One who is *qatil qatil* (lit. killer of a killed; the rhetorical dabah ceased to be used) and *safik dam* (shedder of blood) holds an uneasy place in society. He has no respect for anyone else, because he fears no one else, not even God. One relative who knew Abdallah well said: '*alladhi biykhuf allah la tkhuf minnu wa alladhi ma biykhuf allah khuf minnu*', 'he who fears God, do not fear him; and he who does not fear God, fear him.' Such a man might attack and humiliate anyone (*nakkas*).[11] He has gone beyond all sense of community and is truly 'on his own'.

Abdullah was not simply rejected as *makhlu'a*, a man who had gone beyond the pale. He was not beyond consideration in other terms. Agha men also spoke of him as *nahs*, an unfortunate or ill-omened person; he was *mubtali*, someone afflicted by a trial, morally stricken. In these words there was an acknowledgement of the unresolvable dilemma which he lived out, a recognition of the burden of his role. His violent death was anticipated; and many realized that his death would free them of one who might well bring about other deaths. But when a friend described how he had wept to hear that Abdallah had been shot in a quarrel and might die, he said that it was not right that one such as he should be killed 'like that' (*haram yimut mithl heyda*), expressing a sense of misfortune visited upon Abdallah as much as consequent upon his own acts.

The pitiless rhetoric of exclusion as makhlu'a, an exclusion he produced through his own conduct, had shifted him from the centre of collective honour to the empty world of the isolated individual outside the social realm. Without his own wife and 'house' in the full sense of the term, landless, Abdallah was peculiarly marginal to the aghas whose emblem for a brilliant moment he had been. He was marked by the blood he had spilled for the glory of the beit. He was a peril to others because of his readiness to see agonistic confrontation at every turn. Once, his heroic act had been commensurate with the offence. Now his behaviour was dangerously inappropriate. In the common view, you never knew when he might fly off the handle. He would treat some of the elders disrespectfully, had even insulted the man who saw himself as sheikh ash-shebab on one occasion, but no one responded in kind. Their reserve indicated his re-classification from the status of 'true man' into the problematic, troublesome makhlu'a. Men of honour do not answer to any challenge from such a figure because he is by definition asocial and any response would be therefore totally unwarranted.

Frequently, his actions were cited to demonstrate his role as agent of disruption. On one occasion Abdallah had stopped a car containing a very wealthy member of the agha descent group and an important olive and wheat trader as it came to the entrance to the village. There in the road in front of others, he bitterly accused the trader of being a whore (*sharmut*), coming to the dai'a to take its rizq (everything from which it lived, its wealth and produce) so that he could go away and get fat. The wealthy kinsman, deeply embarrassed by this public insult and as deeply implicated in the deals as the trader, exploded with rage. The killer drew his gun, and so did his kinsman. Bloodshed was only avoided because a very senior man, a famous qabaday and murafiq to the lords who was honorifically treated as the young man's paternal uncle and thus in a strong authority position, sternly intervened and had each taken off to his house.

An enormous row followed, with one or two shebab relatives of the kinsman swearing to wreck vengeance, insulting and cursing in the mode that marks the response to challenges. The seniors of the beit made a formal visit to the offended man's house where his paternal uncle, a man of great reputation and scathing tongue, savaged his nephew for entering into a row with Abdallah and denounced the stupidity of responding to a makhlu'a. The uncle 'shut them up' (*sakkathum*), and from then on they 'said nothing' but replied civilly to the makhlu'a as though the incident had never occurred.

Abdallah's ferocious outburst at the trader, whose prosperity depended upon association with the well-to-do agha, had pointed directly to a serious economic division within the descent group of Beit Abd as-Salam as a whole. The young killer was one of the propertyless, who scratched their precarious living from agriculture, while a few of their kin became rich. He had evoked the central values of 'the village' and 'our rizq' against what he saw as a profiteering alliance with outside interests. Had some other young, penniless cultivator dared to commit this kind of offence against hierarchy I am certain he would have been ridiculed and might even have been soundly beaten. Abdallah played on his own particular kind of marginality and the freedom from constraint he had taken for himself to denounce the kinsman in the name of fundamental, shared values. He put into words what everyone knew, but never said.

He had to be taken seriously, and neutralized. The dangerous economic and social issue of descent group divisions was suppressed by the redefinition of the situation produced by the uncle's insistence that the man of honour does not respond to an insult from one who is makhlu'a. The wealthy agha, who had once been dirt poor himself, played an important role in the local economy of his group: he employed many of the young men in work on the bey's lands, of which he was the manager taking a large cut of the produce; and he owned an olive press on which ten or twelve of them and their families depended for work in the autumn (see Chapter 7). No one was going to argue with that. 'A man has to live', as the saying goes. The senior men, too, were sure to support him. Abdallah was isolated.

What had been briefly voiced was muted. The same marginality Abdallah had used to make his challenge was made the means of ignoring it. There had been no challenge, because one does not answer to the makhlu'a. Indeed, the offended party was himself denounced for taking offence. Peace was restored. Nothing had happened.

A very different example of his behaviour as makhlu'a was his attack on a patrilateral first cousin, in formal terms his very close relation. One night in 1972 Abdallah, by now in his late twenties and no longer a mere seventeen-year-old, woke with a start in the pitch darkness, certain that he had heard sounds outside his stone built, one-room house. Darkness is a dangerous time, a time when enemies come against you, when 'friends' might send word to certain persons that you are in your house.[12] In the night, sounds took on a special menace. Abdallah at once interpreted the noise as a sign of a killer seeking vengeance for the murder. Grabbing his revolver, he rushed out.

There was no one there. He convinced himself, by mysterious processes nobody could later fathom, that it was his cousin trying to steal a chicken – from the sublime to the ridiculous in honour terms – and ran off down to the cluster of poor houses where the cousin lived, shouting his name as he approached. The cousin stumbled sleepily out in some alarm to hear himself accused of lurking round his relative's house to steal a chicken when he knew that the least nocturnal sound would suggest violent and sudden intrusion. When the cousin denied the charge completely, the enraged Abdallah fired a series of shots between his feet, emptying the magazine of his revolver, then announcing with menace: '*Iza wahid da'as 'a-karamti, baqawwasu'*, 'if anyone stamps upon my honour, I shoot him.'

This typical declaration of the 'real man' was much quoted the next day when people told the story, not in praise of exemplary manly readiness it need hardly be said, but as proof of his absolute lack of judgement. To threaten a close relative was bad enough, but over an imaginary chicken theft?! It defied belief. His own actions demonstrated that he was 'crazy', *majnun*, and a danger to anyone at any time. The aghas closed ranks against his representation of himself, refusing any identification with the man who had momentarily been the incarnation of their honour. He was to be denied participation in the agonistic exchanges of challenge and response. Of course, one effect of this strategy was that Abdallah was effectively free of the sanctions normally applying in situations of insult. By a kind of positive feedback he was both liberated from constraint and in the same process bound within a restricting social identity.

Only a few months after that incident a group of friends of the agha family and I were seated under the reed shelter (*siwan*) on my roof, playing cards and enjoying the relaxation of the summer *sahra* (evening socializing) under a warm night sky. We heard fast bursts of gunfire coming from the fellahin quarter just up the hill, and we began to speculate whether the shots announced the signing of a marriage contract, and if so whose, for such a pattern of firing usually indicates a celebration. Suddenly a teenager rushed to the front of the house shouting up to us that Abdallah had just been shot, by the police, or maybe the Palestinian *fedayin* (fighters). It had happened on the plain, or perhaps way off north in Akkar al Atiqa. Was he dead? The boy didn't know. He thought so.

The news disrupted the sahra. An atmosphere of grim unease and consternation at once dominated. Nobody said very much at all as we hurried down into the agha quarter, though one friend murmured to me that he was not worried whether Abdallah died or not, it was the consequences that deeply concerned him. Women appeared on the roofs of the houses shouting questions to each other; small children poured on to the street by the old mosque, racing back and forth with messages from family to family; older men came out in their pyjamas and called out to each other asking for details, furiously debating the possibilities.

The talk was urgent. Were those shots from up on the hill motivated by the original report of Abdallah's death? Joy for a wedding, or joy at a death? Had the fellahin been directly implicated? The eldest son of the murdered man was now an adult and who knew if he was not involved? Was the bloodshed about to recommence? '*In sha' allah* it was the police', said one man. If it was matters would be 'a bit lighter'. The beit could operate the usual patterns of mediation and the influence of the notables. If it was the Palestinians, well, God curse the Palestinians, coming here and taking our land. Still, they were keen not to have major problems with the local population. If not the fedayin, then who? It was all too easy to imagine possible outcomes, all involving bloodshed and loss of life, perhaps a massive retaliation, certainly major social disruption.

Further reports a few hours later confirmed that the incident had occurred down on the beach. Or, more accurately, one of the drivers had seen Abdallah there at sunset with a couple of men in his old blue Opel car. A Palestinian *feda'i* was said to be involved, though in what way it was not clear. Abdallah had been thrown out of a car and left bleeding profusely from a serious wound in the groin. He had 'lost half his blood', but someone had taken him to hospital, and it was thought that he would live.

News that the incident involved a Palestinian marginally cleared the atmosphere. Now the issue was part of the problematic makhlu'a biography but did not compromise the peace mediated with the fellah beit. One man recalled that Abdallah had once associated himself with Fatah and then left them. He had mocked them and taken their name in vain. One night he had brought up his tractor from Beirut and when stopped by the police on the road from Tripoli to Berqayl he had used Fatah's name and flourished the revolver he had got from the organization, daring them to confiscate it. Of course they hadn't. The organization was too powerful in the region.

Now, inevitably, some negotiation with the Palestinians of the big refugee camp nearby at Al Badawi would begin. Another risky set of possibilities certainly, but the fedayin had their structures for keeping order within their own ranks and a local reputation for not getting caught up in needless confrontations with powerful villages (in contrast to the situation in the south of Lebanon at the period). Equally, no group would wish to be drawn into confrontation, given Fatah's high level of military strength. Negotiations were in everyone's interests. Whatever Abdallah's actions – and it was also rumoured, perhaps conveniently, that he had been involved in unspecified but dubious deals with fringe Palestinian elements – they could be treated as the isolated deeds of a marginal individual.

All agreed that there was no cause for instant response, for there was no challenge. Strikingly, for this wounding of a member of the family down on the plain, there was no serious sabb wa shatima from the shebab, no rhetoric of hamasa or seizing of guns.

The next day I heard two of the senior agha men shouting to each other from the roofs of their houses that the shots we had heard from the Zawiya were out of joy at the shooting of Abdallah. The fellahin family of Ali, the murdered man, were letting the whole village know where they stood.

While they were talking, the man who organized the work gang of labourers and heavy machinery drivers down at Beirut airport, on which as many as twenty of the young aghas worked, came back to the village (the sheikh ash-shebab of Chapter 15). He had seen the story of the shooting on the back page of one of the national newspapers and returned straightaway in case retaliatory violence needed to be organized. He wanted to show himself as the leader of the fighting men in a worrying situation; he had his claims as sheikh ash-shebab to assert.

He wasn't concerned whether or not Abdallah died, he said to me, but only about what might happen within the village. 'You know the story', he added, nodding up in the direction of the Zawiya quarter but not publicly saying anything more. Even in this situation – or perhaps particularly in this situation – the rules of social discretion that had been followed in the dispute with the fellah family were observed.

Abdallah's eldest brother questioned whether there was not some treachery here by a young and disreputable man of a different fraction of the family who had run off to join Fatah when it looked as though the police were going to catch up with him for theft. He was a notorious robber and outlaw, though only about eighteen or so years old, and Abdallah's maternal uncle remarked contemptuously that he would betray anyone for a match. It was said that he had told Abdallah that one of the men of Fatah with whom he had had a quarrel had died in Jordan, and then had taken him down to Tripoli where they had met the supposedly dead Palestinian, as if by accident. And it was this Fatah man who had shot Abdullah last night ... Had it all been a trap set by the thief, for who knew exactly what reason? The speaker returned again and again to this possibility: 'treachery, it looks like it, what do you think?' he repeated insistently.

Everyone visited Abdallah in hospital. In this context, group piety was strictly observed. He was one of theirs, and wounded. Women of the closer family were there, scarves on their heads and flower-patterned dresses, some holding large black handbags. Depending on which men came in they either stayed at the bedside or moved slightly away, while the males gave family members time to make sure decorum was observed. The senior men put on their formal clothes: here the leading landowner in his suit and tie, there his elder brother in white shirwal and headdress, another with the long waist wrap, black shirwal, white shirt laced up at the neck, black coat and headdress. The younger men and teenagers wore their newest shirts in psychedelic colours, and when they could afford them, the flared trousers then so fashionable; their hair was carefully combed in waves at the front and of a length that the seniors saw as one of the marks of their sons' decadence. Two of Abdallah's maternal first cousins showed up dressed identically: both with black hair heavily greased back, black sleeveless T-shirts, racing-style shades, pointed shoes, jeans, and thick belts with 'COWBOY' in large letters on the buckle.

The peacemaker appointed by Fatah arrived at the hospital amidst the greatest show of amicability all round. He assured the elders that everything would be resolved to their satisfaction and that the culprit, who had taken some money and fled with the car, would be summarily dealt with. Everything would be returned and compensation paid.

Back in the village there was more news. The adami brother of Ali, Abdallah's victim, had met one of the young aghas with whom he had good personal relations in Tripoli and had assured him that the bursts of firing we had heard from the Zawiya were indeed for the signing of a marriage contract. They had nothing to do with the incident. There was no cause for more ill-feeling. The aghas, gratefully I thought, accepted this assurance at once.

I drove Abdallah back from the hospital one morning on his insistence and against the doctors' advice and my own inclinations. His maternal uncle was with me and disapproved of my sounding the horn loudly and repeatedly as we neared Berqayl, but Abdallah himself and the young men in the other car demanded that we give the sign of celebration and homecoming. The uncle said that it was 'shameful', 'aib, but did not press his objection.

People heard us coming from a way off once we had crested the first line of hills. They knew at once what the blaring horns meant. Everyone has time to get ready: the return from hospital and a critical illness is always a formal and important social occasion demanding due ceremony. Men hurried to change into their best clothes and to shine their best black shoes, and one old hajj was terribly put out to find himself 'not dressed', as he said to me.

The celebrations went on for two days (see Plate 10). Drummers and a reed player were hired, and the maternal uncle hosted all the visitors who came to give the ritual greetings to the sick man outside the small, one-room house Abdallah shared with his unmarried brother. Men sat on stools under the olive trees while young cousins served tea and sweets. Seven or eight of the men danced the *debke*, but it turned out that only two of them could do it with any style or knew the movements, and the rest had to follow their lead rather uncertainly. Abdallah's older brother went round, as was expected, speaking of organizing the young men to take on the Palestinians. It was clear that his threats were appropriate behaviour rather than expressing a real intention. King Hussein was much praised for thrashing the Palestinians during Black September 1970. No actual organization occurred. No one would take on those sorts of odds, and Fatah had dealt smoothly with the affair.

Faced with this crisis, Beit Abd as-Salam acted as if Abdallah was un-ambiguously a part of the social whole and the collective identity. They negotiated with Fatah, agreeing that the man responsible was just a 'criminal' and certainly not representative of the Palestinian organization. Outsiders could see how quickly they rallied round the wounded man, and how meticu-lously the forms of proper, ceremonial behaviour were followed. Not for a moment was he left alone, whether in the hospital or in the village. The constant stream of visitors marked the respect the group demanded. Fellah families who were linked through work, handouts and patronage with the aghas made sure to send representatives to see him, and to be seen. Those who did not go let it be known, with much regret, that they had not heard that he was back – no one had told them.

When Abdallah had recovered from his operation, life returned to normal. He became a familiar sight around the agha quarters again. A revolver was always visible in the waistline of his thin, brown cotton trousers. He now had a limp. His right foot dragged slightly as he walked.

A Story that Should Not Be Told

That Abdallah should be wounded after a squabble over money in a car at the beach had its own narrative logic, doubling back to the original moment of the quarrel and the blow of a knife. The narrative had its own topography, and had imposed its own imperatives upon space: Tripoli, illicit sexuality and the dangers of a chance encounter with one of 'them' in an environment where there would be no one to help you; the beach, a no-man's land where business no one should have might be transacted, a place where no one would go at night but for forbidden acts; the village, where men had to obey all the complex, precarious rules of avoidance under the alert eyes of other men, and where whole quarters up in the Zawiya were interdicted for years to aghas closely related to the killer; the space between the fellah houses on the hill and the road below seen through a telescopic sight and measured by the range of a rifle. The Palestinians were now part of the social and physical landscape. They had been brought into formal relations, and a new field of potential social tension had been created with Al Badawi camp, down on the road to Tripoli.

'News' no longer reached only neighbouring villages and local allies or enemies by word of mouth, creating a regional space of observation and judgement. The story might be on the back page of a national newspaper and bring men hurrying home from their work in the capital, where others might read of the wounding of a Lebanese by a Palestinian up in the far north of the country, in Akkar. Time and duration also took on different significance. Where was a given member of the other group likely to be at a particular time of day? The sound of bursts of firing instantly reminded aghas that the murdered man's son had now become an adult and might have taken the moment for revenge. The night was dangerous for some, outlaws or men who had taken vengeance. Anticipation was always there of a possible rupture of the peace, no one could know when. Time had its own characteristic tensions, which might come to the fore at any moment. The coffin of Muhammad al Abboud still lay in his palace above the old mosque, waiting on a killing for its proper burial. Less exalted deaths brought more immediate, practical concerns for the village as a whole. But all lay within the same set of the narrative of vengeance, however it might, or might not, be worked out.

Abdallah's changing figure was central to all these processes. Once, his shooting the fellah shopkeeper had acted as an aesthetically perfect and transfiguring performance – establishing his social being as a true man, purifying honour, resacralizing family, reframing a sordid squabble in the glorious terms of heroic narrative. In one iconic moment, he had re-established the order of status honour hierarchy. The passage of years and of interests subverted the condition of the hero. The long liminal period in jail came to be seen, not as the prelude to reabsorbtion into the social and narrative world, but as part of a transition to marginality. He became makhlu'a, a condensed symbol of arbitrary violence, one who acted all too often as one who 'needed no one'. His persona was as threatening as the persona of my adami friend, his victim's brother, was reassuring. The heroic aura faded, making it easy to remember the suppressed, discreditable and 'real' beginning of the story of a prostitute and a fight in a car.

In the makhlu'a role and character which he assumed and into which he was compelled, Abdallah stood for the underside of the imaginary of the sacred, hero Fathers in all their virtue and excellence. He was the figure of the burden upon the sons, a burden excluded from the heroic, patriarchal narratives as surely as he came to be from the social centre he had once fleetingly occupied. The Fathers decided the forms of history and shared memory. He acted as if he could retain his significance, would retain it, despite them.

Abdallah had incarnated the group identity and the force of the true fighting man; he would continue to assert it against the group. He would point at contradictions they wished to keep suppressed, refuse the complex rules of avoidance, act as if he needed no one, provoke whatever new crisis might befall, and drag them with him. The fellah elder brother, his role in the world, too, changed for ever, might be adami and stride around in his own space of the Zawiya with his revolver in his belt in a performance of manliness which all complicitously supported. Abdallah would not play the game. He wanted control of his own story, or, at least, the illusion of control. The hero mutated into the transgressor.

He who had been an icon of integrity and coherence became an emblem of discrepancy and discord. The dialectics of the very practices which had constituted his significance transformed him into a particular form of non-significance. The pity expressed in the word *mubtali*, the afflicted one, the man under some terrible burden, was surely an acknowledgement that the affliction was the burden of the narrative upon him, and of the weight of the Fathers upon their chosen victim.

By a harsh irony, Abdallah could be characterized in the very terms my young agha informant used to describe his victim – a menace to his own people. A rhetorical equivalence united murderer and murdered. Both were described as troublemakers, their acts incongruent and incommensurate with their claims for them. The curious narrative symmetry seemed to work its own way out, the two figures linked in an ambiguous complementarity. The transparency of that triumphant moment years before when Abdallah had been hailed as a true fighting man became opaque. What had begun as a classical story of honour, classically realized, had become muted and a source of social disjunction.

The exemplary and demonstrative function of the narrative having been subverted, it ceased to be part of the agha repertoire on occasions such as the sahras. It was a story that could not be 'told', a silence in which the fellahin had their own reasons for joining. Men knew it well and its relevance to events was evident in the practices of avoidance. It had ceased to be a gallous story, not least precisely because it was all too representative of the continuing historical processes of violence relations and could not be transformed by the heroic images and epideictic rhetoric. Like the Icelandic 'berserker', the killer whose honour he had once incarnated had turned into a threat to everyone and a makhlu'a is a makhlu'a for ever. There is no conception that such a man may 'return' to a normal social state. So he had declined from an apparently stable to an unstable and indeed destabilising archetype. His role was still revelatory, but of the tangled and ambiguous practices of violence rather than, in a miraculous way, of the glories of honour and beit. The narrative was disturbingly *typical*, not extraordinary.

CHAPTER ELEVEN

Marching in the Wrong Direction

The dispute between aghas and fellahin examined in the last chapter demonstrated the complex dynamics of those processes. At any given moment men
might find themselves caught up in narrative enactments in which their
capacity to manoeuvre and to act in ways fitting to role and social position
might be cruelly limited, if not exposed as totally lacking. To be so caught
faced many with the near certainty of being discredited in one form or
another. No wonder that much energy tacitly, and sometimes explicitly, was
expended in trying to avoid situations in which one might have no choice
but to engage in enactment although that enactment could neither be sustained nor would be supported by others. Laughter and mockery could
brutally discipline a man who attempted to act as 'a man should', but who
had not the social means to do so.

A poor fellah could thus find himself in a double bind, driven to defend
an honour he could not defend. Yet even the poorest might be part of a
chain of events which would draw in much more significant persons and
might become part of their competing strategems.

Sharaf of the Strong, Sharaf of the Weak

Sharaf, the honour of person and family which is particularly identified with
the control of women's sexuality, was crucial to the public, social identity of
men.[1] It was intimately linked with hierarchy. Beys and aghas who wished to
assert the more 'traditional' sense of a strict order of prestige and rank
regarded speaking of the sharaf of any of the fellahin groups as a source of
mockery or a social solecism. They alone guarded and preserved the sanctity
of their women, while showing deliberate disregard for that of men beneath
them. So the lower orders might be said by such speakers not to have sharaf,
and that principle was illustrated and 'proven' by reference to the violation
of anonymous fellahin victims so necessary to the discourses of power. During
the time of my fieldwork, the girls from the most destitute cultivator families
of a small neighbouring village who still came to harvest the grain on the
widow of Abboud's land near Berqayl were knowingly referred to for their
pleasure value. These were (Sunni) women from the region, rather than the
totally despised Alawites spoken of by the older agha men as having been

theirs for the taking when they managed the beys' Syrian estates. The very poor did not, or could not refuse. Work, money, favour was at stake, and the bosses could take advantage. These women laboured in the fields, not within the privacy of the house and the social conventions of invisibility. They were treated as available.

The sharaf of the mighty was thus linked with their destruction of the sharaf of others; or rather, with the denial that those others either had or might presume to possess such a quality. This theme of sexual transgression was by no means limited to the taking of fellah women. It had a more general significance. For the violation of moral boundaries others could not, or dare not, breach was one of the characteristic images of an important man of power's social role. We remember that Bahgat and Tamimi spoke disapprovingly of the 'disorder' of the beys' houses. It is important to understand that in terms of their power and command, 'disorder' and transgression were experienced and represented as of the essence.

The sharaf of great lords was thus held to take very different forms than that of the social inferiors whose bodies they utilized. Beys were imagined as those who went beyond what ordinary men took as the moral constraints and values in sexual and familial domains. They might, indeed, invert such values. Several of the lower status aghas used to say how a particular great lord, when he was an old man, ordered younger male attendants to service him sexually when he felt like it.[2] This reversal of power – the master penetrated by the servant *because it pleased him to be so penetrated* – did not shame the lord, as it would have done anyone else.[3] It demonstrated the increased arbitrariness and command of the master when he became 'an old man', a time when men usually experience a diminishing of at least a significant part of their household or public dominance. This was an important dimension of the story. Most men recognized as 'old' relinquish their role as household head as the sons marry and their children in turn become young men. But the lord violated that pattern, too, for he required services he had not required before in his full maturity. Then he had been a *fahl*, an outstanding male. As sexual potency disappeared with advancing age, it was reasserted by the perverse command of the potency of others who had no choice but to obey.[4]

The bey's violation was part of the more covert narrative of zulm, his arbitrary and excessive rule, which was a shadow to the public narratives of how he had acted to enforce his will. Men did not approve. But their approval was neither here nor there.[5] The lord violated central values of masculinity, and continued to exercise his dominance in so doing. Any lesser bey would have become an object of ridicule, but the truly dominant figure was represented as being able to reverse the values binding the rest of his society.[6]

Sexual relations within the beys' families were frequently represented in the more private and confidential talk of the middle generation of aghas and by fellahin of my acquaintance as being in transgressive modes: father–

daughter and brother–sister incest, 'passive homosexuality', bestiality, adultery. One of that house was said to have committed such-and-such an act, another was 'known' to be in a no less sinful and disapproved of liaison. These practices, which formed an integral part of the ways in which the lords were imagined to *be*, seem to me to demonstrate the wielding of power as inherently monstrous and desecrating. Such images appeared to exhaust the category of the forbidden, and perfectly complemented stories of gratuitous killing by a lord 'to test his new rifle', or 'because he felt like it'. The ideological proposition was that, just as the lords filled ideological space, so they violated the moral space of others. Their norm was others' perversion.

Great beys defied censure and social judgement in the committing of acts under interdiction to lesser mortals. By the same token, they were figures who highlighted the moral demands and bounds that should not be crossed by 'ordinary' men in sexual and familial life. They were the contrast term by which the acceptable could be unambiguously represented.

In the beys' dealings with the cultivators, therefore, the theme of transgression continued to be central. I have already spoken of the stories of beys and aghas sexually possessing fellahin women. Violation was a dominant metaphor for the public ways in which lord–labourer relations were articulated. 'The bey who took the wife/sister/daughter of a fellah' was a central image of domination as desecration of the subordinated in a sexual mode. The core of male identity of the inferior was irremediably tainted by overt violence.

In such a schema men see themselves as the real object of attack, the woman as a mediatory figure through whom they are injured. She is doubly violated, for in addition to her physical rape she is treated as having no relevance except as the hapless agent showing her men's weakness. 'They have no sharaf' thus expressed a range of practices of power in a concentrated symbol of social shame.

The cultivators of Masoudiya who denounced the rape of the women of their families by the lords thus pointed to their own violation as reason for actions which were treated by the state as civil disturbances and 'peasant troubles' (see Chapter 3). By reaching for the gun, encouraged by political forces in opposition to the lords, they issued their own challenge to the power of the landowners. They asserted their sharaf, or their right to be considered as men like others who had concern for the sacredness of family and control of women's sexuality.

This movement of resistance on the plain was symptomatic of other, parallel developments. The poorest labouring women of the neighbouring village might be viewed as fair game by the aghas, but in Berqayl itself the larger fellahin descent groups, some of them of considerable relative size and with some changes in their economic and social position as I have discussed earlier, were not treated in this manner. They had begun to assert their own rights to position and respect, and not only in matters concerning other fellah families. Circumstances were slowly changing. Should an opportunity present itself, they might claim to participate in agonistic exchange with the aghas, and we shall see an example of this later. They might well seek ways to show that they were responding to social desecration, though this could place them in an agonizing dilemma if they did not have the social capital to live out fully the logic of honour.

At the same time, the adolescents and younger men among the aghas did not always endorse the view of sharaf of their fathers and grandfathers. They were little inclined to see peers of fellahin houses in the terms of total subjugation which present realities clearly contradicted. They knew, and believed, the allegations against the landowners by the people of Masoudiya. Some might disapprove of such behaviour, others might be indifferent. There was no doubt in their minds that property holders should not surrender to labourers, but that did not mean that they did not regard the rape of women as 'aib, shame.

Furthermore, the transgressions of family and sexuality represented as current among certain of the beys, appeared to younger aghas and fellahin more as a sign of decadence, corruption, or something to be laughed at between friends than the attributes of domination. They told stories alleging all the categories of offence. But, as far as I could judge, offenders were as likely to be ridiculed behind their backs and were not, in any case, important figures in their own right. They tended to be those perceived as marginal, either in terms of a whole family group thought of as being in decline, or as an individual who carried no weight in his own beit. The subordinate often had an eagle eye for the failings, lapses and losses of the great; and they spoke accordingly, at least among themselves.

Sharaf was thus by no means a static concept or set of practices. The social implications of the term varied. There was no simple consensus as to its wider meaning in reality, even within the strata claiming status superiority. Fellahin in the village viewed themselves as bound to defend their family integrity as much as any other group. None the less, for the socially weak and unconsidered such defence remained as problematic as ever.

The destitute had little choice and almost none of the means for defending themselves against violation. One of them might none the less take it on himself to act as if he had, hoping to be taken as a man who has self-respect and knows his obligations. For such a man, the control of social form would be unusually hard to achieve. A man with few social or material resources might well find it difficult to give any performance of social integrity that would not be usurped and 'upstaged' by others better placed in the community. He courted one of life's greatest dangers: that of being taken to demonstrate publicly, not a proper concern for sharaf, but the discrepancy between proper assertion of capacity and empty pretension.

Marching in the Wrong Direction

I stood one day outside a bey's house, one of the cluster built on the slopes above the agha area of the village. With me were two of the aghas, men of low personal status as they were mere servants of an important bey, and one of their lord's sons known for his malicious perceptiveness. We were looking down on the road leading to the lower mosque and chatting about nothing in particular.

Suddenly, inexplicably, my companions roared with laughter as a labourer strode by, herding a few cows for his master, an old rifle slung ostentatiously over his shoulder. One of the aghas pointed to what seemed to be a richly comic spectacle saying: 'The man who snatched his daughter from him comes to the village and Hussein [the herdsman] puts his rifle on his shoulder and marches in one direction while the abductor is going off in the other.' The derisive laughter was loud, public and prolonged. The man's daughter had been 'kidnapped' by a young man from another village and this was his public response. When the offender came to the village the herdsman marched off with his rifle in the opposite direction. The mocking *bon mot* was repeated with great relish as the story was taken up in agha sahras or casually on the street to friends.

Even before the abduction, the cowherd and his rifle were an incongruous spectacle in the eyes of my companions. To them, someone who got his living *min wara' al baqr*, literally 'from behind the cow', had no claim to that symbol of male potency and prestige, the rifle. (The phrase is often used by extension to mean the lowest form of peasant status existence; a *ra'i baqar*, a cowherd, is treated as barely superior to the animals he herds.) For such a man to carry a weapon connoting power and hierarchy rather than a knife, the weapon of the lowly, was preposterous in their eyes. The implication of violence, blood and status was amusingly nonsensical.

Their public laughter had an active, disciplining power as *violence douce*. The show of mockery violated his persona as a man ready and able to defend his karama; ridicule patrolled and enforced the boundaries of social distinction, infringed by the sight of the labourer parading the signs of force. The servant aghas, themselves *ipso facto* in what was at best an ambiguous position, were especially compelled to make a comic story out of the cowherd's progress through the public space of the village, to make the event – in which their own mockery had played its subverting part – into a story for telling.

They saw the situation as a joke and made it into a *fabliaux*, changing the significance intended by the performer, taking over the authorship. They reordered his reality, showing his behaviour as the reverse of what he wanted it to demonstrate. Re-enacting his walk and fierce look, my companions shaped the incident into a commentary on the cowherd's social buffoonery for the delectation of the other aghas. In other comic narratives I have cited, the joke derived from the usurpation of power by one apparently powerless, a constant theme in many serious honour stories; here the narrative derision represented a powerful right to crush an attempted appropriation of signs over whose use and meaning the aghas asserted their possession.

The ra'i baqar's tattered clothes, his manner and speech – as clumsy and loud as his livelihood from renting a small plot of land on the side of the hill bordering the cemetery was precarious and intermittent – were not these the attributes suitable to the protagonist of a joke narrative? After all, one major principle of social honour is that manner is as important as the action itself. How could such a man ever imagine he could carry it off?

The kidnapping of his daughter was made a double cause of laughter. Seized from her chaperons at gunpoint? Well, in such cases daughters are always said to be taken against their will. In fact, my sceptical friends inclined to think that the whole thing had been staged to force the father's hand; that it was, in short, a *tamthiliya* or 'pantomime'. This added insult to injury, since it suggested that his own daughter was a willing party to her father's shame rather than the victim of coercion.

Either way the event was made part of a coherent comic narrative witnessing to the cowherd's failure to control the women of his family, something which could also be treated in the many amused accounts sedulously spread around as 'typical' of that kind of person. Hilarity at agha evenings of socializing showed how delighted participants were at this demonstration of social ineptitude by one they wished to characterize as 'by definition' socially inept.

There was nothing at all funny to the cowherd in this situation. What led him, or compelled him, to such a risky display?

His daughter had been engaged (*makhtuba*) to a young soldier in the village whose mother was from the same beit, though his father was an outsider, an old camel drover from one of the *'arab* 'tribal' groups on the plain. The family were dirt poor, strangers and without status, though the boy had got into the army so at least had some sure income. No agreement had been reached about how much the suitor would pay as a brideprice. The father wanted 2,000LL but had been met with a refusal.

The fiancé was involved in a fairly serious accident. While he was in hospital the cowherd married his daughter to the son of his wife's brother, a man from an important village at the top of the mountain. The new groom agreed to the same sum but would pay in instalments.

The marriage was only ten days old when the soldier came out of hospital already informed of events. People were saying that the daughter loved him, that he had paid out money on her account, had given her presents of a watch and a gold ring, and that she had threatened to drink poison if he did not take her away. So he 'abducted', *shallaf*, the girl to Tripoli to take refuge with one of the *sheikh al 'arab* who lived there and from whose *qabila* (tribe) his father came.[7] A small delegation then went down to bring her back, but the sheikh turned them away telling them that his young relative was a good man (*adami*, here stressing his moral correctness and decency) and under his protection. The sheikh certainly could not afford to be seen as one who could not protect a member of the qabila against outsiders, however low in status that individual might be.

I now found out that, by the irony of history, the cowherd had himself shallaf, taken off, his wife in similar circumstances from the mountain village twenty years previously. The point of the marriage of his daughter to his wife's family was to make a final reparation by accomplishing an exchange which would put an end to the never-healed breach in relations.

The next day his mother-in-law appeared in the village from her mountain home. The old lady staged a public scene in the saha, open space, outside one of the shops by the lower mosque, a point of maximum visibility. She had given the girl milk and bread and meat, she had taken her in her arms like her child, they were all *sharamit*, whores, and she demanded a daughter in exchange, 'etc. etc.' said my agha informants drily, relishing the drama playing itself out and anticipating possible outcomes for every situation. The serious dramas of others are often a comic spectacle for those on the sidelines, especially when they see themselves as superior. All the right insults were shrieked, all the predictable rhetoric of injury, all the appropriate gestures of outraged honour. And they were performed by a woman in one of the few public realms where she might publicly appeal for support and denounce wrongful behaviour. That she was classified as 'old', *'ajuza*, and not therefore in her full female role but somewhat in the background and beyond sexuality, made the scene permissible and added extra shame to the cowherd's plight. To be publicly verbally defiled by a woman *fi qalb ad-dai'a, quddam an-nas*, in the heart of the village, in front of everyone, further dramatized the situation. It enlarged the audience and inserted the claims of the other village into the centre of the dispute in a ritualized denunciation using the language of purity, kinship and exchange.

The denunciation served as a prologue and framing for what followed that very night. Four cars came down the mountain road from the village above and took the cowherd's wife back with them. The distraught man now found himself without either wife or daughter. One was surrounded by her publicly enraged relatives in her powerful home village. The other was under the protection of an arab sheikh in Tripoli. It was impossible for him to keep matters within bounds; the plot had ramified, the characters multiplied completely beyond his control. The ra'i baqar was lost in his own story.

Some friends and I met him by chance as we set off for a sahra at a house where we were regular visitors. He was in an almost incoherent state. Would someone drive him down to the police post so that he could make a formal complaint (*shakwa*)? One of my more malicious companions said very gravely that of course we would do it. Were we not ready to die in his cause if necessary? – a humiliating parody of the kind of elaborate rhetoric of *'awatif* suitable to dealing with a bey. He added in a murmur to me: 'poor bloke, he's completely broken' (*inkasarit ash-shawka*, literally the spur of the cock is broken, his power and courage have gone, a quite typical phrase for male social degradation). Another was brutally frank, saying that the cowherd had been a fannas all over the place, showing off about what he would and wouldn't do and now he wasn't able to do anything at all. That would teach him to put on a show without substance.

Eventually the cowherd said he would go off the next morning to the local administrative centre of Halba and make a legal petition, a *da'wa*. Such a petition was his only remaining resort given the forces arrayed against him, but I felt that it was more a matter of a desperate hope and a vague sense of 'the law' as a last refuge rather than any real understanding of what a da'wa was that prompted him. He certainly had no patron to take up his case at the local court and had no way of grasping any aspect of the legal process, or of paying for it. None the less, a petition must have seemed to him the only way to escape from circumstances he could not master, and some access to a mysterious language and authority transcending that of honour and kinship. In the event, he abandoned the idea.

A few days later his wife came down from her natal village escorted by an impressive procession of cars full of men of her beit, a calculated demonstration of power and support, after the mayor of Berqayl had arranged her return in a mediation of the quarrel between the families. Any dispute involving these two locally powerful villages, one at the top and one at the foot of the mountain, might lead to unforeseen and difficult repercussions. Collective honour could be involved through one party's decision to use the incident, declaring integrity at stake and widening the scope for action. Some hothead might want to make a name for himself by an act of violence. The end result could entail a major regional row in which the powerful beits, not to mention the government forces, might feel obliged to get involved. Our cowherd was certainly in deep trouble, and everyone else might be. So it was worth the ra'is's time to mediate, no matter how insignificant the cowherd himself might be.

Not twenty-four hours after, his wife went back up the mountain again, this time on her own initiative and with no procession of cars to stage a public performance of the injured reclaiming their own. And this time the mayor failed to get her back.

There were further complications. An extremely well-known qabaday and family leader in her home village was said to have telephoned using the only phone there to threaten one of the cowherd's close family supporters with exemplary punishment for going around making grandiose, but serious threats about what he would do.[8] The empty boasting (*fashr*) might be dismissed as brainless, even so such people can drag a lot of others with them. Meanwhile the rival politico who had denounced my adami friend for cowardice, demanded to know whether one of the poorer aghas reputed to be active in the shadier side of local affairs had not assisted the flight of the daughter to

Tripoli. He received an outraged declaration of innocence, with mighty and pious oaths that may have done as much to confirm as to assuage his suspicions. The politico thus put down a public marker of his intention to try to mediate the dispute where the mayor had failed. Clearly the case of the abducted daughter was becoming very complex.

A whole background of events had thus preceded our morning sight of the cowherd parading with his ancient rifle. One after the other, these events had reignited a crisis of twenty years before, implicating people well beyond the range of the impoverished fellah. The sheer scope of the problem was sublimely incongruent to such a marginal person. The wretched ra'i baqar controlled neither his social dilemma, nor the authorship of the evolving narrative, much less the comic persona he assumed in the story. His march behind the cows seemed to my companions a hilariously inadequate way of trying to cope with the storm breaking over his head.

So when their laughter rang out as he passed by, in yet another richly comic episode to be related by the aghas, he was already firmly cast in the buffoon's role. Striding off in the opposite direction from his daughter's supposed kidnapper he was the perfect trope of the man who, while giving the show of meeting his obligations of honour, was in fact doing everything he possibly could to avoid them. Running away from the challenge, he was marching determinedly towards invited derision. His performance was usurped by narrators who could present him as the agent of his own unmasking.

The very next day, as if on cue (and indeed perhaps he had been told of events by someone quite eager to stir the mixture?), the kidnapper appeared in the public space before the lower mosque, expanding the narrative by his own dramatization of defiance. His immediate response accelerated the tempo and introduced its own suspense. What would happen next?

The young soldier was in civilian clothes, a formal suit in fact, and with clean white headdress draped casually, but elegantly, around his shoulders. He might be half 'arab and half outsider, but he knew how to dress for the occasion. Indeed, he was acting as if quite capable of showing all the classical insouciance of the great honour stories: 'at his ease', in the sight of all, and more especially of three houses from the beit of the cowherd. They could not but see him. If any of them were man enough …

Nothing happened. The girl's kin did not dare to make a move. Now doubly wronged, they stayed in their homes, 'like women' it was said, not venturing on to the street where men act out their dramas. The source of their shame had decided to expose the kizb of the rifle over the shoulder, the rifle that would never (everyone thought) be used, but which its bearer had probably felt he had no option but to carry. And even that had worked to his harshly comic destruction. The abductor tested the reality of the cowherd's performance, and revealed it to be mere simulation, a tamthiliya.

To be made into the buffoon, exposed in this way to the laughter of others, turned into an unwitting parody of honour, was a cruel outcome.

Moreover, to his audience the buffoonery was inherent in his social identity. In short, carrying the rifle he committed what the American sociologist Erving Goffman has called the cardinal social sin: 'the sin of defining oneself in terms of a status while lacking the qualifications which an incumbent of that status is supposed to possess'.[9] His determined march was, metaphorically as well as literally, 'in the wrong direction', towards rather than away from further loss of face. Events were taken to reveal it to be simulation, nothing but show. They were interpreted as proving that he was nothing.

This incident raises the question of how far a man of his position could even imagine, let alone author and tell, a 'story'? How could he accede to biography and narrative, given the weight of hierarchical mobilization against him by dominant groups? It is almost as if he thought that the very act of appearing with the rifle would somehow be sufficient *in itself*. He seemed to lack any narrative grasp of how the processes might unfold, how to structure others' responses, how they would 'cast' him. Though in a very different context, it has something too of the character of the young killer in the previous account who lost his authorship of the narrative and who also appeared unable to apprehend his act as anything other than a once-for-all and sufficient moment rather than as part of a complex sequence of events.

Those more culturally sophisticated who saw themselves as in command of the narratives and signs of honour, were not going to let the ra'i baqar present even a momentary instant of pretence. They could see how far he had unthinkingly sparked off the whole imbroglio without appreciating the risks.

What was dismissed as the kizb of the cowherd might be seen as an attempt to disguise the undisguisable, impotence as potency, almost perhaps a plea to be allowed to continue a fiction of possessing individual integrity when circumstance and status made it impossible. He, too, felt compelled by his apprehensions of the imperatives of honour at least to affect to have a choice and to be able to act. The only other option would have been an equally damning refusal to do anything save to stay at home. Either way he was in a trap. The aghas' laughter and the young soldier's elegant pose closed it upon him.

The expansion of the story went well beyond his ken. The sheikh al 'arab in Tripoli, and his followers on the plain, were acting as protectors of their kinsman. One of the powerful clans of the village on the mountain was asserting its power to right the wrongs begun twenty years before. There was a legal complaint. The mayor was involved. Everyone was talking.

Mediators were once again mobilized. The experienced politico I have already referred to used his wide range of relations to try to create the conditions for an agreement. He possessed the authority to call the young soldier to him, not least because the latter needed a settlement too in order to move back to the village, and to release his kin from their much-proclaimed, but somewhat burdensome provision of sanctuary. They did not want a protracted quarrel with the mountain clan, particularly since they knew that their opponents were celebrated for their capacity for violence.

When the mediator summoned the 'abductor' to his manzul he berated him furiously in front of an audience of his supporters, family and the English anthropologist. He cut the young man down to size, refusing to countenance even a hint of the cool bravado of the headdress over the left shoulder or playing 'at his ease'. The furious denunciation, expected by the others, used both direct insult and didactic homily: the soldier was a *kalb*, a dog, *bahim*, an idiot, and he was not adami, polite, a good man knowing his place. He should keep good family relations, show respect for seniors, and appreciate the need for mobilizing allies around the justice of his cause, not simply run off and drag everyone else into this enormous mess.

Having publicly asserted the proper form of social life by calling the boy to account, the mediator was ready to face the mountain clan's leader. The girl had been snatched from the great qabaday's village, the husband was his kinsman. The insult had to be avenged and much public outrage had been expressed as in the old mother's furious insultings down by the mosque. Fneidek had to show publicly that it could not be lightly challenged. So the wretched cowherd, at the very opposite of the spectrum of honour from the clan leader, brought down upon his head a collective response represented by this notorious figure. The latter was a famous outlaw, wanted for fourteen or more killings depending on your informant, celebrated for his fearlessness and the fear he caused. Such a man travels by night if he leaves the relative safety of the mountain height where not even the most naive army officer would think of going to bring him in. If he travels by day it can only be by a whole convoy of cars, each one full of his men armed to the teeth. So it was one o'clock on a freezing cold morning when I was first summoned to the manzul because Sheikh Ahmad al Ba'arini had arrived.

That meeting involved much drinking of coffee and tea, the smoking of nargilehs and general talk about the state of the world. Agreement could not be reached easily. The sheikh was not to be moved to mundane questions of financial compensation. His sidekicks did most of the talking, lamenting with the mediator what things had come to, the wisdom of resolving disputes of this kind speedily, the ill-judgement of the ra'i baqar, the stupidity of the soldier thinking he could simply stage such a performance and unthinkingly involve all these other people who only wanted correct relations with the distinguished clans. The talk continued. Eventually the sheikh left without any settlement, but it was clear he would return and that no one had expected him to allow matters to be cleared up at a first meeting.

At the second meeting matters came to a head. The mediator played endlessly on the utter poverty and marginality of the cowherd. 'What was the use of demanding a franc or a million lira?' he asked in a typical hyperbole. The man could not pay. They were dealing with a nobody. Was he even a person at all, a *zeleme*? No he was not. He had no status and money. When the Fneidek side, speaking at this stage only through one of the sheikh's attendants, started by demanding 5,000LL as compensation, they were told that 1,000LL was all they could get, and then the mediator would have to put in 500LL from his own pocket. Much was made of this commitment, of taking on the role of providing compensation himself, something a mediator does not do. He insisted, making it an act of personal generosity in a hopeless situation where he was taking on the burden for the socially insignificant ra'i baqar. It was not long before the other side acceded to his figure of 1,000LL, which in this context essentially represented a face saver for them as much as a recompense.

But the procedure was not yet accomplished. It was at this point that Sheikh Ahmad al Ba'arini finally spoke. He had remained silent, on the sheepskin in the place of honour in the corner of the room, wrapped in his cloak and never leaning near to the rest of us huddled by the small paraffin fire. His subordinates had spoken of him, evoking him as a living incarnation of what a real man was, could do, had done. They elaborated with turn-taking, each introducing a new attribute of, or episode in, the biographical narrative of their leader, a kind of antiphonal singing of his praises. The subject preserved his masterful stillness. This series of references, in all of which we joined, paying tribute by murmurs of assent to their claims for him, or by adding memories which endorsed the extraordinary nature of the qualities of which they spoke, served as a formulaic introduction and framing for the moment when he assumed his own central role.

The sheikh began to hymn his own valour. He performed the quasi-bardic function of the hero who, once he has judged the moment ripe, recites the stories that make his name what it uniquely is. He performed his own story. It was marked by the typical cumulative structure of such narrative acts. Episode succeeded episode, each one being a microcosm of the whole. There was no linear or teleological form. Sequence was not important. New characters were introduced in each different episode, but never any new capacity of the hero who in all of them emerged simply 'as he is'. There was no progression, but a series of illustrative instances organized according to the individual's perceptions of the moment in whatever order seemed to him appropriate on that occasion.

His presence was formidable – a tall man with 'a dark, harsh voice: abrupt cadences, piercing looks suddenly switched from one hearer to another, cutting and precise gestures, everything apparently pared down to its absolute, iconic rightness'.[10] The full, epideictic force, the demonstrative weight was built up as he rose to his feet, re-enacting the occasion when he had turned back a whole cavalcade of cars full of armed men that had come from Zghorta, a small town famous for its aggressive temper, to attack the village of Bezbina where one of their girls had been taken by an 'abductor'. Single handed he had blocked their route, his presence and name sufficient to halt their planned attack. The sheer focus of his voice, the concentration of his look, the dominance he exercised as he strode around the small, bare manzul transformed the moment from a routine haggle over compensation to a demonstration of the essence of the man of honour revealed through the telling of his acts of extraordinary violence.

This devastating show of murajul, performance of masculinity, raised the scene to heroic proportions. Yet there was a strategic deployment here too. 'For its own sake', it was also to establish a rhetorical and narrative ascendancy in a setting in which a prosaic discussion about 1,000LL marked a closure to an affair of abduction among the poor.

The re-enactment vivified and quickened the audience's active memory, of just whom they were dealing with and what he represented. In appearance a dramatic monologue, I see it as essentially dialogic in nature given the significance of the audience's participation in framing, catalysing and endorsing the whole event. The performance, the most striking of the many that I witnessed of the murajul expected of men claiming power in 'traditional' terms, encapsulated a whole universe of male violence and hierarchy. That there were other universes and other practices was 'forgotten' in the glamour of his being. The other reality of the quarrel, the pathetic marching cowherd, the mocking laughter, the outraged mother and the sheikh al 'arab all faded momentarily into the background. The skilled mediator, whose reputation and political influence in part depended on being able to bring such affairs to a conclusion, and who would never have adopted that style of presentation of self since it incarnated quite a different kind of identity, was content to be effaced by this act of dramatic closure.

Other audiences, other voices. To an outsider such as myself the performance in which I had participated appeared grotesquely melodramatic yet powerfully authentic. I was completely seduced by his vivid picturing of the darkness of night, the convoy of men coming down from Zghorta, his leap into the road and the shouted challenge that no one dare take up, so great was his name ... That there might be other versions, other perspectives, key omissions, was swept from my mind in the dramatic representation of confrontation and triumph. A cultural paradigm had taken human shape before my eyes and imposed itself upon me as real, as the only possible truth: *that* was how it was, how he was, how all 'men' were.

Yet when I told the story of the evening to middle-class Lebanese friends in Beirut, university teachers and intellectuals like myself, laughter dissolved the magic of the hero's aura. It was now a story of how extraordinary my experiences were up there in Akkar. I am sure that I must have produced it unthinkingly as something I knew would be 'striking'. In my version, and in general conversations where this kind of topic of 'qabaday violence' arose, such re-enactments and murajul were seen as inherently parodic. Sheikh Ahmad incarnated the urban stereotype of the moustachioed wild men of the mountains and the embodiment of primitive backwardness. Narrated in a Beirut apartment to that kind of audience, his words and gestures imitated by someone like myself, who could never be the author of the original performance and who was situated in a very different social universe, the telling could not but be anomalous and comic.

In its context, of course, there was absolutely nothing comic about it at all. To the sheikh's voice all others were subordinated. The sheikh was what he was. A key figure in a powerful clan, his leadership depended in part on his proven capacity to defend its interests. Violence was a necessary condition of his existence and a key to his centrality. His identity was achieved, that of the clan warrior and outlaw wanted by the government, a man who single-handedly had turned back the convoy from Zghorta, and had killed fourteen men. Narrative and being were one seamless, timeless whole.

The cowherd, bound up in the same narrative, was Sheikh Ahmad's polar opposite. Yet was there some unrecognized or misrecognized truth behind the loud public amusement he occasioned the two aghas that morning? It was the laughter of servants. They worked for the beys in the manzul and on various errands, and part of their mode of interaction with their masters was through joking, telling stories, and generating the comedy which it is inappropriate for men of status to initiate. Notables and men of social position permitted themselves only restrained and occasional laughter; it violated the gravity and weight of their persona. The servants took the low status form of behaviour, and were not respected. They were both poor men. In short, there was more of a link with the situation of the cowherd than they could contemplate. For it would have been difficult to imagine either of them feeling able to take up a public role of challenge and defiance had their sharaf been at issue.

They, too, never carried rifles, which was one witness to their lack of position and regard. But they were part of a group which did represent itself as having the right to bear arms as a mark of social privilege and violence. So if even 'someone like that' was going to put his old weapon on his shoulder and combine it with herding his cows before him, then desacral-ization of one of the primary symbols of status, masculinity, and violence was threatened. Moreover, the cowherd's mere possession of a rifle was also a sign of the times, for there were now many Kalashnikovs and Czech rifles on the market, much cheaper than they had been pre-1970 and the defeat of the Palestinian fighters in Jordan by King Hussein's forces which had led to such a flood of arms for eager buyers. They were no longer rare, or pro-hibitively expensive.[11] Guns could be bought, all one needed was the money – weapons were no longer the monopoly of men of status. The fellahin were armed.

Laughter covered the fact that the cowherd was doing what most men were said to do in reality – dissimulate; using the signs of power without true intention or being able to make them effective; marching in the wrong direction, away from the confrontation one was feigning to seek. Laughter did something more, and quite unexpected. A couple of days after the scene of mockery came the news that the cowherd had shot the young (early teenage) brother of the man who had made off with his daughter. The boy was wounded but not killed. Some said the victim had also shot, or shot at, the cowherd, but no one could or would confirm this rumour or, if it were true, knew who had fired first. The next day, the soldier and his elder brother turned up in the village armed and looking for the perpetrator, who had prudently fled. The police appeared that evening at the mayor's house to get his cooperation in resolving the legal issues now raised.

Shooting the boy was taken by everyone to be an act incommensurate with the offence, to be quite inappropriate in the choice of a socially non-mature victim, and to raise the level of violence in a way threatening serious bloodshed that might be very difficult to control. The cowherd's use of the rifle, thought by all originally to be for nothing but show, thus disqualified him even further in terms of personal integrity.

Death in the Street

That someone may attempt to render visible the 'true' nature of a situation which others are colluding to make socially invisible is part of the tensions marking the interplay of honour and kizb. We have already seen one instance of this in the very direct denunciation of the murdered man's brother by the politico. He pointed straight at the weakness at the heart of both the injured family's *and* the aghas' position in the language of dominant values on virtuous behaviour. That the response was 'not to say anything' but to attempt in turn to discredit him by various strategies illustrated the permanent, structuring ambiguity in the position of both opponents. He may have failed in his primary objective of pushing the conflict to further violence, but no one can have been unaware of the force of his words.

The ice cracked but it did not break. In another setting the results may be dramatic. A beit may have come to an unspoken agreement for whatever reasons that they were not in fact actively engaged in the search to avenge an injury. They may think that their performance in the social arena suffices for everyday practical purposes; that the original event no longer concerned any others who might want to embarrass them; that their way of defining the situation had in fact carried the day. Then everything falls apart with a word:

> One man I knew was walking down the street in town [Tripoli] with a distant relative when the latter suddenly indicated an old man walking ahead of them and said that that was the man who forty years ago had shot my friend's paternal uncle. My friend drew his revolver and killed the old man on the spot. What motivated the relative I do not know. The point is that he forced a definition of the situation on my friend, who had to recognize that his total social identity was at issue. His identity would be degraded if he did not maintain it by wiping out the old blood debt. He was jailed but is now free again, and is himself a potential victim.[12]

This scene in a Tripoli street has the pitiless clarity of revenge stories. The identity of the, to the young man, apparently unknown person walking in front of him was made clear. It was the murderer of his uncle. The young man instantly responded. Blood wiped out blood. The act was carried out before the anonymous city throng, publicly and in the broad light of day ...

Forty years telescoped into a moment that became the new event in what had seemed to be an 'inert' narrative. The now 'hero' was on the instant inexorably engaged in the narrative logic which would now be said to have begun before he was born. A new generation assumed authorship. Nothing was absurd, all was coherent.

His subsequent imprisonment, the carefully orchestrated movements which had always to take account of the possible movements of vengeful others, the ways in which he was spoken of were all typical of men who have played out this role. He, too, had had seven or eight years in jail, and because he was of a poor fellah family there had been little of the support in money, food and tobacco that the more well-to-do gave to their men in these circumstances. Sounds in the night menaced him. His time and space, and that of his family, took on a different definition. Though he answered the summons to honour, and he, too, was only an adolescent when he shot his victim, he had by the time I got to know him also become a socially anomalous figure, thought of as unpredictable and risky company even if not defined as 'beyond the social pale', makhlu'a.

In his tiny shack down on the plain he had the great piles of cheap school exercise books that he had filled up in jail. They were packed with a hodge-podge of 'facts' as he called them, trawled from a bewildering mass of magazines, digests and encyclopaedias. 'They will explain everything in the world', he said to me intently as, by the light of the hurricane lamp, we pored over the blurred pencil lines of his ill-written Arabic script. The ambition to encompass the world from his unique vantage point seemed a desperate attempt to make sense, to impose a universal order that only he could see and only he could construct. No one else could understand it, though it was possible that this stranger might have some grasp of the significance of the project. It was as though he alone had the key to every-thing, and at the moment of killing in one sense I suppose he had. His identity in his own eyes now seemed bound up with this insatiable, and unrealizable, devouring of 'all the facts'. The obsessive pulling on my sleeve for emphasis and the insistence on going through page after page as though I could somehow be a witness to his vision and authenticate it unnerved me and I was glad to leave him.

So if simulation could be a precious instrument in the social working out of manhood and reputation, it rendered men vulnerable to those who wished and were capable of imposing what they insisted was the truth of the social situation. People might feel that the last thing they needed or could afford was to be trapped in the narratives of revenge. They might have wanted at almost any cost somehow to evade the imperatives even while going through all the rhetorical motions, the fine speeches, threats and proclamations, with the accompanying suppressions, silences and collusions. Nothing could ever quite guarantee the performance.

CHAPTER TWELVE

Joking, Play and Pressure

Putting the Screws On

Narratives of power and property developed central themes of attempted seizure of assets and contests in which the capacity to enter into the exchanges of violence was put on trial. Challenges explored and constantly tested 'the limits which distinguish, separate and oppose, but which also allow mutual recognition'.[1]

What I want to explore here are the different forms of putting self and other on trial which occurred routinely as if 'for their own sake', rather than in some challenge also involving material resources. For the subjection of a person or group to pressure (*daght*) of one kind and degree or another was part of everyday life as well as of more obviously political and property confrontations.

Death might take many forms, and dealing death to another had many degrees of pleasure. The potency of one was shown in the impotence of the other. Playing with, and on, those forms and those pleasures is an integral part of male existence. Triumph was a means whereby a man put himself on show to the world, however restricted that world might be.

A 'real man' was always alive to the occasions he might seize to provoke a contest; looking for opportunities to develop an argument, to close off another's rhetorical alternatives and to drive him either to the broken, incoherent language that signified helpless exasperation and loss of self-control, or to equally helpless silence. Equally, he might be cautiously seeking to avoid any such openings where he might be challenged. '*Am yashidd 'aleih* or the more dialect phrase '*am yu'arriq 'aleih*, 'he's putting the screws on him', referred to processes as important in male joking and verbal contest as they were in all the agonistic dimensions of social practice.[2]

Men spoke of ridiculing and exposing someone to mockery, *bahdala*, and of throwing someone off their social balance and into a confusion that rendered him an object of laughter, *tahrij*. Performance types ranged from what participants define as *mazah*, making fun, through to the dramas of formal insult, *sabb wa shatima*, from fleeting banter through sustained joking ridicule to the high seriousness of honour.

The genre of *jaqmara*, performances of prose speech disputing 'in play', could be constructed in a contest through inventive use of many overlapping forms of speech and gestural challenges: mockery, oaths, boasting, tafnis, mazah, insult, and mock displays of manly virtue all played their part. All created pressure through agonistic address to others. The boundaries between genres were themselves precarious and overlapping. They depended always on who could impose (or whether either could impose) his definition of 'what is being performed' at a given moment. Whether exchanges of gestural and verbal violence were to be taken as 'playful' or 'serious' were questions which emerged in practice; frames of social action have to be established and maintained, frequently by collective effort and complicity. Things went wrong.

The capacity to exercise such pressure was part of a man's and a collectivity's identity achieved through the repeated competitive exchange of social life. It was essential to the *savoir faire* of violence: 'We know how to be shebab, how to abuse and fight (*sabb wa qatl*)' was the often-used formula which expresses the cultural archetype of how to exert pressure on others. To 'know how' to be a man was understood first and foremost as being able to act in these two main registers of the performance of offence. Qatl, fighting (or killing), had a central value but had to be expressed in gesture and rhetoric: *how* the act was done was what men spoke of afterwards. To know how to abuse and verbally aggress others is therefore equally important. The mere capacity for a fight or the raw courage for a risky confrontation only become social virtue and excellence if they signified and were given due form and persuasiveness.

A talent for exerting pressure went well beyond merely knowing a set of offensive terms and phrases. Could a young man master the pitch and tones of voice, the facial expressions, body postures and hand gestures, the pacing and control of the rhythm of the encounter, the cutting words of assertiveness and mastery, as well as the handling of the audience? Was there some lack of fit in his performance and in the claims to standing which it embodied? In his teens and early twenties the *shabb*, the young man, was expected to begin to show how well he had absorbed these central lessons of male life, and to essay demonstrations of his own capacities in an aesthetically powerful and 'spontaneous' way, with all the risks that such efforts courted. Play episodes of insulting, ridiculing, arguing and trying to put the screws on someone rehearsed capacities and responses that were required in serious settings. Perhaps just as significantly, they gave men experience of what counted as winning and its triumphs, what counted as defeat and its humiliations, and of that uncertain zone where the nature and extent of injury were established.

The shebab continually tested each other (as did the senior men, though of course on the basis of life experience over many years). Some inevitably showed themselves in practice to be far more successful than others in the rhetorically obligatory declarations of their own skill, calculation, intention and mastery. But even the skilful might not 'hit the target' in the use of an argumentative strategy or in fooling and making a fool of another. A failing of timing gave observers the chance to grin knowingly and draw attention to their faulty aim with a sardonic '*ma zabtit ma'ak*', 'you missed.' The more cunning and adroit were particularly scrutinized for miscalculation and the complacent moment when a too easy assumption of superiority led to failure. At that moment the less skilled had the pleasure of publicly registering a defeat for one of the shebab who has previously distinguished himself too often and aroused a collective interest in cutting him down to size. Those who stood out thus took the greater risk for they were watched more closely and there was greater relish in their discomfiture – a counterpart to the important discursive theme of 'envy' dogging any successful man in the village and acting to diminish claims to excellence.

Seniors as well as peers scrutinized a young man's capacity to make swift assessments of the nature of the audience, the balance of forces, just how far an opponent could be pushed, and what his own limits were. They judged whether he was acquiring sensitivity to the ebb and flow of contest, the momentary hesitation or flaw in the opponents' rhetoric, the time to strike and the time to defend. Everyone required some critical, practical sense of his performative abilities, not least in order to try to avoid being dragged into an unwanted situation by his lack of *savoir faire*. He might be unskilled in the rhetoric of violence but have the nerve for a killing; or he may be rhetorically cunning but have no stomach for a fight.

If seniors used a junior for a serious task, they needed a good sense of his hamasa (commitment and zeal) and his capacity for violence, and that would have been judged in part by his behaviour in the genres of play. In that case they got it right. But in other cases errors were made in assessing a young man's readiness for confrontation (as we shall see in Chapter 15). The processes of reputation therefore began early, growing out of observation of what are often very ephemeral and apparently insignificant contests between the socially immature in daily life as much as out of serious confrontation.

Jaqmara: Mock Fighting with Words

Conventionalized modes of verbal duelling are known in many areas of the Arab world. The more refined styles are staged in different poetic forms appropriate to, and defining of, the particular occasion, the performers competing to outdo each other in linguistic subtlety, metrical skill and poetic representations of their own or their communities' glories.[3]

Scenes of jaqmara in the village were always staged in ordinary speech, and initiated in the flow of social interaction rather than in specific conventionalized phases of weddings or great collective challenges. The arena might be a sahra, a casual encounter in the street, a few men sitting outside one of the shops, or indeed any gathering not excluding the most formal occasions. Judgements of whether or not verbal mock battling was appropriate depended partly on who were the dominant 'insiders' on the particular occasion, since outsiders or strangers would not consider launching into this genre of performance unless given some very strong indication by those on home ground that it was permissible. Furthermore, it was not considered appropriate for jaqmara to dominate a sahra, but rather it should constitute only a phase of the socializing. Too much 'play' was not fitting for male assemblies, particularly if persons of rank were present.[4] Those who wished to show that they were sticklers for social form might well denounce their companions for lack of correct and proper behaviour at an evening when a great deal of mock argument was carried on.

Jaqmara was unlikely to occur on a major occasion such as a mulid celebration in honour of the Prophet or at rituals following someone's death, except when a senior man challenged one of his age (though not necessarily status) peers. No one else broke the formal frame. The senior would launch on some line of speech calculated to provoke another of his generation; two elders might have an alliance and gang up on one of their peers to see if they could exasperate him beyond measure. It was not at all unusual, when people came together for the rituals of death, to see those defined as 'old' (khityariya) beginning a jaqmara with sly references to the age and decay of one of their peers or an account of how life had been 'in the past' which discredited the other in some way and ended with a bad-tempered public outburst. Furious oaths that 'by God, I shall see you on the washing table first!' accelerated the tempo and generated ill-feeling which, at least on the side of the defeated party, might rapidly replace the initial apparently light badinage.[5] To restore some social decorum usually required the amused mediation of their sons, now mature and regulating their fathers' acts rather than vice versa.

These formal and official occasions also furnished a large audience for displays of speech performance and demonstrations of the capacity to make someone mistillim, in one's power. The 'serious' nature of a setting when, for example, men came together to listen to Quran readings after a death, added spice to the unequal contest. It presented a particular challenge, for the ritual frame should not be crudely violated, and offered a particular reward to the man who could play on the tension between such a frame, a 'proper' topic, and jaqmara.

Such confrontations, in my experience, always involved an unequal match and were stimulated by a man who regularly picked on the same victim and regularly won. The local prayer leader of the mosque, the *imam*, a man from a poor fellah family who was treated with scant respect by the aghas, often fell into the trap set for him by one member of this group. Abu Ali, as I shall call the agha, was always on the lookout for an opportunity to 'put pressure' on the imam and had few scruples about when or how he did it. When one man of the agha descent group died – a totally disregarded and impoverished person whose only social credit was that he was a cousin of the mayor – Abu Ali took the chance offered by the large evening gathering in the mayor's reception room on the fortieth day after the death to ask the imam what he thought about the relative merits of the Prophet Muhammed and the Prophet Jesus Christ.[6] Was not Christ, he mused reflectively, perhaps 'preferred' (*afdal*) by God in the sense that he had neither been born nor died in the normal human way?[7]

The imam was, as I am sure everyone anticipated, deeply upset by this notion.[8] Citations from the Holy Book flew between the opponents, along with accusations of inventing supporting verses. The tormentor maintained a posture between serious religious enquiry and impatient interrogation of an incompetent. Eventually the imam, whose literally as well as metaphorically toothless rage was mounting rapidly, leapt from his seat to stand in front of his tormentor while issuing increasingly wild denunciations. His crescendo of fury, made all the greater by Abu Ali's mocking rebuttals of his arguments, led to the imam jumping up and down in such exasperated frustration that he dropped his staff and his turban tumbled off and rolled across the floor, a moment which I took to be the major aim of the exercise.

The room was packed with males of all ages, from the beys and most high status, elderly aghas at one end, to a crowd of male adolescents and children at the other. Abu Ali used the full repertoire of performance to engage the audience, from eye cueing, general appeals both to 'what everyone knew' and to intimate acquaintance with the religious texts, to confident attacks on the imam's exegetical skills. Since the audience was in large majority composed of his own kin, indeed he was in the privileged position of being the maternal uncle of the mayor, he was very much on home and higher status ground against the mosque officient of fellah origin. Through this, as it seemed, totally appropriate dispute he wound up the wretched imam with the greatest ease. This certainly did not diminish anyone else's pleasure in the spectacle, which was taking place, be it remembered, on a formal occasion of mourning and around a significant theological issue.[9]

The fact that he had a rhetorical triumph and was exposing the imam on ground where the latter might have been taken to have some competence – and that of religion, the most serious ground of all – is a link with the scenes of comedy to which I have referred elsewhere. The outraged loss of self-mastery, in this case set off with perfect comic aesthetics by the tumbling turban (itself a metaphor in action of the dispute, since the headgear stood for the wearer's social role), marked the achievement of mastery by Abu Ali. He looked around him in apparent astonishment at the prayer leader's incoherence, the seriousness of his demeanour showing that nothing so improper as mazah or jaqmara was in his mind, but only the totally suitable topic of a delicate point of theology.

That open laughter *had* to be suppressed because it would be a violation of the ritual moment, gave a specific additional tension to the performance. This was part of Abu Ali's skill in generating the scene and playing both by, and at the same time, with the rules. Members of the audience also had to control themselves, and for the younger men particularly, not to mention the anthropologist, it was extremely difficult to behave correctly in due form. It was only later, once we got outside and at sahras over the next few days, that we could explode with amusement.[10]

The particular topics of jaqmara were frequently those of most pressing interest – the current state of electoral politics, for example, the significance to be read into the behaviour of a particular group, or the course of action to be followed in a dispute. More or less any subject on which people were liable to have strong views, or felt obliged to act as if they were already men of some standing or aspiring to be so, might be used to begin the joust. The point was to select a ground on which men might be called upon to assert the primacy of their personal view against rivals, thus staking their rhetorical identity and social weight 'in play' but very much as they would do in a 'real' verbal confrontation.

Activities which did not in general admit as wide and personal a range of possible opinion and interpretation about individual action, such as mechanical work or agricultural practices, tended not to become topics. Men usually discussed olive harvesting techniques, what crops to sow when, or which machinery was best for which job, with sober evaluation and acknowledgement that one had more experience than another. Yet the nature of such a subject was not 'in itself' always neutral. It might well be utilized in the genres of jaqmara and mazah, *provided* that it was made significant to the identity of a given individual.

Let me give one example of such a 'play' dispute over what in local terms would be an unlikely topic. I was present when one of Abu Ali's sons, a young man who knew nothing about motors, worked up another, who had at least three years' experience as a motor mechanic, into a helpless fury and loss of self-control through calculated challenges to his technical skill in mending his broken tractor. Two of the men assisting in the job, one of them the owner's brother, began by confidently riposting in the jaqmara mode of argumentative play. But they were not very verbally astute performers either, and eventually became as infuriated as the main victim by the self-righteous and laughing assumption of a totally bogus superiority by their opponent who mercilessly bombarded them with parodies of technical instruction and interrogation. That the challenger had words as his only weapons but still was able to defeat those who should, in practice, have been utterly secure on their own ground as mechanics made it doubly exasperating. Those who seemed to have the power and resources in the encounter were made impotent.

The half-dozen other shebab present were vastly amused. They knew that the mechanic's command of his trade was not matched by his talent in repartee, the capacity actually being tested. To watch someone being out-talked on what is ostensibly his own domain was, as I have already suggested, a principle of much comedy and its perhaps unexpected emergence around the unpromising material of the tractor gave the audience a lot of pleasure. Several of them spoke of the scene as one of mazah, joking, showing how closely interwoven, indeed virtually indistinguishable, genres could be and how a skilled performer might incorporate this genre switching into his performance. Since defining 'what is happening' is itself subject to negotiation, this is a familiar point.

The scene was brought to an end by one of the older men there, who was himself a construction worker and senior to the shebab present. He had kept out of the jaqmara, except to grin sardonically at the sheer gall of the winning contestant in his outrageous claims to any knowledge of machinery, for it was not appropriate for an older man of higher status to participate in the contests of his juniors. When he did intervene he did not do so in jaqmara style at all, but by drily and authoritatively telling the aggressor that the latter was 'just a chauffeur' and had no business talking about mechanics. He thus shifted the frame and made the talk 'serious'. The fact that he came to the rescue of his younger work colleague and employee, on the other hand, emphasized just how badly the young tractor driver had been defeated.

Yet to understand the dynamics of this short scene we have to go further. Each episode of jaqmara needs to be contextualized as part of a sequence rather than being viewed as simply self-contained. In itself, after all, it was difficult to see how the motor could have become a focus for joking and a rewarding topic, particularly since one party seemed to have no standing in the matter he selected for argument. For jaqmara requires a confrontation over a theme in which each side can claim some competence. What made the challenger successful?

The scene demonstrated that the relatively new world of machine work could in fact be made appropriate material for joking and jaqmara if the *person* and social identity of one of the contestants were to be engaged. In this case the young mechanic (the frenzied younger brother who features in the narrative of the Tripoli conflict in Chapter 15) only a few days before had flaunted his acquisition of the very second-hand tractor, a vital resource, by riding it around in front of the shebab seated by the shop at the entry to the village as if it were a high-spirited horse. His tafnis in showing off the undoubtedly prestigious Massey Ferguson to his peers, none of whom possessed one, was all the more galling to them because he was often the butt of jokes and putdowns to which he usually could not reply as he became quickly flustered. His mode of revenge, both in undeniable material possession and stylistic terms, made the tractor a key element in the (non-verbal) claim to distinction against his competitors, who were now challenged in their view of themselves as his superiors.

His very success in transforming the Massey Ferguson into an instrument in the construction and extension of his social identity in turn furnished those whom he had forced to 'eat it' with the means of response, using the breakdown to attack his too-confident triumph. He had made clear in his tafnis display that he would socially use the tractor in a way that underlined, not its economic significance, but rather his new capacity to put on a show against his peers. In fact the swirling turns on its axis which he executed specifically defied narrow and dispassionately considered economic interest, not only because the manoeuvre made the already badly worn tyres almost bald and unfit for most tasks, but because he could not afford even second-hand replacements. This had been pointed out critically by the other and more sober mechanics present who liked rhetorically to present themselves precisely as being distinguished by a new, more neutral and technical way of evaluating objects and behaviour. His tafnis tarnished their self-image, and they harshly criticized the young owner for making his machine an occasion for what they saw as a demeaning display.

The young driver, who had no real schooling and came from a poor agha family, had shown a real aptitude for the work and was, in respect to some tasks, thought the equal of his very experienced mechanic father. The other shebab were aware that he was likely to be materially better placed than most of them in the not-too-distant future. The disregarded young man was better off and would owe whatever social position he did acquire to the central fact of his work. But what he wanted to do was to turn that advantage into social capital in the mode of tafnis and putting down others, instead of staying on his own ground of competence and affecting indifference to flamboyant display. Had he followed this latter course of action I do not think that the jaqmara scene could possibly have been played.

Form, Frame and Audience

In all contests of jaqmara, whatever the subject, men developed their case by stressing through their posture, tone and emphatic phrasing that at each point they were challenging the claims of the opponent even to have a view on the topic. They tried to 'prove' exactly the opposite to his argument, marshalling the forms of *rhetorical* attack to show that their *analytical* powers were superior (*b'il 'aks*, on the contrary, is an often heard interruption). In such dispute around some political process, for example, every effort would be made to reverse the interpretation of the opponent who was characterized as seeing only the surface of events while the speaker could take apart those same events to reveal the complex inner realities (the process of *tahlil*, analysis).

Protagonists did everything possible to distract and mislead opponents, bombarding each other with assertive claims to authority. Instead of the polite turn-taking of public discussion – where interruptions were introduced with a formula of excuse for 'cutting' (*qata'*) the words of another and speakers intersperse their own accounts with polite phrases like 'have you followed my meaning Abu Fulan?' – breaking in on the opponent was of the essence in jaqmara. The aim was furthered if one succeeded in the classical ploy of using the other's own words against him by turning the meaning and producing a more barbed or elaborated phrase to which he found it difficult to respond.

A performer tried constantly to widen his own options while narrowing those of the opponent whom he attempted to push to a point where he could no longer continue. Soliciting favourable audience reaction through apostrophic address played a major role here. Players made elaborately disbelieving exclamations (with much looking round, throwing of hands in the air, shrugging of shoulders and raising of the eyes to heaven) calling attention to the supposedly manifest stupidity of what has just been said by the other and inviting members of the audience to endorse their huge amazement that anyone could be so unseeing: '*Leik al haki*! '*Ajabak al haki*?! *Ya 'alam, heik biyihki*?!', 'That is talk! Does that drivel please you?! (employing a singular pronoun for 'you', thus treating the audience as a familiar and singular figure). Listen everyone! (using the vocative form *ya*) Can that be what he is saying?!' The speaker then typically went on to address those present directly, detailing the flaws in what had been said and not even deigning to seem to take any account of the opponent's presence.

Those new statements were met by vigorous counter statements about what was 'really' happening and how it had been totally missed by the opponent, who was roundly declared to be incapable of insight: '*ma bitifham shi anta*', '*ma bita'rif shi abadan*', 'you don't understand a thing', 'you know nothing whatever'. With such dismissive phrases go self-praise: '*ma fi hada biya'rif mithli. Bukra hatshuf*', 'No one knows as I do. Tomorrow you'll see'. Negative assertives are at their most economical in single word interjections denying any validity to what is being claimed: 'kizb!', or 'fashr!' for example, 'lies!' and 'boasting!'. And if the opponent seemed to cede a point or was driven into silence after a torrent of questions the terse '*khamant*', 'I thought as much', in tones of grim satisfaction and finality drove home the victory. Performers maintained pressure through loud and insistent delivery, often staccato or with heavily stressed pauses at what they hoped was a particularly telling move.

The key point of the encounter – and in later talk about it, for jaqmara contests frequently became subjects of report – came in one of two ways: when a given participant or participants withdrew altogether because he had been routed, or when he became *mithammis*, which in this context means 'got carried away', 'wound up' – 'he blew up' would be something close to the sense. Now to be mithammis in a formal speech on a public occasion, or in defence of the family or the self was something to be remarked on with admiration and respect. The person is totally engaged and filled with active force in the cause. Person and performance are one. But in jaqmara such a total engagement signified defeat, for it pointed to a full absorption of the individual's passions in a setting where the convention was that 'this is only play' and thus not appropriate for the response of 'real' hamasa. Jaqmara

demanded an awareness and maintenance of *distance* from role and performance (as in fact did many 'serious' confrontations, even though in
ideological terms the actor was affecting to be completely committed). Victory
consisted in making someone lose that distance in genuine emotion. The
loser's reasoned sense of the bounded genre, his powers to achieve calculated
rhetorical effect while being only apparently totally engaged, and his social
awareness, all had been overwhelmed by emotion. He had lost self-control
and broken the frame of play.

How was that frame established in the first place? Jaqmara might be
introduced by an explicit challenge when teasing or provocative jibes had
already begun: '*biddak tjaqmar?*', 'do you want to take me on?', said in a
challenging tone. On the other hand, opponents might move into the genre
without anything more than the cueing that follows from a couple of men
focusing on each other in a rising tempo of verbal confrontation. At a later
stage, when many or all of the participants seemed to be defining what was
happening as jaqmara, whether or not the term had actually been used, one
might throw the challenging phrase 'biddak tjaqmar?' at another when the
speaker thought that he was in a superior position. If indeed he was, he
might attempt to seal his victory by announcing dismissively: 'do you want
to jaqmar or not? You see, you don't. It's all over.' (*khalasna*, 'we have
finished'). Not infrequently there was no obvious winner since no one
achieved a telling final blow, or play was broken off by one side, usually the
one who sees defeat close at hand, saying that the confrontation has de-
generated into empty talk not worth the effort, or members of the audience
expressed impatience with the jousting and were able to impose a suspension
of the contest.

It will be obvious that the genre itself might be in dispute, since one or
several of the participants might deny that they were involved in anything
less than a serious division of opinion. So whether a given scene was 'really'
jaqmara (or described as such at the end of the encounter if things were
getting tense to neutralize hostilities), would be a function of possibly
conflicting definition.

In the social definition of the genre of the event the audience's direct
involvement was crucial, especially at moments of tension when a speaker
seemed to be losing his self-control. They would join in to assert that 'it's
all jaqmara, nothing more'. If the angry loser could not perform properly
then he should not get involved; he'd get no backing from them in acting as
if there has been a genuine insult. A refusal to accept his (or their, for
jaqmara may involve up to three or four people at a time) threat to the 'play'
character of the encounter recalled him to the collectively endorsed conventions in which his individual contest has been framed.

'Cooling out' someone who was perhaps seriously mithammis and making
him realize that he has lost, was something of which most shebab had
experience. They had experience, too, of trying to dissuade one of their

number from a hot-headed reaction to a slight, real or imagined. If they wished to, and were adept enough, they would reassure the loser about the meaninglessness of the whole encounter, flattering him on some other quality they said he possessed. On the other hand, they might rub salt into the wound if their conception of their momentary interests allowed it, and work to accentuate the pain, not least with delighted reporting of the dispute in another forum.

Sociologically speaking, therefore, the role of the audience was as much a practical rehearsal of knowing how to be men as that of the protagonists. The responsiveness, judgement, timing and rhetorical ability they practised in jaqmara are equally important for 'serious' conflict. If the convention is that this is 'play' and does not 'count', this verbal mock fighting nonetheless contributes to the continuous processes of contest and reputation on however small a scale. Men grew up constantly socialized into negotiating what the context for actions and interpretations was to be taken to be.

The boundary between audience and participants was relatively fluid. The former was never passive but interjected, passed evaluative comments and showed approving or disapproving reactions to a particular attack. They acted as judges and their reactions might have great influence on the confidence of performers. Finding even this level of participation too constraining, an individual might abandon his spectator's part altogether to join fully in the jaqmara – because he was unreflectingly caught up in the rhetoric, out of calculation in supporting an ally, or simply because he could not resist the chance to shine.

Not only were the protagonists usually his peers in terms of age group and general status, but they also tended to be from the same or closely related descent groups. More specifically, they also tended to be men who were in regular social contact through kinship, work, sahras and informal gatherings as well as probable membership of one or another level of the violence group which all of these conditions imply. Challenges to family hierarchy tended to be excluded from such play. Brothers, for instance, avoided confrontations with each other until they thought they had achieved adult status and/or were married with their own families. Even then the audience would have to be socially close for them to challenge each other in jaqmara and it might be an ill-tempered affair virtually indistinguishable from a bitter squabble. Cross-generational jaqmara only occurred where juniors identified an older man as having so little social standing that they might engage him in the genre without being reproved by seniors for their *lèse-majesté*.

Jaqmara might have a special quality of ambiguity. Because what was made the subject of argument was indeed 'serious' and almost bound to be subject to varying interpretation and vigorously defended, play on this ambiguity, 'play on play', gave plenty of scope for virtuosity in performance. I can best illustrate this by describing a scene of jaqmara at a sahra held in the poorly furnished one-room house of Abu Nabil, a middle-aged mechanic belonging to one of the lineages of the agha family.[11] It was the time of the 1972 national election campaign. The room was full of men from the descent group, perhaps fifteen to twenty in all, with some coming and going during the course of the evening.

The specific issue was whether the maternal uncle of a young man called Tariq, would vote according to the intentions of the elderly and prestigious father of one of Tariq's maternal cousins, Ahmad, in the elections. Tariq himself was arguing for another candidate whom he supported and he was trying to show that his uncle was bound, for all sorts of complex reasons, to support the same politician and not the one favoured by Ahmad and his family. Both young men were attempting to get their families to go in the direction they had defined as doing most for their personal interests and were trying to play very active roles in competitive electoral manoeuvring. It was a perfect arena and topic for agonistic display.

The argument began in what seemed to be jaqmara mode, the audience setting it up by playful interjections, and 'heating up' both sides. Each young man used the standard appeals to bolster the superiority of his position and highlight the obvious idiocy of the other's, with elaborately patronizing 'explanations' of what was *really* going on so that even one as unsuited to political debate as the opponent might understand it. They 'took the stage': raising voices, sitting forward, gesturing emphatically, showing facial expressions of amazed disbelief or indignation or self-satisfaction as seemed most appropriate, or slumping back with exaggerated assurance and indifference in the face of some new point presented as having great force by its proponent.

After much back and forth, Ahmad and an ally, Talal, began to lose their initial confidence and poise before the insouciant, mocking and verbally inventive denial of all their views and interpretations by Tariq. It was bad enough that the latter kept up a stream of dismissive and patronizing remarks to disparage their every point without apparently being at all fazed by their rhetoric of 'really knowing' politics. Bad enough, too, that he always had a more elaborated and complex reading of his own which seemed to depend on what he claimed was a far greater capacity to see behind the mere surface of what was happening. But the final straw was that he constantly cued everyone present to his mastery of 'playing with the serious' by malicious glances and wicked grins that seemed right on the edge of parody. In other words, he showed that he could both enter into the mode of talk, *and* keep his distance, emphasizing his control of both himself and the others, who were rapidly losing theirs in the face of this exasperating performance.

Finally, in a state of obvious and real irritation, Ahmad attempted to achieve a winning closure by rhetorical evocation of descent group hierarchy and genealogy: 'We are the family of Ahmad Sheikh Mustapha!' he shouted, with a challenging glare. 'Your mother's brother kisses our father's hand!'

The cry: 'We are the family of' and the calling out of the name is the conventional identification of one side in a serious confrontation, and shows the full social identification and commitment of the person to the struggle. Tariq, however, found a reply to this invocation that both acknowledged and then contemptuously brushed aside the challenge: 'That is true – he kisses his hand, but out of respect (*ihtiram*), no more. When it comes to the elections respect will count for *nothing* [with a heavily sarcastic stress].'

Tariq thus both paid tribute to, and flouted, the use of the transcendent family principles of descent and seniority by first paying due service to 'respect', and then claiming that those principles did not in fact englobe and determine the sphere of politics which was the whole topic of the dispute. He allowed the reference to the hand kiss but promptly showed that that was literally 'lip-service' only, the curt *'wa bas'*, 'no more' being particularly rhetorically effective here for its terseness in response to Ahmad's somewhat too heroic and grandiloquent appeal to his name. The rhetorically daring separation (almost subordination) of ihtiram, a cardinal value of status and social ordering, to the practical demands of politics and interest, effectively reversed Ahmad's argument while still presenting his, Tariq's, maternal uncle as preserving familial pieties. So Ahmad's claim was turned against him and relocated in a different frame within which it did not have precedence.

Having staked his all, his father's name, on ending the contest and being mortified to have its significance and appropriateness finessed, Ahmad found himself without further recourse. He turned out to have closed his own rhetorical space. Moreover, the trumpet call of name and house was in itself an indication, not of the speaker's strength but of his vulnerability. For the proud invocation was not fitting in 'play', being reserved for moments when one was putting oneself on the line 'for real'. Ahmad had unwittingly demonstrated that he was slipping out of frame. The result was anger and mere 'shouting', completely inappropriate in a sahra. Ahmad and Talal, the other relative who had his own reasons for wanting to see Tariq defeated in jaqmara, ended by resorting to what amounted to crude threats which had no appropriate linguistic or performance 'turn' to them. To which Tariq could reply with infuriating cool and flattening scorn simply: *'ghalat'* (wrong! a mistake!), thus contrasting his economy of utterance with their excess. Awareness of that loss of course made them yet more infuriated. Tariq then brought his performance to an end with a stereotypical boasting coda: *'as-siyasa? ana ikhtira't as-siyasa!'* 'Politics? I invented politics!' a classical piece of *superbia*.

Tariq naturally spared no theatrical effect in his retellings later, edited and phrased at his leisure with no one to say him nay. The performance he had given could itself be re-presented at other sahras, a comic version of a 'heroic' victory against the odds, and as such a serious point scored. More than that, he managed to make the whole electoral process seem nothing more than a rhetorical contest in which what was at stake was word play alone. The question became 'who was better at disputing' rather than whether or not there was anything of serious import to dispute about. What was signified was subordinated to the form and manner in which the signifiers were articulated.

Tariq's reputation as someone to be reckoned with in such a context went up a notch. So perhaps did the attentiveness with which others looked for a chance to bring it down again. His quick-wittedness and gift for exploiting the weaknesses of others in verbal performance was dangerous, even to him. There were people who murmured that he was a man who took pleasure setting folk against each other, which indeed he did and which he instanced to me as part of his mastery of language manipulation. The line between his virtuosity in performance being feared and admired, and his being taken to be a *fattan*, one who causes serious internal strife in a community by operating on its vulnerable points, was a thin one.[12] There was a suspicion that he was *jaban*, a coward, an accusation sometimes muttered by shebab who were worsted by him in word contests. He showed himself almost too obviously to be a skilled performer with language and in reading others' weaknesses. This was taken to indicate a weakness of his own in physical confrontation or readiness for a fight. Certainly he was not mobilized at moments when the fighting men were summoned into action. His emerging identity was thus anchored on words in performance, rather than on words and physical deeds of agonism.

Choosing a Victim

Great fun was gained by the aggressive, teasing joking which men used on each other, probing for a weak spot. There was little of the supposed ideal of honour of picking on an equal, though you got more credit if you could manage that well. The challenge was frequently directed at one who was not very quick or good with words or able to respond effectively (for example the young mechanic). Men were looking for those who are vulnerable or those against whom they had launched successful attacks before. Easy targets existed to be hit.

On one typical occasion two maternal cousins, young men in their early twenties, united against one of their peers (also a maternal cousin to both). The latter's main characteristics in the eyes of his peers was his physical strength and lack of shrewdness, but he was putting on airs during the election period and sounding off about who he would and would not support, as if anybody thought it was important. This was both unwise, since it invited a challenge likely to be too sharp for his capacities to respond, and a perfectly standard tactic. Men had to try to make themselves seem worth something in the electoral marketplace, and the point was simply to have the behaviour noticed by one of the candidate's supporters who might then try to buy his vote. This kind of behaviour was thus highly instrumental and virtually required at elections if anyone hoped to profit. At the same time, and as was the case in any claim to status, one would be judged merely to be a fannas and a fool unless such proclamations of one's value at least stood a good chance of persuading enough people to go along with them.

This was definitely not the case with the young man in question. He was the third of Abu Nabil's sons, and he and his brothers were obviously not succeeding in uniting around one candidate. Their father was ineffectual in such matters and clearly had no real idea either how to maximize the various possible advantages of possessing five sons, how to turn those votes into money, or how to 'talk up' what his family could do. The brothers, individually and collectively, were thought to have no social judgement or status. Finally, and damningly, they were considered not even to realize that that was what men thought of them. So the young man was in a sociological catch-22: compelled to act in a way which would in fact demonstrate that he could not really act in that way at all, a dilemma which in different ways was all too familiar.

His routine but ill-advised attempts at self-aggrandizement led to a public hazing before an appreciative audience of agha shebab outside the small shop of his paternal uncle, also a man with no status with the group. The whole scene had been set up by two of his cousins when they saw their potential victim approaching. One turned to the other immediately, with a complicitous glance at the rest of us, and said: 'Biddak tjaqmara?' 'Do you want to jaqmar?' It was a dull day, and time for a little diversion. Here was the perfect opportunity ...

The combined attack made by the two cousins was easy enough to carry off, given the inequalities in verbal and intellectual dexterity. The victim was encouraged to give his views on the electoral situation, and then deluged with contrary opinion, each attacker feeding the other lines for a further assault and cueing each other and the audience with hardly suppressed grins of self-satisfaction. The crescendo of knowing analysis culminated in the mocking tone and patronizing disdain typical of so many encounters: *'Hey da shugle ma bita'rifha anta'*, 'that (politics) is business you know nothing about'. The victim's predictions about what would happen were derisively slapped down and he was told in the standard boast: *'Ana rabb as-siyasa. Bukra hatshuf. Sajjil hikayati'*, 'I'm the lord of politics. Tomorrow you'll see. Mark my words.'[13] The formulaic phrases used were delivered with a pride which was both a play on contests in general, and serious enough for the amusement purposes at hand. *'Kanu 'am yujaqmiru 'aleih'*, 'they were giving him a bad time', and doing so in the certain knowledge of victory. The victim was made, and made himself, the instrument of their effortless demonstration of superiority.

This exploitation of the exploitable by the exploitative was a regular feature of everyday male relations and the discourse of power, and we should recall the extreme case of the lord shooting the hapless boy 'just because he felt like it', *'heik'*.

Certain individuals achieved a dominance over a particular other whom they made the regular butt of bahdala, mockery, tahrij, kizb, and an often especially aggressive mazah. The mode of challenge and response governed the encounters, but the winner was nearly always the same, except on the rare occasions of a real misjudgement by the superior party. These pairings were well recognized and several senior men of the older generation had their 'partner' in such scenes, while among the shebab these relations emerged in later adolescence through mutual testing.

Harm and Humour

Mazah or joking might take on a deliberately damaging form which made the whole genre frame ambiguous. Then the question might be raised as to whether a person's words and actions were really 'joking', and thus licensed, or whether there was an attempt to 'harm' (*yadurr*) the other. If there was, then the permissible bounds were considered to be overstepped and too-confident aggressors might find that their skill and tactics backfired, earning them the disapproval of their peers. What was 'harm'?

As always, situation, relation between participants, and the nature of the audience were crucial. If we remember the real terror of the young man who was grabbed and wrapped in the Lebanese flag that covered the coffin of Muhammad al Abboud (Chapter 2), and the loss of face of victims of jaqmara, we can see that real emotions, feelings and reputations were at stake. But in each case I think that the social test influencing men's judgement as to the admissability or otherwise of a challenge as joking depended on whether the confrontation stayed within the arena of the specific without affecting any other interest of the persons concerned. So although people might mention a given scene for a couple of days, a particular battle was held to be of no real account outside the frame of its occurrence. It was, by definition, 'not serious'. But if someone's interests were put at risk, for example by a 'joke' that actually entailed material loss or what was taken to be some compromise of the other's integrity, then 'harm' was being done. That was sanctioned by overt disapproval and talk against the perpetrator who might find himself confronting a degree of general censure and lose all the pleasure of his victory.

The young mechanic who had bought the second-hand tractor had, over time, become the expected victim of the man who harrassed him over his competence in his work. The two of them often got into such encounters, always instigated by the confident joker who seldom had any trouble in 'winding up' his verbally unskilful opponent.

One day the tractor owner received a phone call from Beirut, or ostensibly from Beirut, saying that he should go to the capital for work.[14] He dashed off immediately despite warnings that it might be kizb since no one else including the work team leader had had any indication of urgent business. Everyone else seemed to think that the ruse was transparent. No one except the eager mechanic seemed to have any doubt that the message was a deception.[15]

The young man returned the next day, angry and crestfallen. It had been kizb after all. The wasted journey cost him two days and 40 lira he did not have (a serious loss representing four days pay on average). Everyone in the work and family groups knew about it of course, and all were certain that his usual opponent was the cause. No one showed much regard for the dupe, who had not listened to advice or critically examined the circumstances as a man should, and whose social judgement in the general view was exasperatingly poor. But it was clear that people thought the phone call was what one leading mechanic tersely called *mazah wihish*, a dirty trick, a rotten joke. You did not 'lie' about work opportunities, and clearly the spread of any such practice would have been potentially highly prejudicial to work relations.

The unspoken boundaries of the genre were crossed. The material loss of money and work-time, new but increasingly important factors in individual and collective life, were crucial in the strongly disapproving verdict on the incident. If mazah violated personal *maslaha* – 'interest' here in terms of maintaining a family, since the mechanic's wages went immediately to his father – then it became *wihish*, dirty. Although successful in the narrow sense that his opponent had fallen for the ruse, the joker too had misjudged the situation. The 'victor' had overreached, exposing himself in turn to severe criticism. His mazah, and his reputation as someone very quick to cause trouble for others, counted against him.

Pure Humiliation

The singling out of a man who was judged by an audience to be inferior to the initiator of the 'pressure', very often in several respects such as courage, family position, wealth, social rank or performance ability, was thus routine. The point is that such occasions were often the subject of telling and repeated narrations, even if only on one or two occasions before they became absorbed into the unspoken record of social relations and identities.

The leader of the work-team at the airport, sheikh ash-shebab of a large section of the aghas and future rival of his influential and prestigious paternal uncle for authority within a large section of Beit Abd as-Salam, had a younger brother who was extremely maladroit and regarded as rather backward.[16] The senior man, who was also the eldest of what constituted an important group of brothers, constantly berated his socially handicapped brother in front of those of the team or kin who were around. Any mistake or fumbling execution of a command might lead to a stream of loud imprecations against him and a tremendous show of verbal violence. There was no mazah. It was pressure, daght, pure and simple, certainly without even the semblance of a response from its object who was doubly disbarred from retaliation as both junior and incompetent.

Apart from a personal reaction of embarrassment and discomfort caused by what seemed to me to be displays of vicious fury at the helpless brother, I was puzzled. I could not see the reason or need for these repeated assaults which contradicted my notions of how the 'real man' and leader would behave. No one else said anything, for no one might interfere in such hierarchical family relations unless he were an extremely senior and respected relative. Very occasionally such a man did permit himself to murmur the usual placatory formulae: 'basita', 'it's nothing', or 'malish', 'never mind', when one of these outbursts took place in his presence. Otherwise the shebab themselves remained completely silent, looking away or at the ground as if withdrawing from a performance in which their presence as audience was none the less important.[17]

After an especially intense outburst one day, I asked a young team member why the leader persisted in this pattern of public humiliation of his younger brother in front of others. My question was in fact out of order, as what one brother does to his junior in public or otherwise is no one else's affair. Asking the young man to comment was at least implicitly asking him to pass judgement on someone on whom he depended for work and of whom he had no right to speak in anything but terms of strong support given their family relationship. Moreover, he and I were not in a privileged relationship of private confidence. My interlocuter was naturally uneasy. He eventually muttered, without looking at me directly, that 'perhaps it was important for him to show how he could treat people'. We quickly changed the subject.

The implication appeared to be that a leader, in this case the sheikh ash-shebab, needed a figure such as the socially disabled brother on whom to rehearse and exercise his performance of total command of the situation. Unlike other relations, where one person came to be recognized as mistillim to another only through mazah, however harsh, this was a link established in the hierarchy of the patriarchal family. He demonstrated a willingness and intention to insult and dominate the weaker brother without mercy and without restraint in a theatre of public humiliation. With all other members of the group there were kin links, political alliances to be made with their families, labour to be relied on, and potentially complex consequences to any major row the leader might have. The hapless brother served as a way of acting out his rage which was blocked in various degrees with respect to his subordinates and other kin.

The Play of Triumph and Desecration

Laughter joined with agonism, and play with seriousness, nowhere more intimately than in the arena of the card game. In this highly framed activity men's capacities for the play of confrontation were tested before a critical audience. And it was all 'just a game'.

Cards were usually part of those informal evenings of talk and social exchange at the house of one who kept a manzul, however modest, open for friends and visitors. The host had to bear the costs of tea and sugar, to be the first to pass round cigarettes and sweets, see to people's comfort and solicitously look after the gathering.

The saharat were regarded as the 'informal' social occasions *par excellence*. Even when composed mainly of kin and close associates they were meant to represent a free quality of coming together for talk and sociability. Men sat on chairs arranged around the walls of the manzul, passing their own cigarettes or loose papers and tobacco to each other despite the host's insistence, exchanging gossip, swapping notes on the olive crop, the latest harvesting arrangements or whatever. Children whispered to one another, sitting on their fathers' laps or in a corner; the younger male adolescents chattered and joked among themselves or stood silently waiting to be sent on errands for their seniors, offering tea, coffee or cigarettes around at the host's or an elder relative's instructions.

Their mothers and sisters prepared the drinks, and sometimes glanced in the window or hovered, half visible by the door. If those gathered together were very regular visitors and/or close kin (the two are nearly always the same thing) the senior woman of the house might enter to respectful greetings and sit by the door (never, of course, going round the room shaking hands and greeting each person in turn as men of any status will do). She managed the 'back stage'.

Etiquettes of turn-taking were observed, unless an argument developed. Card games alternated with other activities of general talk, jaqmara, tamthiliya, or went on at the same time with comment passed between players and non-participants who might or might not manifest any interest in the game. Once I heard complaints from a man who, though he affected to fancy himself as a connoisseur of proper form, was actually known for his bravura parodies of others' foibles and for his delight in fantasies of discovered treasure, as well as for loud sung obscene rhymes on sexual licence.[18] This dubious champion of propriety stalked majestically from the room saying: 'Do you call this a sahra? There is no proper talk, it is all just insulting and shouting.' The remark caused further amusement, coming from such a source, and the verbal games continued.

'Evenings' were archetypally referred to as incarnating the model of relaxation (being *murtah*) and friendship (*sahaba*) shared among men, and it is a cliché of letters to absent companions to include in the rhetoric of memory and community formulaic phrases about 'those unforgettable and eternal saharat'. The sense of suspension – of agonism, of interest, of hidden purpose and calculation – is vital to the notion of an ease which is held to pervade 'those unforgettable occasions' which are in retrospect conventionally treated as idyllic interludes.

Men arranged to meet later with someone who regularly received people at his house. Perhaps the host let it be known that people were welcome on a particular evening. Men exchanged news of where a sahra would occur. These occasions relieved the gloom of the cold nights from November through to the beginning of the spring agricultural season, after which men were usually either too busy during a long working day to want to do anything but sleep early, or were away harvesting or busy on building sites in other regions of the country. Some continued to meet when they could, often on the roofs of their houses on summer evenings, despite the early morning start to work.

It was in this setting of the sahra that cards generally belonged, and not at what are defined as more public, formal encounters such as weddings or mulids. Periods of funerals and mourning excluded 'play' and occasions for laughter by kin and neighbours. Cards, the radio, joke-telling, or any festive gathering infringed the boundaries of respect and *huzn* (mourning) if played within whatever people took to be the same quarter of the village as a house where a death had occurred. (I participated, none the less, in more than one argument when the shebab started 'play' of some kind, despite protests from others present about the lack of 'respect' for the mourning of a neighbouring beit.) Conventionally, the card game was excluded from the universe of status and ordering in and of the world. As we shall see, disordering is its principle.

The space of the manzul had to be adjusted for the game. Players moved down off their chairs on to the floor to play, and losers at once resumed their seats on being replaced by new players. To understand this shift in position we need to grasp what 'the floor' signifies in social practice. Chairs and sofas, relatively recent forms of domestic arrangement, were not felt to be appropriate for playing a game. In a room that was furnished in the 'modern' style, where people were sitting up on chairs and sofas, the floor became a space where the only proper interaction was one wholly defined by the idea of 'the game' and the suspension of the ordinary practices of social hierarchy. Traditionally, everyone sat on rugs or mats on the floor and 'informality' or 'play' needed little spatial adjustment. With the introduction of furniture 'the floor' becomes more specifically marked in terms of meaning.[19]

When I began to play in the mayor's manzul a table was brought as a polite gesture to my assumed cultural preferences and status. It was taken for granted that as a foreigner and as a man of different class and experience I would feel it unfitting to 'go down' on to the floor. As it turned out, we abandoned the table fairly quickly. Players manifestly felt an awkwardness about quite how they could or should behave, player–spectator relations were disrupted, and a self-conscious hesitation crept into the spontaneities of the game whose gestures were impeded when the table and chairs imposed restrictions.

The group engaged might be a regular meeting, always at a friend's house several times a week in the winter, or it might have a relatively fluid composition. Some attending played almost every time, others intermittently and yet others never. Losers gave up their place to new players who wanted a game, and in this way everyone present may at least have the opportunity to participate. Games were for four players and were nearly always a version of whist called *tarnib*, or sometimes hunt-the-lady, *likha*. Games were played in a highly stylized manner. Players in tarnib smashed their cards on to the floor with a melodramatic flourish of the hand when their partners played a suit they wanted followed. They shouted rhapsodic commentaries and accompaniment in a kind of parody of the war cries of epic tribal battles and the shouting insults of the young men. The last few tricks were played in a quick series of blatant disclosures of who was to lead and with what, accompanied by a crescendo of gloating expletives ending in a triumphant roar of self-congratulation.

'Cheating' was conventionally expected. Players swore the most sacred oaths that they had played the ten, not the eight their opponents claimed; they exhausted the repertoire of winks, nods and eyebrow movements, and took any opportunity to see the opponents' cards; and they tried to blind the enemy with a stream of running banter and insult, often of dazzling speed and apt turn of phrase.

The moment of victory and defeat signalled the beginning of another phase of play. In raucous glee winners would heap opprobrium in emphatic scorn on losers while indulging in paroxysms of self-praise. Losers were quite likely to mirror this behaviour by rounding on each other with savage denunciations of idiocy, lack of sense, skill, and strategic capacity. Anyone unfamiliar with the institutionalized forms might well take this theatrically convincing display of challenge and humiliation for the highest seriousness.

If losers attacked each other, their words and gestures were as nothing compared to the mockery of the victors. Winners were expected to indulge in a play of insults which was prodigal, elaborated, and exceeded all bounds *except* those of direct sexual reference to the women of the players' families about whom there was no 'joking'. The losers were left on their own in the joking nightmare of triumphal vituperation. Their role was to suffer for their loss and only muted protest was admitted. Anyone who could not tolerate the humiliation, and there were times when the limits of the game seemed to have been breached in a genuinely angry reaction, would find that he lost yet more in the eyes of the company. A player had to bear the unbearable, show self-control in the situation of play and endure a pantomime of the hell of the man of honour.

I was told by my village card partners, fellah and agha, that 'we' do not go in for some of the practices 'they' in the poor labourer settlements on the plain or 'up in the mountain' do. 'People say that we used to, but not any more.' Men with whom I played cards in the village told me that 'in the mountain' 'they' put a donkey saddle on the losers' backs and rode them (*yerkabuhum*, a term with strong sexual overtones) round the manzul; or they hung stones round the victims' necks and whipped them round and round. 'They' relate to each other as 'they' do to dumb brutes.

On several occasions in poor fellah houses on the plain or in the Jurd I saw burlesques of sexual violation following on card games. Winners lovingly prepared mock phalluses by twisting headcloths into long, thick and pointed shapes; or a man would bind the shaft of a broom between his legs and elaborately caress it prior to 'raping' the losers in groaning, orgasmic parodies of anal and oral penetration, with much gasping, moaning and frantically rolling eyes. They would use the left hand in a pantomime of wiping shit from themselves on to the faces of the sullen losers, before miming shaving off the victims' moustaches and the beard on their cheeks. A victor would sing stock obscene songs in a falsetto, beseeching tone and with leering intensity: 'Doctor, please help me, who can cure me? I've a pain in my stomach, examine me ...'. Singers sometimes appeared to act out a dual role as enticing female and then penetrating male. In two instances a winner took out his penis, exposing himself to the audience and the 'submissive' losers, in one case rubbing the glans on the tip of the staff tied between his legs before 'shaving' the victim.

The card game explored the nature of conflict, giving and receiving injury, sustaining and forfeiting masculinity. Men abandoned their due place in the social order when they went down to the floor. There were no honourable draws, and even less honourable losses. Language and gesture were given full licence and what would be unpardonable insult outside the game became the norm. The purities of personal integrity were polluted. There was nowhere to hide.

Men were really 'on their own' in a theatrical, agonistic world where pure chance in the fall of the cards conjoins with trickery, dishonesty, skill and the use of rhetoric to produce an outcome with but one certainty: a triumphant pair of victors and a wretched pair of vanquished, bound to be desecrated. A man of honour will not endure insult – 'ma fini ithammil', 'I will not bear it'. But the player has no choice. His will is subjugated absolutely to the game.

The violations were systematic, complex and performed with enormous relish for the equally enormous pleasure of those acting and watching. There was a delight in the tahrij and other elements 'for their own sake', for their apparently gratuitous character, and the pleasure of humiliation. The opponent was broken, *inkasar.* [20]

Desecration became in play as much a spectacle as it was in situations and narratives of challenge and confrontation, but without effect beyond the framework of the game itself. Men act out a comic transformation of the nightmare of being unmanned. Their beards are 'shaved'; that which is taken to stand for the essence of their male persona, that by which one swears the most compelling oaths and the most sacred invocations, is forfeited; the moustaches too, worn by most mature men and which likewise they would never cut off, are removed. The victim is animalized, both in the use of the saddle and in the subjection to animal, unbridled and unnatural passion;

penetrated, feminized, made into the passive object of public desire and act. The privacy of licit and illicit sexuality is made open in the most shameless way. The rapist glories in screwing the partner, just as he lovingly smears his face with 'shit'.

'Cards' were thus a play on the nature of the person and of the boundaries of male personhood in which the hell and the heaven of masculinity were produced as a game. Everything which destroyed a man's name was represented and parodied in a display of the vigorous workings of the monstrous and grotesque phallus, itself the object of laughter and a caricature of mastering sexual power to which all 'losers' were subjected. What was in agonistic exchange the shame of the defeated was here controlled by laughter and unambiguous framing 'down on the floor'. Victims were compelled to bear actions which were bearable because not 'real'. Humiliation ends when they get up off the floor.

The figure of social death was made a performance with its own atmosphere of misrule.[21] Cards were practice for life. The game as an exercise for reality represented men's existence and identity in a specific mode which, though highly controlled, had great freedom of action. Men honed their skills, challenge, deception, rhetoric, cunning and performance which had to be employed in the everyday world. The pretences and ruses of the game were much closer to the actual daily practices of sharaf, karama and distinction than the superb clarities of the honour stories or murajul of great hero figures. The latter were by definition the preserve of the magnificent few, dramas in which most men played only supporting roles, roles they often felt compelled to perform by the chief protagonist, whether they wished it or not. The 'cheating', mighty oaths that guaranteed nothing, 'shouting', threats and pre-emptive attacks of cards were far more familiar in the mundane routines of masculinity. The game, though bounded, derived at least part of its comic force from its approximation to experience, to men's desires and fears.

'Playing cards' was shadowed by the complementary relation between the obscene pleasures of domination and the awful vision of what it really was to be mistillim. Men knew, had witnessed, participated in, enjoyed inflicting or suffered the wounds of defeat and the tense uncertainties of living out agonistic exchanges. It was no accident that those lowest in the social hierarchies were closely identified, by themselves as well as others, with the extreme forms of tahrij performance. Being 'ridden' by those in power and subjected to unbridled violation was an image of domination with which they had an affinity. In play they became masters of the performances of violation; in practice, they found themselves subjected. Their tahrij created a comic metaphor out of victory and defeat by making both 'unreal', and power itself a spectacle to be laughed at; it made them full players in the game of subordinating and penetrating those who have no recourse; and it was a frame within which they acted out with a particular clarity and force the fundamental social relations in which they are compelled to live. Laughter laughs at terror.

Senior men preserved a certain distance from the boisterous vulgarity of play. Men of standing in the community tended either not to play at all when in their mature years, or left the game indulgently to their dependants and juniors, or played decorously with moderated badinage and insult. It was not thought appropriate for them to accede to the principle that rank and place in the world are abandoned on the floor. One agha who spent most of his time in Tripoli, a leading figure in his family with an important role in the 1958 revolt and a reputation as a qabaday, expressly forbade joking and tahrij when playing. Cards, he insisted, were to be treated in accord with the maintenance of all the rituals of hierarchy and respect.

Those men of higher status who were willing to play without tahrij seemed to use the game partly to set up a frame within which they could socialize with members of other groups with whom they had or wished to establish some relations of social exchange or political alliance. The ra'is baladiya, for example, used to play with another senior member of the council from a fellah family. Mockery was kept low-key. They got together on occasional afternoons, not in the relative privacy of evening sessions, outside a shop in a public space up in the fellah quarter of the village where they could maintain a key relationship at a visible level of easy familiarity. A casual, shifting audience of one or two or half a dozen might sit around to chat, offer each other tobacco tins from which to roll a cigarette, raise issues that just might need the council's attention without having to make any formal representation. Any passer-by would offer greetings to those sitting to be returned with the appropriate degree of warmth. Such sessions kept the ra'is informed and enabled him to speak as if on equal terms with the fellahin. Card games were important for the maintenance of his village networks and showed he could be 'humble'.

Those who had largely moved from the public arena into old age played two-handed card games together, passing the time, grumbling, making tart observations on mutual failings and unflattering reminiscences of past inadequacies, often goaded on by mischievous grandsons for whom the mocking cackles and discomfited mutterings of the khityariya (the aged) were a source of amusement. The old men played during the day; they had little to do and would not play at saharas with the shebab, for no one would feel able to indulge in the insulting and tahrij with such elders. For them too, playing cards has its own rituals. Each player puts on his black headdress for the purpose (see Plate 9). Increasingly marginalized through age, they played formal, but inconsequential games.

Teenagers and children watching the game learnt what it was to be in an arena, and some of them learnt much more and much faster than others. For the younger shebab, not yet commanding independent resources in the world, and still uncertain of identity, the game was a bounded space where they could show themselves off, rehearse challenge behaviour, score points, achieve victories and in defeat demonstrate self-control when others were trying their best to break it. The permitted excesses suited their social position and trained them in the forms of confrontation and simulated confrontation. And all was ephemeral. There were no narratives about card games. They vanished with the evening. That was a lesson too.

CHAPTER THIRTEEN

The Perils of Display

... whereas at the level of the subject the appearance deceives precisely by pretending to deceive – by feigning that there is something to be concealed. It conceals the fact that there is nothing to conceal ... it deceives by pretending to deceive ... like the Jew in the Freudian joke ... who reproaches his friend: 'Why are you telling me that you are going to Cracow and not to Lemberg, when you're really going to Cracow?'[1]

The seriousness of play and being able to play in the ways I have described were fundamental in daily life. One's capacity to present oneself as angry, competent, intending something, uncalculating, in control, was an essential part of narratives. Men spoke of how they 'made themselves out to be' in part from a strategic or tactical need to establish themselves in the eyes of others as knowing the ways of achieving their purposes. But they did so in part too because that was how men spoke of themselves. It was an essential trope in the rhetoric of personhood and agency, not least in a man's self-persuasion and self-perception, and, quite frequently in the judgement of others, his self-deception.

Thus those who were marginal and of low status might speak of themselves as 'really' having such a capacity, though no one else realized it. They only appeared to be unknowing, unseeing, insignificant, as befitted their social position – but that was a ruse which enabled them to outwit the dominant while gaining credit for behaving correctly in the eyes of the superior. At the very least the subordinate might perceive himself as hiding his 'true' self and thoughts from the one who falsely thought he could 'look into' and violate him at will.

The presentation of self as an actor who produces events in the lives of others was a basic element in the way men narrated social identity, virtue and excellence. My question is whether the telling of such stories did not witness to the integration of the subordinated into the discourses of power and the agonism of male social relations, though laughter and irony might modify an individual's or group's self-conception to a significant degree.

The complementary risk was that such performances would be either publicly or privately challenged. Putting on a show often required collaboration in a specific act or pattern of deception; any such presentation of self might then be discreditably classified as lying (kizb), boasting (fashr), or showing off, tafnis, and thus adversely affect a man's standing and reputation. Performing in its various modes and senses was a permanent feature and subject of talk and evaluation. Since people used these terms of their own and others' behaviour, and that use was as much part of my enquiry as understanding the varying kinds of behaviour for which the terms may be taken to be appropriate, much semantic overlap and frequent ambiguity confronted any attempt at understanding these ways of creating and realizing social forms.

Play and Display

This self-consciousness about modes of performance finds expression in the word 'tamthiliya'. The term means theatrical performance, display, histrionics, and can be used negatively to discredit someone as 'nothing more than' a *mumaththil*, an actor. Or it might be employed positively in evaluating a skilful manipulation of a situation to create an outcome where the emphasis was typically placed on the instrumental aspect, the achievement of a goal through the playing of a part.

In a less instrumental mode there were one or two boys in their early teens who had shown skill as mimics and who were called on to stage comic scenes for their elders on occasions of *farah* (joy, pleasure) such as weddings, the return of someone from hospital or celebrations of the birth of a son. At some point outside the main festivities, when only the more immediate family were present and the atmosphere was less formal, the boys were cajoled, willingly, into presenting their tamthiliya, here very much in its sense of 'a play'. They rehearsed together and produced often sharply observed vignettes of stereotypical encounters between a pompous lord and a wily peasant, an incompetent barber and a terrified customer, or a parody of cowboy life taken from some television film, for example, or broadly suggestive scenes between a doctor and a woman patient.

The world acted by these as yet socially immature boys who were not quite ready to be reckoned as part of the shebab, was always comic. It was appropriate for them to be 'players' since they did not count and were in the process of becoming rather than having the realized form of the mature man. They no longer played as children do. They had passed the phase of being indulged and had become rigorously subordinated in the patriarchal family, kissing the hands of their elder brothers, serving not speaking. For the moment they were not recognized as having anything 'serious' to say and from that position could play the world as if without intent, goal or any purpose other than inviting laughter for its own sake.

'Tamthiliya' used to classify the behaviour of adult men was a different matter. It was always presented as part of a project which might need a fair degree of continuing collaboration by others in order to achieve a goal or to initiate, even to sustain, a key relationship. Men who involved themselves in tamthiliya had to be willing to play along. They needed an ability to 'read' the options and the improvisatory capacity to react to the shifting requirements of the social interaction being performed. A man had to know how to use language: *Lazim biya'rif yahki*, he must know how to speak. In this context haki, talk or speech, was employed to mean effective words and not 'empty gabble' as it may be understood in other settings. To say of someone that 'he does not know how to speak' might be taken as merely a factual observation; some men did not know how to employ the style, and observation of reactions, that would sway others.

The particular notion of speaking and performance conveyed by tamthiliya was closely associated with a weak or ambiguous social position. In the rhetoric of honour and place it was not proper for a man to be thought to need to 'play' in this manner. For those who have little more than their wits to live on the ability to operate in this mode may be a vital element in their battle for social survival.

Abu Abduh's Hajj

In this battle Abu Abduh was an old campaigner.[2] Outlaw, servant, and discredited son of the great hero of his agha house, he had become a virtuoso of dramatic performance, a connoisseur of those aspects of others' characters upon which he could attempt to play in order to maintain and, if possible, improve his severely constrained place in the world. At his level, even the smallest gain might make a difference, and ingratiation was a necessity of which he was fully, and cynically, aware.

Hobbled by his outlaw status, and heavily dependent on his bey for the always delayed implementation of the promise to intervene with the courts and other powerful men for pardon, he was always looking out for some opportunity to make himself less totally subject to the lord's pleasure. One means was the cultivation of his paternal cousin, the mayor (his grandfather's brother's grandson). The latter was also a neighbour, his house only fifty metres or so away from Abu Abduh's one-room dwelling, and he was a regular visitor in the mayor's manzul. Occasionally, some opportunity for gain was put his way, and while I was there the mayor arranged for Abu Abduh to be entrusted with the guardianship of an olive grove in the hills across from the village. It had been bought from one of the beys by an outsider, part of that movement into the region by entrepreneurs which was becoming evident at the period. This man, who was known as hajj as he had made the Muslim pilgrimage, was a businessman from Tripoli who presumably thought that his contact with the ra'is al baladiya was as reasonable a guarantee of local support and protection against thieving as he could get.

He had not been told, of course, of his new guardian's rather particular qualifications for the job; these included knowing every trick in the book when it came to cheating on measures; harvesting secretly; breaking agreements; procrastinating on deliveries; fixing his own private sales months ahead of the harvest to obtain ready cash, and appointing nightwatchmen who were chosen because he regarded them as either too stupid or having too much of a shared interest to cheat him in turn, but certainly not for their vigilance on the owner's behalf (as an outlaw he dare not spend the hours of darkness in the grove lest someone inform on him and the gendarmerie arrive).

Abu Abduh appeared to his new boss as a model of etiquette and deference in his 'awatif, those elaborate phrasings of etiquette so characteristic of formal meetings. But he also presented himself as a man of some account in the dai'a: 'he had his markaz, his own place in the world, by the grace of God he did!' As time went by, the outsider, who became ironically known as 'the hajj of Abu Abduh', in tribute to his being the unknowing dupe and instrument of the outlaw, seemed delighted with his respectful overseer. The powerful was mistillim, in the power of the weak and, without realizing it, a perfect joke situation. All of Abu Abduh's associates were elaborately briefed on what to say and how to behave to sustain his illusion of respectability and reliability. The plot was simple enough for me to be a participant, and a valuable one too, for the appearance of a European greeting his worthy and trusted friend and engaging in elaborate mutual politesse was both surprising, given that one rarely saw Europeans or foreigners in Akkar at all, never mind as residents, and a gratifying additional guarantee of what a good relationship the mayor had brokered. When Abu Abduh and I met, apparently by chance, though in fact after careful rehearsal in which I was instructed exactly how to react and what to say and at a moment timed to coincide with the hajj's arrival, we would embrace and kiss on both cheeks as if we had known each other for years and were intimately acquainted. To the businessman hajj, who was treating me as an equal and a man no doubt of some status in his home country, this seemed to afford considerable satisfaction. Then one or two younger cousins would go into elaborate paeans of complimentary rhetoric to the owner, hailing him as a father to those fortunate enough to be associated with him. To the more educated city entrepreneur such language must have had an archaic sound, being full of flowery phrases, saturated in marks of deference and hierarchy, and spoken in what to a man such as the hajj would have been the characteristic 'heavy' rural accent of the 'backward' Akkari villagers. Indeed, he would comment to me about the underdeveloped nature of the area and the village in front of the others and how uneducated they were. I would assume that this actually made it difficult for him to perceive any ironic intent, since it would not be at all easy to get beyond the steam of rhetorical utterance to judge intention, patterns of cueing and forms of performance.

My role, impressively anomalous as I have indicated, was to sit with appropriate dignity and murmur endorsements of the sincerity and worth of village people, together with what other felicitous inspirations should come to me at that moment. I authenticated what was said, as if from the different world of the English academic and as if speaking the hajj's language. Privately I was being educated into the practices of performance and deception in such a way as to be of the greatest use to others while not apparently compromising my position as 'truth-teller'. There was also that flattering identification with the people I was studying against those with whom I might in other circumstances be identified; it was a satisfying mark of some level of incorporation and diminished in my own eyes for a moment the ambiguities of my position. And there is no doubt, either, that I had a hostility which was as much personal as political to those who were taking over part of the olive and citrus areas of Akkar and bringing in Alawi day labour to replace local workers. I too, I told myself, wished to absorb outsiders into the benefit of the village and for the private welfare of Abu Abduh who had succeeded in making me an accomplice. My participation was part of our relationship. For he offered information, insight and a commentary that seemed to my anxious ears to unlock the realities of intention behind the appearances. I could make return by becoming an actor in his tamthiliya. The pleasure of a play on my own identity and role both came from and gave me an ephemeral sense of being in control of a situation that depended on what I would call 'righteous fraud'. It was fun.

Further tamthiliya, as everyone referred to these encounters, were put over on the hajj in the months that followed. Of course, each performance might follow exactly the same lines as all the others in terms of roles, turn-taking, complimentary etiquette and so forth. Yet each time there was always some risk that a clumsy or incapable, or malicious, performer might threaten the long-term project. Furthermore, Abu Abduh had to exercise a constant vigilance over the nuances of our meetings with the hajj, for in mobilizing his fellow actors he had made himself dependent on them. They might tire of the collaboration, mischievously threaten him with their withdrawal, or in some way use his use of them to exact a return he was unable to give. So the outlaw took care to keep up a stream of small services – invitations to smoke a nargileh with him, eat a simple meal, drink tea, or more generally supporting his allies in tamthiliya whenever they too had some project – while monitoring their (I should perhaps say 'our') behaviour with the hajj.

Abu Abduh issued a furious denunciation of one of the thicker of the shebab whose sense of social nuance was notoriously ill-developed. This fool – Abu Abduh's word – had come along to the olive grove one day and said that he had something to talk over with the hajj and that it was none of Abu Abduh's business. He had not used all the 'awatif so scripted for the shebab who had anything to do with the relationship and had simply tried to exclude the outlaw from the mysterious matter at hand. The precariousness of Abu Abduh's position made him almost morbidly anxious about any lapse in conduct which might imperil this precious relationship and source of income.

He saw it as essential that there be no deviation from the framework and performance which he had constructed around a constant demonstration of ihtiram, respect, for him before the hajj. And he was only too aware that others in the descent group, whatever their protestations and sense of his maslaha, might sabotage his link with the hajj out of spite (*jakara fih*) and malice aforethought. So he made a great show of lecturing the offender and of telling others of the ham-handedness of this buffoon who had spoilt the scene with his patron. It was important to him to mobilize support to neutralize the effect of this threatening intervention both by putting pressure on the disobliging fellow actor, and by maintaining others' cooperation in fooling the owner of the grove.

Spoiling the Show

Anyone who cannot play in this arena is potentially disruptive. There were many who were slow on the uptake and simply not reliable for whatever reason. It was inevitable that I should be such a one and that the role of unwitting spoiler not infrequently fell to me, whenever my ignorance of local relations inhibited my use of the requisite acting skills, supposing that I possessed them. In fact, my participation could and did introduce unexpected elements into a tamthiliya already demanding considerable collective co-operation in staging and 'bringing off'.

I am chagrined to recall my misreading of a drama involving a sickbed. A very senior man of the aghas, a famous hunter, sent word that he was ill, and I at once hurried to his house to make the *ziyara*, formal visit, that is the correct form on these occasions. Each visitor bears witness to the validity and significance of the network of relations and the kinds of people who make it their business to assist are public markers of the social standing of the sick person. Word is sent out by any family with pretensions to status. Sickness is important news, *khabr*, and one can of course tell a great deal about the state of relations and hierarchy by seeing who does not come to the house (and who later claims if pressed '*wallahi ma 'indi khabr*', 'truly I had no news of it'), or sends only a junior male, or visits in person. This is a public setting and visitors are expected to dress formally as in the case of a man of importance the whole hierarchy of the family is present and it is quite likely that others from outside the village will arrive if word has travelled fast. The sick notable was guaranteeing my presence since in his case the news arriving with a young child often employed on such occasions, acted like a summons.

All the notables of the more closely related family groups were present as expected. The sick man – a formidable and assertive figure of the classical hunter-murafiq type with a domineering manner, staccato and harsh vocal delivery and emphatic gesture – was propped up in bed. He was regaling the audience with narratives about the times when he had been wounded in fights down on the plain disputing landownership on behalf of the bey. A bullet had struck him here (showing all of us the scar), and he had not so much as murmured. A knife had been jabbed into him here (another scar) in a different fight. He had made not a sound. But now, this illness and this pain, he could not help groaning aloud. Which he did. Never before in his life had he moaned with pain, but he did so now. This confession of weakness, quite startling in him and contrary to all his public performance, testified to the extreme and unusual nature of the moment. His evocation of his own heroic past raised the event of the sudden affliction beyond the level of the ordinary and rhetorically compelled participants to deferential acknowledgement of his condition. The notables in the audience murmured consoling words, reflected on the bitterness of life, occasionally invoked the name of God, and framed his complaint with a chorus of proverb, truism, and conventional saying. The younger men were attentive and completely silent, only busying themselves with serving tea or coffee and handing round cigarettes. Visitors came, sat for varying periods of time, and left. The names of others were mentioned, and it was explained that they were, for the moment, out of the village but that their wives had sent word using one of the small children that the husband would be told as soon as he returned. It was as though men were being enrolled into the scene, and it was quite clearly not one in which alternative modes of address or behaviour were available as the notable's definition of a crippling pain imposed tight constraints on what could be done or said.

He called my attention to his suffering, and I felt obliged to suggest going to the hospital in Tripoli where a doctor could examine him to find the cause of this acute abdominal discomfort. To me this seemed a logical proposal, and one of some urgency, but he resisted strongly, a fact which I unreflectively put down to villagers' reluctance to entrust themselves to hospitals or outside agencies in crises whether of health or otherwise. Other seniors joined in to persuade him, and it appeared that I was changing the frame of the occasion in a way that he did not seem to have anticipated. None the less, the appeal to medicine, specialized care, and to the importance of what the English ustaz suggested, won the argument.

'Going to Tripoli' meant organizing three or four cars, for this is an integral part of the collective occasion and it was appropriate for the notable to be accompanied by a convoy of men of the family. The 'patient', as he had now become, would only stay for some hours at the hospital and refused point blank to remain overnight. He had to be picked up later after observation, again in a convoy, and ceremoniously conveyed back to the dai'a.

When I had parked the car in which I had driven him, I went back to his house after a short interval as was expected. To my astonishment there was a great deal of laughter, behaviour totally excluded from the previous high seriousness of his agony. He remarked to me sardonically, and to much general amusement: '*Heik biddak ya ustaz Mikhail? Heik biddak?*' He had been entertaining the crowded manzul with the story of how the nurse had insisted on taking his temperature rectally. The comedy was relished; the great hunter face down with a thermometer up his arse, was the colloquial tone. Is that what you go to hospital for? '*Heik biddak ya ustaz?*' All of a sudden he seemed much better. I was pleased, amused and puzzled.

A day or two later the abrupt cessation of pain and the transformation of atmosphere were explained. The laughter had a double quality to it, or so I was instructed. Didn't I realize that the illness was a tamthiliya, said one of the family with a grin? The notable had had a row with his wife, much younger than he, and she was threatening to go off to her family. There were huge confrontations, of which I had known nothing, scandal loomed, and the old hunter had produced the illness in an attempt to neutralize his private crisis which was about to become known to a wider audience by staging a public one. He calculated, said my friends, that everyone important in the family would rally round and formalize the scene as one in which he would have full attention and be able to assert his position in the collective so as to pre-empt his wife's possible course of action. It would effectively bring closure, at least temporarily, to the domestic problems which threatened to become public. Other senior women would feel obliged to put pressure on the wife too. Certainly no one would be in a position to challenge him as to his illness, his position in the hierarchy guaranteed that.

The double play in the situation, making the tamthiliya into a joke form, was initiated by the break of frame unknowingly introduced by a performer who did not apprehend the true nature of the situation. The ustaz had, without realizing it, trapped the notable in his own scenario. The latter had not foreseen that the Englishman would 'literalize' the story; take it at 'face value' and in his own foreigner's frame of reference; make 'the illness' rather than the social configuration the sole focus of his attention; and would insist on medical treatment in the Tripoli hospital.

The rectal thermometer thus became a condensed comic image for the way in which the notable had been forced to 'take it up the arse', control of his own narrative being lost to him in ways he had not imagined. It showed the risks of enrolling someone who did not know the practices of social form well enough. The foreigner had taken him 'seriously', but in a foreign rather than a local mode, and the dominant figure was hoist on his own petard. The old hunter's own play on the social situation was subverted by another kind of playfulness created, not by the deliberate plan of another actor, but by a combination of circumstance which he had himself set in train by sending off the messenger to summon my presence. Since there was already a shadow comic dimension in the anomaly of one so well established in the hierarchy resorting to tamthiliya at all, and in the 'hero' doing what heroes do not do, namely drawing attention to his pain by comparison with wounds gained in fighting and emphasizing his vulnerability, the incident of the thermometer triggered a rich appreciation of the play of events.

These two anecdotes, of the hajj and the hunter, point to the hazards in the mobilization and control that tamthiliya presents to men at opposite ends of the scale of family hierarchy. They also indicate the kinds of pressure upon performance that is asserted in the community. Others are required to play certain roles by the protagonist, who disposes of different means of incorporating them with greater or lesser certainty into the design. He may do so by an overt appeal, as with Abu Abduh who has to arrange and rehearse his fellow actors, anxiously hoping that he can rely on their collaboration because of his past demonstrated assistance in their schemes and an assumption of willingness to go along with them in the future. Or he may be in a position to rally support on far less uncertain grounds and conceal the 'real' significance of the scene which is being played out. The hunter can compel participation and tacit collaboration that needs no rehearsing (indeed some may remain unaware of the ulterior purpose altogether and take the 'sickness' to be perfectly genuine, as I did). Either way there is an element of persuasion, of obligation, even of force, involved. Demands are placed on others for what may be a relatively long period of time, not least on their skills in performance and sense of appropriateness.

Playing at being serious is a serious business. Real interests are at stake. Men are reflexively engaged, for the tamthiliya becomes a metalanguage, commenting on and modifying the practices of what it is to be in relations with others. In the case of Abu Abduh, the scenes with his hajj became in turn a subject of talk. They were comically re-enacted for the benefit of others who were to be brought in on the joke as second-order accomplices. He played out his role in sahras as the joker who could, in a particular setting and circumstances, use dissimulation to take power over the more powerful, a role which itself witnessed to the insecurity of his place and his need to have others 'go along' with him.

My own experiences of being drawn in, wittingly and unwittingly, illuminated the demands routinely made on people to interpret settings and scenes, and spontaneously to find the right mode of response, a considerable test of social perception. My social innocence and ambiguous reputation for telling the truth, due to a limited command of the skills required for elaboration, artifice and swift reading of possible scenes and evolutions of plot, meant that I might easily give the game away, either because of clumsiness or because I had not even realized that there was a game. 'Hatgarrasna ya ustaz?', 'are you going to compromise us sir?', I would be asked. And compromising someone by knowingly or otherwise exposing what they have said as kizb or as a stratagem is dangerous. It is something people fear. To unveil someone's secret (garras) or the shameful truth of a particular design might have profoundly serious implications for status and social relations. So behind the lightness of tone there was a real concern, and a drawing of my attention to the fact that 'face' and more might be involved in even the apparently least significant moment. Thus it was a serious lesson on social interaction when a friend exclaimed, in only half-mock exasperation, after my truth-telling in a situation which all his confederates had instantly understood depended on kizb for its proper realization: 'How long have you been here? A year? Listen everybody, he's been here a year and he still doesn't know how to lie!' Someone who cannot 'play' may make others lose control, subvert their performances, transgress their sense of the possible and make the calculation of risk even more fine a question.

Compromise was not the only possibility. My position might also become a resource to be used in a performance both serious and comic. I might present, at a given moment and for anyone quick enough to grasp it on the wing, a golden opportunity to display an unexpected mastery of situations through spontaneous seizing of control from those apparently possessing it, subverting and reversing roles.

Two incidents soon after my arrival demonstrate the form that such ephemeral but real refashionings of power might take. They also illustrate the impromptu brilliance necessary to 'bring it off', the capacity so much admired and so crucial for anticipating the challenges that might arise in everyday life.

On my arrival there was a certain competition to be associated with a stranger who by that position, mode of introduction and what was understood of his background might constitute some kind of social asset as well as whatever more personal interest might develop out of his curious and ill-defined role. It was appropriate for the sons of men of the aghas to act as quasi-attendants on me, subordinate and respectful but of course knowing the way things were in ways far beyond my ken. Since you do not often meet social innocence of that degree in north Lebanon the pleasure was spiced with this even rarer experience.

Some days after my entry into the village one of the sons of the old bey, whose family lived mostly in Beirut and Tripoli but would spend time in the dai'a in the spring and summer or during elections, invited me on a kazzura (an outing, an enjoyable trip purely for the pleasure of it). He proposed a drive to Bsherri, place of the few remaining cedars of Lebanon high in the mountain due east of Tripoli. As a tourist resort this was completely outside the social range of the shebab who could never afford such visits and did not conceive them as part of their possible life chances. They were totally out of place there except as drivers or waiting on one of the beys. The young bey fancied the trip; I had a car while he did not, and he could use me and the occasion to show off in front of the village lads and emphasize a privileged relationship between the privileged. Or so he thought.

As we drove past the mosque and the great tree over the spring at the entrance to the social space of Berqayl we were spotted by those sitting around the little shop at the roadside where there was always a group of the agha young men idling away time and watching the world go by, something my passenger had counted on. He had not counted on one of them swiftly

The Beirut workplace, after a 14-hour day laying the new airport runway. At any given time some 18 or so workers might be involved. The worker, centre, has a finger bandaged after losing a joint in an accident. The one sitting on the right has had time to change into his best shirt to go to town.

ABOVE. The hunter and his dog in the Jurd. An old murafiq of the beys
and known as a great hunter.

BELOW. A leader of the young men, boss of the Beirut airport work group. We were having
a picnic beneath the poine trees. The man on the right is about to pour the coffee.

The leading notable of the aghas, owner of a large farm on the plain. Sitting in a room newly built for a young married couple whose marriage he had arranged.

The point of the story. Abu Asad at the climax of a tale. He and his first cousin on his right had spent 20 years as tractor and harvester drivers on the Saviers estate. He was now an orphan, living in the market-place, but light-hearted, still...

Examining the new rifle, the most expensive in the village. The old murafiq at the back has put on his formal clothes for the visit to admire the weapon and show his attachment to its owner, the Beirut work boss centre. Children, as always, are taking it all in. The gun was dismantled and inspected many times as visitors arrived.

A group of young members of the ... all of whom had emigrated to Kuwait. The mayor centre front row in tie

Abu Walid placing his revolver in his only son's hands for a photograph. Having just posed with the gun he insisted on a photo of his son with it. His old father's stone built house is behind them.

ABOVE. On seeing that I was about to photograph Abu Asad, who had invited me to eat meat at his house that morning, his sons and their first cousins immediately grabbed whatever weapons they could find with which to strike a pose. The invitation, a costly one given his extreme poverty, was part of our pattern of reciprocity and indicated his wishing to honour a visitor who in turn behaved to him with courtesy when he might not have anticipated it, and showed concern for the health of his children.

BELOW. The author smoking the *nargileh* at a formal invitation by an Agha family.

leaping into the road and stopping us: 'Where are you off to *insha'allah*?' Had
I been there longer I might have lied and evaded the question in any of the
standard ways which would have been conventionally used by anyone to fob
off such an enquiry. The bey tried to do so, but my naive truth-telling gave
the real answer that we were off to the mountain. In a flash the young man
was in the back seat of my battered VW Beetle, grinning all over his face and
announcing his undying enthusiasm for our company, the honour it would
be, and his duty to accompany me. My host said, and it was an acknowledgement of defeat had I but realized it at the time: *'Hatigi ma'na ya 'Abdo?'* ('Are
you coming with us then Abdo?'). The answer was that he would go anywhere
with the ustaz Mikhail and Mustapha Bey, follow us wherever he might be
at our service. These replies came with vast sanctimonious enthusiasm as he
lauded the bey to the skies in all the fitting 'awatif of subordination, but in
what to me was such an overblown way that even I felt nervous at the
transparent play of it all. Compliments flowed as the grin grew wider and he
kept up a stream of talk all the way.

At the restaurant to which we went in the beautiful resort of Bsherri
visited by wealthy Lebanese, the bey who had invited me to lunch did the
social equivalent of exposing his Queen at chess. As I looked at the menu
and admired the dramatic view over the mountains, he advised me to take
half a chicken and a dish of aubergine (*nusf farrug wa sahn bitinjan*). Abdo fell
on this opening with ruthless speed. 'What!? This was a lord's invitation? Of
course ustaz Mikhail should eat this dish and that and the other. The table
should be covered in dishes. Did not Arab, and especially lords', invitations
know no bounds?' Classical virtues were invoked, imagery of the table and
the sacred link of guest and host swamped the bey who almost visibly
drowned in the rhetorical tide. The table was duly covered with food,
demolished with particular enthusiasm by Abdo, and the bill was obviously
many times more than half a chicken and a dish of aubergine would have
cost. I enjoyed this all the more as some inkling of what might be going on
dawned on me.

All the way back the defeated bey was subjected to recitals of the glories
of his house, his own qualities as sheikh ash-shebab and Hatim Tayy, a
legendary figure of generosity. I was given the most outrageously complicitous
smile in the driving mirror. Game, set and match to the village boys.

In the days that followed Abdo told the story in sahras and wherever he
could and 'nusf farrug wa sahn bitinjan' became an instant catch phrase for
miserliness. The delights were many. First, he had hijacked the whole trip in
front of the very audience (myself) before whom the bey thought that he
would be the one to parade his rank. The latter was thus hoist on his own
petard. Abdo finessed the fannas (the show off) and did so as a member of
a group of a lower social status, the aghas, whose champion he made himself.
Secondly, his use of language and social manipulation were infinitely superior
to that of his supposed superior. Sitting 'in the back seat' he actually

conducted the whole trip. Every compliment was hollow, yet just so calculated as to be unchallengeable, at least by the unskilled victim who had so disastrously misread the possibilities of the situation. Abdo employed the 'awatif and rhetoric of hierarchy as his instrument in the control of the bey, making it very difficult for the latter to operate and yet giving him no obvious means of calling the miscreant to account as he was on the surface saying all the right things. That included complimenting me, which further restricted the lord's freedom to respond since everything was taking place before the stranger. Thirdly, he could play on the codes of generosity and the invitation with virtuoso ease. He was entitled to join us, as it would be incorrect to refuse him once we had said where we were going and that it was an 'azima (invitation) to me. Abdo would be there as my attendant and companion. Moreover, he acted as the very mouthpiece of the great Arab tradition of generosity and feasting, specifically discomfiting the host with his evocations of transcendental virtues of Hatim Tayy and days of glory. None of this could be denied.

The bey was compelled to fulfil the conditions of Abdo's verbal performance that followed on the uttering of the fatal phrase 'nusf farrug ...'. The bakhil (miser) was forced to act as if he were prodigally open-handed, having condemned himself out of his own mouth. Abdo, out of his own social setting but not out of his social depth among the Lebanese bourgeoisie and tourists, had the wit to play also on the code of the 'Western' invitation: the menu, from which a few dishes are carefully chosen, the privacy of host and guest. This was all exhuberantly subverted in the name of the imperatives of Arab ways and a true invitation.

In every department therefore he was the winner. He had picked his victim unerringly, because there were a couple of the lord's sons with whom he would probably never have tried it on so blatantly. I was a perfect stooge and witness all in one, and of course was integral to the whole operation. So Abdo appeared as in a special relation to me, as guardian and educator of the Englishman who was to be especially linked to his descent group and prised from the clutches of the beys who felt that he naturally belonged with and to them. My innocence was the ideal foil, as my vindication of his account was the perfect guarantee of truth. Had I been displeased and willing to show it there would have been difficulties but I clearly gave enough behavioural clues on the drive to show that I really had no objections at all.

This same young man had accompanied me to Tripoli in my VW a week or two previously. Not knowing the city I headed off in the wrong direction on one of the boulevards and executed a quick U-turn on Abdo's directions. There was an immediate and imperious sound of a police whistle. A young constable came over in full uniform and utterly in control of the situation. He began to note the infraction and assert his function as agent of the law. Abdo jumped from the car and gave him a lecture on the importance of tourism to the country, the Prime Minister's own orders that visitors were to be welcomed and treated with the maximum helpfulness since they did so much for the Lebanese economy. Here was an Englishman, a university person to boot, being treated in a way that defied the rules of hospitality and the state (I do not remember if God was invoked but I do not think so). Moreover, *'ihna min Berqayl'*, 'we are from Berqayl', a large and important village, so the 'tourist' was suddenly revealed as part of a local universe of relations in some unimaginable way. The constable, by now looking battered and uneasy, tried to insist on my infraction and his duty as he was threatened with loss of face in public and taken by surprise by the torrent of words, adjurations and rhetorical questions from a younger man with no official standing whatsoever. He would continue. At that point Abdo said peremptorily, as if fully in control of the situation: *'Ar-raqm ma'ruf. Wein az-zabit?'* ('We know your number. Where is the officer?'). His dismissive look at the number on the policeman's epaulettes, and obvious willingness to continue this outraged performance to an officer who might well find the spectacle of a foreign visitor with who knows what position or links, was sufficient to crush resistance. We drove off, I bemused and Abdo exultant.

The incident immediately became a story in which one of 'us' (of Berqayl, of Beit Abd as-Salam) turned the tables on one of 'them' (the city, the state). The man in uniform was challenged on his own ground in response to his challenge based on his official functions, and he was routed. Speed of reaction, an instant assessment of the disposition of resources, was used to surprise the other in his own over-confident deployment of authority by someone apparently in an inferior position (a parallel with the previous story of the invitation). We were in the town, the *balad*, and yet could invoke the weight of the village, the dai'a, against the representative of the central power, and win. The name of Berqayl could be introduced to show the officer he had completely misconceived the context and implications of what he was doing. The revelation that I was English and at an English university was a further blow, as he must have assumed the driver in the car with Lebanese number plates was local, my moustache and short hair and general build not being obviously 'foreign'. He had misread both actors and situation. Abdo's employment of his own police number and the threat against him of his own higher authority was the final coup. Narratively speaking, it played the epigrammatic, clinching role of 'nusf farrug' and was often used later to invoke the entire scene.

The fact that the constable was acting quite correctly and on his turf made the victory one even more to be relished. The encounter was essentially between two persons who did not know anything about each other outside the frame of the face-off. One of them was able to introduce elements which moderated the apparent frame of the action in ways quite unanticipated by the other. The third figure turned out to be English and not what he seemed to be – Akkari – as well as being classified as representing a category of privileged stranger (foreign tourist). Abdo played with the rules and overthrew the one who thought he was the master of the moment. The challenge was thrown back on the challenger; the initiative and advantage seemingly with the policeman was snatched from him by rhetorical adroitness.

Both incidents pivot on the capture of a situation from the actor who presumes himself to have the power to define its nature and appropriate course (in which case it would become a 'story'), very much as in honour stories. The hero of the stories, also usually their narrator to audiences from his own agha group, plays with the language of the other who knows or fancies that he knows himself to be in the superordinate position. Abdo was not like the great sheikh qabaday in his *murajil* (show of manliness) performances, with a reputation and a large force behind him. He was at this time one of a small set of brothers, the fourth of them and therefore very junior, living on his wits as much as anything for he had left school but had no training and only very intermittent work. What he did have was a devastating sense of timing and rhetoric, sharpened in the day-to-day encounters of which, after all, these stories are only two. He made one situation, the invitation, into a test of wit and nerve; the other was thrust upon him and he converted potential embarrassment, for if I had had trouble with the policeman he would certainly have been described as being at fault back home by his shebab rivals happy to discredit him, into a different kind of reversal of authority.

In both sequences there were other possible outcomes. Abdo had summed up the young lord correctly and I have suggested that he probably would have been shrewd enough to avoid those of the old bey's sons who were quite sufficiently mal'un (cunning) to put him in his place. The policeman might have been more flexible, or well connected, or simply brutal. Many of the other young men of the village would have been capable neither of the first response nor of the dexterity and temerity required had they blundered into a confrontation. A lightning fast appreciation of the potentialities of a situation, a refusal to accept the apparently dominant hierarchical framing of a situation as given, and a capacity to 'turn' an encounter into an event by mastery of performance alone – all these qualities were on show in the two episodes. That 'nusf farrug wa sahn bitingan' and 'ar-raqm ma'ruf' became catch-phrases, repeated with enormous relish and laughter and used as condensed evocations of these comic triumphs, testified to the more general significance of Abdo's brilliant seizure of the moment.[3]

Compulsion and Performance

Tafnis is a counter in the rhetoric and calculation of power and show, obligatory as much as idiosyncratic in the cynical view of many. Men viewed 'it' in resignation or delight or both, as an inevitable part of their lives and the world in which they moved, of the style of things. A man has to stand out. He must shine, dazzle, glitter. To sink into the background is to be anonymized, reduced to nothing, to be someone who has no weight and who will not be able to further *maslahtu*, his interest. Inevitably in such a context, the idea of mere showing off rather than demonstrating the reality of one's social identity becomes crucial. Fannas is a word used rhetorically to assert that such-and-such a person is one who is only putting on appearances; or as one who, even if he has rizq and a beit behind him, is still not truly the man of real weight and markaz or social station he affects to be. So the same behaviour a man adopts to show that he is not *hayyin*, easy, or *khafif*, light, may be adduced by rivals to 'prove' the opposite. Supporters and allies will, of course, assert his authenticity and deny the charge. Those among the poor labourers and cultivators upon whom social insignificance is imposed in the hierarchy of status honour are also, of course, likely among themselves to denounce the beys and aghas lock, stock and barrel for their lies and showing off, insisting that kizb and tafnis are the true reality of all the performance of the 'higher' groups.

The 'show' of personal distinction was often spoken of, and I think experienced, as being a double burden. On the one hand, men routinely complained that they were 'forced' to act that way in the village 'to live'; and on the other hand, as a complement to this idea of compulsion, that they could easily be trapped within their own tafnis so that even while knowing that the 'reality' was otherwise they would feel obliged to act 'as if' it were as they proclaimed. In so doing they would inevitably fail, victims of their own performances and show. Double burden, double bind.

'Are we going to sit here and just fannas to one another?' one of the agha young men exploded in exasperation at a sahra when the others, in a boastful discussion, were comparing the social and political weight of the daiʻa to that of the new President Franjieh's home town of Zghorta in a neighbouring northern district. The speaker issued a furious call to realism and proportion, warning of the dangers of empty talk, self-deception and the collective illusion that was being proclaimed. Zghorta was now manifestly predominant, he argued. The village could not begin to compare with it. The talk was all meaningless bravado. Why did people feel obliged to pretend otherwise?

His point, I think, was crucially bound up with the fact that the gathering was entirely one of members of the same beit, kinsmen who knew each other all too well. There was no need to act with the kind of self-aggrandizement and flourish that might be assumed in front of outsiders. No one could be fooled, and yet there was still a collective illusion being produced. Here they all were, trumpeting a manifestly false equality between Berqayl and Zghorta, an equality with no political, economic or social basis, and, moreover, an equality in which nobody in the room really believed.

Even the most experienced might be caught by their own mistaken judgement of a situation into asserting more than they could possibly deliver, thus being vulnerable to the deflating criticism of tafnis. Indeed, one important tactic of political competitors was to try to goad the opponent to just such a rash public display, to make them lose their control and over-commit themselves in an unthinking way (this has much in common with the play of jaqmara).

The leading political figure in the agha family at the time of the 1972 national elections was viewed by some as furnishing a classic example of this kind of self-induced failure by falling into the trap of tafnis (see Chapter 7). A candidate on the 'popular list', a member of the other major agha family now based mainly in Tripoli, had made an impassioned appeal to the leading notable on the grounds of healing 'family' divisions, a sacred theme. The notable was vulnerable to this charge. He was not supporting the candidate or the new, and in his view, dubious politics of the popular list which threatened the interests of beys with whom he had been long associated. Challenged in the highly charged language of shared descent and solidarity and under public pressure, the leading political figure of the aghas *ithammis*, that is he became 'fired up' by passion. Reacting to the competitive atmosphere in which men were outbidding each other in proclaiming their willingness to sacrifice for the beit, he went beyond all the others, and his capacities, by saying that he would be the first to join the cause 'and would bring fifty cars with him'. 'Fifty cars' in this context referred to the long cavalcade of vehicles sweeping around Akkar with the candidates, cavalcades which were expertly assessed for the make of car and the number of passengers and the money it must have cost the organizer – all indices of the degree of a candidate's public backing. So fifty cars represented a huge band of supporters, and an equally huge financial outlay.

This promise hung around the notable's neck like an albatross. For a whole series of reasons, of which more later, he was both unwilling and quite unable to muster such troops for a cause to which he was in any case fundamentally opposed. Opponents regularly reminded everyone of the 'promise', making sure that it was not forgotten as the giving of the notable's word. He had been rhetorically out-manoeuvred by the candidate, since he could hardly cite his links to the beys against the appeal to 'family' interest, and had lost control. He was driven into a proud assertion of what he would and could do, and made himself seem a fannas to those who sceptically assessed his political abilities faced with this new challenge. He lost prestige with the beit, since people felt he had made a serious error of judgement and had revealed a lack of adroitness in responding to someone who was in fact an opponent, though appealing to him as a member of the same group.

Opponents were always ready to take advantage of such a lapse into language that could not be made good in order to expose the emptiness of a man's words. During the same elections one man I knew well, from a poor section of the agha descent group, heard a couple of others, who backed a particular bey who had been a Parliamentarian for some years, cursing his preferred (bey) candidate and saying they would 'close the village against him' (*sakkar ad-dai'a 'aleih*) and 'stamp on his neck' (*da'as 'a rabtu*). Such threats were conventional, formulaic expressions in the rhetoric of challenge. He decided to respond by taking it at face value and making it a 'serious' statement of intent rather than merely a conventional use of words with no real intention of realization. My friend staged a public scene. He invited the bey to a formal lunch, an *'azima rasmiyya*, together with most of the *kubbar*, or big men, of the aghas, sure of the latters' attendance since no one wished to slight either a potential winner or their kinsman (his father-in-law was the celebrated hunter of whom I have spoken, a man whose presence would compel that of others). As the guest of honour arrived his host fired off two full magazines of bullets from his revolver over the bey's head, traditional greeting of the highest public honour, thus making unambiguously clear to everyone that he was feasting the candidate in the most ceremonial of ways. People who did not already know would investigate the meaning of the ritual shots, and the whole village would be aware within minutes of what was going on, and against whom the display was directed. The other aghas who had so unguardedly spoken of the bey could do nothing whatever. Their tafnis discredited them, and made them less effective in the support of their candidate.

A scene of this kind was only an obvious example of the dialectics of how men showed themselves to others, and how they might be reflected back to themselves. The tissue of daily life was shot through with the colours of tamthiliya and tafnis. There were tiny, micro-events in which men found ways of drawing attention to themselves for an instant's gratification of the need they felt for acknowledgement of their particularity. A man wanted to borrow a set of prayer beads of unusually fine quality so that he could spend a couple of days running them through his fingers in front of others. Or he might try to get hold of the more recently available expensive (by local standards) cigarette lighters which were much in vogue and flash them around, making sure that people knew how much they cost.

I hung my corduroy jacket on a chair in my house one day, and one of the shebab put it on while I was out, and swaggered round the public space up near the cemetery. When I showed an uncomprehending exasperation, he explained simply: 'I have to do it to live here.' He had been demonstrating that he had a privileged relationship with the stranger by flamboyantly acting the peacock, and showing too that he had been able to outsmart any others who had the same ambition. Feeling by this time that I had had enough tafnis to last me a lifetime, I remarked with approval that his studious elder brother, who was the only one in the village training to be a teacher, did not indulge in all this nonsense. I was swiftly corrected: 'You think my brother isn't a fannas because he never sits outside the shop and doesn't talk much and people in the family think he is weak and sickly? You should see him at the top of the village [in the quarter of the fellahin], he's the biggest fannas in the whole village, talking about how he'll organize these and those votes and who's going to pass exams, etc. etc. Up there he makes himself the lord of the village (*rabb ad-dai'a kullha*). Watch him.'

The brother indeed picked his audience carefully, doing his number only among members of the fellahin among whom he could make a greater appeal with his learning than he could among his own agha group, where it counted for little. Though he represented an innovation in career in village terms, his style of behaviour was firmly within the local mode of showing oneself to be significant and standing out from the crowd. Unable to transform learning into social capital in his stratum – for there was no existing way of doing so – he found a way of making it operate among those for whom schooling was seen as a possible path to changing life chances, however modestly. As I began to observe him with the fellahin families I realized that his style of presentation was indistinguishable from that of anyone making claims about influence, importance, what he had already accomplished and the powerful men he could reach. His language was inflated and grandiose, his posture changed from that of the withdrawn and modest figure of his own quarter to an assertive, patronizingly smiling indulgence of those less gifted. The younger brother was quite correct.

The younger brother was also vastly amused, both by his sibling's transformation and by my naivety. Tafnis creates a highly spiced mixture of social drama and entertainment. It is not only that a man may suddenly turn to you, eyes alight with anticipated pleasure, and say 'khallina nefannis 'aleihim', 'let's go off and put on a show in front of them'. Off you go on whatever display he has decided to extemporize, hoping to make the audience 'eat it' and to have a story to tell maybe for a day or two. There is also the possibility that he will say 'khallih yefannis 'aleina', 'let him show off in front of us'. It has been a boring afternoon, perhaps, and this is at least a diversion. We'll go to the saha where our acquaintance is sitting and pretend to go along with all his bravado and claims to prominence with our enthusiasm and respectful interjection. We'll act the audience part, but actually be the controlling performers, without him knowing it. He will think he has us in the palm of his hand (yistilimna); we will know we have him in ours (istilim, to have control over, the whip hand, possess, is the most common word employed in these situations).

In this particular instance there was a very serious dimension to the joking. The person called a fannas was a man one of whose younger brothers had been killed by a paternal first cousin. The victim had for a long time been involved in robbery and various acts of violence, causing major problems to the aghas. He had threatened and extorted money from various beys who were linked to his relatives in estate administration and the organization of violence. He was said to be afraid of nothing, and thus to know no limits. He had all the qualities of the archetypal qabaday – brave, ready to take on anyone, tough and able to impose himself on others – but he was also unpredictable, and showed none of the sense of the collective good and interest which is so crucial to a career as an qabaday honoured and respected by his peers. Rather, he put the collectivity at risk. Instead of being a shield against danger, he involved his kin in situations of risk and potential loss. Living out the paradigm of 'the man who needs no one' in so literal a way he imperilled the social order.

Unsurprisingly, he had been classified as 'crazy' and 'makhlu'a', asocial. A formal peace had been guaranteed within the descent group by the victim's own father after the murder. He had said there should be no revenge, for his son was beyond the pale, he should not be reckoned as a proper member of society, and the beit should not be torn apart by a cycle of internal bloodshed.

Yet blood still called for blood in the minds of many, whatever the social fictions involved and the terrible dangers inherent above all in this kind of dispute. His death was seen as 'shameful' by some of the young men who briefly alluded to it in my company, though he had died before some of them had been born. And the narrative detail supplied by one teller that the dogs licked his blood as he lay in the road in the heart of 'our' quarter highlighted the shame and impiety. The image of the unclean animal drinking the blood of a man who had at least begun his life as a paragon of virtue and violence seemed to cause a deep sense of repugnance.

There was strict avoidance between the cousins, but for the older brother not to act was nonetheless a permanent unspoken diminution of his identity. The (what was taken to be) deliberately assumed 'silence' on the matter by the surviving youngest sibling seemed to some to be a mark of a serious intent and further highlighted the ambiguous reticence of the elder brother. This was the man who sat in front of the shop at the saha by the old mosque, gun ostentatiously on hip, holding forth about affairs, going on deputations to appropriate outside political figures, always treated with proper respect by agha notables, and generally being a paradigm of a man of value and place, *qima wa markaz*.

His tafnis was a desperately serious business, guaranteed complicitous support by kinsmen who deeply feared the possibility of savage disruption within the beit by a revenge killing. The murder, whatever the dangerous character of the dead man, had created a situation both personally dis-honouring and collectively embarrassing. Endorsement of the performance of virtue and manliness was intimately related to acute awareness of the precarious base upon which it rested since collective interest might still not prevent vengeance, whatever an aged father's words and everyone hoped. At the same time, the elder brother, caught in this trap, seemed, at least to some of the men of the descent group, to cross the fine line between the per-formance demanded of him and 'putting on a show'. He had become liable to the concealed mockery of those such as the man who urged me to join in the pleasures of letting someone lay it on for us without realizing that we did not take him seriously. So although the tafnis was in part created by a collective interest, a fundamental ambiguity persisted beneath the apparently playful diversion of our behaving as if we really took him for what he only seemed to be.

CHAPTER FOURTEEN

A Killing in the Street

Puffing up the Lord

Many people relished the mimetic dimension, playing a role for the pleasure of it. They used such playing as a reflexive commentary on their own and others' ways of being in the world. The detachment, irony and frequently comic realization of a part was central in the constitution of men's experience of everyday life.

What men were frequently giving, as I have already suggested, was a performance of a performance, or claiming that that was what someone else was doing. Interaction with the beys was a major arena of such demonstrations. Young agha shebab would provide hilarious parodies of how they had played on the appetite for deference, the vanity and self-image of a bey for their own aims. The elections of 1972 gave them the chance to demonstrate their skills by, for example, spouting exuberantly elaborated rhetoric in speeches of stupefying pomposity and canvassing support for him with virtuoso mock seriousness, while being vastly cynical about a would-be electoral candidate's illusions of his political chances.

There was a world of parodic, sceptical energy in such tamthiliya. Jihad and Ahmad told a sahra audience of their agha kinsmen with great delight of how, in a café in Tripoli in front of an audience of patrons, most of whom would recognize their victim, they had noisily drowned Nadim Bey in extravagant compliments of 'awatif and put on a huge display of tafnis. Nadim was a young lord known for his arrogance and patronizing manner of dealing with the aghas, the older of whom contrasted him most unfavourably with his predecessors to lament the passing of the 'good old days'. Moreover, he was related to the house of Abboud Bey and the duty of taking vengeance for Muhammad al Abboud lay on him. His swagger therefore related to an expectation never spoken of, but always shadowing his cultivated bravado. He had a brother who had received a university education in America and who was regarded as far more sophisticated. He occasionally visited Berqayl, where he was unfailingly polite to everyone, and did not participate to any real extent in local questions of politics, revenge and estate management. The two siblings thus formed a complementary couple of a kind I have mentioned above.

The lads reported that they had done everything to please the bey. He had been flattered beyond measure, encouraged to 'puff up' and to preen himself as they poured on the compliments (*nafash*, an often-used word referring to a bird puffing up its feathers, or to swelling someone up with pride by excessive praise). 'What wouldn't we do for him?! We'd shoot and strike (*qawis wa darab*), make speeches for him and only him. Was he not the sheikh ash-shebab, the acknowledged leader of all the fighting men of the region? Was not his branch of the beys the noblest of all? Were we not from Berqayl, capital of Akkar?' Wickedly accurate parodic imitations of his walk, lordly look and elaborately relaxed posture when seated produced huge mirth as the young men re-enacted the scene in all its grandiloquent rhetoric and expansive gestures.

All these conventional formulae of power and hierarchy were gleefully staged for us, and characterized as 'shouting' (*'iyat* from *'ayyat*, which really means yelling and raising up a storm of empty noise). The whole thing was kizb and tamthiliya, but how he had showed off! How he loved it! *And* it put them in his favour so that he would pay them to act as chauffeurs and 'mobilizers of opinion' at election time, because all candidates needed men to go around singing their praises in these terms. They were demonstrating what they could do, and in so doing were usurping the control of the bey even as they seemed to be deferring to him.

In their version the laugh was on the lord who carried out his own performance unaware that it was realized only through the kizb of his subordinates. They know that all *siyasa*, politics, is 'just show', nothing but 'talk' and lies. Why not out-perform those who take themselves for the leading actors? The shebab 'really' understand what is going on. In the comic narrative, they presented the ambitious young lord's appetite for tafnis as his source of weakness; it made him vulnerable, because a fannas, endlessly concerned with putting on his own spectacle, is ill-equipped to distinguish that of others. He blinds himself. Unable to see through their tafnis to the manipulation behind it, he could be used.

The Tripoli café was a suitable arena for the show, since it was a social space for men of different classes, many of whom would know the identity of the others; the élite of the social hierarchy, lawyers, officials, businessmen and politicos, would meet there, seeing and being seen. The two young villagers were alive to the nature of their urban audience, and they enthusiastically acted out what they presented as their triumph in the city. They were aware, too, that it had been gained by playing on urban expectations of how rural shebab behave in attendance on their beys. More than this, the young men played with the rhetorical forms marking hierarchy, holding them up as an object of mockery. The language and style in which one routinely deals with lords was itself the wider point of their mockery. In short, they revelled in their capacity to play in several dimensions at once, and to present that capacity to an amused, admiring, and participating audience in the sahra.

Having been reduced to tears of laughter by such a *tour de force* of narrative performance I can vouch for its power. What sort of power is it exactly? The humour converting inferiority into superiority is created by the ideas of reversal and unique insight: 'we' in fact define the situation and control its evolution while the one who imagines himself the protagonist is unconscious of the true manipulation being practised upon, and not by, him. We have the manner and the forms under control. How satisfying it is to play upon the style required of the bey who *must* parade in town, to establish himself as someone who is literally and politically 'in view', conspicuously attended by his faithful shebab. The young bey is no grizzled political veteran, still less a mal'un and cunning fox who can see through you. This lord is at the beginning of what he hopes is a political career. He has to find ways of entering on to the scene. Furthermore, he is someone who rides roughshod over the forms of respect for those lower in the hierarchy when he deals with the family and this invites revenge. So he is, and only Jihad and Ahmad see it, a spectacle for us even as we enable him to put on a spurious show for others (almost 'at' them, given that it is agonistic and designed to outshine anyone else in the café).

At one level all of this was a 'truth'; the scene in the Tripoli café and the comic narrating in the sahras were built out of and created certain social realities. They also used those realities for purposes of sustaining what is, in another dimension, a fantasy – namely that we master the master.

What was magically obscured in the comic re-enactment – so much appreciated by the very well-disposed agha audience, relishing the opportunity to deride one who infringed on their self-respect – was precisely the performative aspect: that acting the expected role of the subordinate puffing up the superior *did* contribute to making the bey what he was and wished to be. Their eulogies and aggrandizement did sustain his necessary public image. Eveyone in the village might know him as a fannas, someone who delighted in putting on an act, but then tafnis was not always and everywhere the enemy of real power. The bey's style of authority *was* confirmed by the young aghas who were doing what was required.

They required it too, for they wanted those jobs as chauffeurs and gunmen, and the local status as well as cash that went with such positions. There was a material need and interest which was both revealed and masked in the laughter. The comic narrative and performance made the acting out of (real) dependence a subject for display to their peers and seniors. They were 'replying' to any anticipated criticism for working with Nadim Bey from those supporting a different lord, by taking a comic distance and claiming merely to be using the bey for their purposes. The laughter restores their (apparent) autonomy and violates the lord's control, though they clearly felt that they could only laugh at him privately or in his absence and not to his face.

The lord concerned may or may not have been aware of what they were up to. I have already said that he had a formidable reputation for self-centredness and arrogance blinding him, among other things, to coded mockery; so we may easily imagine that his preening in the café was devoid of any trace of doubt about the tribute proper to him. Does it matter? Perhaps, if others in the café were sensitive to the style of the eulogies and picked up on the excess (even in a mode where 'excess' is so difficult to judge), or were cued in by behavioural signs from the two lads. In any case, the bey most probably felt he had got what he wanted. The balance of power was clear. His family's estates tied senior agha men to him. The shebab depended on the election for money. As long as there were others who might show themselves just as adept at flattery, they had to convince him of their effectiveness. His public display was assured.

Demonstrations of Beauty and Excellence

The young men were thus contributing to Nadim Bey's sense of markaz, of social 'station' and significance in the world. If they were helping to make his social place, he was quite capable of putting them in theirs, and of demonstrating upon them the force of hierarchy and exclusion in which there would be no laughter. The young lord had been raised and trained in the micro-practices of power, and lost few opportunities to exercise it on subordinates.

The city was very much his territory, and he dressed in the style appropriate to one of the gilded youth – expensively. The gold bracelet, neck chain, costly open-necked silk shirt and the flared trousers spoke money and leisure quite as loudly as any 'shouting' by attendants. Such a costume had become *de rigeur* for many younger beys who made visible their membership in the high-consumption, highly competitive world of the Lebanese bourgeoisie. It was a costly necessity for them, part of the means of claiming and maintaining status in the ruling stratum to which they either aspired or felt they belonged – part of their social distinction.

I met Nadim Bey by chance on the street one day in Tripoli where I had gone with one of the young parodists from the café scene. The bey was on his social parade, we had some shopping to do. But a trip to the city was still an occasion for one of the shebab when in the company of a foreign visitor and invited to a meal in a local restaurant, a rare experience for most people from the village for whom the concept of 'eating out' was one associated exclusively with middle-class society in the towns. So young Ahmad, my companion, had chosen to put on his best clothes for the kazzura, the leisurely wander around. They were the best clothes of one who only made money from giving taxi rides to day labourers from the village down to the plain in an old Opel and from occasional service for a bey. His shirt was in cheap quality synthetic fibre with vivid green and yellow patterns, and the wide flare of his ill-cut aubergine-coloured trousers proclaimed their price as surely as did the lord's finery.

Nadim Bey and I exchanged banal greetings. He turned condescendingly to the young villager and said something to the effect of: 'My dear Ahmad, with someone like you wearing trousers like that, what *are* people like me going to put on!' This effortless act of verbal humiliation, this fleeting moment of *violence douce*, kept him in practice in the use of an arrogant sarcasm which substantiated hierarchy for an instant in a cheap pair of trousers. It had a physical effect. Ahmad shifted nervously and flushed. I felt a bodily tension. Neither of us found a way directly to challenge the derision. It was only when the bey had sauntered off down the street that I insulted him, now joining Ahmad in ridiculing his pretentiousness and haki as making him unworthy of serious response. We recast events, enabling ourselves to mock his remark and his clothes as typical of a fannas, thus justifying ourselves and turning discomfort to comic criticism for our own benefit, but 'when his back was turned'.

The attack on Ahmad's way of dressing when he was showing himself in public 'at his best', related closely to more overtly and physically coercive forms of domination. One fellah, who was giving me a long account of oppression by the beys and aghas in the recent past, added to the scenes of arbitrary power, murder, false imprisonment, and land seizure, the story of what happened if one of the labourers was seen wearing a new shirt. A couple of the aghas (he named them, both men by then probably in their late fifties; they confirmed what he said to me) would grab whoever wore the new garment and throw him to the ground. The bey they accompanied would literally 'stamp' on him, *da'as 'aleih*, a fundamental iconic act and idiom of power (da'as is a very common word for what a superior does to an inferior; one stamps on the honour of another, *da'as 'a-karamtu*).[1] The aghas would yell at the victim: 'You've a new shirt? You've nothing, no money. You've been stealing olives.' Then they would rip the shirt to pieces off his back. The narrator added: 'so no one could go to Beirut'. Access to the city, claims to civilized status, were denied in the act of tearing the shirt apart. Fellahin had no right to be in a position to dress for the capital. To the beys and aghas the labourers had no means to 'dress', except by theft, which would be publicly punished. As we have seen before, stealing was the only way for the dominant groups to represent the acquisition of property by the fellahin. The shirt was illicit by hierarchical definition and a sign demanding punishment, for the user had no right to the sign's use.

With Ahmad, in the streets of Tripoli, I had witnessed a contemporary transformation of the 'traditional' scene of power. He was effectively told that he was pretending to what he could not autonomously claim – 'fashionable dress'. It was not proper for him even to ape the clothes of his superiors, or at any rate he would be informed that that was all he was doing in his poor boy's version of a rich man's style. His cheap shirt and the aubergine-coloured trousers made him vulnerable to the cutting remark from someone who saw himself as embodying 'taste' and the hierarchies that taste expresses and maintains. The bey policed the boundaries of power with his barb. His ironic amusement punctured Ahmad's pride at being able to participate in the new conventions of how shebab might present themselves, and did so before an audience, the Englishman, who was presumed to share the bey's pleasure. He shattered Ahmad's 'show' with a few words, casually and publicly. He had no necessity to hide his mockery but used it to the face of his victim.

In the dai'a itself the young lord could equally use his tafnis as a weapon to break the etiquette and conventional forms of respect. On one of his many visits during the elections, when seated in the mayor's manzul with some of the senior men, supporters and murafiqs of his family, he coolly adopted a posture of what seemed to me calculated effrontery. He lounged at elaborate ease in the reception room, idly flipping around in his hand his rosary (*misbaha*) with its glittering golden tassle and amber beads proclaiming its high cost. One leg was crossed on the knee of the other so that the sole of his shoe was directly 'in the face' of that very reputed elder, the famous hunter murafiq of Muhammad al Abboud.

There was already indirect violence in the manipulation of the misbaha. Where the beauty of rosaries, much used by older men and a subject of some discussion among local connoisseurs, was usually judged in terms of the quality of their beads, the workmanship, age and – most important – the genealogy of those through whose hands they had passed, here the point became the sheer display of money value. Decoration of the bey's person had become the main function much in the same way as his silk shirt and gold neck chain. The casual twirling of the misbaha around his hand was the style affected by those of his class and age who used the beads as an appurtenance testifying to wealth. Religious and traditional reference were subordinated to modern consumption in a demonstrative assertion of indifference to sacred meanings.

The young lord's posture offered a specific offence. A man's *qa'ida*, his way of sitting, is always noted. On a public occasion of an official visit, as this was, politeness dictated upright posture, legs uncrossed and together, the back held straight. Only among close friends and at informal moments would a man cross his legs in the 'foreign' way (though always with the sole of the shoe to the ground) or slouch back against the cushions. More specifically, to present the sole of the shoe to someone, to have it 'in his face', *fi wijhi*, is seriously degrading to that person in front of an audience alert to any such sign of disrespect. The social ritual of 'respect' was unambiguously transgressed.

The young lord was showing off with a vengeance, his tafnis was highly directed. The posture insulted a man who was his senior in terms of age, who was highly respected (*muhtaram*) and a companion of the lords for many years. By extension, it offered injury to all the aghas present in a double manner. In terms of the conventions of address it was a gross infringement, and clearly a knowing one. More than that, the posture asserted a difference between codes – that of the village and that of the class with which the bey identified, a superior class characterizing itself in part by standards and forms outside those of the rural classes altogether. Thus his pose was perfectly 'natural' in the context of his class and lifestyle, and perfectly calculated in the context of the manzul whose proper social standards of respect it subordinated through violation to a 'higher', other code.

The mayor was deeply embarrassed. But he was closely linked to the bey in economic and land management ties and had long relations with the family. The elder who had found himself directly faced, and defaced, with this gesture was silently outraged, remembering as he said afterwards in justification of his non-response, his service with the old lord, father of this young jackass (*humar*). After the departure of the guest everyone immediately commented on his tafnis, boastfulness (fashr), and what we unanimously agreed was his total failure of social grace. We all seconded the affronted senior in his refusal to answer the insult and not deigning – how rightly, we insisted – to reply to this vulgarity. In his absence, the one who had tried to demonstrate his *maîtrise du jeu* to the point of playing with the rules was downgraded to a station below his audience. We could judge him by 'traditional' standards and reduce his violation of social form and transgression of our status to signs of the decay in his line from the great days of his father and grandfather. He was 'just a fannas'.

My account tends to stress the element of compulsion, of choice denied, of power closures operating either through the sheer weight of the discourse, or through the coercive force exercised by the dominant. This is too simpleminded and deterministic. In this brief encounter in the manzul there were at least three levels of risk involved for the bey: of an immediate reaction to his violation creating some order of crisis; of a later price paid for the offence; and of unintended consequences flowing from the flagrant display of commodity values and 'modern' manners.

First, respect for the mayor might inhibit a verbal response or a walk-out by one of the seniors, but a young intemperate agha might stalk from the room in furious reaction to the bey's challenge. At election time there are often shifts in allegiance, possibilities of more advantage to be gained elsewhere. The shebab were coming to play a greater if unacknowledged role because of the new labour market and work options. They might see themselves as more independent of the lords than in the past.

The second level was that the criticisms expressed after his departure might be or become not merely rationalizations of subordination, but consensual judgements on significant matters of status and social form. By those standards the audience denounced the bey and rejected his imposition of insulting behaviour. The fact that no one had responded to his challenge in the manzul at the time could well be presented as proper etiquette and respect both for their host and for their own past, linked by the offended hunter to the 'great days' of the old lords when such a thing would never have happened. And though I say carefully that the bey was downgraded only in his absence, with an implication of below-stairs muttering confined only to the servants, yet that too can be interpreted in a different way. Unaware, unconcerned, or affecting unconcern, the young bey might one day have to reckon with the opinions of the aghas he had so slighted. Concealed social judgements can have dangerously long-term consequences. If interests changed in an ever more economically volatile situation, then the tafnis might be paid for at a later date. There might be a reckoning, particularly if a dispute were to arise with any section of the agha family, by no means unthinkable given election divisions, traditional attachments to different lords' beits, and hostilities that could break out over property relations.

The emphasis on the money value of clothes and misbaha focuses the audience's eyes on new consumption patterns and fashions dependent, above all, on the translation of wealth into status goods and status honour. Such a sequence of course grossly simplifies and reduces social complexity, but seems to invite such reduction to one standard of value: you have money or you don't. People might reflect that access to money is not restricted to the lords, however much a jibe might discipline Ahmad's self-presentation. True, the bey still has that which makes possible though not inevitable the conversion of wealth into power, his land, and his family history of controls, alliances and violence. Yet if one refuses to respect the 'traditional' forms and to preserve the fiction of a shared privilege in which money is relegated to a minor role for it is status honour that really counts (issues which I will explore in Chapters 15 and 16), one may jeopardize one's own capacities to mobilize support in a crisis. For if one implies that others can be bought and sold in what is treated as nothing more than a market situation, why then they may well take the lesson and go off with the highest bidder. The tafnis might later be seen as more expensive than it appeared on the Tripoli street or in the manzul.

Finally, Nadim Bey's very insistence on the cultural displacement and instability of local forms and their effective subordination to his wider élite universe had its own dangers. The Weberian idea of 'beauty and excellence' in the superiority of the ruling status honour groups is at issue here. If the young lord's deliberately offensive posture is an embodiment of power relations, it at the same time draws attention to a dislocation in the forms and proper ordering of those relations. The sole of the shoe facing the older man suggests not just an indifference to the old criteria of virtue, but a positive pleasure in negating them, the pleasure of gratuitous transgression. Now it is quite true that his behaviour might be taken to be an instantiation of the power principle I have elucidated of 'going beyond' the values and capacities of others, of deliberately and arbitrarily showing that the ideal typical man of power can do 'as he pleases'. If such a man wishes to 'break' people (*kassir*) by some insult great or small, he does so secure in the knowledge that he has shown in the past that the price for defying him is

too high to pay. But our young lord had no such individual past on which
to call. He was behaving as if he was something he was not. He had the
status of bey, but not yet the biography of a true man of power. Was Nadim
Bey capable of fully realizing the persona he assumed, or was he really 'all
show' and a fit object of laughter?

The Killing of Tewfiq

Nadim Bey tested subordinates. He demonstrated his power upon them, as
the episodes I have narrated make clear. Men discussed whether or not he
was a man of courage and whether he had the calibre to assume the task of
taking vengeance for Muhammad al Abboud, the relative who had died when
he was just a small child. There was uncertainty about how far he was
prepared to go.

Walid, a young agha from the beit which was mostly based in Tripoli, had
worked for Nadim Bey. Walid was widely viewed as someone who was
becoming unpredictable and a danger to his family. He was developing like
the young man who had taken revenge for the wounding on the plain (Chapter
10). He performed as the very type of the young qabaday afraid of nothing,
ready to shout, challenge and demand satisfaction at any real or imagined
challenge, and provocatively self-assertive. And he was very determined. Jamil
al Asmar, a local man who had once had links with the Popular Front for
the Liberation of Palestine, told me that Walid 'kissed my hand twenty times'
to get into the organization. Jamil's own two sons had joined with him but
fled as soon as they were confronted with the realities of guerrilla training.
Walid stayed. He had been on operations in Israel itself, his exploits were in
the newspaper under the *nom de guerre* 'Abu Khaldun'. No other young man
in the village had done *that*.

Walid's older brother, Tewfiq, who was in his thirties and still not married,
tried to rein the younger man in, but Walid was intractable. Tewfiq was a
bodyguard himself, and was often to be seen sitting outside the house of the
sheikh ash-shebab of one section of Beit Abd as-Salam to whom he was
related by marriage. He would complain about how difficult it was to find
a wife, and the others would respond with joking and teasing which he took
in good part. Men felt he was basically 'a good man', but not very bright nor
possessed of much social acumen. Still, he did his job, carried his gun,
presented himself well in public in his suit and correct manner, and tried to
control his brother who made everyone uneasy.

Walid had done jobs – many of them routine but others God knows what
– for Nadim Bey. They had disagreed over something – money, most people
said – and the young tough guy went around the village and Tripoli threatening
that unless he got satisfaction he would do something terrible. He spoke of
shooting, of what a man had to do when challenged, of how he could not bear
the situation any longer, of his anger. Tewfiq told him to shut up, to control

himself and pay no attention to Nadim who was just a worthless fannas. Walid ignored him. He was 'angry', *za'lan*, and no one seemed to think that this was merely a ploy to achieve what he wanted. He meant business. Just as a lord's attendants make a point of going around 'talking him up' so Walid was going around very loudly doing the opposite. He was taking up what he presented as a challenge. Other senior men joined his brother Tewfiq in the campaign to silence him. They were fearful in case Nadim decided the public insulting had gone too far and determined to react with violence. Men discussed the issue quietly in small family gatherings, cursing the danger which Walid was courting, danger which might involve them all.

I returned from a day or two down in Beirut and my VW was surrounded by screaming children as I drove up to the front of my house on the road just above the old mosque. 'Tewfiq is dead, Tewfiq is dead', they were yelling. I smiled and said that I knew a typical piece of kizb when I heard it and paid no attention. It was not until my companion's eldest son ran over excitedly and swore on the life of his father that I accepted the truth of what they were shouting at me.

The story of the murder was simple, at least on the surface. Tewfiq and Walid had been sitting together in a café in Tripoli. Nadim Bey had gone by with some friends, a coincidence that was too convenient to be a coincidence at all in most men's view. He had taunted the brothers through the window as he passed by with some of his kinsmen, and had challenged them to come out. Others said that Walid had shouted insults at Nadim (and some who gave this version opined that Nadim had known that his appearance would be quite enough to provoke an outburst which would give him his excuse to act). Walid had risen to the bait and rushed out drawing a gun. Tewfiq had run after him to break up the whole affair. But he was unarmed, and some said that one of the younger beys, who was supposedly a 'friend' of his, had persuaded him to leave his revolver in the bey's apartment rather than take it with him on the street 'in case he was stopped by the police'. But really it was part of the trap. Tewfiq ended up dead on the pavement with six bullets pumped into him as he lay on the ground, said the boys: Nadim Bey just pumped them into him. And he knew Tewfiq had no gun. Walid was shot too and had nearly died but was in hospital and would live. But he could not walk properly. Everybody was meeting. Word had been sent to Beirut to the men working at the airport. The sheikh ash-shebab and his brother, related to Tewfiq's family by marriage, were expected back.

The immediate family were in mourning, and issuing threats about what they would do as soon as Walid came out of hospital and recovered. The men grew their beards as a sign of intention to take revenge. At Tewfiq's burial the leading member of the descent group, a school inspector who resided in Tripoli and who was also a candidate in the upcoming parliamentary elections, gave a fiery speech. He proclaimed, as everyone assumed he had no choice but to do in the circumstances, that the family would not complete the rites that should accompany a person's death (such as the readings of the Quran) until the blood of Tewfiq had been avenged.

Others said that the whole affair was Walid's fault. Everyone had warned him. What was Nadim Bey supposed to do? Nothing? Things had gone too far and he had shown he was prepared to respond to a challenge and was not just a fannas. Now we had to deal with all the possibilities of a tricky situation. Cynics commented that as long as Tewfiq's family were shouting and insulting and making a huge performance out of their intentions that meant they were in fact looking for a deal: some land on the plain and perhaps a private taxi. It was sad that Tewfiq was dead, but Walid was a menace and a financially profitable deal would be in their best interests, though they could not possibly say so publicly. Men who stay silent are the ones who really intend to do something. I was approached by the younger beys of a different branch from that of Nadim who were staying in the village and unwittingly caused great unease by reporting the offended family as 'not saying anything'. This was at once interpreted as a sign of trouble and determination on revenge, with further untold consequences affecting bey–agha relations in general.

The sheikh ash-shebab returned and days were spent mulling over the implications: what should be done, by whom, where, when. Scenarios were constructed of possible ways of taking revenge. Heated debate took place over whether or not it was legitimate to kill Nadim's older brother who had an advanced university degree from America and was thus more 'valuable' to the family than Nadim. 'Why take silver when you can have gold?' was how one phrased the choice. Others denounced this view as quite contrary to the code which, in their version, only allowed for killing the killer. What would be the best place? Some favoured the courtroom. It was public, and a fit responsiveness to the very public killing and wounding outside the crowded café in the city. It would be an appropriate setting to assert the sacredness of honour over mere law. Everyone would see how the family defended itself.

Walid returned from hospital and stayed in bed in his house. I visited regularly, as was appropriate for anyone close to the family. He had been told he would not walk properly again, he would be partially crippled because a nerve had been severed. There were moves to get a distinguished surgeon in Beirut, to whom I had an introduction, to operate quickly in the hope of restoring him fully to health and to the possibility of becoming his brother's avenger. A decision had to be taken immediately before the nerve atrophied. But no decision was ever reached. 'Perhaps they want him crippled and out of action', said one sceptic thoughtfully. 'They'd rather have the land and the taxi, and he's just a menace.' My interlocuter felt that a settlement might hold if Walid were out of the way. The coldness of the calculation shocked me, but was part of evaluations of possible outcomes and strategies in which all were engaged, evaluations that always marked such events. Walid was not simply 'an individual', he was pre-eminently part of a group. The group had to decide how to manage a complex situation involving blood between them and an important house of beys without seeming publicly to be doing anything less than what honour demanded. So there had to be much shouting and insulting while men tried to work out what the options were and to anticipate the consequences of possible negotiations.

Other branches of Beit Abd as-Salam that had no marriage relation with their agha 'cousins' felt no compulsion to join in a major collective action. Walid's actions were strongly disapproved of and men recalled how often he had been warned. Now poor Tewfiq had paid with his life and something would have to be done, that was certain, but they did not want to get involved if they could avoid it. The mayor's branch was particularly troubled because they were attached historically to the house of Abboud Bey, managed Nadim's estates, and valued these political and economic links far too much to put them at risk on Walid and Tewfiq's account. The elections were approaching and there was a great deal of work to be done and money to be made which was vital to their interests. None of their members attended the meetings and discussions of possible action, and they spent much time going over the stupidity and social idiocy of Walid, and the immaturity of the young man who becomes intoxicated by violence and carrying a gun. There would be negotiations, they said, and that would settle it. There was no chance of Nadim Bey being jailed – it would be self-defence and political connections would get him off in any case. Every effort was made to play down the affair and to nullify any effect of relations with the beys as a whole.

Nadim Bey might be a fannas, arrogant, boastful and insulting. But those traits were now manifestly demonstrated in blood to be the marks of a man of serious ambitions to power and the capacity to respond to a challenge as well as to issue one. Since there was more than the hint of a plan in the killing, he was clearly either more cunning than he seemed or had the advice of men who knew how to go about staging such a scene in the middle of the city before a large public. Walid had set himself up, and been set up. His insults and threats had been answered and Tewfiq, who everyone saw as the hapless victim, had been lost. Nadim Bey had shown himself to be what he claimed to be: a real man of honour.

So if Jihad and Ahmad mischievously vaunted their own skills in puffing up Nadim in the Tripoli café, their humour ultimately rebounded upon them and upon a major section of the agha descent group. Those who fancied that they showed a mastery of performance and a capacity to play with the conventions of respect themselves were deeply implicated in the workings of power and violence in ways of which they were by no means the masters. Their rhetorical position as joking outsiders concealed, at least partially from themselves, their own subjection to those same practices which in fantasy they escaped. Nadim's action, and all that it entailed, presented them with a reality test their play could not meet.

PART FIVE

Imperatives of Work

CHAPTER FIFTEEN

The Challenge of Work
and Wages

Even if it is not perceived clearly as such, the most degrading work always remains something more and other than a way of earning a living, and unemployment is so intensely feared only because economic deprivation is accompanied by a social mutilation.[1]

In this final section I shall turn to the significance of work and wages for the practices and narratives of hierarchy, social ordering and value. It was a significance which young men such as Walid rejected, or at least subordinated to what (they acted as if) were unchanging narratives of confrontation.

The narrative of exchange of violence constituted by the death of Tewfiq and the wounding of Walid highlighted an internal agha dispute about the very terms in which to establish identity and personal value. With fatal rhetoric and performance of anger, Walid defined Nadim Bey's conduct as a challenge: he, Walid, would not be treated in ways inappropriate to 'the man he was'. His karama, his integrity and honour, was at stake, let others try to deny that as they might. He had no choice. Walid's senior kinsmen, on the other hand, contested his definition of the issues as well as his right to set the bounds of the social truth of the situation.

They attempted to curb him in three different rhetorical modes. In the first they collectively refused to recognize the existence of a challenge which demanded a response; some said that Nadim Bey was a worthless fannas not to be taken as a worthy opponent. In the second, and complementary, mode they treated Walid as an immature and thus subordinated young man, who must be urged towards self-control through appeals to the weight of family hierarchy. But in the third, a marked rhetorical shift, his elders evoked the distinct concerns of work, pay, need and 'interest' as elements integral to the proper mapping of Walid's situation.

Walid, however, refused the restrictions and closures his elders sought to impose through the three discourses. He could not and would not bear the lack of respect from this fannas, Nadim Bey. He saw himself within the narrative terms of the agha qabaday, a champion in the agonistic exchanges to which a true man is bound. Family would not silence him, far less the calculation of mere money, so foreign to honour and the hero's role. For that

he showed nothing but contempt. He would achieve his place in his own and
the collective story. And that place, as so often happened, turned out to be
not the one he had imagined.

He acted in the classical manner and according to the idealized accounts
of karama, as if there was no space in his biography as qabaday for considerations of job and income. Devoted to the master narrative tradition of
excellence and identity which excluded work and wages, he maintained the
ideo-logic of heroism, rejecting any realistic calculation of the balance of
forces, the odds in the challenge, and the possibility of the trap.

His seniors, aware of possible disaster, urged the pragmatic force of the
new economic realities. They had become very conscious of the impoverished
nature of Akkar and of the degree to which financial exchanges and financial
necessities impinged on a group. The younger were all in the labour market
and some were in the same situation as the poorer fellahin with nothing to
sell but their labour. They spoke of finding work as an imperative, and of
their lack of the training and qualification vital to prestige occupations. They
had to find jobs.

The labour market was no abstract mechanism of anonymous forces in
the life experience of men like Walid. It was intensely personalized and
personalizing. The younger generations were still closely implicated in the
relations between their fathers and the beys. They often owed their positions
to such links. The lords controlled access to many of the much desired
'posts' in government service as well as to more casual employment. To
'enter' a job usually meant ties to someone who had the power of 'entering'
people into positions. The demonstration of that capacity was a central
function of a patron whose public standing would in part depend on the
numbers he was said to have placed in various positions of varying degrees
of prestige and difficulty of appointment.[2]

Getting the job thus meant entering into a double dependency that was
related both to the patron and to the job structure and the hierarchy it might
entail. At the same time it also often meant moving out of the confines of
a world in which 'being from Beit Abd as-Salam' was a primary mode of
identification with which to face those whom one might encounter. In the
different workplaces with which the younger aghas were becoming familiar
that proud boast counted for nothing in terms of how they were judged.
Family name and reputation might have but limited value to them in their
jobs as taxi drivers, panel beaters, furniture maker apprentices, construction
workers and mechanics in Tripoli or Beirut or some other smaller town
where demand and opportunity took them, or while they drove around
Lebanon during the harvest season with small combine harvesters and
tractors. 'Being an agha' would mean nothing outside the social range of
Berqayl itself.

A capacity for violence still offered 'a career open to the talents'. Monetar-
ization and the labour market had not diminished that possibility. A man

who established a reputation among his peers for answering challenges and defending his name and that of his kin could find such conduct a path into a job with its own prestige – bodyguard, labour organizer, assisting in local politicking, defending property boundaries, waiting on the boss in the salons of the city, all duties which might require physical force and verbal aggression. Yet even a bodyguard and attendant on a bey increasingly held status as an individually waged employee using the lord's revolver and the lord's car simply as a routine part of the job.

Though 'respect' and the capacity to instil fear remained significant in many areas of male social life, other, more generalized ways of achieving respect existed too. Now, men were expected to have work and not to 'sit' unemployed. A man should provide for his own nuclear family or contribute to the extended family budget. He should earn money to keep his wife and children properly, and bring back clothes, goods and food from Tripoli. 'A man had to live', he 'had his own interest' in personal and family benefit, 'he had to look after himself'; the clichéd phrases expressed a powerful, and sometimes ambivalent, awareness of changing experiences and life conditions. Above all, they acknowledged a *need* which was the antithesis of the central values in the rhetoric of status honour. The familiar phrases articulated a more individualized sense of identity and interest, one less subordinated to the cult of the status honour of the descent group.

Wages might enable men to achieve a more predictable and calculable place in the world, to imagine a future whose absence was so often dolefully proclaimed. A man who acquired skills by watching others, picking up the knack of doing particular tasks from his kin or colleagues, and who was steady on the job, having the ability to cultivate good relations with bosses or show himself worthy of trust and promotion, might attain the financial means to expand his interests. Higher wages were a way to recuperate landholding that had been lost over the years, or to profit from the speculative buying of crops ahead of harvests, or to make loans to the young beys desperate for spending money in the city against olives they would illicitly take from their father's groves come the harvest, or for investment in agricultural machinery. A young agha might even dream, putting it a different way, of buying back 'the grove of the orange' so many years later. This time it would be simply a cash transaction, a matter of market value, but it would carry its own possibility of status.

Of course, money did not 'in itself' bring prestige and standing. A man had to know how to use it, a complex and also competitive form of practical knowledge. He had to know what to buy in order to demonstrate to others his ability to go beyond the necessity of work into the luxury of choice. Attendance in the reception rooms of the great beys had long accustomed the aghas to the ostentatious display of wealth and influence; for forty years the château of Abboud and the villa of his son had been practical demonstrations of the lifestyles of the powerful. During the boom decade of the

1960s, when Beirut became the undisputed finance capital of the Middle East and shops had been flooded with the latest in luxury goods and consumer durables, men had become quite skilled in assessing the sheer expense of furnishing the stage of social taste and influence, and the means for playing a role. The key question was always simple: what did it – a slot on an election list, a lord's apartment, the Cadillac or Buick, the silk tie, the Italian shoes, or a fellah's new shirt – cost? The answer was an index of social place, the rise or decline of powerful men, or the relative wealth and pretension to public appearances of a member of the lower stratum.[3]

Money, as everyone had come to realize, posed a certain threat to the values of status honour. *Anyone* might now buy the signs and appearances of status, whatever his genealogy or personal conduct, if he had the cash. Buying the signs of status might gain a man nothing but gossip and mockery. If a man of little public esteem obtained access to cash, he might buy consumer durables, a tape recorder, a radio, or even a television; he might furnish and decorate a reception room which imitated the style of those who saw themselves as above him. They, and men of his own status, would certainly attempt to turn his show to derision. It was better, those fellahin who had acquired money and some small property through employment and prudent purchases of land told me, to invest it and not to bother with furnishings and changing the house. Never mind the world of lies and envy.

A sense of what house furnishing might be was none the less being established. Those same men, whether fellah or agha, who cautioned against envy might well buy these new objects for the private world of their own house. They had access, limited but real, to patterns of consumption and lifestyles from which they had hitherto been rigorously and even coercively excluded. One agha who lived in Berqayl (though he belonged to Beit Khalid, the descent group most of whose members were resident in Tripoli), invited me into his house. He was in his twenties and had a trade. When he was in the village he was not seen much in the street but stayed at home and sought no public role. He wanted the English anthropologist, his guest for the first time, to listen to the tape recorder playing tapes of President Nasser's speeches or Um Kulthum's music, and pointed out his ornate new coffee tables with marble tops, the heavy upholstery of his large wooden-framed armchairs, his mirrors with gilt frames, his decorative pictures of stags and European country scenes, his china in a cabinet.[4] The anomalous stranger would understand, and could be appealed to as someone who had seen how people in the village were just 'liars', and that it was better to stay 'quiet at home' and live this new life in these new surroundings 'for oneself'. His was a world constructed with care to conform to ideas of taste thought to be typical of persons of some higher class.

But aside from myself, who else might he invite into his elaborately furnished room? The young owner told me that it was not 'for people'. In that space which he made personal rather than social, he could indeed practise a difference of lifestyle, but 'on his own'. In this very personal, and self-contradictory way, he transformed the paradigmatic claim of the hero to 'need no one' into a new, domesticated mode. On the one hand he rejected the public performance, contest and violence so valued in the honour narratives, while, on the other hand, rhetorically representing himself as truly autonomous and constrained neither by men's opinions nor their envy, precisely a hero's attributes.

Work, wages and the labour market as driving forces in men's lives, yet often deeply imbricated in personal lines of status and power, made it difficult to decide how to act and react in the rapidly shifting world of Lebanon in the 1960s and early 1970s. Agha shebab often expressed an ironic, self-critical ambivalence when they spoke of their dependence on occupations and wage work. Oh yes, they might show off with the car or the revolver and boast of their place and stations and how they 'knew everything', but that was just 'empty talk'. Their modern continuation of the heroic style was shot through with practical cultural unease.

The younger men were unsure of the forms of their social life, the defining shape of their social spaces and the degree of mastery they possessed to define forms and spaces. As one of them, a central figure in the narrative which follows, said to me with bitter and amused contempt: 'Look, you saw what I was saying over there and all the showing off about the Buick and being a chauffeur? Kizb, my friend. What am I? I'm a taxi driver, that's what I am.'[5]

Performance out of Place: the Rifle, the Knife and a Woman's Mockery

One of the younger agha men, Nabil, had obtained a job in Tripoli driving a bus for a private, Christian girls' school which was run by a woman director. He liked to present himself as a chauffeur without equal, but was personally held in no great respect by his peers and elders who regarded him as a show-off, shallow and lacking in judgement. This was his first job in Tripoli. Though a married man and the eldest of five brothers, three already of fighting age, and as such potentially a significant figure, in fact he had not been able to translate this resource into prestige. Indeed, the fraternal group as a whole was regarded as socially ineffectual and troublesome.

Word came to the village in the late afternoon. One of the drivers reported that Nabil had got into a fight with a drunken friend in Tripoli who wanted to cadge a ride on the bus with the schoolchildren. Nabil had refused. Shouting had led to an exchange of blows, a fracas in which Nabil had been kicked in the stomach. He had collapsed, said the narrator, had fallen out of the bus onto the pavement, and had been rushed to hospital. The incident might have had serious consequences, as Nabil had had a major stomach operation not long before.

Only a short time later, having been judged well enough to go home, Nabil arrived back in the village proclaiming the outrage. The rhetorical field was entirely his, for no other version from an acceptable source was available. The reaction was instantaneous. The sheikh ash-shebab, three of Nabil's brothers who worked on the Beirut airport team and two friends who were also kinsmen, at once loaded up three or four rifles into the boot of the leader's car and departed for Tripoli. In the car with them, highly visible and immediately to hand, they carried heavy sticks.[6]

The sticks were conventionally carried when men wanted to indicate the relatively limited level of violence they intended, to offer a sign of the order of confrontation they wanted to define. That only one car set off was a similar sign of the scale of the event in their definition. Two cars would have constituted a major eruption of village shebab into the alien space of the city for some dangerous purpose of collective violence. This level of intrusion, in turn, might have crystallized overwhelming opposition to them in a setting where they had no obvious allies. The rifles were out of sight, for emergency use only and then, as we shall see, more for threat than use. Firing would be the last resort. These were the practical 'rules' which the shebab were following, taking them also to be more or less understood in the urban milieu of the poorer quarters. Whether they would be so apprehended in a well-to-do private girls' school was not a question whose possible significance seemed to have been considered.

When the men returned from Tripoli a couple of hours later in the evening, they went at once to Nabil's house, built next to that of his father and adjoining his brothers' rooms. There they found Nabil's paternal uncle and his first maternal cousins, together with those of Beit Abd as-Salam who supported the shebab leader or owed jobs to him. Initial rallying of support nearly always occurred in the residence of the offended person or his family head; there people hastened to demonstrate their readiness to act. As expected they found what amounted to a council being held about the ma'rika, the affray.

Their story, told by the sheikh ash-shebab with much murmured support, was as follows. They had driven off to the school, leapt out of the car, loudly demanding to know where the offender was, and berating and insulting the other chauffeurs there, threatening them with the full force of Beit Abd as-Salam if they failed to stand by their wounded colleague. One of Nabil's brothers, an adolescent perhaps eighteen years old, lost whatever self-control he had and went for one of the chauffeurs. The leader of the group made it absolutely clear that the man subjected to assault had nothing whatever to do with the affair. The leader went on to say that he had seized a rifle from the boot and, grabbing the boy by the scruff of the neck, had pulled him violently back, a pre-emptive action for he had feared that someone present would draw a gun. The scene had ended inconclusively with mutual recrimination and a promise of further consequences.

It was obvious that not only had the row been with the wrong people, but that the young brother was being singled out as the cause of what was essentially a reverse. The leader's narrative showed his energies directed towards correction of a mistake by one of his own side. Rhetorically the boy's rash behaviour could account for a failure to bring the confrontation to a satisfactory resolution; his hamasa was defined as disruptive of the proper form of riposte. Since he was a very junior figure at the gathering who had no ability to handle difficult social situations, even among his peers, he could only remain silent while his faults were denounced.

The sheikh ash-shebab thus attempted to impose his coherent narrative at the same time upon a rather incoherent series of events and also upon those present, who were in any case an audience self-selected to support him. He had taken pains to explain his resort to the rifle as an attempt to restrict the scale of the ma'rika rather than to enlarge it. He presented himself as trying to keep things in proportion and at their right level, an important part of such a person's capacities in the organization of violence. His was a claim to correct social judgement by overruling a headstrong young man who had so nearly pushed a conflict into bloodshed. The narrator's unspoken argument appeared to indicate his trust that the other chauffeurs would understand his real intention.[7] The tactic was a risky one dependent upon the correct decoding of the unverbalized message signified by grabbing the rifle. The leader had had to make an instant response to an unwelcome development, exactly the situation such men have to show themselves able to handle. The ploy had been successful. (I assume that he hoped that the fact he brought only one car whose passengers were only carrying staves had also immediately registered with their opponents.)

The strenuous interjections of assent and outrage by the shebab who had taken part, as well as by others present, none the less concealed a real rhetorical difficulty in the narrative. That the other school drivers were not offending parties and could not be described as such was an embarrassing element to be rather ineffectually glossed over. Neither the phase of insult and abuse nor the infuriated assault by the young brother had been directed towards the proper target. There was no obvious model of what would constitute action commensurate to the offence in these circumstances. The men of Beit Abd as-Salam had rushed off to the school and treated the other chauffeurs as responsible and, in addition, as if they constituted 'a group' on the paradigm of a family violence group, which they obviously were not. The drunken 'friend' was absent, and no one quite knew how to situate him socially, since his only tie was an individual one to Nabil. The participants had never considered confronting his kin, nor had they searched for his residence in the city for the very good reason that in an urban quarter they would have been intruders to be seen off by the local shebab, whatever their cause. Their narrative had no real centre or proper sequence. In the absence of the man who had struck Nabil, the hot-tempered brother was turned into the narrative focus. He had became a rhetorical figure of disorder and incommensurate response, diverting attention from problematic elements in the account.

The narrator, the sheikh ash-shebab, was in a dilemma. Narrative expectation of his role was clear: he had to appear to seize control of the situation. Yet the situation was one which in fact was beyond his control, since it took him out of the local space and groups where he might be expected to demonstrate mastery. Nabil's return to the village, calling for support and redress, had placed him in a very difficult position. Since he actively sought to fill the role of leader of the fighting men of a large section of Beit Abd as-Salam he was virtually compelled to set off for Tripoli with a maximum show of force. Not to answer the call of response to the challenge would have exposed him to a charge of not living up to his claims; it could have lost him the support of Nabil's family, three of whom worked for him at different times, both in general and in the forthcoming elections when he wanted to gather support for his candidates. His instant response had been the decision to set off in a car full of junior men, none of them known for their quick grasp of events, taking them into an urban arena where bounds might well be very difficult to set and control. Even allowing for the account of the initial outrage given by Nabil, the leader might well have played for time given that he privately had as low an opinion of the injured man as most people in the room. Anyone who did not support him, either because they did not want to get dragged into an affair by Nabil or because they did not wish to reinforce the leader's claims, might consider that a better option, whatever the value of hamasa and avenging bloodshed.

The call to arms was his responsibility, praiseworthy and showing his fitness to lead, but it was also vulnerable to criticism. He might tell the incident with the rifle as a mark of his ability to handle a sudden deterioration in the encounter, but the very fact of the rifles in the boot of the car might also be read as foolhardiness. What if one of the chauffeurs, equally short-tempered, had drawn a revolver when his colleague was attacked, in response to the rifle flourished menacingly in front of him? Was the sheikh ash-shebab perhaps too eager to act in accord with his image of his role as leader of the violence group and author of heroic narrative, and too eager to assert his persona in a dramatic confrontation?

The first to comment upon the account was a man from a closely related family section who was also a neighbour, an additional appropriate cause for his presence. He was a quiet figure, much respected for his taciturn self-control, his experience as an qabaday with the beys in the past, and his avoidance of unnecessary trouble. His group of five brothers and their redoubtable old father certainly did have an established social position among the aghas. Like so many of those present, he was a tractor driver and mechanic. There were many reasons, therefore, to take his intervention seriously. His carefully framed remarks took the form of a seemingly impersonal comment: the ma'rika showed how difficult it was to know exactly how to handle such a situation in town. The best weapon in Tripoli, he said, was a knife. It scared people off and prevented their coming too close, whereas a gun meant shooting all around.

At first, I thought his words nothing more than a kind of pedagogic effort directed at the shebab to make a key distinction between weapons. A knife can strike only 'at arm's length', effective only within the range of the body of which it is the limited extension. The blade creates a visible zone of possibilities, enabling opponents to make their own judgements about what may happen, permitting them to be held off. The gun, above all the rifle, extends space in a qualitatively different way, creating a field of fire and threatening another sort of violence which implicates others much more randomly over a much wider area.

The qabaday's commentary, more significant than I had originally understood, contained a veiled reproach quite as much as a lesson in the suitability of different weapons. In his careful, almost technical evaluation, he had found a way to express something which, phrased differently, might otherwise have been too openly and challengingly critical: why if the sheikh ash-shebab had wanted to avoid actual physical violence, while seeming to be ready for it, had he chosen the wrong weapons? Knives would have been more appropriate, precisely because of the limits inherent in their use and the communicative ways in which they were interpreted.

The comment went to the heart of the matter, coming as it did from one esteemed for his known experience in such affairs. The whole point, he continued more explicitly, was to calculate how to gain recompense for insult *without* getting involved in a cycle of violence. He made rhetorical appeal to what 'everyone knew': namely, that behind the shouting and threatening a dispute could be performed and managed to avoid serious violence with fist, stick, knife or gun in ascending order of intensification. He shifted rhetorical focus away from hamasa and the bungled attempt to restore honour to the more abstract calibrations and control of violence. These calibrations had been evoked by the sheikh ash-shebab, but the commentary questioned whether guns should have been taken into Tripoli in the first place.

Nabil himself, not a man reputed for his careful reflection on these questions, joined in the discussion to deflect the criticism with a rhetorical shift that appealed to an 'essential' contrast between the rules, practices and morality of confrontation in city and village. The trouble with fighting in Tripoli, he mused, was that you never knew who in the crowd was with you and who against. He described the crowd as 'just a bunch of individuals', each with his own interest, maslaha, 'and no one would help you unless he had his own good reasons' (it is worth noting that this is exactly the complaint voiced in the dai'a in disputes when someone does not get the support he hoped for; here it was being used as if characteristic only of the urban universe). Nobody would jump in to drive someone off, he said, or to prevent one of their own from getting at the man they were threatening.[8] Here in the village, he went on, you could count on what people would do but not down there in the medina. 'There's nothing worse than living in a place like Tripoli', he ended.

'The crowd' (zahma) was a concept alien to the identity of 'the village', and antithetical to the precise definition and placing of each inhabitant in a face-to-face community. It was taken to be a crucial distinguishing mark of the city by villagers used to knowing everyone's identity and characteristic behaviour and knowing, moreover, their probable allegiances and responses. The rhetorical figure of 'the crowd', which by synecdoche stood for the city, generalized the issue to a difference between modes of life. It appealed to a strong, shared identification of 'we in the village' against the individualized, impersonal anonymity of Tripoli where one 'never knew what might happen'. Nabil presented to the assembly two vital elements in the urban arena: the absence of proper intervention and the unpredictability of others.

This move to a higher level of abstraction, following the respected neighbour's coded critique of the weapons chosen, served a fairly obvious tactical function. The broader narrative of contrast between village and city masked the failure of the expedition with a proposition to which all present could at once agree. The failure evident, I am convinced, to everyone, would not be defined as such in the context of Nabil's father's house and the presence of the leader who had rushed off to defend the family. The standing of the sheikh ash-shebab was at issue, whatever the impetuous boy had done, and in this framework the former represented the group as a whole. 'Tripoli' shifted the discourse, enabling the group to close rhetorical ranks and to speak as if any fault lay with 'the city'. They attempted to absorb the misreadings and miscalculations that occurred in the unfamiliar setting of the school and the job into familiar narrative forms and rhetorical conventions for constructing events.

All the speakers that night and for two long evenings that followed addressed indirectly or directly a central aspect in the practice of violence: how was it to be kept within appropriate limits and who decided what those limits were? What were the right signs to give and receive? How could one maximize the predictability of an encounter while appearing to throw aside mere calculation for the pure violence of the honourable man? They laid great emphasis on the ritual and aesthetic aspects of the performance. In this kind and scale of confrontation it would be counted a failure of judgement if serious physical violence occurred, whatever the shebab might have said during the course of their 'insulting'. The young brother's impetuousness did not cover him with glory. It marked him instead as thoughtless, immature, a boy still under the sway of emotions, still unaware that performance is often predicated on the notion of *not* doing what you say nothing can stop you doing. Words and gestures were to be inflicted on the other in this type of encounter, not blows.

The idealized construction of reason and control had its own rhetorical dimension, as did its dialectical counterpart – the appeal to blood and hamasa. Reason, with whatever difficulty, was supposed to subordinate passion, older men to command younger, even if only the better to choose the moment for violent retribution. This way of talking was an important element in the way men spoke about violence and manhood, and was related closely to ideal social conceptions of what a man should be. But the speakers also knew of many cases where such reasonable processes had not occurred. More particularly in this instance, they were justifying behaviour which was *not* necessarily going to be taken as demonstrating these qualities at all. In part, the appeal to the ideal obscured the precarious nature of the narrative.

The audience was a large one, drawn from three of the four beits of the agha descent group. They heard the discussion with great seriousness, the male children of all ages following their lessons in the forms of violence with great concentration. They were learning now as much as they had previously learned from listening to the shebab's insulting and threats on hearing the news. Adolescent boys and young men joined in with fervent expressions of readiness to confront any insult to the family.

Only one participant used the moment of the second or third meeting in Nabil's father's house to subvert the tone of high seriousness. I noticed that a young man, who clearly wanted me to notice, was asking a whole stream of questions, uttering sober exclamations of amazement at the ways of the world, and interjecting endless conventional affirmative phrases such as *wa'allahi ma ba'rif* (By God, I don't know). He vigorously shook his head at appropriate moments, sat aggressively forward, hands planted on knees in the characteristic attitude of the assertive champion of status, and at the same time showed by quick eye signals that the whole occasion was affording him a huge and barely suppressed pleasure.

The young performer, one of Nabil's maternal cousins, was parodying the ritualized interpolations as his young kinsmen competed, each to show himself a more mature and involved participant than his fellows. He was living up to his already established persona as one who had the wit and mischief to play on social incongruity. It was a show of power, ephemeral of course, but power for a delicious moment all the same. *He* could see what was going on, and *he* was going to refuse to go along with it in a way which would make the scene a comedy, while using all the rhetorical instruments of seriousness. The just-disguised laughter separated him out from the others, enabling him to construct in the performance his identity as one who could perceptively manipulate the situations supposedly controlled by his peers.

The senior men appeared unawares of the parodic effects of the game, and it was not appropriate that they should pay any attention to him. But the shebab certainly were not. Some of them were in a suppressed but visible way exasperated, in my view not least by the performer's capacity to produce a comic distortion of their public role-playing in a masterly and unctuous show of wholehearted support using all the 'right' phrases. That he had not gone down to the city himself added to their irritation, as it was meant to do.

The playing with the rhetoric of violence and solidarity was its own form of critique, all the more effective because it turned people's consciousness to the discrepancy between the ideals of self-presentation and a misjudged riposte. The ironic mode undermined the shebab's attempt to maintain an idealized image of themselves as the young fighting men, an image one of their number persistently subverted. The 'comedian' used ritualized language to expose its inappropriateness to *those particular circumstances*, each slight variation in his tone and glance demonstrating that he was playing with both audience and accepted rhetoric. By calling attention to what was 'invisible' he played on the failure of the shebab to be what they wished to be in their own eyes. He gave himself a pleasure at their expense, pleasure which was heightened by their impotence. For they could not stop his performance without themselves seeming to be in breach of the required norms, given that his impassioned contributions were so commensurate with the seriousness of his apparent sense of outrage. Within the dominant frame of the occasion, he thus won his own playful but serious challenge.

On the next two evenings meetings were held at the home of Nabil's father. Senior family men of neighbouring and related groups were present, endorsing the incident as a proper reason for formal collective action. Once the sheikh ash-shebab had led the expedition they were almost bound to show solidarity with him. These family heads appealed rhetorically to the hazards of 'the city' and acted as if everything had gone well, as well as it could have in the circumstances. Since all present were 'insiders', the collusion was easily sustained. The sheikh ash-shebab and his trusted younger brother were constant visitors. He continued to assert his primacy in the rallying of the young men and to show how devoted he was as champion of the *'ailat*, the family, at all times.

By the second evening, however, the driver who was at the centre of the argument was noticeably downcast (*kashish*). Nabil had lost his job, in his version because he had quit in exasperation at his mistreatment; others stated privately that he had been kicked out as an unreliable nuisance.[9] His mechanic father, who never participated in public politics and was always described with much affection but no great respect as very adami, was properly truculent in defence of his eldest son, saying that in any case no 'real chauffeur' was interested in a lousy job for which he only got 200LL a month.

Unfortunately this defence immediately raised problems. A first maternal cousin, who also worked for the school, was present and he now apologetically declared his own obligation to carry on for the sake of an extra 60LL on top of social security: his family could not do without it. This defence of the practicalities of a wage and family 'interest' was highly embarrassing. The imperative of regular income and social security conflicted with, and even overrode the sacred duties of family solidarity. His statement directly focused attention on the increasingly present tension between the poetic ideals of honour and the prosaic demands of livelihood in the labour market, funda-mental demands which the rhetoric of riposte to a challenge had thus far occulted.

The discourse of material necessity directly threatened the hegemony of the status honour discourse. That the cousin should have placed both sets of rationalities on an antithetical level was bad enough, but to give precedence to interest and income, contradicted public norms which subordinated money claims of status honour. A contradiction better kept tacit had been made explicit. Nabil had characterized the city as the place where people supported you only when they had some individual interest, yet here was the cousin evoking precisely that same principle of which 'we in the village' were supposedly innocent. And, finally, the cousin's practicality threw doubt on the father of Nabil's attempts to dismiss a 'mere' 200LL a month.

The young man who had parodied the earlier discussion gave me in private his version of what lay behind the whole affair. Nabil, he said, owed the director some 1,300LL, borrowed to improve his small breeze-block house. His father, went on my informant, owed someone else about 1,000LL on the tractor plough and other implements. So they were quite seriously in debt and dearly needed the money. The job had been vital, and anyone with any sense would have taken care to stay on the right side of the school head at all costs. It could easily take Nabil and his father a year or so to pay off the debt, even if they were able to do so in regular monthly instalments. '*Miskin Abu Nabil, ya di'anu*', he said of the father, 'poor Abu Nabil, what a loss!' Then he added that he was sure the director had set up someone else for the job and arranged the whole incident to force the troublesome Nabil out. This mode of demonstrating insight by exposing what 'lay behind' everything as the cunning of one manipulative individual was a characteristic mode of local interpretation.

Commentaries turned sour. The outlaw, who lived 'in the mountain' and who was regarded as socially 'dead', was a first paternal cousin of Nabil's father. He turned up at a neighbour's house when only four or five of the shebab of Beit Abd as-Salam and myself (and none of the brothers involved) were present, grumbling furiously about the whole incident. 'What use are murajul?' he fumed. 'It's all pa-pa-pa and to-to-to and sleeping for months in the wadi among the rocks' he added with scathing bitterness, exaggeratedly puffing up his cheeks for the nonsense syllables he used to parody the young men's mouthings about their prowess. '*Qus ukht al murajul 'akrut*' (roughly, 'fuck murajul, the bastard'; literally 'the cunt of the sister of murajul the bastard'). For him, the rhetorical performance of blustering threat only led to an unglamorous reality – sleeping rough, as he did. He employed his own degraded biography as a strong rhetorical figure pointing epideictically to a conclusion opposed to that of the shebab.

From his outsider's position he attacked the theatre of manly self-representation, ridiculing its self-defeating, self-deceiving show. He used what had become a common trope for the perceived decline of the aghas, their self-entrapment in the coils of their own rhetoric. The mayor's grandfather had given away a priceless olive grove for his word. These young men now squandered themselves in empty words incapable even of the grand gesture of the past. His evocation of the world of the mountain, barren, solitary and beyond society – the only reward for murajul – was a poignant comment, coming as it did from 'a dead man' who had made his now wasted life out of miscalculated and dishonourable violence.

Other fractions of the agha descent group exposed other vulnerabilities of the narrative which protagonists were seeking to establish. The mayor's large beit was in some tension with those most immediately involved because of divisions over the anticipated village baladiya elections and the parliamentary elections of 1972.[10] Moreover, since the mayor's house and allies were unconstrained by close attachment to the sheikh ash-shebab through work or influence, had no important kin links with Nabil, they were able to reconstitute events as a subject of comedy. Humour distanced them from the call to arms and subverted the evocation of challenge and response. They remade the confrontation in Tripoli into the tale of a dirty deed, provoking much amusement at sahras. Nabil they described as a jerk and a wastrel, a hopeless trouble-maker of whom one could expect nothing good. Their version featured, not an insult to be avenged with hamasa, staves and guns, but just the sort of nonsense you would expect from that clown, putting on his big act in the city and creating a needless imbroglio. He had got exactly what he deserved. In open mockery, they distanced themselves from the ma'rika.[11]

The richest humour was derived from exploiting an incongruity that had been suppressed in Nabil's original narrative. It had been learned that the female director of the school had asked her hapless chauffeur: 'What? Are you going to bring qabadays here to the school?' The reiteration of her devastating challenge epitomized the discrepancy between city–village responses: murajul were 'out of place' in the town. In a school, before the woman who was the head of the institution, the performance of manliness was still more inappropriate. She represented progress (taqaddum), culture (thaqafa) and education (ta'lim). With every repetition of her remark Nabil was represented as out of his social depth, out of time as well as out of place. The director could be made a figure of transcendent values, respected and acknowledged as superior to the ways of the village where their absence was endlessly lamented. The formulaic confrontation of insulting and the show of rifles could be presented by the mayor's group as in every dimension the wrong form of challenge.[12]

Nabil had a job. He was a bus driver, and that was all. Acting as if 'being a man' was involved was mere buffoonery. Another logic and rhetoric prevailed, that of the job and the work hierarchy. Foolishly he had mixed the two, failed to discriminate, and got what he was asking for. The stinging remark said to have been made by the director reduced the display of force to gross misjudgement and ignorance of social form. Rather than appearing as the admired figure of the courageous, tough, 'true man', the qabaday figured as a blunderer who committed crude and clumsy coercion devoid of social awareness; he was a character from a limited world of rural values that could only be an object of mockery in the school. Nabil's failure to respond, his silence before the terse and ironic rhetorical question of the director, was a sign of the qabaday's impotence.

We can now see the precariousness of narrative space when both work and violent confrontation contributed to the founding event. The major actors attempted to circumscribe that space, more properly to circumlocute it, and to define its major topographical features in terms of the logics of blow and riposte, hamasa, and all the vital qualities of 'men'. But this story proved impossible to establish beyond a narrow audience of those immediately concerned.

The sheikh ash-shebab had exercised a key choice by reacting at once as if an imperative of honour was at stake. But that choice proved increasingly difficult to present in convincing rhetoric as the right one to have made. He had to be seen as a leader. He grabbed opportunities to act and had put Nabil's family under an obligation to him by demonstrating his authority over the young men and instant response to an insult. Yet given the consensus with regard to the chauffeur's character and the problems that might follow a move into the relatively unknown world of a girls' school in the city, a man of judgement might well have hesitated in order to think on various courses of action. He might have counselled an appeal to 'the family' and spun the matter out to test opinion. Furthermore, he himself was involved in the organization of semi-industrial work and knew better than most how men were being compelled increasingly to acknowledge that the world of work had its own imperatives, the chief of which was that a wage was a pre-eminent maslaha thrown away by none but fools. He had made a rash move. The outcome had not been a great success on any count. He had to try to reconcile two different narratives, of virtue and interest, agonism and oc-cupation.

The intense rhetorical efforts of his shebab to show in formulaic language and formal demeanour that they were indeed 'the shebab' were both justi-fication and a heightening of the significance of a situation whose dubious nature was actually more and more difficult to conceal. However, the sharp perception and wonderfully judged acting of one of their number pointed at the comic possibilities inherent in the processes of constituting a narrative of Nabil's fight. The young parodist produced his own reflexive and comic performance, built on the incongruity and incommensurability of narrative and action.

The outlaw's grim denunciation, on the other hand, had exploded murajul from within, showing that its consequences were quite the reverse of the illusions of the shebab. His was the narrative in which collective self-deception and the biography of 'a dead man' were fused. He made of himself an icon of social exclusion, speaking with the only authority to which he could lay unassailable claim, that which derived from his solitary place outside society, 'in the mountain'. He could also draw on the fact that he had been for twenty years a tractor driver with Nabil's father, his first paternal cousin, and had a relationship with him of great closeness and privilege.[13]

The mayor's sahra could be an open arena for the comic devaluation and redefinition of the whole narrative space. Laughter here, apart from anything else, endorsed the mayor's political judgement in staying aloof from the fracas in which his rivals were implicated. The refusal to treat the matter as one on which the entire descent group could or ought to be mobilized took the form both of ridiculing the instigator of the crisis and of relocating the language of murajul in the city to a subordinated and encapsulated position. It became an inappropriate performance marking out the fundamental social error of the narrators. Instead of the surface coherence of the sheikh ash-shebab's account, the mayor's laughter suggested nothing but a mess.

Narrative, serious and comic, was an appeal for support. Local politics and intra-descent group influence were at issue. According to one's interest Nabil's fight could be made into either an insult which all good men would wish at once to avenge, or a messy scuffle on a bus caused by a troublesome nuisance who deserved everything he got. The response of the sheikh ash-shebab similarly was either appropriately honourable or ludicrously misjudged. Modes of narrative presentation were not mere reflections of positions already occupied or taken. They were also weapons in a set of more or less important struggles going on within the wider group.

Work and the labour market thus confronted men with challenges of a different kind in different social spaces and under different constraints from those to which they were accustomed. Obedience to *need*, defined in terms of a wage and a job, and a material value defined in terms of labour power and skills, appeared to be a contradiction of the narrative principles of social life. That contradiction was mediated by personal links and the continuing importance of personal violence, but it was consciously present. We shall see in the next chapter how narrative transformations might nonetheless be attempted which would magically restore the primacy of status honour over the logic of the market and the calculation of financial worth.

CHAPTER SIXTEEN

Horsemen on Tractors

The Chauffeuriyya

The changing labour market brought in new considerations of the disposition of time and the ways in which time could be measured and given value; it introduced new and problematical perceptions of action, choice, project, investment and the future; and it posed questions concerning the relation of the worker to the family and pertinent to the pooling or division of a family's material resources.

Wages might mean acknowledging the need for a source of income just like everyone else, including the fellahin. But there was another side to the matter. Wages were also the way to regain land, to speculate in olives, to lend at interest to prodigal and impoverished young beys, to buy one's own tractor or car, to furnish a house with the new consumer durables still hardly to be found in Berqayl in the early 1970s. A somewhat different kind of social status was emerging: of money and what a man could make it do for him.

To take commands, obey routines of fixed hours, lift and carry, and go here and there as required, might be galling to a 'real man'. On the other hand, to be called 'a good worker' and perhaps 'one who gets work for others' was becoming a serious tribute. Everyone said that a man of honour did nothing for money. Increasingly, however, one could do little without it. Practical measures led most men, including young beys of impoverished houses, to the world of work where agonistic exchange might well be treated by others as simply 'out of place'. Value, virtue and excellence took on different, often blurred meanings.

Work, kinship, politics and violence were not clearly distinct spheres of life. Every job required the use of influence and a patron: entry into the army, harvesting the fields on a landlord's property, becoming a trainee mechanic, joining a workshop making furniture, operating a bulldozer on a big construction site, or driving a school bus in Tripoli. This required a sense of how to make connections, a certain social finesse. If one could bargain for a revolver as part of the deal – and there were those who did – then the role of a part-time bodyguard and protector of property became an integral function of the relationship.

Younger men spoke of keeping their money to themselves and planning their own futures; they complained that kin made working in the village very difficult because of all the claims, not infrequently competing, they made on one and the expectation that one might do the job for less than the going rate; landowners from one's own family should be treated like any landowners, as bosses with opposing interests to the drivers. At the same time, the clusters of brothers working together and the choice of people for the airport work team showed how closely tied were kindred, work and politics in the broadest sense. If one was not going to follow the lead of the sheikh ash-shebab in the elections, one was not going to keep a job.

Work began to suggest other forms of temporality and biography, other narratives of lives developing over time, lives represented in terms no longer those of the values of the companion to the lords. And yet the narrative of 'being a man' ready to defend and challenge might at any time impinge on work, presenting urgent dilemmas of social judgement and commensurability.

Being 'in work', or, just as significantly, being 'out of work', had become crucial. 'Unemployment', a relatively new term, appeared as a state of being as much as an absence of occupation. Lives were coming to be apprehended as structured and framed also by the market, however personal relations might remain. Only one man out of an active male population of eighty-seven in the whole of Beit Abd as-Salam was classified as 'unemployed' by informants who gave me a list of occupations, but most of the drivers and workers in my period there had practical experience of 'sitting' – the idle days between jobs.

'Sleeping in the house', or 'sitting', these terms were expressive of lack of activity, activity which in the world of 'being a murafiq' was so central and took such different and esteemed forms. Every value with which the young aghas had been inculcated said that a man had to act. 'Sitting' represented a kind of limbo, without dignity and without any arena in which one might either confront or collaborate with others. 'Sleeping in the house' confined one to the woman's sphere and as a dormant figure, a doubly anomalous position. Some men tried to pass it off, saying that a given job 'didn't suit them, they didn't need it', but this was socially unconvincing and taken to be mere empty words.

Money and manliness became integrally linked. The fathers' generation knew it. They needed the productive sons to contribute to the foundations of the unit of patriarch and cluster of sons which ideally make up 'the beit of X'. Added rooms, now above, now adjacent, now facing the father's house, were tangible signs of the constructive power of cash.[1]

Men of fellahin origin also had access to jobs other than unskilled manual labour. With wages they could build houses in breeze-blocks, distinct from the stone, wood and mud dwellings still inhabited by the poorest in the early 1970s. They might even add a small balcony, a sign of luxury in the use of space, and put flowering plants on the wall in earth-filled jerry cans. They could buy new clothes for themselves and their children at the time of the great Muslim festivals when formal visiting was required, and decorations for a reception room where people could admire (and envy) the cotton-covered armchairs, the electricity supply, the fan in the summer and the gas fire in winter rather than the old paraffin stove. They exhibited as many signs of equality of appearance with the aghas as money allowed. Those who became carpenters, iron workers, or builders, could achieve such signs of prosperity. Some of these men used their profits to buy small plots of land themselves. Work made that possible too.

Young agha men knew how much they had in common with fellahin contemporaries in terms of their place in the market. That awareness translated itself in situations of family and status into even more ferocious declarations of superiority and their unmatched capacity for violence.

Many of Beit Abd as-Salam under the age of forty-five or so framed the historical narration of their own place in life and that of their family in terms of a transition from the primacy of land to the primacy of wages, and their biographies in terms of jobs. Tariq was about twenty-two years old, the youngest of five sons and two daughters. His father, he told me, had to give up his holdings in Syria after the land reform of 1958. His eldest brother was already in the police at that time, a much desired post with guaranteed employment and certain opportunities for other, not strictly licit, gains. It required a powerful mediation to arrange such an opportunity, and the father had had it. 'We had money and servants in Hamidiya,' he said, recalling proudly how magnificent the reception room had been and the long stays of the lords who came hunting in the region and stayed for a month or more. His grandfather had been the 'head of the family' of his time, and there were stories of how he had physically beaten up a couple of the beys and defied the greatest of them to dare take on Beit Abd as-Salam after some quarrel. 'We were independent. We never worked for the beys, not like the others,' he would insist.

When his family came up to Berqayl after the loss of their property in the Syrian land reforms of 1958 which deprived the beys of their holdings, his father began to deal in olives with the beys. Then the old man bought a tractor. One son drove it, and the next opened a small shop selling butagaz, paraffin and petrol. The place did not do too well, so the son in charge of it sold up and got into the army through his father's connections. (While I was in the village he had to leave the army because of an accident and for some months stayed at home on disability allowance.) His father sold the tractor and bought a Morris car to use as a taxi taking people back and forth to the plain. The car ownership, very significantly, was shared with a man from a fellah family who had some money to invest in a speculative venture, and 'he ruined the motor' driving it in Syria. Two other brothers were 'chauffeurs', one driving a tractor and the other currently drove a school bus. 'I spent eight years here and took the school certificate,' Tariq told me. 'Then the family sent me to the religious college in Tripoli to be a sheikh. After ten days I left and went to work on the airport in Beirut for two years.'

Four months as a 'mechanic' with a French company which also ran the airport contract followed, then he went back to building the runway. Sometimes he took a threshing machine around at harvest time as well.[2]

Tariq's 27-year-old maternal cousin, Ali, left school when he was nine. His father had always been a wakil for the beys but had no land himself. For two years Ali was a tractor driver with Nabil's father in Syria and on the plain, though there was little winter work. That was 100LL a month. Then he had six years in Tripoli as a mechanic repairing cars, after an introduction to the garage owner from a relative who worked there. By the end of the time he was earning 60LL a week. Four years were spent driving the big caterpillar tractor belonging to an uncle in Baalbek, Zahle and the plain in summer, 'working day and night'. In the winter he ferried sand and pebbles to construction sites and 'might get some sleep'. Or he would take a tractor off on odd jobs. That gave him 300LL a month.

Why had he gone into the army then, given that the pay was slightly less? 'Just like that, really,' Ali said. 'You get a uniform, wander around and take the air, and get 290LL a month.' His wife stayed with his father in the latter's house and he visited when he could. He was just finishing a two-room place of his own built on to one side of the existing house. 'Actually,' he told me, 'the best thing to be is a mechanic, but there's no way I can open my own garage and there are a lot of mechanics, so I stay in the army. The engines are new, not like the rubbish in civilian life, and I'm happy at the moment.'

Ali's next youngest brother, Ahmed, had had three years 'sitting in the house'. He worked for nine years in an olive oil can factory in Tripoli, but had an endless series of minor accidents and hand lacerations and left. Now he too was an army mechanic and chauffeur. Of the other three brothers, one was the first from the village to go to teacher training college in Tripoli and the two younger ones were still at school, though the elder of them did a bit of driving as well.

'Chauffeur': cars, taxis (official and otherwise) tractors, bulldozers, dumper trucks, vans, heavy-duty lorries, school buses, whatever had wheels and a motor seemed to be included.[3] Men were often therefore able to work both in agriculture, services or construction. There were thirty-four men who classified themselves occupationally in this way, seven of them being owners or owner-drivers of taxis, private cars, or agricultural machines. If we allow for the fact that at least four of the fourteen men of Beit Abd as-Salam who were in the army worked in transport, we can see that nearly half of the active male population of the group were spoken of as 'chauffeurs'. Groups of brothers were significant here too: Abu Nabil and his four working sons; Abu Khalid and two of his brothers; the three al-Hassan boys; four of Abu Osman's sons. The clusterings were such that the largest fraction of Beit Abd as-Salam, Beit Abd al Latif, had thirty-two of its thirty-seven working males as drivers or as work organizers whose position depended on machine ownership.[4]

To be known as a chauffeur a man had to know the mechanics and be able to do repairs under critical eyes comparing him with others. He was expected to be able to take the clutch, or the gears, or the whole engine apart, and to have the right network of contacts to get jobs he could not manage done for him. He had to be able to talk, knowledgeably, about the machines and swap stories. He was expected to know what kind of tractor was good for what job, the costs and capacities of all the new models, and to talk with assurance and eventually some connoisseurship about any car on the street. Most important, he had to know the limits of his own competence. It was no use affecting a skill one did not possess, since one could so easily be exposed as a fool.

When it came to talk about engines and doing the repairs on a vehicle, men dropped any idiom of kizb or tafnis altogether. Where a father and son were both mechanics the latter might not hesitate to correct publicly a job his father was doing – in other circumstances an almost unthinkable challenge to paternal authority. The father might well ask him to do it because he recognized his son's specialities. Others would evaluate their work very frankly and objectively in front of them. Male hierarchy took on a different form in this context.

A man could earn the title 'chauffeur' the hard way – driving all over the cereal growing areas of northern Syria as far as Aleppo and the Gezira area, or going as far as the Iraqi border for three summer months, sleeping under the harvester; or over the mountain into the Beqaʻa valley and Baalbek area; or to the Zghorta region due east above Tripoli with only his own skill and wits and the landowner's name to defend him against thieves. He was obliged to deal with people with whom his work had often been arranged through a third party. Running repairs depended on cobbling something together from whatever parts could be cannibalized or on inspirational 'making do'. Landowners wanted the harvest in, and the driver had to keep the Massey Ferguson or the International, and himself, going as many hours as he could in the hot sun and chill night, sometimes miles from a village.

A driver might make money as a bey's chauffeur for a period, or as a full-time job. That meant wearing a suit, carrying a gun, sitting in attendance, waiting around at all times and then sweeping his boss off in a Cadillac, Buick or Peugeot depending on his master's status. The family would expect him to train younger brothers or cousins, to let them watch him at work, or to arrange for them to join the workshop of a skilled mechanic in Tripoli. Listening to the conversations in the back seat of his car as he drove along, or in the reception rooms of the well-to-do, he could back his opinions with the weight of reports of what the influential were saying and doing; or, more often, of what they said they were doing while actually doing quite the opposite. But he *knew*.

Work exchange was important: one would help his kinsman or colleague on a day off or when he was 'sitting', and the other would reciprocate (providing the two men were not competing for the same job); each would help to keep the other's machine running. A man who had no tractor or car of his own might repair another's vehicle with a tacit understanding that he had a claim to work with it at some stage when a job came up. Such exchanges, the loose but real sense of a community of work experience, a grasp of mechanics, and a proper awareness of one's status, could draw the drivers together as colleagues if need arose.

Drivers might invite their workmates from a building site, workshop, garage, or the army vehicle pool, back to Berqayl on a formal visit. They were 'colleagues' and 'comrades', *zumala'*, a term used locally of a man for whom the host claimed special status relating to work and friendship outside the realm of the kin.[5] Other chauffeurs would respectfully attend, marking by their behaviour and the tenor of the occasion their own value and seriousness as men in the community. A father might insist on his young son's visitor smoking a nargileh, something which the young normally never did in the presence of their seniors, and would provide a large meal served in the reception room. If their visitor was of some standing in the profession and was respectfully addressed by the title of *mu'allem*, then the father would completely take over the occasion. He would welcome and make much of a man of such worth and would show a maximum of respect and attention to someone who taught the skills so important in this economy.

The older chauffeurs knew that a serious demeanour, a suit, a pair of dark glasses, a Belgian revolver in the waistband, and a heavy imitation gold watch carried real weight when they purred up the road past the mosque in the Buick belonging to the beys. They would leave it to a kid to swirl his Massey Ferguson round on its axis for all the world as if he was a great horseman on a tractor, and would drily comment on the expense of ruined tyres. Style and form remained important to them too, but they demonstrated their status in appropriately modern ways of dress and ornament.

All the drivers in agricultural work shared common problems in dealing with their bosses. Owners and employers, whether from Berqayl or outside, often held forth on their employees 'unreliability', complaining that they could never depend on them. Drivers would be stopped on the road and fined 100LL for not having licences, fines they would want the boss to pay though they would not have told him that they did not have the necessary document. Men bringing their own machines would describe them as being in perfect working order when all too frequently that was not the case. Days were lost for repairs. At other times it would turn out that the chauffeur could not raise the money to hire the plough he had described as his own. Or the landowners claimed that the chauffeurs would quit their work with no explanation and no warning, either for several days or indefinitely, saying simply that they were 'tired'.[6] There was nothing the boss could do. It was often difficult to find replacements at no notice, not least because men with these skills went into the building industry rather than agriculture, and they were left with a harvest to bring in and no workers. Then if they did get a replacement, the first driver might reappear with the equipment and a dispute would erupt that was even more difficult to resolve if all the parties were from Beit Abd as-Salam than if they had no kin ties.

One working group returned unexpectedly in the village over a month before they were due. They had made the long journey back from north of Aleppo and were exhausted; the harvester would take several days to follow them. Why had they returned early? The machine had broken down many times; it was too far away and the work tired them out, so they quit.[7] In any case, all except one expressed a dislike for 'the Syrians'. Another man I knew very well also left his Syrian employers, from whom he had negotiated 1,600LL for a two-month work stint, to bring back his vehicle for repairs and was not sure whether he would be able to fulfil the terms of their verbal agreement. It was not uncommon to find a man saying that he had walked out of a job, infuriating his relatives who were working with him as well as the employer, because he was fed up, or it was Ramadan and he simply could not cope with fasting (which his colleagues alleged he never did anyhow).

Drivers had to haggle over wages for a harvesting job or a season's engagement, which was always paid on a daily basis. One owner might offer only 5LL and the driver would argue for 7LL with 10LL in the spring when there was intensive work to be done and someone who could plough well was much valued. If the boss could find someone he felt able to rely on who would do the job for less, the first man lost his income. 'A man has to live', and appeals to shared interests *vis-à-vis* the owners would be made to try to avoid others offering their labour more cheaply.

Relations between drivers and landowners became quite strained in the two years of my fieldwork. Beys with land on the plain tried to bring in tractor drivers from elsewhere in an attempt to be free of the collective constraints and problems that dealing with men from Beit Abd as-Salam imposed. They wanted a more strictly economic relationship, less encumbered by the web of bey–agha history. The region was changing. Businessmen from other regions wanted an easily controlled workforce taking its wages and doing the work on time. They were often unable to grasp the complexities of local social relations and found themselves subject to different forms of what they saw as cheating, theft, obstruction and violence.[8] The idea of getting in outside drivers was also not without private appeal to the managers and landowners of Beit Abd as-Salam itself, since they were frequently tangled up in competing claims of relatives to monopolize this or that job.

The chauffeurs reacted to the threat. Some spoke vaguely but with passion about forming a union: first, to block the importation of 'outsiders' into the beit's territory, geographical and economic; secondly, to stop them being manipulated against each other; and thirdly, to deal *en bloc* with their employers, especially where those employers were kin trying to use that leverage and the code of duty and family loyalty to influence a deal. A union might strengthen the all too permeable barrier between work and wages on the one hand, and the importuning of a powerful relative on the other. The problem was, of course, that a driver might very well wish to claim those same family ties himself in order to claim the 'right' to a particular job in the gift of a kinsman. So the arguments for a union had disadvantages, as everyone knew.

More ambitious schemes were mooted. If a syndicate were established it would put huge pressures on the landowners at harvest time. The chauffeurs could refuse to bring in the crops or allow watchmen on the holdings, or to let in other drivers to replace them. This was the suggestion of the qabaday neighbour who offered the advice on using a knife in Tripoli to which I have referred in the previous chapter. He personally would go round the other villages in Akkar and say 'to avoid trouble between you and Berqayl all you have to do is not send any labourers to Berqayl this year'. We did not need rifles and sticks, he added, but we did need a sha'b, real people. You could get a couple of the men from each beit in Berqayl, he said, waving aside the fellah–agha distinction, and completely screw the beys simply by not letting any of them near the village. The beys and other owners would be forced to give in and grant the drivers a third of the harvest as well as the daily wage – a kind of sharecropping by violence. The language used, 'by force', 'whether they like it or not' and 'we'll close the region against them', was typical of honour confrontations and brought the idea of conflict and social stratum into the heart of the work setting.

The man who had refused to support Nabil, on the grounds that he had a family to support and could not afford to lose his job, objected that some of the landowners were from Beit Abd as-Salam itself and so should not be compared to landowners from another region. 'What if they are?' retorted one of his younger brothers, who made his living as a tractor driver. 'We need to live too. We've got kids to bring up.'

There was an element of quasi-class conflict here, mixed with conflicting interests over property ownership. Voluble supporters of the idea of a union borrowed from the language of the Syrian baathists active in Tripoli and on the plain and from Palestinian leftist rhetoric. But the same baathist ideology was opposed by the same drivers when they felt that the labourers down in the poor coastal settlements were being encouraged to rise against the system of property represented by the great landowners. In that situation, all the sections of Beit Abd as-Salam at once supported the rule of the beys and the property regime. The rhetoric of a union was therefore never translated into action. There were too many cross-cutting ties and relations with the beys and 'outsider' landowners and within the agha families for such a major collective confrontation. But it was spoken of, and the tensions it expressed were in people's consciousness.

There were unpredictable delays in projects, such as the one at Beirut airport, that led to lay-offs at very short notice. If bad weather stopped work no one was paid. Days were very long, starting at dawn and going on till early evening. Men were doing very heavy work out on the piste in great heat. The drivers also alleged that the charges which were deducted at source for rent and meals in the cheap four-room apartment – where up to twenty-five men might be sleeping packed together on mattresses in every available space – were too high. Each man had to pay about 15LL a week for rent and another 12LL for food. Each had to provide his own work clothing, shoes and equipment. A semi-skilled worker received 11LL for eight hours work and then one-and-a-quarter time, so he might make 16–17LL per day on a six- and sometimes a seven-day week. Drivers got no overtime at all, which was a reason several of them gave for leaving. Disputes blew up.

The youngest of Nabil's brothers, a boy of about sixteen, lost his temper when his older relatives and employers failed to (or could not) pay him money he claimed was owing. The adolescent stormed off to the public space by the old mosque in Berqayl, the main arena for confrontation and denunciation, and began to insult his employer and kinsman, to everyone's shock. For an adolescent to shout and swear against the forceful and important sheikh ash-shebab in that way contradicted all the norms of hierarchy, whether of family or work. One of his brothers, who was a couple of years older and also worked at the airport, heard what was going on and leapt on him furiously to give him a real beating in front of everyone and to reassert the 'respect' of his embarrassed family.

His maternal uncle (the outlaw who had driven with their father in Syria for so many years) heard the screaming and cursing from his house just near the mosque. He hurried down and tried to pull the boys apart. But the elder would not stop thrashing the younger, who had drawn a knife and was trying to stab or fend off his assailant. Their uncle pulled out his ancient Second World War English service revolver, a monstrous thing with a long barrel, and began to hit the attacker with it, to no avail. Finally, he cocked the gun and told him he'd blow him away unless he stopped. The younger brother escaped, bleeding, howling with rage and waving the knife, and ran off. He spent the night outside the village 'in the mountain' with his outlaw uncle before he dared return home, where he feared worse assaults from the others of his family. The row continued in the house, loudly, for several days.

The boy felt that the exchange should be a simple one: money for work, as if other elements were not in fact present by the very fact of kinship and the way the work was organized by the sheikh ash-shebab. He had done the job. He wanted his money. When he did not get it, he reverted at once to the classical form of public insult in response to a challenge, thus combining the social logics of work, of confrontation and of hierarchy in a problematic mixture. In so doing, he followed the code of display and public denunciation, but over an issue in which he could never be supported by others in public and in reference to wages which were not regarded as part of the arena of karama and personal integrity to be defended by force.

Men found it hard to come to a social consensus over just how disputes should be regulated in the work setting when so many factors might be involved. They could not easily decide what was at stake, or what were the appropriate forms of conduct, and that ambiguity could be very dangerous.

The young man had grown up in a household dominated by machines and mechanics. The whole nuclear family was defined in relation to such work. The father, Abu Nabil, was a wonderful mechanic on any machine, except his own car, an East German wreck which in my time there never worked.[9] Every Sunday, his day off from work in the company where he was employed, he was there, seated on the ground behind his small house dismantling the engine. If it was raining the only room they had became a sort of workshop with parts, grease and rags everywhere all over the central space between the large bed, the cupboard, table and four or five chairs.[10]

This car was his chief project and leisure activity. Every month or.so it would be rebuilt and pushed up the hill early on a Sunday morning, to be run down again in a stench of burning cable, clouds of filthy diesel fumes, or on one occasion, a burst of flames. Covered in oil, he and his sons would push it back home and start again. The car – 'the only East German car in the whole of Lebanon' he would say with a rueful grin, 'I thought it would be cheap to run' – defied everything he could do to it. The vehicle became a symbol of an unsurmountable obstacle and an investment that led only to loss. 'We used to eat chicken', one of the younger boys said to me, drily, 'but now, with our machines, all we eat is beans and rice.'

Nor was that Abu Nabil's only problem. He had a harvester that was impounded in Syria by Customs. Rival beys' families promised to get it for him. There was the election of 1972 coming up and they were competing for his family's votes. But he never took them up on the offered deals, and there clearly was some additional problem he was concealing. The harvester had ruined him financially. He had been well off before, owning a caterpillar tractor. He was the first one in the whole beit to own a car, and used to drive the richest of the aghas on important errands. One of the earliest 'real mechanics' and chauffeurs of Beit Abd as-Salam, he had made 20,000LL from the harvester for its two seasons, or so others estimated. Now his family did not even eat chicken.

Abu Nabil had other problems over and above his debts. His health was not good and he had breathing difficulties, but never dared to stay at home when he felt ill in case he was fired. He had lost three fingers in a work accident and was fortunate to be still dextrous enough to do all the repairs demanded of him. Most drivers had the same job insecurity. Accidents were a hazard of the trade. There were worse eventualities than lost fingers. Tractors had no cabs or protective bars. In wet conditions or on a hill terrace they could be unstable and dangerous. One teenager of Beit Abd as-Salam was confined to bed for life, his back broken when the machine toppled over as he was ploughing on tricky terrain, crushing him beneath it. Stories of major injuries and deaths were common. Safety regulations were usually non-existent.

Axles were regularly broken, gearboxes went, second-hand tractor tyres dried inside and cracked. Oil pumps ceased to work and engines burnt out; clutches were exposed to heavy use and failed, ploughs and harrows were badly damaged on rough land. The list was long. Yet despite all the difficulties, machines were thought of by many, senior and junior men alike, as a good investment. Moreover, they were part of a new order displacing one dominated by the notion that the purchase of land was the obvious priority for anyone seeking security, prestige and returns. The aghas had seen and spoken about Abboud Bey's success with the early use of agricultural machinery. He had prospered greatly, and machines appeared as a formula for change and profit, though men seemed to forget the depth of the human and capital resources he could command and the security derived from all his other enterprises.

Two brothers who had regularly driven for him had profited from his death by keeping possession of caterpillar tractors and threshers, and had made renting them out the foundation of their own prosperity. Now they employed others from the family and were important figures in organizing work locally. The skills of the chauffeur and the mechanic had been appreciated very early on as a result of this historical link with Abboud's modernization programme. Beit Abd as-Salam had developed a group speciality in skills which could be used, either in agriculture, or in construction and other jobs.

'Driving' thus already had a very positive history in Berqayl by the time of my fieldwork. One senior agha, who had become rich as manager on the landholding of Abboud's widow and had put some of his money into one of the four mechanized olive presses in the village, advised a young kinsman to buy a tractor and a thresher if he wanted to invest his wages. The senior man offered to guarantee him; there was no reason to buy land for the same cost.

Men would heatedly debate the issues of investment choices and the relative advantages of different options: should they buy land, or olives ahead of harvest, or would the money be better put into acquiring a tractor, and if so what make of machine for what sort of work and conditions? One of the elders of the beit, who had spent forty years working for the beys, advised a nephew not to lend to the young lords at interest as that was forbidden by Islamic law. Instead, he should put his wages into property in Tripoli and take rent – a much better proposition. Members of the older generation were therefore quite as likely to downgrade the significance of land as a source of prestige and money as were their sons.

Such choices and decisions were central to the younger wage earners. As adolescents or unmarried men, they would begin by giving all their wages to their fathers and receive a fixed sum as an allowance. After a year or two, they would keep what they were paid and give a certain amount to the family, retaining control of their own funds. They would say that they were saving for their marriage, or to build a house at some rather vague time in the future. They could thus control the money on an individual basis, any

financial arrangement with a brother in a tractor, for example, being set out
on a strictly legal basis establishing share ownership and not as an undivided
enterprise among family members. None of them could afford irrigated,
tree-planted land, and they were as sceptical as the seniors about the value
of growing cereals or other cash crops on small plots except as a side
investment. One of the brothers who had taken over Abboud's machinery
on his death spoke of making 15,000LL profit on a harvest season in Syria
after paying out his expenses of around 4,000LL for the two drivers of his
harvester. He found a receptive audience. That was an excellent return.

Leader of the Fighting Men

The identity of Hassan, the sheikh ash-shebab, was founded on a combination
of bringing work for kinsmen and in a readiness to act 'at once'. He had a
history of taking on opponents, of furiously challenging anyone, even the
most powerful lords if he felt that the aghas were affronted.[11] So it was to
him that men ran shouting hysterically as they burst into his main work
room where we were all sitting while various mechanical tasks were being
done: 'Women are being raped! Blood is being shed in the heart of the
village! And you are sitting here doing nothing!' The army and police had
moved against Berqayl in 1972 because groups in the village had cut the road
to the mountain in a dispute with the government. Hassan rushed from his
house with the other mechanics and myself, grabbing rifles and shrieking
that blood was being shed in the heart of the village. Once in the heart of
the dai'a at the old mosque he hurled his name in a crescendo howl at the
qaimaqam (senior governorate official) who stood in the middle of the road,
impeccably grey-suited and elegant: 'I am Hassan Abd as-Salam!' he screamed,
on a deafening rising note, as if the name itself should paralyse the man who
had dared to penetrate the village at the head of an armed force.

The qaimaqam, confronted with the posse of armed men and as aware
that more rifles were trained on him from the fellah quarter up on the hill
behind as he was of the lines of armed government forces down in the olive
groves below, said simply: 'The shame of it, the shame of it.' This refusal to
participate in the discourse of honour in Hassan's terms, while implicitly
asserting a higher code of order, had the effect of blocking the rhetoric of
name and insult which the young men used to define the situation in terms
of challenge and response.

The official himself was unarmed. He had carefully come into the village
without an escort. He wished to talk. The notable of Beit Abd as-Salam,
who had many connections in Tripoli and already knew the qaimaqam,
advanced to parlay quietly with him. Though some villagers blazed away
from up on the hill and the army returned fire, everyone realized that the
fire was in both cases being directed well over the heads of the opposition
and was to preserve *amour propre*.

The talking continued. Hassan had forcefully played his role, but had been effectively countered. He had to yield to senior notables of the agha beit who came forward in their most formal dress to denounce their sons for disorder and civil strife, and to demand peremptorily that they return to their homes.

Faced with a barrage of the most scathing and public denunciations by their own fathers, the shebab, white faced and very tense, slowly began to drift away. But they, too, had done their job. They had shown that the village was not to be trifled with. But they were also made very aware that the older men would do anything to avoid a full-scale armed confrontation with the government.

As central to Hassan's position as a capacity for violence was practical expertise and the control of work opportunities. He was permanently on the lookout for second-hand dumper trucks, cement mixers, tractors, trailers, threshing machines and harvesters for use on construction sites or on the estates and landholdings of Akkar, the Beqa'a valley, the Koura and Syria. There were bargains to boast of: the truck trailer he had bought for 1,200LL that he swore was worth 3,000–4,000LL; the 'surplus to requirements' cement mixers picked up for 200LL each from a ministry official. Every tractor or vehicle hired from him by the airport construction company was worth 40LL a day in rent, of which the driver only cost a quarter. Machines meant money.

The younger brother, who acted as his number two in organizing work on all his jobs, despaired of what he saw as a failure to realize that one needed capital and a reserve fund, and a calculation of future eventualities. 'You always reckon the maximum and never think of all the possibilities which could make it the minimum', he said earnestly to his older sibling. They had just been obliged to hand back a Russian harvester because they could not continue to make the payments.[12] But the work team leader was off the same day to look at an old threshing machine when the one they already had was causing them expensive problems, and he was thinking of buying a Russian caterpillar bulldozer too. He had made 1,500LL in two days on a job at an engineering school just above Beirut a few days previously, a windfall that would finance more machines. He would have a sudden idea – that the steering mechanism of an old Desoto would work in a broken-down dumper truck, for instance – and it would fail. Hours of work would lead to nothing. But he could always point to schemes which had succeeded, at least for a time, and carry on to the next one.

His brother, Khalid, who had lost a finger on the engineering job and spent time in hospital, grimaced in disapproval of his elder's expenditures. The younger man had spent a year in Saudi Arabia working with another brother who had his own mechanic's workshops and construction business there, but he had found the hours and what he saw as very poor pay no real incentive to stay, so he had come back to Berqayl. He did not like the absence of planning and placed a high value on securing his family income. 'Might not becoming an army mechanic be better for me?' he asked me one day. He would be free of family entanglements and have a guaranteed post for life.

The sheikh ash-shebab acknowledged their differences and his own lack of careful planning, 'but that's how I am'. The constant self-invention through new projects had another very practical dimension. I have already mentioned that he was using his capacity to find work for others to bind families to him in terms of election votes for the candidate he favoured. Long before the vote he was making promises of places in military college and of positions he would obtain for faithful clients 'just by telephoning' – the standard boast of the ease with which a patron could arrange what he wished. The more jobs he had at his disposal, the larger the number of the shebab linked to his fortunes. But these arrangements did not always turn out successfully. Men sometimes came under great pressure from other kin or as a result of other established social obligations to follow another course of action and left the work group. Bitterness and a public break in relations would follow. The sheikh ash-shebab would not speak to them for the period of estrangement, nor offer them later jobs as they arose. None of the men from the mayor's fraction of Beit Abd as-Salam, Beit Ibrahim, associated with him because it was thought that he might challenge the mayor in baladiya elections and because in the past the two sections had had a series of differences. Others from other fractions were ready to take his lead, reasoning that the wages were crucial to their social position and overrode other considerations.

Hassan had never opened a manzul, a 'traditional' strategy that he rejected in favour of a different form of assembling a following. But he sought the signs of status and influence, and they could be costly. He organized a formal invitation for two of the election candidates he supported and invited a large number of beys and men he hoped to have as allies. It was the most public occasion of its kind among the aghas for years, and had the added benefit of discomfiting his first paternal cousin, the leading notable and landowner who was supporting another candidate. (no. 21 in Figure 1). He 'showed himself off' in the lavish feast which signalled his very public bid for leadership. Shortly afterwards we went on a 'secret' expedition to an arms-dealer in another village at one o'clock in the morning to purchase a very expensive rifle. After much haggling, and the pretence of a break in negotiations altogether, the deal was fixed for 1,100LL, an enormous sum. The weapon was unique in Berqayl, no one else had one like it, and the cost was about 400LL more than a Kalashnikov. All the next day men of the agha descent group who were in any way linked to him came, often in formal dress, to admire and examine the rifle, and to compliment him on the purchase (see Plate 16).

He thus filled the time with a stream of projects, all requiring the mobilization of others in one way or another. The younger aghas were always being summoned for repairs in the reception room of his house. Its main function became that of a workshop. He spent nothing on consumer durables or new furnishing, nor did he keep an open reception room: work was his space of mobilization, it was where he was 'on show', cajoling, ordering, harassing, arranging, deciding.[13] Some privately questioned his judgement. For him, however, each machine acquired and each job taken on held out the promise of work.

The family exasperated him, he said, launching into tirades against their failure to *work*: 'They'd rather lease out land for 1,500LL or so of profit than work it themselves for a return of 6–8,000,' he fumed. Movement, change, agency – the acquisition of machines that was his brother's complaint was for him an integral part of his claim to the central role in a narrative of status and manhood.

Hassan would harangue the shebab furiously: a man is identified by what he *does*. That meant work. That was the only way of securing a future. Never mind about the past. In this rhetorical mode appeals to glorious memories were derided, though in a crisis he would be the first to shout the name of Beit Abd as-Salam as a challenge to any opponent. He never hymned the immutable qualities of older generations, but rather furiously attacked his aged father whenever the latter began to speak of his days as the great companion of Abboud Bey. Memory negated the present, and the future.

Transfigurations: High Cranes and Tango

The sheikh ash-shebab had worked for some seven years in Latin America. His reasons for going were said by his father to be tied to the murder of Muhammad al Abboud in 1953. The son had been a young man at the time and was determined to avenge the bey by killing the other landlord accused of his murder in open court, a favoured place for public revenge. But the police had got wind of the plan somehow and arrested the youth and an accomplice. Abboud had paid to get them both out of jail after two months. The father sent his son to Brazil to get him out of danger.

Hassan explained that on the jobs in Brazil, Uruguay and Argentina, he had always acted as if he were a skilled worker, though he initially had no skills at all. Employers had to be fooled if he was to be anything more than just another anonymous migrant worker. He had to make all the judgements about what level of work he could deal with at a given moment without revealing his ignorance. Backed by one or two friends on site, he had dealt with sudden difficulties in a technical vocabulary and in a foreign language.

His narrative of bluff emphasized the speed of comprehension which this secret apprenticeship demonstrated. Everything had been done '*as-sakat*', he said to me, 'silently'. Hassan portrayed himself as a classical hero figure, alone in a hostile environment. Under observation, yet himself the real observer; acquiring knowledge without the realization of those whose skills

he appropriates; having nothing but his own autonomous ability and accomplishing everything, though only he understands what is happening –
these are the hallmarks of a true man. The audience knows how the narrative
will end. The wonder lies in the extraordinary means of getting *there*, there
being both the reproduction and representation of the narrative itself and of
his vividly present identity as hero-author.

Now Hassan truly had become what once he only seemed to be. He
could organize and carry out anything from dangerous high crane work on
apartment blocks, much in demand in Beirut and Mount Lebanon, to building
an airport runway, which was in fact his current main project just south of
the capital.

There was a second achievement, however, one in which the appropriation
of form and aesthetics were the prize. The hero boasted of how he had
watched the Argentinians dancing the tango. He observed in silence, and
intuitively 'knew' how to perform its intricate movements and rhythms. One
evening he imperiously took his partner to the centre of the floor. They gave
a virtuoso demonstration of the rigorous, passionate, improvisatorily complex
world of the dance. The other dancers stopped to watch in astonishment as
he dominated the gathering through his style, command of rhythm and sheer
allure. 'He must be a native Argentinian,' everyone said. 'No one else could
tango like that.'

The two narratives, though they are really part of the master narrative of
his identity, can be linked immediately to major themes in the discourse of
power and the subject. Under the hero's gaze the mysteries of construction
and of dance are revealed. The tango narrative concerns a flamboyant public
show. The display of form and aesthetic are fundamental. Others are so
dazzled by his dancing that they can only stop their own. They became
passive, unable to equal his potent display. The eroticism of the tango, an
exotic cultural form for which there is no equivalent in the society back
home needless to say, was part of a sexual pre-eminence asserted publicly
before others. Hassan violated the boundaries of Argentinian identity in a
triumph where, this time, an artistic order of skills was required. The narrative
demonstrated his command of improvisatory imagination and cultural knowledge.

What my friend was doing in repeating his stories was to constitute his
own ta'rikh and sira (history and biography). The two narratives were not
about a past, but about his powers in a constantly acted-upon present. It was
thus entirely logical that when I asked him to 'tell me about his life', naively
expecting both a stream of talk and an 'autobiography' corresponding to my
own unreflective expectations of what that would be, all I got was an impatient
refusal. 'I look forward,' he would say. 'I only think about the future. What's
the point of going back over things?' He had already shown me 'what he
was'.

The shebab saw his competence at drawing up projects and arranging work as part of his identity, a primary reason for respect in addition to interested attachment to a provider of wages. What he had learnt by his 'extraordinary insight' he taught to them, transforming their skills and competences. The glamour of the protagonist made possible for his Lebanese village followers the magical subordination of the hard realities of labour on the site to their own criteria of honour and excellence. It gave them a way of telling that life, of narrative placement and transformation, and confirmed the continuing validity of the familiar mode of constructing identity. The shebab thus had deeper reasons to be amazed by their leader's capacities than mere material interest, however important that was. They wanted to be amazed. They needed the validation that the narrative transfigurations of the hero reasserted against what were indeed heroic odds.

CODA

The Roses of Life

The sense that life as a whole is absurd arises when we perceive, perhaps dimly, an inflated pretension or aspiration which is inseparable from the continuation of human life and which makes its absurdity inescapable, short of escape from life itself.[1]

Or we may think, on the other hand, of the '*Lebenslüge*' (vital lie) of the individual who is so often in need of deceiving himself in regard to his capacities, even in regard to his feelings, and who cannot do without superstitition about gods and men, in order to maintain his life and his potentialities.[2]

Configurations

Figures in a landscape began this book: forms, images, representations which gave shape to powers and properties. Figures were constituted, negotiated and embedded in narratives, narratives in the dialectics of social relations. The empty palace and the Minister's coffin made up another potent figure of a different kind: a form of expression deviating from the normal, a deviation at once exceptional and typical of domination.

The book ends with transfigurations in a landscape: transformation and glorification combined in a narrative that makes a migrant worker a charismatic force, the labour market a theatre of personal powers. The objective constraints of that market were transformed into the material for a demonstration, or a claim to demonstrate, the capacity to transcend them. The claim was made in terms of what were locally apprehended as the narrative structures of life, and as 'a certain kind of enacted story'.[3] The whole of this study has been an attempt to explore the conditions of existence and the many dimensions of those structures and practices.

Palace and worker might be perceived 'in reverse'. The first as nothing but a sign as empty as the building; the second as no more than a mechanic struggling for work and a very local influence. Both contained contradictions, and those inherent narrative incongruencies, incommensurabilities, and incoherencies to which I have constantly drawn attention. Neither was stable. Each might be subverted – but in certain ways and under certain conditions.

Instability of figure and social life has been my leitmotif. I have attempted to show that discrepancy and discontinuity had become central to the rhetorics and narratives of everyday practice. I mean this in three senses. First, that men were acutely conscious of different discrepancies and discontinuities in their lives, self-representations and histories; secondly, that they played on these dimensions in narrative and metanarrative, while at the same time expressing the conventional feeling that they had, contrary to the ideology of hierarchy, 'no choice'; thirdly, that specific historical processes rendered intensely problematic conceptions and practices of hierarchy and status honour taken to be 'immemorial'. I am making an analytical claim for the centrality of these elements and have constructed my own narrative and rhetoric around them.

There is an important historical point to make concerning the issue of stability. As the beys' dominance developed and physical force became identified as essential to hierarchy, power and status, men were constantly probing for weakness and testing each other's capacity to press claims. They sought position in a highly competitive universe of contest over revenues, property, labour and the benefits of the state. The establishing of reputation through fear was fundamental, the significance of narrative and repetition in that process, great. We can, I think, assume that joking, parody and ridicule of those held not to be able to sustain the claims they made must have played their integral role in such agonistic relations.

The joking and reversibility at that stage nonetheless existed, in my view, within a social universe whose structures and narratives were perceived to be fundamentally transparent and stable. As powerful beys became yet more so under the French, and as losing rivals dropped or drifted downwards into client roles or obscurity, the congruence of social reality and representation I think would have been high. My reading of the Mandate period as encapsulated by Abboud Bey, who was at once both great 'feudalist' and great capitalist, is that the 'immemorial' was fully constituted at that time under the French. Land and property were crystallized into legally established private estates. State powers were personalized. The possibilities for at least proto-capitalist rationalizations of agriculture, technology, investment and labour controls went together with a systematic incorporation of physical coercion exercised through the use of attached staffs or status groups into local and national power. The subjected subsistence cultivators, labourers and share-croppers, deprived at this stage of whatever holdings they still possessed, were more thoroughly bound to the persons of landowners and aghas. Status and personal honour were commensurate with the always contested dis-tributions of property and the macro, as well as micro, exercises of social, economic and cultural powers. Reiterated narratives asserted, commented on and represented grounded realities of everyday life and the emergent political order.

As the decades of the 1950s and 1960s developed, however, I suggest that joking, parody, and indeed the repetition of narratives in general, took on a different significance. Abboud was a great landowner, but also a great investor in the city. His peers followed the same pattern. Moreover, Syrian land legislation in 1958, the year in which Abboud was killed and Lebanon suffered a brief civil war, deprived many beys of their major holdings. The agriculture sector was becoming less important in the country as a whole. Beirut dominated that Lebanese space within which Akkar was increasingly a relatively and absolutely impoverished zone in all the dimensions the IRFED team could think to register. The costs of beys' lifestyles and political participation increased exponentially as the tertiary sector boomed and patterns of luxury-conspicuous consumption flowered.

Not only was it more and more difficult for individual beys' families to maintain social position in the contexts of Tripoli and Beirut, but their collective interest in preserving landholdings intact upon a father's death, previously the social rule, decreased. Sons were tempted to sell individual parcels for personal expenditures. If land prices rose steeply in irrigated areas as 'outside' investors with sufficient capital began to develop citrus groves, the temptation to sell was even greater. Fathers saw their progeny ready to dismantle the property and the social, as much as financial capital of what had been built up with such force, cunning and planning over many years.

When a leading bey died in 1972 no one was surprised that his many sons argued intently about what they should do with his properties, in accord only on the fact that they would divide them and each sell if he wished rather than maintain a collective patrimony. They had no interest in pursuing their father's strategies of local power, strategies which in any case they saw as failures. Shocked aghas and fellahin alike predicted the social end of their 'house' as a result. Some of them also had a material concern, for the bey's family put a considerable sum of money into the village economy through wages. That would end.

The dying and funeral of the old bey was marked with certain breaches of the all-important form supposed to govern such a key moment. Public display of freedom from constraint on the part of some of the family, as in visits to Tripoli cafés when convention demanded that they remain at home with their rapidly declining father, caused much censorious comment. Huzn, grieving, required abstaining from activities such as card playing, listening to the radio, joking and social visiting. But as the old man lay in an adjoining room all these behaviours were occurring in his reception hall. Moreover, there were few visitors. This too was much commented upon, for it was a brutal display of the loss of power and the reading of the beit's future as being no longer central to the village.

Laughter made its subversive entry into the procedures of public death in multiple forms, running now on, now below the surface of rite and transition, as if created and highlighting contradictory social forces. A venerable senior agha, much privately mocked for his insistence on the minutiae of social form, arrived in full formal dress with a written prayer he said he had spent two months composing in honour of the dying lord. This tribute from another time was greeted with barely muffled hilarity by those of the family and retainers sitting around. He was encouraged with a typically mischievous mock seriousness to read on, and on, and on, while young men spluttered behind their hands and shouted to each other to listen well to the wonder and wisdom of their elder.

In the following days dhikr rituals of rhythmical repetitions of the Names of Allah became scenes of general hilarity as individuals who lost control of themselves provided ideal butts of delighted mockery for the shebab. The young men who joined in, parodying the movements of their elders, had to shut their eyes tight in case they burst out in uncontrollable laughter. Young beys sat around in tight waisted shirts, gold neck chains, flared trousers and gilt-buckled shoes, for all the world as if they were off to a Beirut party, as several of the senior men said with contempt. 'This is huzn not farah (rejoicing)', one of the sons reprimanded the company severely. But he promptly ruined his standing by posing ludicrously inappropriate questions about adultery and sexual relations with a woman within the forbidden degrees of relationship to a religious sheikh, questions understood to relate very intimately to his own life. The sheikh replied emphatically that it certainly was not licit. He went on to add tartly that the beys should not eat with their left hands, as they were doing from a dish of meat, but only with their right. The left was polluted.

Play was created out of the sacred and the transition to death. Many saw the disorder as an expression of social 'confusion'. The funeral had become not so much a solemn ritual repetition of the forms commensurable with the demands of religion and of power as an ambiguous recognition of key disarticulations in relations.

One bey in his thirties meditated on what he called the 'solitariness, confusion and uncertainty' of the lords. He did not know what to do and had veered between the idea of being an insurance agent, a space engineer and half a dozen other occupations. Having settled on air space control management he had found out it was no use to anyone here in Lebanon. 'We're all like this.' He told me his father and uncle did nothing but go to the cinema and the cafés as a retreat because they could not accept the changes. They all visited each other, talked about each other, hated each other, and all wanted to know what the other was doing. Their lives, he went on, were built on patterns of relations, not on possessions. Now that had shifted, and they were caught in an anachronistic striving to maintain an intensity of relations and lifestyles that no longer had a social base. Once you could interpret the present in the idiom of the past, in stories of the Caliphs Umar and Ali, etc. etc.; time was telescoped, as he put it. Now such stories no longer validated, authorized or guaranteed the present.

Aghas, too, represented this discrepancy between what had been and what was. The 'had been', whose major narratives all dated from the Mandate period and the 1940s, took on the character of a golden age of timeless virtue which was increasingly perceived as time bound and historicized, a 'then' not a 'now'. Fathers had been landowners and lords' companions; wielders of guns, knives and staves; possessors of names and authors of the deeds that constituted those names – deeds of violence. Sons were mechanics, if they were lucky, paid gun carriers rather than proud murafiqs given land or gold Turkish lira 'out of respect', tractor drivers, army privates and corporals (sought after but at the same time lamented as 'without a future' and only an option because of 'the curse of poverty'), or unemployed. The nightmare on the brain of the living lay, as I have already suggested, in the double bind the fathers and history, a different history, imposed on the sons: Be like us. You cannot be like us.

How could the repetition of narratives coexist with the wider history that unfolded in this period? Reiteration seemed still to ground virtue and descent, yet only if the collective 'vital lie' of acting as if nothing had changed could be sustained. In this context, repetition took on a more magical form, as the relation of narrative and enacted story to what was narrated and enacted became intensely problematic and discrepant. The 'as if' necessary to social life was revealed as a strategem, as a white lie necessary to group existence in terms of dominant group representations, a nostalgia rather than a present force. To adapt Marx's *Eighteenth Brumaire* again, we might say that in the heroic narratives the aghas found 'the self-deceptions that they needed to conceal from themselves the ... limitations of their struggles'. But now the concealment was only partial. The very bases of narrative and enactment were in question, ambiguous, as much a source of incongruence as of coherence.

Here an often bitter comedy arose that threatened to become the dominant narrative mode, destabilizing heroic narrative altogether. Society was perceived to be structured as a joke, and lived, at least in part, as a joke. The gap between act and narrative, social reality and agents' consciousness, was no longer a matter of individual failure to establish congruence between seeming and being, it was a collective experience. What possible acts and what possible narratives could bridge such a gap? How might reality and consciousness be articulated, if not through comedy?

Repetitions of narratives which ordered and objectified social life and historical consciousness now made the inevitability of 'lying', the contradiction of heroic transparency, seem the nature of life. In such a context the figure of the low-status joker, the buffoon, was as likely as the classical hero to be seen to represent a collective situation. The marginal picaresque teller and liver of discreditable and discrediting tales, whose every narrative inverted the virtues of the murafiq, or the expert player with words whose only quality was that he could play with words but nothing else, were less marginal than I at first imagined or than they were characterized as being. Their play on genre, language and convention brought into the light of social day the ways in which the entire mode and principles of narrative enactment themselves were 'misrecognitions' (to use Bourdieu's term, *méconnaissance*) of reality.

That play was ambiguous. Such misrecognitions were still founded in social practices of power. Violence was still a career open to the talents; the beys needed their bodyguards; no sphere of life was free of the possibility of agonistic exchange; the state did not have a monopoly on violence and its institutions, army or *Deuxième Bureau* being the most locally relevant, were accessible only through personal links; law was subject to utilization by the powerful; shebab grew into repeated scenes of insult and confrontation. There was much to reinforce the significance of the rifle and the gun as key symbols of masculinity. On another level, the joking that was frequently brutal, degrading, subverting and distancing was also frequently a reinforcement of the canons of what a 'real' man of honour was and would have done. Jokers dealt in acts which showed, and narratives which told of the violation, desecration and pollution of persons in an often obscene idiom. Such narratives were the blasphemous side of the sacred narratives of power of an Abboud, a sacred which itself depended on the capacity to desecrate and pollute the persons of others. Joker and bey were dialectically related in what Kenneth Burke called 'the paradoxes of the Absurd'.

It was thus no accident if the main joker figures were as eager defenders of the rules of proper conduct in confrontation as the sheikh ash-shebab. Theirs was a double vision and double experience. Their own sense of seeing behind the seeming and 'really knowing' was itself a kind of impotent power. It paid tribute to the very world upon which they saw themselves playing with such virtuosity.

Agha consciousness of discrepancy between claim and reality was nowhere more acute than in terms of the hierarchical position which supposedly placed them above the fellahin, but which in practice increasingly existed more in formulaic language than in reality. A discourse of status honour and being, of differences between the two strata given in the nature of things, was no longer the secured foundation of social place. Work and wages were part of the change. Some men of fellahin origin had begun to achieve material positions superior to some aghas; beys were increasingly likely to employ both, and to anticipate less problems with a fellah. The very terms were themselves at issue. Certain fellahin descent groups had the numbers and the arms to make defending themselves in any case of attack a practical possibility. The flow of arms on to the Lebanese market in the early 1970s gave an enormous boost to the acquiring of weapons, until then effectively monopolized by the aghas. They might challenge the use of the term 'fellah' as meaning anything more than a description of an agricultural worker, and no longer regarded by some as in itself constituting a life status. Even if very many remained poor, that was also true of aghas whose claims to status appeared merely empty bravado and 'lies'. There had been fellahin qabadays, and fellahin labour organizers. Why not fellahin narratives after all?

All these elements were stressed to me when I visited the ornate and anomalously ostentatious three-storey house of fellahin brothers up on the top of the Zawiya hill. Its balcony looked out over the houses and valley below as if in imitation of Muhammad al Abboud's palace. Two were shopkeepers and a third was in the army. The upstairs room to which I was ceremoniously ushered was dazzlingly illuminated with batteries of lights, rows and rows of tiny lamps. Models of buildings done in seashells, a common feature of poor houses, were on every available surface. One was a large mosque complete with two tall minarets and praying figures, glittering under its own special set of lights. Another set of lights was strung across the concrete arch which bisected the room, and a third on the balcony outside made house and inhabitants visible from miles around at night. Binoculars were eagerly thrust into my hands so that I could admire 'the view', the only binoculars any villager had ever produced. I self-consciously did so. The armchairs were large wooden constructions with very heavy velvety gold embroidered coverings, plush and manifestly costly. The floor was imitation marble and covered with tables under whose glass tops coloured postcards of scenes and views from many countries juxtaposed Australia with Brazil, Nigeria with France, Scotland with Switzerland. Ornamental frames surrounded Quranic texts and photographs of the brothers on the walls, beside calendars of the Bolshoi Ballet and posters of lush Alpine valleys. Every available space was filled.

This flagrant display of objects and money might be ridiculed by those who saw the brothers as peers not superiors, and who derided their pretensions to look out over anyone, binoculars or no binoculars. The house was nothing but a grotesque piece of building paid for by the illicit gains of a bandit brother, so said resentful and envious Zawiya neighbours. In its, to me, wild parody of the villas of the Lebanese bourgeoisie, the house made claims that perhaps no one else would acknowledge. But it made claims none the less.

Other families in the Zawiya saw an end to what they called tyranny, and evoked past narratives to make a contrast with a present they saw as inexorably shifting away from beys and aghas. The latter had nothing but 'show'. The beys were 'finished', a phrase some older men used with a kind of nostalgia. They had sons who did not have regular jobs in the electricity company, construction or the army. The poor level of education seldom led anywhere. They had few overseas migration connections of any worth. Unemployment had become a key word and poverty, cursed poverty, was given as description of a condition and as a cause of 'everything'. Looking back, at least there was 'order', these men said, and at least there had been 'good beys' from whom one could claim benefits or subsistence or a favour. But now? What could they do?

Hero and Buffoon

The shift of the order of the hero to the order of the buffoon was explicitly personified by men in the village who referred to one particular father and son relation. The agha father, always spoken of by my informants, aghas and fellahs alike, as the true 'standard bearer', the *bairaqdar*, had been the closest and most esteemed companion of Abboud Bey.[4] The often-repeated stories of his excellence were always given as supremely exemplifying everything for which the aghas stood, everything they were. He was *the* figure of the autonomous hero. As murafiq his reputation was unparalleled. Courageous and a by-word of silent forcefulness, he had acquired a landholding of some ten hectares of olives through the 'respect' the lord paid to him in honour of his services in outfacing the lord's enemies, controlling labourers, and maintaining the prestige of the bey's name. In him, seeming and being were one.

Everyone, bey, agha or fellah, knew of Abd ar-Rahman Said. His name alone was enough to protect his olive groves from thieves. He had no need of guards or watchmen since he was who he was – that is how he was frequently spoken of to me many years after his death. The lord offered him marks of his esteem, gold on some occasions, land on others. He was a true qabaday. Such a man is not paid, the very notion would run totally counter to the idea of excellence, respect and prestation. Rather he was acknowledged and publicly recognized for what he was by these material yet so symbolic signs. Honour in this narrative served to accumulate, not to dissipate property.

Abd ar-Rahman Said died some time early during the Second World War, leaving a baby son. The child, later known to everyone as Abu Abduh, inherited significant resources from his hero father in olives, almonds and irrigated as well as unirrigated land. In Abu Abduh's version, conflict over the inheritance followed almost immediately. His mother wanted to marry again, to the wakil who looked after the land who was from her own fellah beit. She aimed to keep both the property and her son. The dead father's four sisters, not surprisingly, wanted to control the inheritance and leave the small boy, the ultimate rival in ownership, to his mother. The sisters got into a violent quarrel with their own father, who backed the boy's rights against what he saw as their strategy to deprive him of them. The boy grew up nursed by one of the paternal aunts. His mother had married the wakil, and aghas disapproved of one of 'their' paternal descent being brought up in a fellah household.

When he became a teenager in the late 1950s, Abu Abduh began to use the income from the olive groves inherited from his much-talked of father to go to Tripoli and Beirut with friends for a good time. Cars were just starting to be a more familiar sight in Akkar. The capital was in reach, if you had the cash. Local society was growing more and more monetarized, and a village youth could aspire to a local version of ostentatious consumption

THE ROSES OF LIFE 307

if he had the means. Clothing styles were changing and the young men no longer wanted to wear the baggy trousers, shirts with the draw-string at the neck and waistcoat of their fathers. The objects consumed had changed. In a rapidly developing economy Beirut was furnishing a whole world of fashion and leisure hitherto unknown to the young men of Berqayl and beyond their social and economic means. They could still only participate at a low level of expenditure and could not rival the lords' sons whose own investments in city entertainment and styles were considerable and increasing. Still, a youth with money, land and no controlling father might well think he could afford to take his ease and act at his own pleasure, and that of his friends. He exchanged his olive grove, not for an orange in a time of famine, but for a different kind of luxury in a time of plenty.

The son's 'grand gesture' of autonomy was to spend to excess. He threw his money into clothes, cafés and visits to brothels for the group of shebab who surrounded him and loved the trips he organized. The young man was one of the first generation to participate in the swiftly developing economy of late 1950s Lebanon after all, and the 'generosity' that helps to create social distinction could take new forms for the adolescent agha from the impoverished northern province.

When the money ran out, he sold some land to an important agha from Beit Khalid who had acquired land and considerable financial security through his association with Abboud.[5] Then he sold some more. And finally, inevitably, the last grove went. It paid for the public display of a young man eager to establish himself as a social figure of some importance before his peers who acknowledged his importance to them through accepting his generosity in this new form. The older men regarded his spending as mere fecklessness rather than fabled generosity. The son, in their eyes (and his own later), 'wasted' the material inheritance of his father's reputation and the weight of his social station. The olive groves could be translated into cash, the cash into 'pleasure'. All that had been concentrated could be dissipated.

He would lament to me how he had been alone in the world and how the older male relatives who should have protected and looked after him had instead exploited his foolishness (a variation on the themes of Chapters 8 and 9). They had ruined his life. The older men, in his version, used the younger and profited from his immaturity and naivety. They were implicated in his loss of land, a loss in which they had a direct interest and benefit. So for him the narrative could in fact be read to demonstrate how the patriarchs undermined the son of the 'standard bearer' and how economic interest easily triumphed over the supposedly sacred rules of family. They had duties towards any orphan, but particularly one who had no siblings and who was the sole descendant of the greatest man they had ever produced.

The narrative was one of the destruction of substance and incommensurate exchange – the son gave away his property 'for nothing'. Honour and excellence in that older generation of 'the time when' were represented as avenues to material acquisition (though never in a calculus of financial reward), not at all as a source of self-deceiving gestures. This ancestor-father, who stood as a metaphor of the ideal collective personality of the agha status group as a whole, was represented as acquiring through honour and excellence what the son disposed of for only the most ephemeral social return among his socially insignificant peers. The young man devoured the fruits of the father's honour in useless gesture, rather than the father's gesture depriving the son of land.

The idea of reversal is central to the narrative. In the telling, the son emphasized constantly to me how he had become the opposite of his father, as others were ever eager also to inform me in denunciations of his foolishness. They were pleased to rehearse his biography to him in public as a moral tale of loss caused through a lack of reason, judgement and self-control, the type-case of the disaster which youth unguided by age can cause. Abu Abduh himself would sometimes refer to his own life in just such a way, lamenting his brainlessness. But there was another kind of reversal upon which Abu Abduh's narrative depended. He always gave an additional gloss of betrayal and connivance by those who acted in a way diametrically opposed to what true 'family' behaviour should be. They were hypocrites, these censorious seniors who had profited by his foolishness rather than constraining him. He had been 'eaten' by his own relatives, who feigned indignation at his behaviour when all the time they had profited from it. These older men appeared to be defending Beit Abd as-Salam, he said; they acted as if they were men of integrity and position, but in reality that was all a façade and a show. Behind the performance of respect and status they had 'the souls of slaves'. 'Just watch them', Abu Abduh would say to me, 'acting as if they were true aghas. But when they meet a real man of social position they crawl like servants.' Their seeming and their being were quite opposed. I should not be fooled by appearances and fine words. He would show me the break, the fissure between what they feigned to be and what they truly were. Everything was its opposite. Behind the performances of language was a reality of what? Nothing. In his eyes, he alone saw the family for what they really were, because he had a unique insight and could see behind the artifice of seeming.

Abu Abduh's own life was taken to be exemplary of the gulf between social significance and social insignificance: the father he had never known but who existed in miraculous narratives of agonistic excellence and pure dominance, and himself, working as a servant for Jud Bey when he might have been a major local landowner. The hero father had a buffoon son. Abu Abduh had become a figure of reversal. He was notorious as a joker, a player of roles, an enactor of uproarious scenes of cowardice and public disgrace. He would perform hilariously funny scenes centring not infrequently on robberies carried out by himself and an accomplice, and always on a situation or person being 'turned' and comically transformed. He would make himself the central actor of a tale in which he foolishly challenged a Kuwaiti in a cinema who was taken to have affronted Abu Abduh's rich woman employer, only to find that the opponent was of huge size. Abu Abduh ended up howling on the floor while the blows rained on him, a howling pantomimed with enormous energy while the rest of us sat shaking with laughter at the spectacle.

The hero's son was not only a landlord's servant, he was also an outlaw who dared not sleep in his house at night but went off into the hills only to reappear the next morning in the village. If the police were to come they would come at night, such things have their rituals and conventions, and he could not stay with his family in their one room not far from the ra'is's cluster of buildings in the Marouche, at the time when any man of any worth would be in his house.

Abu Abduh had come to this precarious social position through a series of ill-judged moves and the cunning of one of the lords. When his money had run out he had been made a kind of policeman for the baladiya council, a post arranged by his relative the mayor. For several years he had held this position, earning himself a reputation for harshness among the fellahin in the process. Then his conduct had become too unpredictable for the comfort of the mayor, who had to work with leading members of fellah families. Abu Abduh was persuaded to go to Kuwait, where one of the mayor's brothers already worked. There he became a chauffeur for a woman of a leading family. That, at least, was his version and it was embellished with stories of sexual exploits that some of the younger agha men found deeply educative. He had eventually returned, after more unspecified problems, and had become attached to the house of Jud Bey Ibrahim.

Beit Jud were the opponents of Abboud and had a dispute with the old man and his now dead son's widow, a woman of an influential family and position in her own right. In Abu Abduh's version of what transpired, he himself, another man of Beit Abd as-Salam and one of the bey's sons had been instructed to set fire to the shutters and doors stored in the basement of the late Muhammad al Abboud's villa, causing a great deal of costly damage. Legal action had been taken against them, and the bey had persuaded the two agha men to jump bail, while his own son appeared for trial and was imprisoned for a few months. Abu Abduh and his companion were outlaws and wanted men as a result of their flight. The bey promised that 'when the time was right' he would get them a pardon. Ten years had passed since that promise, and there was no sign of its, or his, redemption.

The Roses of Life

On that first morning when I was taken round Muhammad al Abboud's palace, one of the young fellah men, Abd al Aziz, had been wrapped, terrified, in the Lebanese flag from the dead Minister's coffin. His wildness and excitability were well known to the adolescents of the village: *sheikh shaitan*, the devil sheikh, as they called him. He was always good for a laugh.

Abd al Aziz was now in the army and studying for his baccalaureat, though he had no real expectation of passing it. I saw him one spring day, walking studiously along a track near his father's field, dressed in his uniform and reading a book. It was a common enough sight – a young man immersed in his study and wandering along a path on his own, reading, untroubled by others. He greeted me with his customary great warmth. I responded, and asked the name of the author. Ronsard, Abd al Aziz said, showing me a collected edition in French of the great poet's work, a set text for his examinations. 'Listen, ustaz Mikhail!' he enthused. In his loud, raucous voice and with great, rapturous portentousness he recited the famous line: '*Cueillez dés aujourdhuy les roses de la vie*', 'gather this very day the roses of life'. He gave a shout of laughter, his face transfigured by a huge grin of delight – in the language, the sentiment, the poetic imperative, and in a rueful, wildly amused recognition of the infinite unlikelihood of ever fulfilling the poet's urging.

When I learned several years later that Abd al Aziz had been killed in the Lebanese war, those moments in the palace and on the path came painfully to my mind. His laugh at the image of gathering the roses of life, and his screams as the flag was wrapped round him by his merciless, joking companions, are the sounds of all that time.

Maps and Figures

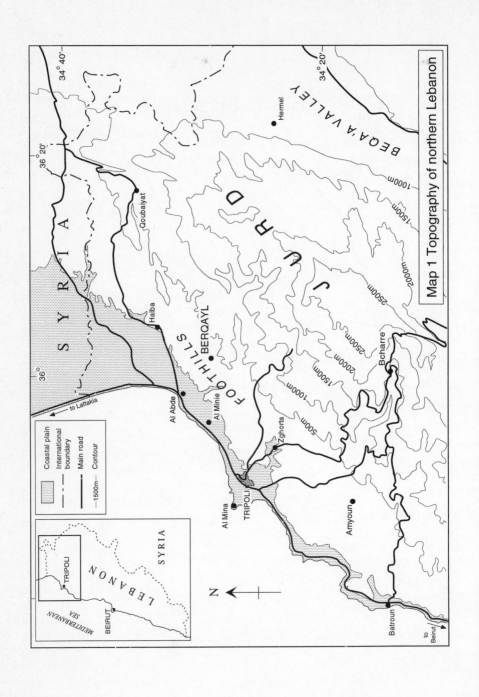

Map 1 Topography of northern Lebanon

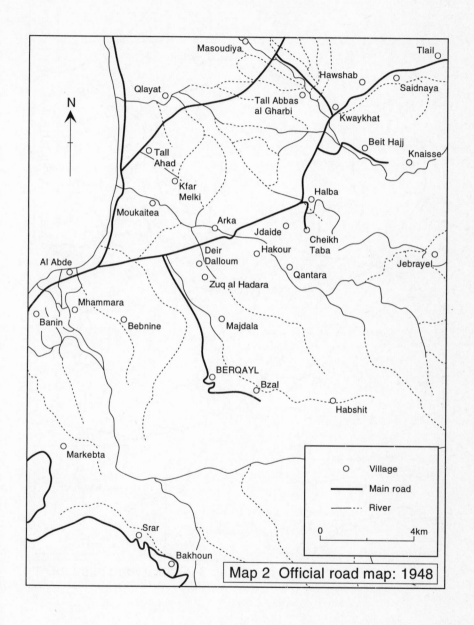

N

Masoudiya
Tlail
Hawshab
Qlayat
Saidnaya
Tall Abbas
al Gharbi
Kwaykhat
Beit Hajj
Tall
Ahad
Knaisse
Kfar
Melki
Halba
Moukaitea
Arka
Jdaide
Cheikh
Taba
Deir
Hakour
Dalloum
Jebrayel
Al Abde
Zuq al Hadara
Qantara
Mhammara
Banin
Bebnine
Majdala

BERQAYL
Bzal
Habshit

Markebta

O	Village
▬▬	Main road
–·–	River

0   4km

Srar
Bakhoun

Map 2 Official road map: 1948

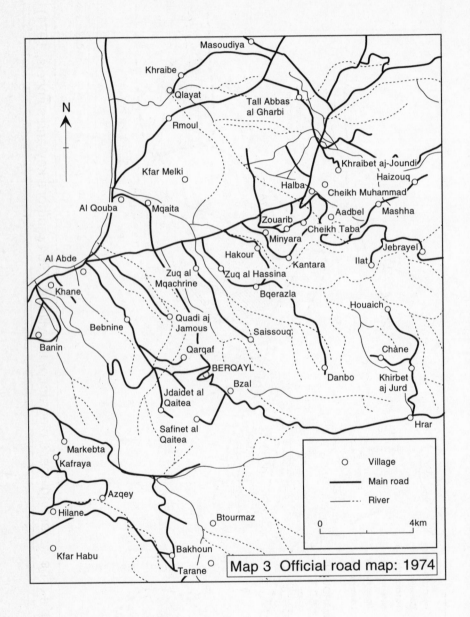

N

Masoudiya

Khraibe

Qlayat

Tall Abbas
al Gharbi

Rmoul

Khraibet aj-Joundi

Kfar Melki

Haizouq

Halba

Cheikh Muhammad

Al Qouba

Mqaita

Aadbel

Mashha

Zouarib

Cheikh Taba

Minyara

Hakour

Jebrayel

Al Abde

Zuq al
Mqachrine

Zuq al Hassina

Kantara

Ilat

Khane

Bqerazla

Houaich

Bebnine

Quadi aj
Jamous

Saissouq

Chàne

Banin

Qarqaf

BERQAYL

Danbo

Khirbet
aj Jurd

Bzal

Jdaidet al
Qaitea

Safinet al
Qaitea

Hrar

Markebta

Kafraya

○   Village

Azqey

──   Main road

Hilane

Btourmaz

─·─ River

0   4km

Kfar Habu

Bakhoun

Tarane

Map 3 Official road map: 1974

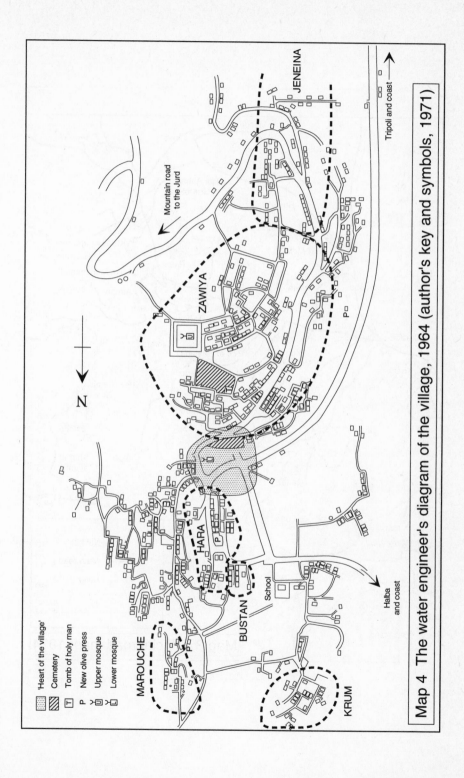

Map 4 The water engineer's diagram of the village, 1964 (author's key and symbols, 1971)

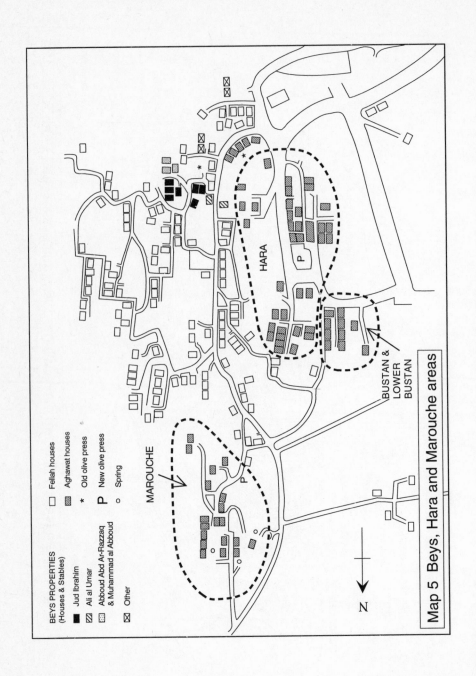

BEYS PROPERTIES
(Houses & Stables)

■ Jud Ibrahim

▨ Ali al Umar

▦ Abboud Abd Ar-Razzaq
& Muhammad al Abboud

⊠ Other

□ Fellah houses

▨ Aghawat houses

* Old olive press

P New olive press

○ Spring

MAROUCHE

HARA

BUSTAN &
LOWER
BUSTAN

N

Map 5 Beys, Hara and Marouche areas

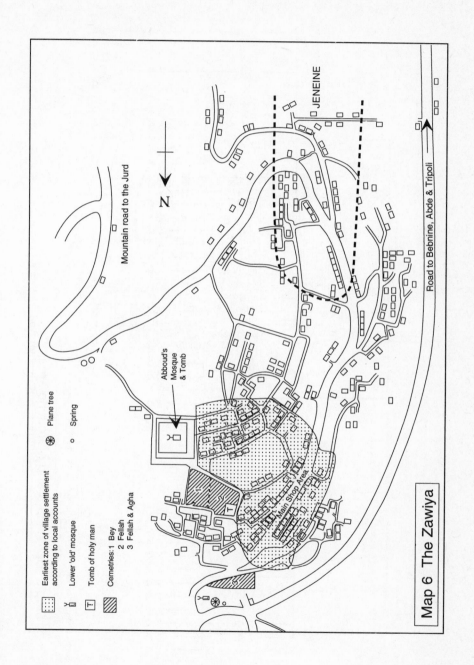

JENENE

Mountain road to the Jurd

N

Road to Bebnine, Abde & Tripoli

Abboud's
Mosque
& Tomb

Main Shop Area

⊛ Plane tree

○ Spring

Earliest zone of village settlement
according to local accounts

⌐⊡ Lower 'old' mosque

T Tomb of holy man

Cemetries: 1 Bey
         2 Fellah
         3 Fellah & Agha

Map 6 The Zawiya

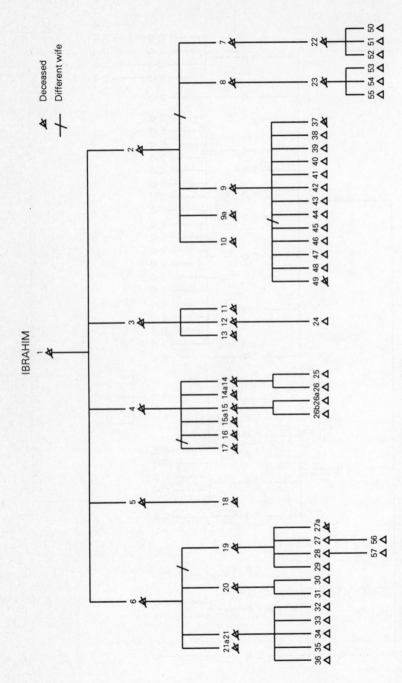

Main informants: Nos 38 and 24 (males of working age only given as 'Beit')
a and b indicate commonly omitted persons

Figure 1 Beit Ibrahim Abd As-Salam (males only)

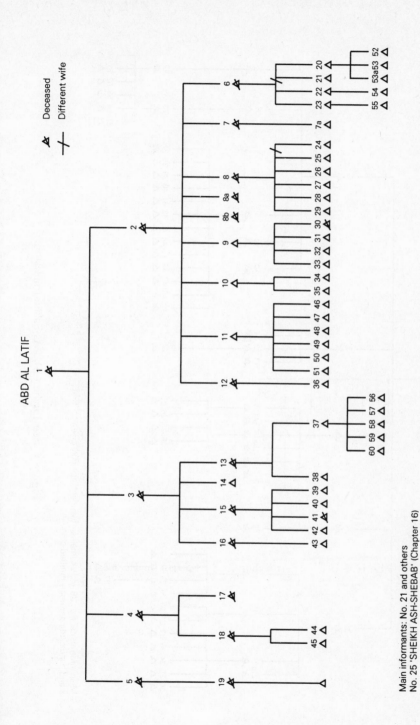

ABD AL LATIF

Deceased
Different wife

Main informants: No. 21 and others
No. 25 'SHEIKH ASH-SHEBAB' (Chapter 16)

Figure 2 Beit Abd Al-Latiof Abd As-Salam (males only)

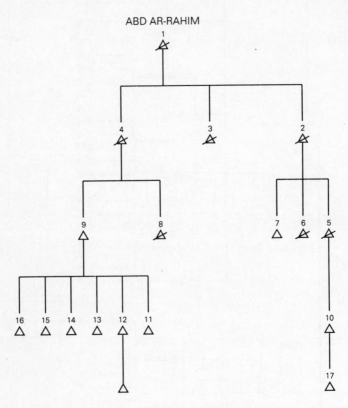

ABD AR-RAHIM

Main informants: Nos 9 and 10

Figure 3 Beit Abd Ar-Rahim Abd As-Salam (males only)

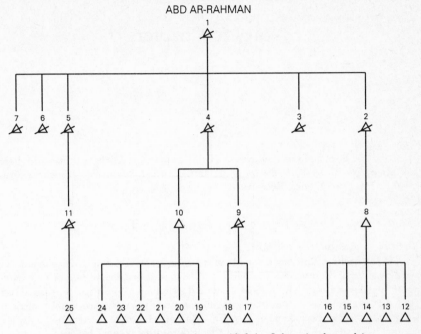

Figure 4 Beit Abd Ar-Rahman Abd As-Salam (males only)

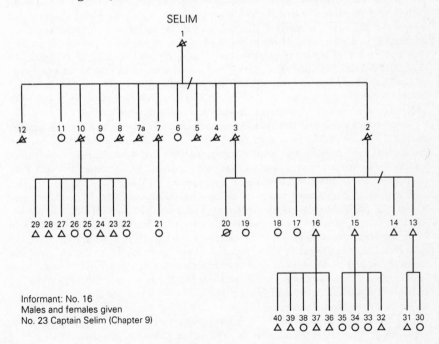

Informant: No. 16
Males and females given
No. 23 Captain Selim (Chapter 9)

Figure 5 Beit Selim

Notes to Chapters

Preface

1. *Bekawat* in the Arabic plural.
2. For the inspiration behind the use of this contrast of gallous with dirty deed see J.M. Synge, *The Playboy of the Western World*, Act III. In J.M. Synge: *Plays, Poems and Prose*, London: J.M. Dent & Sons, Everyman's Library vol. 968, 1959, p. 165.

2. Figures in a Landscape: Two

1. For a discussion of this major report see Chapters 3 and 7.
2. The American Embassy reported the killing to the Department of State in a document classified as 'Restricted' on 29 July 1953. The official described the crime as 'a flare-up of feudalism'. On 23 July, three days before the elections, Muhammad al Abboud had been shot five times as he was leaving the Presidential Palace. He died in the American University of Beirut hospital on 25 July. 'The assailant, who readily surrendered ... was a fanatical follower ... of Aboud's [sic] rival in the Parliamentary election.' No evidence proved that the act was carried out with the rival's foreknowledge, though he was arrested along with several 'henchmen'. Elections were postponed until 9 August. 'Blood vengeance by kinsmen of the victim is expected. The father of the deceased, Aboud Abdul-Rezzak ... has refused to permit burial of the corpse until retribution has been effected.' The killing shows the 'tribalistic nature of politics still prevailing in certain sections of Lebanon'. All deputy candidates at the meeting with the President had firearms, and the Minister of Public Works had had to resign after two machine guns were discovered in his car. United States/ National Archives and Records Administration/C-Washington DC, 783A. 00/7–2953, July 29th, 1953. (From copies held in the Centre for Lebanese Studies, Oxford.)

   Elections for Beirut and Mount Lebanon were held on 12 July; those for South Lebanon and the Beqa'a on 19 July; those for North Lebanon were due on 26 July. Male voting was, for the first time, compulsory. 'Virtually every candidate had his coterie of ward-healers, taxi drivers, bribers, fixers, thugs and pan-handlers, propagandists and rumor-mongers, who roamed the streets with all the trappings of gangsterism.' 783A. 00/7–2053, July 20th, 1953.

   When the Akkar election was held, Bashir Osman, supported by Abboud, defeated Suleiman al Ali, Muhammad al Abboud's rival. The report back to Washington notes that 'the Lebanese government transferred all administrative officials so that influences which might have been partial to El Ali were removed'. El Ali himself was still in jail. The report continued: 'At the Abboud estate in Akkar, the sealed lead casket of the victim is still unburied because of the oath made by the victim's father that burial will not take place until retribution has been made. It may be noted that the residents of the Akkar district, including the Abbouds and the El Alis, are of Kurdish extraction and it is well known that Kurds take their blood feuds seriously.' 783A. 00/8–1353, August 13th, 1953.

   Finally, the Embassy notified the State Department on 4 December, 1953 of the public execution of the assassin the previous day. The Judicial Council had sentenced Suleiman al Ali and his brother Malek to 10 and 20 years prison respectively, over vigorous protests from those who defended them. (The sentences were later commuted.) Abboud had visited the American Embassy in Beirut to complain that 'internal security in the country has evidenced a steady deterioration since the departure of the French in 1943'. 883A.52/12–453, December 4th, 1953.

The Embassy thus saw the killing as part of an over-determined Lebanese political world that was at once tribal, feudal and Kurdish.

I am most grateful to Dr Carolyn Gates and Professor Irene Genzier for their help in tracing these references, and to the Centre for Lebanese Studies, Oxford where the copies I consulted are stored.

3. Most local accounts give Abboud's age at the time of his death as seventy-eight.

4. Abd al Karim was killed in an argument over money with others who were allied with a Palestinian group during the civil wars. I was told in 1983 that he had become an impressive fighter and that his shooting, in which I think another of the disputants died, was regarded as a ridiculous end for a young man who fulfilled so many of the local criteria of the successful leader. My memory is of a self-possessed teenager who never indulged in boasting, as his peers often did, and played little part in the joking routines. He wanted to take the baccalaureat but did not succeed, though he seemed to be serious about his school work. I owe much to his quiet attentiveness and help.

5. It will be obvious that I have to use English rather than Arabic tenses. We move from the past continuous, into the perfect tense and the precise location in the time of '1953', through the simple present that is also continuous (the coffin is here now, and always), into a conditional future and the subjunctive mode.

6. In other contexts and to other persons the story of Muhammad al Abboud had no meaning, was merely a short footnote to modern Lebanese history, unknown, or 'forgotten'. That forgotten, in the case of figures on the Lebanese political scene, that it seemed to require a certain amount of active suppression and silencing. One did not refer in public to the affair, though 'everyone knew'. More than social politeness was at stake. To refer to the story was to invoke practices and relations of power contradictory to what many wished to maintain and what many often deeply felt were appropriate modes of Lebanese politics. It was also too sharp a reminder of the fact that, nonetheless, such practices existed and might even be argued to be essential to the workings of power, rather than aberrant or marginal. Any interventions that I have made at conferences before a Lebanese audience that have drawn attention to such events have been greeted with an interesting mix of silence, disinterest (what I have taken to be disapproval) and/or an urging to continue and to say things which interlocuters felt unable to say, given their own positioning within particular social and political networks. In the latter case it is not Muhammad al Abboud *per se*, but the more general points the narrative might be taken to demonstrate, which arouse the encouragement.

7. The Minister might have tried to kill his rival, the other obvious, taken-for-granted possibility. Withdrawal from the election in the context of acute contest was highly unlikely as it would have meant a public admission of fear and submission to his opponents' will and power. The attempt might have failed. The Government might have tried to rig the result anyhow, had it looked as though Muhammad al Abboud was certainly going to triumph. Moreover, if one moves outside the story so totally accepted as a canonical account of 'fact' by my informants, one might accept the opponent's claim that the act was one of a blindly devoted follower, an unanticipated, individual decision motivated by fanatical personal loyalty and having no sanction by others. This was precisely the narrative of those accused, though it was interpreted as exactly what they would say in the circumstances by Abboud's supporters.

8. Alasdair MacIntyre, *After Virtue: A Study in Moral Theory*, 2nd edn, London: Duck-

worth, 1985. I discuss MacIntyre's notion of narrative in Chapter 4. In speaking of 'heroic society', that is the society of Homer's *Iliad* or *The Odyssey*, Macintyre leaves open the question of whether or not such societies ever existed. And he is also careful to say that 'epic and saga are certainly not simple mirror images of the society they profess to portray'. Poets and saga writers stand outside their characters from whom they are distinguished by a 'kind of understanding' which the characters do not possess. My use of MacIntyre's work does not imply that I wish to use the construct 'heroic society', let alone so categorize the social world in which I studied and lived. More specifically, I am concerned with the ways in which people told themselves and the world in narratives rather than with the writings of poets. MacIntyre's reflections have been of enormous value to me in helping to define the directions this book has taken, but are, of course, addressing a very different set of issues.

9. For a discussion of immortality in the aristocratic and democratic orders see Claude Lefort, *Democracy and Political Theory*, trans. David Macey, Oxford: Polity Press, 1988, Chapter 12, 'The Death of Immortality'. Citing Canetti on Stendhal, Lefort writes that immortality had become in Stendhal 'a question for the law, that it has become the most private aspect of human life, and that it has nothing to do with making a glorious appearance in the public space.' (p. 281)

10. The question of choice arises here. I was not inevitably bound to frame, structure and write the book in this way of course, though by the fantasy common to anthropologists – or perhaps all writers? – it has sometimes seemed to me that it could only be *thus*. And, as part of that fantasy, I felt that external realities imposed this view upon me and that I could not but focus upon these topics in these ways – a common anthropological rhetorical move experienced by the writer as 'objectively the case'.

11. This book has sometimes seemed like a kind of archaeology of a world vanished beneath the layers of the Lebanese wars. It speaks of a 'twenty years ago' and a 'then' with which it is difficult to trace any link of continuity. The violence has been so great that a book loses all relevance – moral, intellectual or political. My notes, at such moments, appear to be traces of an ever-receding past. It is as if the world they record is effaced in the very act of remembering here; or memory becomes nothing but a pious offering to something – though what is not clear – now gone, crushed under foot by years of conflict. Yet sometimes they come forward into the present, as if that present only serves to make notes, memories and images stand out in greater detail and with greater force. Some Lebanese friends, seeking collective ways of narrating an out-of-joint present, encourage me and themselves to re-present work such as this and local histories and ethnographies in an attempt to shed light on recent horrors. Their project is to make sense out of what has frequently seemed nonsense. How does one talk about 'Lebanon'? How may it be imagined? How was it narrated, and did those forms of narration themselves constitute one powerful element in the 'what happened'?

12. The phrase is from Rom Harré's, 'Language games and texts of identity', in John Shotter and Kenneth J. Gergen (eds), *Texts of Identity*, London/Newbury Park: Sage Publications, 1989, p. 22.

13. The reader will have noted that the text shifts at the beginning of this second chapter from an impersonal authorial presentation to the subjective voice of the first person singular, and then to the collective voice of 'the young men'. The polyvocal strategy is intended to bring the reader at once to see the importance of multiple voices throughout what follows, without disguising the mediations effected by my writing.

14. I revert to the classical introductory trope of the arriving anthropologist and the multiple cultural shocks he experiences. But here this mirroring of 'what happened on that first day' is already framed by the opening scene of a summer evening long before the anthropologist's appearance.

15. These differences are easily blurred, and in practice do not emerge with the neat analytical clarity for which one yearns in the field as much as in the text that follows. As MacIntyre says, we have to allow for the idea of a moral vocabulary as a good deal more incoherent than we find easy to recognize; there are disagreements and alternative interpretations of 'the same' virtue (MacIntyre, *After Virtue*, p. 135). And, we might add, of everything else. None the less, I try throughout to indicate differences without slipping into too schematic a presentation.

3. Contexts and Contests

1. Mission IRFED – Liban, *Étude Préliminaire sur les besoins et les possibilités de développement du Liban*, texte provisoire (in typescript), Vol. 3, 'Le Liban Nord et Tripoli' (n.d.), II–5–2, (my translation). The final printed version, under the title *Besoins et possibilités de développement du Liban* was published by the Ministry of Planning in 1960–61.

The report notes that its division into zones follows an analysis of geographical and social, rather than political, boundaries. Thus its use of the term North Lebanon does not absolutely coincide with the area of the governorate of the same name, though the differences are relatively minor.

2. I shall discuss the IRFED document in greater detail in Chapter 7 below.

3. *Loc. cit.*

4. *Ibid.*, II–5–3.

5. *Ibid.*, II–5–4.

6. The most detailed studies on the geography of Akkar available at the time of my research were those by Paul Sanlaville. He insists on the variety of geographical features and zones, the diversity of its relief, climates, vegetation and agricultural regions. The plain receives about 800 mm. of rain a year, though the records are limited. Until the middle of 1964 none of the 208 villages of the administrative unit (the *caza*, a division of a *muhafaza* or governorate), which included the plain, had electricity, not even the main town of Halba. At the beginning of 1965, thirty-one villages were still not served by any road. There was practically no system of drinking water. One twenty-bed hospital served the whole area. P. Sanlaville, 'L'Evolution de la plaine du Aakkar', *Hannon: Revue Libanaise de Géographie*, Vol. 1, 1966, pp. 71–82. See also his 'Les régions agricoles du Liban', *Revue de Géographie de Lyon*, Vol. 44, 1969, pp. 47–89.

7. II–5–C–4.

8. Shebab is a word which occurs at many points in this book. It is translated as 'young men', but frequently means any man capable of actively contributing to collective resistance or aggression by a group. One says of a man in his fifties or sixties who can still use a gun, face down an opponent and make himself respected that he is 'still a *shabb*'. One addresses a group of men with the vocative phrase '*ya shebab*' and speaks of the shebab of a family, village or town quarter. The word may, of course, have a specifically generational sense referring to the socially, as well as biologically, 'young', often meaning unmarried or yet without children, but those who are no longer boys, *awlad*. The meanings in use will emerge in the course of the following chapters.

9. Akkawi's movement was crushed after the Palestinians had been defeated by the Jordanian army in 'Black September' 1970, and Hafez al Asad has displaced a more leftist figure as President of Syria. I draw the information on Ali Akkawi from the article by the late and much lamented Michel Seurat, 'Le quartier de Bab Tebbane à Tripoli (Liban): étude d'une "asabiyya urbaine"', in *Movements communautaires et espaces urbains au Machreq*, Beirut: CERMOC, pp. 45–86. On Ali Akkawi see pp. 62–6.

10. The French language newspaper *L'Orient* thought it worthwhile reporting on 12

November 1970 (p. 14) that there was no new incident to report from the region. Syrian Baathists had denied that Syrian-backed Palestinians, the *Saiqa* movement, were at the base of the 'agitation'. Two days earlier, on 10 November, the newspaper had written of armed confrontations on the Syrian frontier where a peasant had been expelled from working the fields of an owner and had threatened reprisals against him. The qaimaqam of Akkar had been obliged to intervene. There was a risk of a chain reaction. Only the week before there had been trouble in the village of Tall Bire against the al Ali brothers, large and influential property owners in the region. *L'Orient*, 10 November 1970, p. 1.

11. The revolt on the plain of Akkar had begun to preoccupy the Lebanese press. *L'Orient* noted on 11 November 1970 (p. 2), that the proprietors had submitted a memorandum to the government and threatened to enforce their own law and order if the government did not act. The newspaper's correspondent in Tripoli reported that the peasants in revolt were attached to what he called the Union of Peasants of Akkar, an organization which is active at the heart of the grouping of leftist parties in Tripoli (citing the Communist, Baath and Parti Populaire Syrien groupings in the northern port city of which Akkar is the hinterland). The fear of 'the left' in Lebanon, which preoccupied many at this period as the Palestinian movements gave it a new energy and significance, marked much of the writing. On the other hand, of course, the revolt in Akkar was seen on the left as a sign of hope and of a more general politicization of the wretched of the earth.

12. The report runs from pp. 3–11. As in newspapers throughout the world, the rest of the supplement (pp. 12–23) contains pieces on the ruins of Roman temples, Paris fashions, film star gossip, pop music, consumer goods and comics.

13. Dr Saghiyeh was from a locally well-known family. In the Parliamentary elections of 1972 he became the head of the first 'popular' or *sha'abi* list ever to stand in Akkar. It was also the first list in which the two Sunni places were not occupied by beys, but rather by men drawn from the more established descent groups of two major villages of the Qayta' region – Fneidek and Berqayl. No candidate of the list was elected.

Dr Saghiyeh was assassinated in August 1974 by one Akram Ali Dib, a gendarme and reported in the press as a bodyguard of the then Minister of Agriculture, Suleiman al Ali, the one-time rival of Muhammad al Abboud (*L'Orient*, 23 August 1974). The victim was the subject of the cover story of the Arabic magazine *al Sayyad*, of 22–29 August 1974, under the title: 'The danger of "the revolution" in 'Akkar', *khatar al thawra fi 'Akkar*. Noting that the real struggle is that between the clans of the Jurd and the beys of the plain for political dominance in Akkar, the writer says that the main issue is the question of 'a wretched existence in which neither old or young is spared'. He links the killing to Saghiyeh's role in organizing the fellahin against the beys on the plain, and to his political links on the *sha'bi* list with one of the Ba'rini clan in Fneidek at the top of the mountain.

14. In an important paper on land tenure in Lebanon produced in 1972 it is stated that 45 per cent of operators were owner-operators on the plain of Akkar, whereas in Akkar as a whole (i.e., including the mountain and plateau zones) the figure rose to 66 per cent. Others were renters, sharecroppers, or a combination of the three types. The paper gives the mean size of owner-operator holdings as 2.8 hectares, or rented as 1.2 hectares, and of sharecropping as 0.6 hectares, but these figures are for the whole of Akkar and are not broken down into plain and other zones (Thomas Stickley and Kazem Sadr, 'Land tenure in Lebanon', Department of Agricultural Economics, Faculty of Agricultural Sciences, American University of Beirut, 1972). The paper is a condensation of an MSc thesis in Agricultural Sciences at AUB by Kazem Sadr in 1971.

15. I might add that having a written agreement, between kin investing in a seasonal contract for example, seldom seemed either less productive of acrimony or to diminish the possibility of disagreement over management and the division of the harvests. One might

argue that what was described as the rise of written agreement among kin in fact indicated a trend to recognition of individual interest and the weakness of sanctions on behaviour by the group in more purely informal terms. Men thus sought a document which might, if necessary, be produced in court. But going down that route in the event of serious disagreement might turn out to be yet more unpredictable, costly and disruptive than arguments and furious disputes whose resolution might be brokered by family mediators. The situation was messy.

A sharecropper is called in arabic *murabi'* and this was the term used locally. It literally means sharing a quarter of the profits or losses of an agricultural enterprise.

16. The survey gives the production costs per hectare for the most common crops in Lebanese lira: cucumbers – 1,235; tomatoes – 1,645; peanuts – 793; wheat – 167; chickpeas – 407; and watermelons – 580, all at 1971 prices.

17. According to Saghiyeh's figures, 2,067 were Sunni Muslim, 1,473 Alawite (a heterodox Muslim sect whose main area of settlement is the Alawite Mountain which borders Akkar to the north and from which many poor labourers in north Lebanon came), 7 were Shi'i and 1 Orthodox.

2,570 persons had Lebanese nationality, 185 Syrian, and 793 were 'under study', that is, were effectively stateless and of course peculiarly vulnerable to pressure by powerful lords or state agencies.

18. Sanlaville noted in 1966 that such 'external' capital had been engaged in well boring on the plain 'for some ten years', and some 300 wells had been sunk. Characteristically, such projects were carried out with no planning or regulation and wells were dug at 40 to 60 metres depth, often close to other wells, wherever owners wished taking as much water as they felt they needed. The result was a tendency to salinization (Sanlaville, '*L'Evolution*', p. 80).

19. I found it impossible to find any figures for the extent of such holdings, but it was certainly true that they existed and people would sometimes say that such-and-such a grove or plot had been sold by bey X to Tripoli family Y.

20. This regional name was used to delimit an area in the Ottoman system of tax farming.

21. To 'be a horseman' was to be a man of valour and quality exemplified in the *chevalier* image of both a natural and a social quality. The man reputed as the finest horseman of the main agha descent group, a murafiq of Abboud, had a name known throughout Akkar among the older generation. Invited when he was only about seventeen or so to be one of the 'traditional Arab horsemen' organized by Nuri Said Pasha to entertain prestigious guests at the negotiations of the Treaty of Versailles in 1919, he proudly showed me the photograph of President Wilson's wife presenting him with a medal, equally proudly displayed.

22. *Al Jarida al Rasmiya* (The Official Gazette), No. 28, 6 April 1967. Official figures for Akkar as a whole for 1965 give a total population of 139,033, identity card holders broken down by the following categories: Sunni 62,735; Shi'a 541; Druze 3; Maronite 28,868; Greek Catholic 1,975; Greek Orthodox 39,310; Protestant 1,256; Latin 27; Armenian Catholic 27; Armenian Orthodox 52; Chaldean 0; Syrian Catholic 2; Syrian Orthodox 3; Jews 0; Others 4,234. *Al Mudiriya al 'Amma*, Statistical Bureau, 1965.

23. In terms of space, the water engineer's diagram (Map 4), or the map from aerial photography (not shown), or the tourist maps of 1948 and 1974 (Maps 2 and 3), of course represent the village for specific purposes in their specific ways. All maps are part of state projects. The first is a practical guide for siting water supplies and sanitation as part of the follow-up to the IRFED programme which had noted that there was no piped drinking water in the village in 1960. The second is a map essentially for the government and military. Like the IRFED report, it requires measurement and precision of all the phenomena to be mapped, including the distribution of individual dwellings, and a maximizing of information

about settlement, topography and communications. The state requires that it be accurate as a source of knowledge and, where necessary, as a resource for intervention in case of disorder. It is as if, in mapping, the state could assert an all-seeing power it in fact never really possessed, over territories which constantly threatened to escape an inherently unstable control. Finally, the general terrain maps show how the road system has shifted, but requires little information on Akkar, since this was a zone defined as outside the interest and eye of the tourist or Lebanese seeking beauty or leisure.

24. Twenty-eight constructions were *zariba*s, stables or animal shelters with some storage, and some of these had also once been inhabited by fellahin families.

25. Purchase of foodstuffs and material goods was often carried out in the market of Bab Tabbane in Tripoli, the point where taxis stopped on the way into the city centre and the point from which they set out again for villages in the Qayta' region. The cars plied their trade from the mountain to the city quite regularly and people wishing to go to town waited on the road by the lower mosque for a taxi that had a spare seat. Transport was cheap and drivers from the village could also buy goods for relatives or friends. The range of produce in the market was much wider than in the village of course, so many local shops sold only a few canned goods, tools, simple practical needs such as matches or nails, lighter and house fuel, cigarettes and tobacco.

26. I have discussed village space and social practice in Chapter 8, 'Forming and Transforming Space' of my *Recognizing Islam*, London: Croom Helm, 1982, pp. 164–91.

27. *Kazzura* covers a range of social pleasures, including going off on a trip, wandering around town, just making a journey or taking a stroll for the fun of it, for no specific purpose or goal.

28. There is a hint here of another version which would derive supposed Circassian origin from the name Jurakis (close to the Arabic 'Cherkess'). It is not impossible that another melding occurred which combined different families, some of Circassian origin and some said to be by association.

29. The nature of the accounts indicates that the 'brother' relation between Beit Khalid and Beit Abd as-Salam might have its historical origins in separate arrival in the region. The move down to Tripoli of the former, who had in the earlier generations been established with houses in the village (which remained in their ownership), seems to have begun in the 1920s.

30. The four beits had very unequal numbers of men in the total of their genealogies back to the founders: Beit Ibrahim had 63 males (over 18) all told in five generations, of whom 34 were living; Beit Abd al Latif 57 in five, with 39 living; Beit Abd ar-Rahman 24 in four generations, 16 living; and Beit Abd ar-Rahim only 17 in five generations, with 10 living. These numbers were slightly variable, because different informants would sometimes leave out men from previous generations who were defined as 'mad', or who had died unmarried, or emigrated leaving no children behind.

31. I do not use the phrase 'call to arms' metaphorically. When the army and police entered the village during a crisis in which some groups of villagers had blocked the road up to the mountain, young men ran screaming "*'a-silah, 'a-silah*', 'to arms! to arms!' from house to house of Beit Abd as-Salam. They howled imprecations at men not swift enough to move, and shouted how the army was 'in the heart of the dai'a, raping women and shedding blood' while sluggards did nothing. Neither act was, in fact, occurring, but both stood for the extreme cases of penetration and violation by the armed force of another. In more socially restricted crises adolescents would rush around spreading the news and urging instant armed attendance at the house of the one involved (see p. 292).

32. Thus a poor agha who tilled the land of others as an agricultural labourer could be described as 'fellah' by others, referring to what he did for a living. (If he was a day or

casual labourer he would be a *fa'il*, an *'amil* or a *shaghghil*. He could be both a *fa'il* and a *murabi'* or sharecropper, not to mention a *naqqi zeitoun*, olive tree pruner, and *natur*, agricultural watchman or guard of the groves at harvest time.) But he would never be described as 'one of the fellahin'. If he worked his own land, or land leased from others, he would be called a *zari'* or cultivator. Similarly, a man from a fellah beit might become a shopkeeper or driver and of course be known as such while still being fellah in the broader collective sense of the term.

33. Nineteen were in the army (or, in the case of two of them, retired) earning between 2,500LL and 4,000LL depending on rank. Eighteen had full-time employment in government service, or the Electricity Company in Tripoli (those working less than full-time are classified under workers above), the International Petroleum Company or another company in Beirut or Tripoli at around 1,500LL plus a year. Most of these jobs had been brokered by beys in return for support. Seventeen were drivers, earning up to 2,500LL annually, depending on luck and their employers. Twenty-four worked as carpenters, iron workers or in some kind of artisanate, one of the sectors with better incomes (see below), and twenty-one I have classified as 'others'. Of these, nine were described as having 'nothing', *sifr*, either because they were old without family, or sick, or the victims of an accident; one was a sheikh who earned a small income of perhaps 2,400LL reciting the Quran at funerals or mulids (celebrations of the Prophet Muhammad's birthday), writing talismen and engaging in divination. One was an 'arab doctor' who pulled teeth and managed on 1,000LL or so a year; one was a bey's servant, one the mosque imam, or leader of prayer and washer of corpses, another the sheikh for the upper mosque, and these all earned perhaps 1,200LL to 1,500LL. The numbers were made up by two garage owners (one in Tripoli and one on the road to Halba on the plain), a political operator and henchman of a leading bey, a property investor and shop owner, a man living off the rents from his buildings, an ex-policeman who owned an olive press, and, finally, a farmer who had made 'a pile' through allegedly dubious means.

34. See Chapter 9 for a narrative of village foundation by fellahin families and their displacement by the beys.

35. Ali was killed as a result of wounding one of the aghas in a squabble and during my time in the village this blood remained a source of unspoken but ever-present awareness (see Chapter 10). Abu Walid himself, a man of great probity and generosity, who lived out an all too difficult social role with hard won dignity, was murdered during the Lebanese civil wars. 'It was', another friend who had known him well said to me when I returned for three days in 1983, 'the only death I could not find any explanation for at all'. He was shot in the back driving his tractor home after working on the olive terraces and the killing did indeed seem to have been totally capricious. His murder left his young widow in poverty with their only son. Father and son can be see in Plate 18. Abu Walid is pictured handing the four-year-old his revolver prior to my taking the photograph he had requested. I cannot express the sense of futility and sense of desolation his death brought, and still brings in writing.

36. A feddan might be made up of a mixture of types of land, dry or irrigated, and was the area of land worked in a day by one or a pair of oxen; the actual area varied according to the soil, rainfall and other factors. Latron states that in the Beqa'a valley and the Akkar plain a feddan was about seven hectares, but in the Homs and Hama region where rainfall is more limited, it extended to up to forty-five hectares. See André Latron, *La vie rurale en Syrie et au Liban: étude d'économie sociale*, Beirut, 1936, pp. 14–17. Meaning varied according to local practice, context and convention.

A shunbul in Akkar was the load of a camel, which had been the major transport animal on the plain before trucks and lorries largely displaced it. The shunbul of barley was about 100 kilos, that of wheat might be between 100 and 150 kilos, and that of maize was 130 kilos. A shunbul of land was the amount necessary to produce such a measure, and also varied. Latron, *La vie rurale*, pp. 10–13.

4. Narratives, Powers, Persons

1. For MacIntyre 'the concept of a virtue ... always requires for its application the acceptance for some prior argument of certain features of social and moral life in terms of which it has to be defined and explained. So in the Homeric account the concept of a virtue is secondary to that of *a social role*, in Aristotle's account it is secondary to that of *the good life for man* conceived as the *telos* of human action.' A. MacIntyre, *After Virtue: A Study in Moral Theory*, 2nd edn, London: Duckworth, 1985, p. 186.

2. The question of recognition of what is due to a man relates to a discussion of honour. 'In many pre-modern societies a man's honor is what is due to him and to his kin and his household by reason of their having their *due* place in the social order. To dishonor someone is to fail to acknowledge what is thus due.' MacIntyre, *ibid.*, p. 116.

3. *Ibid.*, p. 124. MacIntyre's ideal typical construction enables him to pose certain questions in moral theory. I am not making any analogy between his 'heroic society' and the actual historical (part-) society I studied, but rather with using the issues he develops to frame a way of writing about that society in terms of narratives in practice.

4. *'Illu qimtu'*, literally 'to him his value', was a commonly heard term of praise or assessment of social position. Such a one was 'not insignificant', *minnu hayyin*; he 'has a social station', *''indu markaz'*.

5. This statement requires qualification. I was once shown, but not permitted to keep for detailed study, a long poem of the history of the Mir'abi family: *At-tajliyat al hamidiya 'an al athar al as'adiya wa ma'athir sarah al ayyam al mir'ab al kiram* (*The praiseworthy revelations of the As'adi traditions and exploits of the élite of the times, the noble Al Mir'abi*; no author's name or date. As'adi refers to a distinguished ancestor of the Mira'bi, Ali Bey al As'ad (later Pasha, d. AH 1243, AD 1827 or 1828), who was several times *qaimaqam* or head of the adminstrative district of Tripoli in the early 1800s. One verse states that the text was written at the behest of Muhammad Bey al Muhammad and the poem praises his founding of the religious school or *madrasa 'ilmiya* in the village of Mashha in AH 1311, AD 1893–94. It thus seems reasonable to date the composition as the last decade of the nineteenth century.) The book, bound in black leather with the title in gold on the spine, was hand-written in formal calligraphy on 245 pages. This was possibly the bey's own copy and I was unable to track down any others. The text consisted of a verse history of the beys since their coming to Akkar and praises their great deeds (see Chapter 5 below). Other beys may well have commissioned their own poets in the past as part of their claims to pre-eminence. This poetic genre of *madh*, or panegyric, seems to have been well established, as it was in so many parts of the Arab world. In his thesis on the modern history of Akkar, Faraj Tewfiq Zakhlur mentions political gatherings in the first two decades of this century at which poems appear to have been an integral part of the public rituals of the occasion, and the composition of published or publicly recited poems to mark major events such as the loss by the Ottomans of Tripoli in Libya to the Italians in the campaigns beginning in 1911, or the coming of the French to the region in 1919–20. See Zakhlur, 'Ta'rikh 'akkar as-siyasi wa'l iqtisadi wa'l ijtima'i, 1908–1943' ('The Political, Economic and Social History of Akkar, 1908–1943'), PhD thesis, University of Saint Joseph, Beirut, 1984, pp. 19, 20, 41 and 42.

I was not aware of any still-current local examples of such poetry nor did I ever hear extemporized or repeated praise of an individual in verse. I was not allowed to keep the book in my possession. It was regarded as 'very valuable' by its owner, one of the aghas, who had not previously revealed its existence to anyone and who was thus 'giving away a secret' in showing it to me. The use of gold leaf decoration at the beginning of verses, as well as the nature of the book dealing with 'old times' and 'history' (*zaman* and *ta'rikh*) and its provenance with the lords, reinforced his jealous guardianship. He himself was not a skilled reader.

6. Barbara Herrnstein Smith points out that 'the form and features of any "version" of a narrative will be a function of, among other things, the particular motives that elicited it and the particular interests and functions it was designed to serve'. Speaking of versions 'constructed in order to advance the objectives of a particular discipline', she makes the important point that: 'None of these latter versions, however, is any less motivated or, accordingly, formally contingent than any of the other versions constructed to serve other interests or functions.' Barbara Herrnstein Smith, 'Narrative versions, narrative theories', in W.J.T. Mitchell (ed.), *On Narrative*, Chicago/London: University of Chicago Press, 1981, p. 217.

7. Michael Herzfeld has provided a major treatment of rhetoric in social practice in his *The Poetics of Manhood: Contest and Identity in a Cretan Mountain Village*, Princeton, NJ: Princeton University Press, 1989.

8. See Evelyn A. Early, 'Catharsis and creation: the everyday narratives of Baladi women of Cairo', *Anthropological Quarterly*, Vol. 58, No. 4, 1985, pp. 172–81. Early stresses the ways in which episodes are negotiated through narrative occasions in everyday conversations with friends, and how certain stories become canonical and repeated over the years. Even the most apparently local of accounts may articulate a relationship with a wider social and cultural universe.

9. The *Rashomon* effect is well known. In Kurosawa's famous film – woman, bandit, woodcutter and samurai ghost all have their radically different accounts of 'what really happened'. The specifically forensic nature of the stories is to the fore as each witness is giving evidence to a tribunal seeking to establish 'the truth'.

10. Stan Royal Mumford, 'Emplotment of historical narratives in the Nepal Himalayas', in H.L. Seneviratne (ed.), *Identity, Consciousness and the Past: The South Asian Scene*, special issue series of *Social Analysis*, No. 25, Sept. 1989, p. 53. A particularly interesting treatment of the question of 'why certain temporal and historiographic forms appear in a particular social and cultural setting' is John Bowen, 'Narrative form and political incorporation: changing uses of history in Aceh, Indonesia', *Comparative Studies in Society and History*, Vol. 31, No. 4, October 1989, pp. 671–93.

11. Edward M. Bruner, 'Introduction: the opening up of anthropology', in Edward M. Bruner (ed.), *Text, Play and Story: The Construction and Reconstruction of Self and Society*, Proceedings of the American Ethnological Society, 1983; reissued by Waveland Press, Inc., Illinois, 1988, p.10.

12. They were still rivals with another branch of Abboud's descent group. Moreover, one of the sons was said to have been involved in burning the stored wooden window shutters, frames and doors from Muhammad al Abboud's villa some time after his death. Two agha men, who had already participated in different extortions and general strong-arm tactics for the beys (and on their own account), had carried out the arson with him. He had served a short jail sentence but both his accomplices had fled before the trial could be completed. In the version of one of them, they had done so at the old bey's (father of their fellow arsonist) suggestion. He led them to believe that he would get them off later whereas if they waited for the guilty verdict they might get a heavy sentence from which he would not be able to extricate them. They thus became wanted men and outlaws who 'slept in the mountains' to avoid capture, and were totally dependent on the old bey for a hoped-for pardon that never materialized during his lifetime, though it was often promised. This account is quite typical in its celebration of the bey's cunning at the expense

of his own dependents, as much as of his opponents, an admiring tale told by a victim and instrument whose own life had been severely affected by the manipulation he so vividly recounted (see Chapter 16).

13. No doubt the beys' families, or at least some of them, had family papers, though no one seemed to be able (or perhaps willing) to indicate who might possess such archives. When I enquired about the documents left by Abboud I was told that they were still tied up in legal questions of inheritance and that it would be 'difficult' to get them. I thus did not have access to the kind of material on which so much history of Mount Lebanon has been based. The archives of the Islamic courts in Tripoli only began to be worked on extensively for local history purposes during the Lebanese wars that began in 1976, Farouk Hublos's published study being the most obvious example. This owes a great deal to the enthusiasm and interest of the late and much-lamented Dr Marwan Buheiry and sociologists such as Mas'ud ad-Dahir, to both of whom I am very grateful for conversations and advice.

14. On the death of a person others will attend readings of the Quran, especially on the first, third, seventh and fortieth evenings. Though recitation of verses from the Book and sometimes the singing of hymns, or perhaps the *dhikr* (repetition in rhythm of certain of the Names of God) are the main ritual acts, gossip, talk and narrative frequently intrude. *Mulid*s, celebrations of the Prophet Muhammad's birth, were social occasions offered by a person in thanks for some success, or the birth of a son, or as an act of piety not infrequently interpreted by others as being in imitation of, and competition with, another who had held such a celebration.

15. I only made notes of two occasions, both mulids, where one or two men embarked on stories of the first four 'rightly guided' Caliphs. A friend also told me that when he was a child his widowed aunt had told him stories of Antar, heroic fables that are well known in Arab culture. But I never heard them told at meetings of adult males. One friend did have a repertoire of three jokes around fictitious characters, and he told all three of them again when I returned for three days in the spring of 1983. But otherwise laughter was always at some account of what were presented as actual events and persons known to the narrator and usually to many of the audience.

16. On one occasion I laughingly said to a fellah friend with whom I was engaged in a lighthearted, bantering kind of conversation that he was 'just like X'. As soon as the name was out of my mouth another participant, a young agha who frequently acted as one of my appropriate escorts, shot me a devastating look of disapproval and with much joking changed the subject. I had mentioned the name of the man who had killed my interlocutor's brother some years before and on whom no revenge had been taken. This appalling *faux pas* occurred despite, or perhaps even because of, the instruction I had been rigorously given in the necessity of avoiding the subject. The two men had become so linked in my mind that a moment's relaxation of concentration and the fact that I had to learn what to others was given practical knowledge, was sufficient to bring the association out into the open.

17. Old widows in families I came to know well would sometimes stay in the room if I was there on my own with no other men except those of the house. Occasionally a young wife would stand by the door and interject the odd remark from time to time. But I neither anticipated nor had the chance to speak with women.

18. Such a type by no means monopolized the representations of power. Beys, including the Minister, might be spoken of differently, with a stress on their intelligence, control of assets in Beirut, alliances with members of the upper reaches of the Lebanese political élite. This more obviously 'bourgeois' model stressed what I think was seen as a more recent kind of order. Abboud straddled both. Other leading families, such as the Franjiehs and the Gemayels, not infrequently had sons, one of whom became the leader while the other played the role of tough guy and 'enforcer'.

5. Fathomless Ocean

1. Rafiq al Tamimi and Muhammad Bahgat, *Wilayat Beirut*, Beirut: Matba'a al Iqbal, 1979, p. 230. The work was originally published in two parts in 1916. All references are to the later edition.

2. 'The *Medrese-i Sultaniye* in Beirut … was apparently organized after the model of the Galatasaray *Mekteb-i Sultanisi*.' Engin D. Arkali, "Abdulhamid II's attempt to integrate Arabs into the Ottoman system', in David Kushner (ed.), *Palestine in the Late Ottoman Period: Political, Social and Economic Transformation*, Jerusalem/Leiden: Yitzhak ben Zvi/E.J. Brill, 1986, p. 78.

3. Muhammad Rafiq Tamimi came from a well-known family of landowners in northern Palestine. He and his brothers were educated in schools in Istanbul and some of them, including Rafiq, became Ottoman officials. They joined the regime of the Emir Faisal, son of the Sherif Hussein, in Damascus when he took over there and where one of the brothers became head of the police. Rafiq was secretary of the Fatat party and a member of the Syrian Congress which offered the crown of Syria to Faisal. When the French carried out their military takeover in 1920, he fled to Palestine. He was condemned to death *in absentia* by a military court. I am most grateful to Albert Hourani for kindly providing the above information. The report on the condemnation of both Tamimi and Bahgat by the *Conseil de guerre de Damas* in July 1920 appears in *MDAE*, Série E–Levant 1918–1929. Syrie-Liban. Vol. 35, Dossier général, Dec. 1, 1920–April 14, 1921.

4. After the Druze–Christian violence of 1860 in Mount Lebanon in which some 15,000 Christians were killed, British, French, Russian, Austrian and Prussian representatives under the Ottoman Foreign Minister's presidency met to decide on a special administrative unit for the area, but excluding Beirut. For this 1861 agreement establishing the *mutasarrifiyya*, or special governorate, see Engin Akarli, *The Long Peace: Ottoman Lebanon, 1861–1920*, London/ California: I.B.Tauris and Centre for Lebanese Studies/University of California Press, 1993, pp. 30–33.

5. See Akarli, *The Long Peace, passim*.

6. 'Until 1864, Beirut remained the seat of the Province of Saida, which included Latakia, Tripoli, Nablus and Jerusalem, in addition to Beirut and Saida. In 1864 this area was incorporated into the Province of Damascus. In 1887 the same area, except Jerusalem, became a province in its own right, called the Province of Beirut.' Akarli, *ibid.*, p. 31.

7. Title page of Part Two of *Wilayat Beirut*.

8. *Wilayat Beirut*, p. 230. Authors' punctuation. At the asterisk they have glossed the Arabic word *al-bahma'*, as 'the land in which one cannot find a way'.

9. *'Al mir'aba hum qawm amjad wa fursan ajwad*. Emir Haidar Shihab, *Lubnan fi 'ahd al-umara' al shihabiyin*, A. Rustum and F. Bustani (eds), 3 vols, Beirut, 1933. Rhymed prose or *saj'*, as in this case, was characteristic of such writing. Tamimi and Bahgat for the most part avoid it. Scattered references exist to Akkar in Sheikh Tannus bin Yusuf ash-Shidyaq, *Akhbaru'l A'yan fi Jabal Lubnan*, 2 vols, 2nd edn, Beirut, 1954. He refers to the killing of the head of a powerful Shi'ite *beit*, Sheikh 'Isa, by Shadid Bey, the governor (*wali*) of Akkar, in 1778 (p. 173). It would appear that the Mir'abis were important in driving the important Shi'ite clans out of the Akkar altogether. The phrase 'fled to Akkar' occurs in many of the references.

10. *Wilayat Beirut*, p. 232.

11. They refer here to the plain. Most settlements are on small hills above the winter flood levels and not on the plain proper.

12. Population statistics for Akkar at this period and for Lebanon as a whole have always been problematic, not least because of the different interests of those presenting the figures to show that one or another religious community was preponderant. A brief discussion of

the issues is contained in J.M. Wagstaff, 'A note of some nineteenth-century population statistics for Lebanon', in the *Bulletin of the British Society for Middle Eastern Studies*, Vol. 13, No. 1, 1986, pp. 27–35.

Tamimi and Bahgat's figures are very close to the official Ottoman statistics for 1914 (Ottoman figures in brackets taken from Wagstaff, Table 3, p. 33, where the total should read 41,788 and not 29,578 as printed): Muslims (Sunni) 18,307 (19,920); Greek Orthodox 12,819 (12,573); Maronite 8,208 (8,333); Catholic 669 (671); Protestant 360 (391 'other Christians'). The main sources to be consulted are Kemal Karpat, *Ottoman Population, 1830–1914: Demographic and Social Characteristics*, Madison, WI: University of Wisconsia Press, 1985, and Meir Zamir, 'Population statistics of the Ottoman Empire in 1914 and 1919', in *Middle Eastern Studies*, Vol. 17, 1981, pp. 85–106.

13. Tamimi and Bahgat do not give a source for these figures, but presumably they had access to official records of conscriptions and I think we may assume the numbers are accurate. They certainly represent an extremely high proportion of the 'active' adult male population. The effect on the available labour force and on regional demographics must have been considerable. References to the Ottoman period by old men who spoke to me always focused on the taking away of young men for the army by force, the surrender of land to the beys to get a man released from military service, and the disappearance of those who never returned from the war.

The high number of Akkaris who voluntarily joined the Lebanese army was a feature both of local discussion, journalists' articles and intellectuals' discussions about the region during the period of my fieldwork. It was taken to be a mark of the poverty of the population which had so few alternatives. We shall see later what part this played in the occupational structures of Berqayl.

14. Hublos notes that al Qayta', al Jumeh and al Dreib were names of regions that were sometimes treated as one by the Ottomans for tax purposes, and sometimes divided into these three sections, each with its own boundaries and villagers. These boundaries were often used for tax farming purposes. Administrative arrangements varied considerably through the nineteenth century and the three divisions ceased to be used officially from 1887 but remained in popular use. See F. Hublos, *Ta'rikh Akkar, al idari wa'l ijtim'i wa'l iqtisadi*, 1800–1914, Beirut: Dar al Ha'ira, 1987, pp. 33–7.

15. A *dhira'* is a unit of measure which Wehr's dictionary gives as a cubit, 0.68 of a metre in Syria.

16. The Russians, for example, had set up schools in six Christian villages with teachers brought in from Palestine and providing free books and exercise books. Each school had 5 or 6 teachers and 150–200 pupils, mostly Greek Orthodox. Then there were the American missionaries who had established five mixed schools which were now closed because they did not have state authorization. The Jesuits had three other foreign schools, the Italians one, and it was to these that the Maronites sent their children. The rich sent their offspring to the American schools because they thought them better. Competition for influence and clients between foreign powers through educational insitutions was typical of the period.

17. The 'lack of security' in Akkar is a constant theme in many of the sources. See *MDAE*, NS Turquie, *Politique Intérieure Syrie-Liban*, Dossier Générale XIII, Doc. D44.1 for a French report of 1912 on fighting over mountain pastures.

18. The history of changing taxation in the nineteenth century is detailed in Hublos, *Ta'rikh Akkar*, pp. 95–118. He adds a tax on owners of roofed dwellings, though some of the poor might be excused it and about half the inhabitants were exempted (p. 112). In addition to labour dues, which included the use of draught animals, there were payments on flocks, fruiting trees and one-third of the total produce went to the landowner, as well as the tenth of the fellah's share. Bribes to government officials and customary dues on marriage and at the time of religious festivals were common.

19. *Wilayat Beirut*, p. 248. It is also worth noting that the aristocracy of Mount Lebanon observed elaborate and minutely detailed gradations of etiquette for meetings or communications of any kind. Order and address were very live issues in group hierarchy, as they always are, and no doubt, by contrast, the Akkari landowners appeared to lack all proper sense of vital social rituals. See Nasif al Yazigi, *Risalat ta'rikhiyya fi ahwal lubnan fi 'ahdihi al iqta'i*, Harisa: Matba'at al Qiddis Bulus, 1936, especially pp. 268–72 and 338–9. The allusion to 'every vice' repeats the still common representation of the beys as by nature disposed to incest, adultery, pederasty and sexual violation.

20. *Asala qisasiyya*, a phrase which they may well be using ironically, refers to noble origins spoken of in the form of narrations or tales.

21. On *Wilayat Beirut*, p. 255, Tamimi and Bahgat comment that very few of the beys knew Turkish. Only those who in the byegone times went to the *madrasa al 'asha'ir* (like Abboud, MG) know a little of the language.

The *'Asiret Mektebi* was 'a five-year secondary boarding school established in Istanbul in 1892 specifically for the sons of Arab tribal notables. 'Abdulhamid (Sultan Abdulhamid II) was its honorary director. ... The graduates were expected to rejoin their tribes and to serve as teachers or officials in the area.' (Engin D. Akarli, "Abdulhamid II's attempt', p. 80). This was part of a policy of integrating Arab groups more closely into the structures and institutions of the Empire. The beys of Akkar would not have been described as 'tribal', though they might have been classified as *'asha'ir*, or 'clans', so it is not absolutely certain that the uniforms worn in the photographs of the young beys (see, for example Plate 4) are of that school. For photographs of Imperial educational institutions of the period see Carney E.S. Gavin (ed.), *Imperial Self-Portrait: The Ottoman Empire as Revealed in the Sultan Abdul Hamid II's Photographic Albums*, Cambridge, MA: Harvard University Press, 1988, pp. 155–91. I am grateful to Dr Eugene Rogan for these references.

22. This subject has been much discussed. See, *inter alia*, Zouhair Ghazzal, *L'économie politique de Damas durant le XIXe siècle: structures traditionnelles et capitalisme*, Damascus: Institut français de Damas, 1993. For Mount Lebanon, see Dominique Chevallier, *La société du Mont Liban à l'époque de la révolution industrielle en Europe*, Paris: Librairie Orientaliste Paul Geuthner, 1971, and Akarli, *The Long Peace*. Also Tarif Khalidi (ed.), *Land Tenure and Social Transformation in the Middle East*, Beirut: American University of Beirut, 1984 (especially Part III: Early Modern). Though officially abolished in 1839 the system in fact continued through the century in Akkar.

23. Hublos, *Ta'rikh Akkar*, pp. 41–7.

24. *Ibid.*, pp. 67–82.

25. *Ibid.*, p. 81.

26. *Ibid.*, pp. 170–71.

27. *Ibid.*, p. 250.

28. Hublos notes that Tripoli merchants had been buying up iltizams at least from 1856 onward (Hublos, *Ta'rikh 'Akkar*, pp. 170–71). The earlier period of the Egyptian occupation of Ibrahim Pasha in the decade of the 1830s seems to have been noteworthy for the access Tripoli notables acquired to property in Akkar. Ibrahim Pasha subjected the beys to a greater degree of control than before, suppressing opponents ruthlessly.

29. Hublos, *Ta'rikh 'Akkar*, pp. 229–30.

30. The CUP was formed by junior army officers in 1906 and spread through provincial centres of the Empire. The Committee initially sought a reformed Ottomanism and 'supported the ideology of Ottomanism, of a Turko-Arab nation and state'. Philip S. Khoury, *Urban Notables and Arab Nationalism: The Politics of Damascus 1986–1920*, Cambridge: Cambridge University Press, 1983. See also Rashid Khalidi, 'Society and ideology in late Ottoman Syria: class, education, profession and confession', in John Spagnolo (ed.), *Problems*, pp. 119–31.

31. F.T. Zakhlur, 'Ta'rikh 'akkar wa'l iqtisadi wa'l ijtima'i, 1908–1943' ('The political, economic and social history of Akkar, 1908–1943'), PhD thesis, University of Saint Joseph, Beirut, 1984, pp. 17–21.

6. Precarious Archaism

1. E. Achard, 'La Plaine d'Akkar', L'Asie Française, Vol. 23, 1923, pp. 63–9 (annexe on irrigation and animal husbandry by Capitaine Mieg).
One report optimistically presented Akkar as a vast granary capable of feeding a population of three million as well as producing crops for export. As such, this rich plain extending south from Aleppo to the Beqa'a valley would stimulate the ports of Lattakia, Alexandretta, Tripoli and Beirut, consequently encouraging investment in railways and other public works. 'Note sur la Cilicie et la Syrie' from the Agent Général in Constantinople. MDAE, Série E–Levant, 1918–1929, sous série Syrie–Liban–Cilicie, Syrie–Liban, deuxième partie, June 22–December 29, 1922. Vol.190, Dossier général, Politique intérieure.

2. All these phrases are taken from Haut Commissariat de la République Française en Syrie et au Liban, La Syrie et le Liban en 1921, Vol. 2, Paris, 1922, pp. 1–16.

3. MDAE, Vol. 191, January 1923–May 1924.

4. J. Luquet, La politique des Mandats dans le levant, Paris: Éditions de la Vie Universitaire, 1923, p. 142.

5. J. Luquet, Mandat A et l'organisation du Mandat Français en Syrie, Paris: Éditions de la Vie Universitaire, 1923, p. 163.

6. Luquet, Le Mandat A, p. 169. Weulersse refers to the bold hopes for cotton as a major cash crop on land converted to plantations. After the First World War cotton famine the French administration made serious efforts to bring in American and Egyptian varieties, to establish experimental farms, to distribute seeds and set up factories for ginning. On the Akkar plain alone fifty-thousand hectares were planted in cotton. But the French discovered the perils of the commodity market: 'the collapse of the market and the world crisis put an end to these dreams'. J. Weulersse, Le pays des Alaouites, Vol. 1 Tours: Arrault et Cie, 1940, p. 231.

7. Luquet, Le Mandat A, p. 164.

8. For the history of the Mandate see S.H. Longrigg, Syria and Lebanon under the French Mandate, Oxford: Oxford University Press, 1958.

9. Achard was himself an agronomist and part of the Missions d'enquête économique of 1921. For the problems in obtaining qualified personnel see 'Personnel français en Syrie', 15 March 1921, in MDAE, Levant 1918–1929, Syrie–Liban, Vol. 53, Personnel administratifs, March 1921–February 1922 (Série E), p. 5. There were no specialists in olives or tobacco cultivation for Lebanon and the Alawite region. loc. cit., p. 3.

10. Surveys sent direct to the High Commission and to the Foreign Ministry in Paris could also be published in L'Asie Française, a journal as likely, under its grandly imperial name, to print articles on Cambodia or Indo-China as Achard's report on the obscure plain of Akkar. The most modest enquiry contributed to the global colonial discourse.

11. Archives Militaires de Vincennes (hereafter AM), 24 C3 Levant, 1917–1939, C.R. Opérations for Mieg's appointment as sous-gouverneur, and MDAE Série E, Vol. 52, August 1919–February 1921, for a document of November 1920 noting his appointment at Homs.

12. André Latron, La vie rurale en Syrie et au Liban: étude d'économie sociale, Beirut, 1936, p. 7. In 1971, after years of highly monetized market relations, local calculations on measures were still made by the tabbe, shunbul, ock and keile. Toufic Touma, writing of Mount Lebanon in the latter period of the nineteenth century, notes one unit of measure said to be 'a certain number of times the length of the belt' (zinnar) of the peasant, which varied between

five and seven metres since the material was wound around the waist several times. See T. Touma, *Paysans et institutions féodales chez les Druzes et les Maronites du Liban du XVIIè siècle à 1914*, Beirut: L'Université Libanaise, Vol. 1, 1971, p. 347.

13. Jacques Weulersse, *Paysans de Syrie et du Proche–Orient*, Paris: Gallimard, 1946, pp. 254–5. He notes that in this region the latifundia attained *une ampleur et une perfection* unequalled anywhere else.

14. Jacques Weulersse, *Le Pays des Alaouites*, Vol. 1, pp. 362–3.

15. Jean Donon, 'La question foncière en Syrie et au Liban: les réformes réalisées depuis l'établissement du mandat français', *L'Asie Française*, Vol. 23, 1923, pp. 22–8. This information appears, in a slightly different form, in Achard's 'Notes sur la Syrie', published as a supplement to *L'Asie Française*, July–August 1922.

16. All quotations are from Donon, 'La question foriciere', p. 22.

17. *Loc. cit.*, Donon, 'La question froncière, p. 23.

18. Latron, *La vie rurale*, pp. 129–32.

19. Weulersse, *Le Pays des Alaouites*, p. 224.

20. *Ibid.*, Vol. 1, p. 364.

21. Latron, *La vie rurale*, pp. 81–2.

22. Luquet, *La politique*, pp. 161–2. Huvelin suggested a reorganization of the land tax (the *wergho*), as had been done in Egypt. 'We would see many large proprietors selling lands they currently neglect but which would be too burdensome to leave unproductive.' Then, he says, the Mandate could use 'the old Quranic rule' which authorizes the state to take back *miri* lands which have remained three years without being cultivated. P. Huvelin, '*Que vaut la Syrie?*', *L'Asie Française*, supplément December 1921, pp. 15–16.

23. Edmond Rabbath notes that at the end of 1919 there were armed encounters between different groups and the French troops at Tal Kalekh on the Tripoli–Homs road. July 1922 saw what he describes as the beginning of a rebellion in the region of Tripoli. 'Brutal and murderous' campaigns were necessary against the rebel Sheikh Saleh in the Alawite mountain in 1924 (E. Rabbath, *L'Évolution politique de la Syrie sous Mandat*, Paris: Marcel Rivière, 1928). Zakhlur ('Ta'rikh 'akkar as-siyasi wa'l iqtisadi wa'l ijtima'i, 1908–1943', PhD thesis, University of Saint Joseph, Beirut, 1984) notes that the beys used armed bands of men, *'asabat*, for their own purposes (p. 37), as the Ottomans had previously done for guarding routes (p. 27). Effectively this is what the French also did, not least because in 1920 they only had 100 horses and 50 infantrymen as government forces in the region (p. 74).

24. AM, 24 C3, Levant 1917–1939, C.R. Opérations.

25. AM, 20 C3, Levant 1917–1939, C.R. Opérations (1926–1927), 'Notes sur les secteurs'.

26. Lieutenant Vertier, 'Notes sur l'Akkar', Tripoli, 30 October 1927 in AM, 20 C3, Levant 1917–1939, 'Notes sur les secteurs'.

His report includes a brief survey of agriculture with comments on low productivity (only six to eight times the amount of seed in cereals), primitive technology and rudimentary methods. Vertier gives the population as 16,770 Sunnis, 7,190 Maronites, 9,462 Greek Orthodox, 486 Greek Catholic and 1,027 others – a total of 34,935. He cites no source for his figures; and since the administrative boundaries of Akkar had changed since the final Ottoman period, even the roughest kind of comparative assessment is impossible.

Abboud, the Sunni representative, was a member for North Lebanon governorate in the First Representative Assembly (1922–25) set up by the French, the *Majlis at-tamthili al awwal* and in the Second Assembly (1925–26). He was a deputy in the First Assembly of Deputies (1927–29), and in the Second (1929–32). His son Muhammad al Abboud took Abboud's place as deputy in the Third Assembly (1934–37) with an equally pro-French stance. Muhammad continued as deputy in the Fourth Assembly (1937–39) and in the Fifth

(1943–47), serving for different periods as Minister for Security in both. He was elected again for the Sixth Assembly (1947–51) but lost his seat in the elections of 1951.

27. Weurlersse, *Les Pays des Alaouites*, Vol. 1, p. 364. Though he is writing specifically about Alawite areas, I think it is clear that his comments are meant to have a more general application to the latifundia as a whole. See also his *Paysans*, pp. 250 and 178 for his views on 'the *fellah* of the Orient', stripped of essential peasant virtues by an Ottoman Empire that left nothing but a 'dust' of divided tribes, sects and towns behind it.

28. Weulersse, *Le Pays des Alaouites*, Vol. 1, p. 377.

29. There is now a large and growing literature on this topic and I shall only cite two of the more recent studies. James Clifford, *The Predicament of Culture: Twentieth-Century Ethnography, Literature and Art*, Cambridge, MA: 1988; and Chris Bongie, *Exotic Memories: Literature, Colonialism and the Fin de Siècle*, Stanford, CA: Stanford University Press, 1991.

30. For details on Abboud's active collaboration with the French against the large majority of Sunni notables at the time, see N.W. Atiyeh, 'The attitude of the Lebanese Sunnis towards the state of Lebanon', PhD thesis, University of London, 1973, pp. 112 and 121–2. She describes him as 'the only example of a Sunni notable giving his full support' to the promulgation of a Lebanese Constitution in 1926, a Constitution on whose Drafting Committee he was a member. Vol. 1, p. 124.

31. Zakhlur, '*Ta'rikh*', p. 63.

32. Zakhlur, *Ibid.*, p. 75.

33. For accounts of the many legal opinions in the Islamic court dealing with disputes over land and inheritance, see Zakhlur, '*Ta'rikh*', pp. 96, 97, 99 and 101.

34. Abu Ali said that even before these incidents he had been 'with Abboud' for four years from the age of ten. But he had frequently run away from Syria back to the village, only to be returned to the bey.

35. Letting animals loose on an opponent's fields was a routine way of carrying on what men reported as a constant sniping and jockeying for dominance. Other means would be to destroy crops at the threshing ground (something of a favourite as it could inflict serious and very public economic damage as well as the loss of face), harassing other cultivators, or dumping rocks all over cultivated land.

36. My informant was an outlaw who had worked for Abboud as a young man as both driver and gunman.

37. This fellah beit was held to have a sheikh or holy man founder. One or two of them wore simple white *kewfiyyas* round their heads in a style locally indicating a religious dedication associated with their family, though seldom any specific community function.

38. I should note here that Beit Abd al Hamid was shortly after these events riven with a feud which had continued ever since and had caused four killings within the beit by the time of my arrival in the village. Men were waiting for the killer of the most recent victim (several years before) to emerge from jail and were anticipating that the cycle would, sooner or later, continue. No one spoke of any attempt at peace-making and it seemed to be accepted that where such a cycle began in a beit it was essentially without any terminus except by the physical removal by death or migration of one fraction.

39. The use of direct speech in such private narrations was typically restricted to formulaic utterances of challenge and oath. In a more public version of this kind of narrative I would have expected greater use of direct speech, gesture, imitation of an actor's voice, and a dramatic closure achieved by some terse and splendid phrase of fearless defiance, as well as dwelling on the heightened rhetoric associated with blood-shedding and direct contest.

40. Friends would occasionally monitor the level of knowledge and information they gave me to that which they thought relevant for me to participate in social life without

committing a serious mistake and embarrassing someone or a group by an unwitting reference to a suppressed subject. Thus a man might say to me, very much on the quiet: 'You know about Bedr?'

41. On several occasions men asked me privately, in lowered tones and somewhat obliquely, whether I was aware of 'the Bedr incident'. They seemed to be monitoring the extent of my knowledge, wondering whether I needed to be told to avoid causing embarrassment by some public remark I might make in ignorance, or ensuring that I grasped the context of a particular reference they had made.

42. He himself had made 'a lot of money' in the 1960s, in ways that were held to be secret and suspect by everyone else, a fact of which he was well aware. He lived on the plain away from the village, but was much visited by other fellahin who thought he could broker favours for them with different beys with whom he had dealings. Of his grandfather, whom he described as 'an qabaday', he said that the beys had flung him into prison on a false murder charge because he was managing land up in the Jurd and was so feared that he obstructed the beys' scheme to take it for themselves and register it as their property. The grandfather died in jail.

43. See Chapter 9 for an example.

44. The term *shaddad* was used carrying the same meaning as fellahin but with the connotation of not being from the village but from 'outside'. Some used shaddad especially for those with a pair of cows. *Muzari'* was used as a synonym of fellah.

45. On Muhammad al Abboud's role in the negotiation of a proposed treaty with France in 1936 see Atiyah, 'The attitude of the Lebanese Sunnis', Vol. 2, pp. 149–51.

46. Antoine Messara notes that landed proprietors dominated the Assemblies up to 1943 when lawyers were of equal number or sometimes exceeded them (*La structure sociale du parlement libanais, 1920–1970*, Beirut, 1971, pp. 161–8). One man might, of course, be both a landowner and a professional and have close relatives in the bureaucracy and upper reaches of the managerial levels.

47. I have copies of three such notes dating from 1931 and 1932 sent to one of Abboud's two main murafiqin. In the first he demands that 'our son' take one of the local sheikhs his yearly allowance of 700 Turkish qirsh and get a receipt for it. In the others he insists on this errand being carried out as he has heard that the allowance has not been delivered. (Perhaps the agha was hoping to pocket the cash?) And in the third he peremptorily requires the payment of ten gold Ottoman lira to another sheikh and a note of the receipt 'without any delay'.

7. Underdeveloped Periphery

1. Mission IRFED – Liban, *Étude préliminaire sur les besoins et les possibilités de développement au Liban*, Vol. 3, 'Le Liban Nord et Tripoli', n.d., p. II–5–D–1. References to the two-volume published version are in standard numbering. North Lebanon was a governorate, a *muhafaza*, and the Mission's divisions of the country followed the lines of administrative borders. Thus the region of the Koura to the east of Tripoli as well as Tripoli itself form part of the same volume in this preliminary study.

2. 'From 1950 onward the Lebanese economy experienced nearly 25 years of accelerating expansion ... there may have been an overall growth rate of 7 per cent a year, 1950–74 ... the major role continued to be played by the tertiary sector (trade, banking and services), which increased its share from under two-thirds of national income to nearly three-quarters.' Roger Owen, 'The economic history of Lebanon 1943–1974; its salient features', in H. Barakat (ed.), *Towards a Viable Lebanon*, London: Croom Helm, 1988, p. 33.

3. See Michael Hudson, *The Precarious Republic: Political Modernization in Lebanon*, New York: Random House, 1968; Leila T. Meo, *Lebanon: Improbable Nation. A Study in Political Development*, Bloomington, IN: Indiana University Press, 1965; Abdo Baaklini, *Legislative and Political Development: Lebanon 1842–1972*, Durham, NC: University of North Carolina Press, 1976.

4. Berqayl and the Qayta' region were in general anti-Chamoun. The latter had been a powerful opponent of Abboud and his son.

5. République Libanaise, Ministère du Plan, *Besoins et possibilités de developpement du Liban*, Vol. I, Beirut, 1960–61, p. 17.

6. An excellent account of social transformations in the south is contained in Selim Nasr, 'La transition des chiites vers Beyrouth: mutations sociales et mobilisation communautaire à la veille de 1975', in CERMOC, *Mouvements communautaires et espaces urbains au Machreq*, Beirut, 1985, pp. 87–116. Nasr points to the growth of unregulated agro-export capitalism (fruits and chickens) linked to urban commercial credit interests, the collapse of sharecropping by 1970, and the marginalization of cereals. He identifies a permanent crisis of the small peasantry, indebted and hyper-exploited by brokers, merchants dealing in machines, seeds and fertilizers, usurers and small local banks.

7. Nasr describes the Chehabist period in the south as for the first time bringing the state into sporadic contact with the peripheries through a reorganization of the territorial structure of administration and political representation. He notes a diminution of the power of the big families. Nasr, '*La Transition*', p. 90.

8. Apple trees had furnished a key cash crop in Mount Lebanon after the post First World War collapse of the silk industry, but they were little grown in Akkar. That the Michmich fellahin were starting to produce apples for the market indicated more of a shift than the report acknowledges.

9. The planners thus reverse the usual stereotypes of mountain society and describe it almost as much at the very edge of humanity and culture as Tamimi and Bahgat had represented Halba. It has lost its 'traditional' life without gaining any new forms of order and custom.

10. The authors do not seem to have perceived the shift from virtual 'indifference' to 'stubborn resistance' in their description as at all contradictory. When talking of 'tribal' peoples in the development discourse it is possible to write of opposed elements as if they were completely congruous.

11. See Ministère du Plan, *Besoins*, Vol. 1, pp. 76–82. The authors note further that the population working in agriculture represents roughly 50 per cent of the total and agricultural revenues only 16 per cent, but they go on to point out that some agricultural workers have other activities which improve their incomes without, they add, leading to a comfortable life.

12. *Besoins*, Vol. 1, p. 94.

13. There are one or two moments where the Lebanese reader would understand such discretion without any further reference. The experts would have liked to study the town of Zghorta in the Koura region because of its preponderant role. Unfortunately this was not possible 'because of many obstacles of a psychological and political order at the time of the enquiry'. (Mission IRFED – Liban, II–5–3–1). The town's influence on the local environment is restricted by 'local circumstances' (*ibid.*, II–5–11). These discreet references are to the fact that Zghorta was effectively out of bounds to government forces and had strongly opposed the new President during the 1958 'troubles'.

Those same troubles are evoked in a brief footnote explaining that 1958 was not included in certain statistics for 1950–1957 'because of its exceptional character' (Ministère du Plan, *Besoins*, Vol. 7, p. 77, note 1).

14. A comparative study of wheat farmers in Akkar and Baalbeck in the early 1960s came to quite a different conclusion. The author found that: 'the population covered by the study holds no cultural, social, or other situational factors that prevent the adoption of farm innovations, provided that the recommended practice is economically profitable, feasible within farmers' existing facilities, and that its advantages are understood by farmers through suitable teaching methods.' Wajih D. Maalouf, 'Factors associated with effectiveness of the result demonstration method in promoting adopting of fertilizer practices by wheat farmers in Baalbeck and Akkar counties, Lebanon', PhD thesis, Cornell University, Ithaca, NY, 1965, p. 142. Maalouf was a director of agricultural extension work in Lebanon from January 1960 to June 1963.

15. Some questions are deliberately avoided, such as the nature of the political measures to be taken. But the nature of the modernizing discourse itself excludes and suppresses much in the very construction of the illusion of a globally surveyed universe.

16. The front door gave on to a long narrow hall with chairs facing each other on either side and a television set, a rare commodity, near the end. Here he received visitors, talked to fellahin wanting work or discussed village and regional matters with callers. There were two rooms on either side of the hall: a kitchen on the immediate right of the door, and then a bedroom; on the left was a small bedroom in which men prayed at the appropriate times, with another bedroom and bathroom next down the hall. The formal reception room faced the visitor at the end of the hall and was only used for high-status visitors. The house was thus in practice a rather awkward mix of spatial forms as the intimate domestic spaces were fairly exposed to visitors, contrary to local patterns.

17. We shall see more on the question of 'wasting' and 'eating' land in the two following chapters.

18. This quasi-adoption was not uncommon in analogous situations, with the adoptee having expectations of acquiring ownership of the property from the uncle.

19. Several men spoke to me when we were alone of keeping a 'diary' in which they recorded 'everything', 'things no one else knew', something out of which I could make three books. 'One day', each said, 'I will show it to you'. No one did. It was as if this idea of a totally private document of concealed record, the only *true* and full record of 'my life', served as a fantasy of the isolated subject imagining a hidden total knowledge of, and thus in a sense power over, the social universe. Muhammad's notebooks of agricultural management are a variant of this powerful notion, though in his case I did actually see some of the text.

20. Other works I have consulted show that Muhammad's experience is typical of the overall agricultural processes in Akkar during this period. Ahmed Hlaihel, '*Étude de géographie physique appliquée à l'aménagement dans une région du Akkar*', Thèse Cycle 3è, Université de Lyon III, 1982, especially Chapter 8, 'Occupation humaine du Akkar'. Marie-France Naufral-Giappesi, '*Contribution à la connaissance de la région du Akkar, Liban*', Thèse 3é Cycle, University of Paris, 1978. On the reconceptualization of agriculture, managerial routines and administrative procedures, see D. Holmes, *Cultural Disenchantments: Worker Peasantries in Northeast Italy*, Princeton, NJ: Princeton University Press, 1989, pp. 44–5.

21. Irrigable land that was worth 2,000LL a hectare in 1952 was valued at 10,000–20,000LL in 1972, and up to 25,000LL near Abde where the coast and inland roads divided north of Tripoli (Ministère des Ressources hydrauliques et électriques, 'La situation foncière dans la plaine d'Akkar', Beirut, 1972, p. 23).

22. Such agreements, *sanad*, were always in writing. One for 1971 reads as follows (in my translation from the Arabic): 'I, the undersigned of the people and inhabitants of the village of Berqayl, testify that I have decided and acknowledge to have sold to X 20 shunbuls of olives only for the sum of 1,200LL and that I engage to deliver them on 15 November.

And if I delay the handing over I shall pay 125LL for each shunbul and I assume responsibility for any damage or loss. And as evidence I have myself drawn up this written agreement before witnesses, and God is their blessing.' The servant who had brokered this deal told me that the bey's sons were short because their father only gave them 150LL a month and they could not steal as much as usual this year because someone had leased all the father's land.

23. I was told by an agha who had worked for Abboud that the bey used to bring in fellah watchmen from different surrounding small villages so that they would not agree among themselves to steal olives as Beit Abd as-Salam did. My informant remarked with a laugh that Abboud was too intelligent to leave the task to Beit Abd as-Salam, and no one would beat up a watchman brought in by Abboud.

24. The combination of rises in productivity, prices, markets and land sales is noted by P. Sanlaville, 'Les régions agricoles du Liban', *Revue de Géographie de Lyon*, Vol. 44, 1969, pp. 53–4. He remarks on growing purchases by Beiruti businessmen.

25. Sanlaville in 1969 suggested that some kinds of citrus, such as the orange called 'baladi' gave relatively low yields, were only little demanded on the market, and suffered from many parasites. New groves had to be planted with improved varieties and less density of planting. He puts lemon groves as one-third of the plantation of citrus in the Tripoli region. See Sanlaville, 'Régions', p. 52.

The Hajj certainly had reasons other than his low opinion of the shebab for his decision not to move into this area of agriculture.

26. A paternal cousin of my informant gave a somewhat different version. In this account the olive press owner had initially been very successful because his links with four or five other villages from *Deuxième Bureau* days got him many opportunities to buy up olives both ahead and at harvest. But the men working with him had a reputation for causing a lot of disputes, and he had become 'very difficult and demanding', wanting all the profit. Some had left him, including several of the beys, and now he only had a minority of the Berqayl owners supplying him with olives.

27. This condensed version is taken from notes in English taken at the time of our conversation and rendered as direct speech to give some sense of its tone and form.

28. The son was said by members of his own family never to have communicated with them after his flight from the village.

29. The association of emigration with 'anger' and force is developed in Chapter 9.

30. See Chapters 16 and 17.

31. Sanlaville noted the progressive eviction of cultivators under 'modernization'. See Sanlaville, 'Régions', pp. 53–4.

32. Naoufral-Giappesi, quoting Ministry of Agriculture figures, says that in 1970 sharecropping only covered 38.6 per cent of cultivated lands, where it had been the dominant type of arrangement. Naoufral-Giappesi, 'Contribution', p. 133. Another Ministry report of 1968 suggested that 50 per cent of land on the plain was cultivated in plots of two hectares.

8. Famine and Memory

1. Karm is also a word often used of land planted in vines, which are grown in the Akkar only in a few very limited areas, or to provide grapes for purely private consumption.

2. Zamir says that 'over one-fifth of the population of Mount Lebanon, most of them Christians, died of starvation or disease'. He refers to the fact that remittances did not come in during the war, a factor also commented on by Tamimi and Bahgat; commerce and silk production, the economic foundations of the Mountain though not of Akkar,

collapsed; there was high inflation and, factors which count for a great deal in the stories recounted in this chapter, 'corruption and profiteering'. See M. Zamir, *The Formation of Modern Lebanon*, London: Croom Helm, 1985, p. 36.

In a detailed article covering the whole of Greater Syria, and thus including Akkar, Linda Schatkowski Schilcher lists eight basic factors which she views as contributing to as many as 500,000 deaths in the famine period: 'The Entente powers' total blockade of the Syrian coast; the inadequacy of the Ottoman supply strategy; deficient harvests and inclement weather; diversion of supplies from Syria as a consequence of the Arab Revolt; the speculative frenzy of a number of unscrupulous local grain merchants; the callousness of German military officials in Syria, and systematic hoarding by the population at large.' See L. Schatkowski Schilcher, 'The famine of 1915–1918 in Greater Syria', in John Spagnolo (ed.), *Problems of the Modern Middle East in Historical Perspective: Essays in Honour of Albert Hourani*, Reading: Ithaca Press, 1992, p. 234.

She notes: 'As it is now, the famine is an event which has remained historical lore', an observation that is very relevant to this chapter and to the local level at which I am treating the subject.

3. Schatkowski Schilcher quotes from an account in *The Near East*, Cairo, 4 March 1916, in which escapees from the Syrian coast to Cairo spoke of how the 'poor picked up and fed on orange and lemon peel and also chewed pieces of sugar cane, and when the rains stopped the women and children went out into the fields and picked weeds and other green stuff that sprouted up, in a desperate endeavour to keep body and soul together'. Schatkowski Schilcher, 'The famine of 1915–1918', pp. 230–31. This echo of the grove of the orange story in the bald account of the famine's horror reminds us of the general regional disaster to which the local narratives refer. The agha gets a piece of orange – at a price; the poor scavenge for the peel.

4. I use the word glamour in the old sense of enchantment, a magical aura. *The Shorter Oxford English Dictionary* definition 'a magical or fictitious beauty attaching to any person or object' conveys the quality of being that some men are held to possess and which narratives are taken to demonstrate.

5. I should perhaps note here that local pronunciation is manzul and not manzil, which is much more common in other areas and is the form usually given in dictionaries.

6. The phrase is Hayden White's in *Tropics of Discourse: Essays in Cultural Criticism*, Baltimore/London: Johns Hopkins University Press, 1978, pp. 2–3.

7. *Adami* is difficult to translate. Barthélemy gives *poli, affable, humain*, Barthélemy, *Dictionnaire Arabe-Français. Dialectes de Syrie: Alep, Dames, Liban, Jérusalem*, fasc. 1, Paris: Librairie Orientaliste Paul Geuthna, 1935, p. 5. Claude Denizeau, *Dictionnaire des Parles Arabes de Syrie, Liban et Palestine*, Paris: Éditions G.-P. Maisonneuve, 1960, p. 4 has *homme honnête, brave homme*. Hans Wehr, *A Dictionary of Modern Written Arabic*, J. Milton Cowan (ed.), Wiesbaden: Otto Harrassowitz/London: George Allen and Unwin Ltd., 1966, p. 40, defines the slightly differently vowelled version of the word *adami* with a long initial alef (*alef mamduda*) as 'human; humane;' and then 'poor, inferior, meagre.' Much depends, as always, on context. Said admiringly of someone the term indicates indeed his human qualities, a certain moral strength, an absence of pretension, an honesty, trustworthiness and observance of the appropriate social duties. On the other hand, it is often used of someone who has little social status or public esteem, although he does his best and is certainly a man who attempts, however limited his position, to do what is proper. Phrases such as: *adami katir ya khtaitu* (he's a decent chap, poor devil) or *adami miskin* put the stress on a man's misfortune or poverty.

8. For French treatment of the famine and French help for the Lebanese, see the highly coloured account 'La famine au Liban et l'assistance française aux Libanais pendant la

grande guerre (1915–1919)', *Supplément à l'Asie Française*, Février 1922, pp. 3–14. For a less overtly propagandistic version, see also Jean Donon's report: 'La rescision des ventes de guerre au Liban', *L'Asie Française*, No. 198, Janvier 1922, pp. 16–21.

9. He used the word *shaqfe*, a Syrian dialect word, meaning 'a bit'; see Barthélemy, fasc. 2, p. 399.

10. During this period oranges and citrus fruits were being introduced in areas along the coastal plain of what we now call Lebanon. The profit per hectare was reckoned (in piasters) to be 5,200, compared to 3,931 for olives, 2,700 for vines, and 1,905 for mulberries (cocoons). See Isma'il Bey Haqqi, *Lubnan: mabahith 'ilmiyya wa ijtima'iyya*, Fouad Bustani (ed.), Vol. 2, Beirut, 1970, p. 459.

11. Hublos suggests that a very important reason for this process was the changes in land law by the Ottoman state in 1858. Beys were able to take over *mawt*, that is to say 'dead' land, if they cultivated it. This gave them a way of increasing the scale of their properties and socio-economic dominance. He sees such a trend as a compensation for the lords' loss of judicial power over the fellahin. I am not convinced that *in practice* their judicial power really was lost, but the general point is a valid one. If in the eighteenth century cultivation was limited to the *tall*s, or small hills rising from the plain here and there like islands on which settlements such as Halba were built, by the twentieth century the coastal area had displaced the mountain in terms of production. See F. Hublos, *Ta'rikh 'Akkar al idari wa'l ijtima'i wa'l iqtisadi, 1800–1914*, Beirut: Dar al Ha'ira, 1987, p. 148.

12. Olives are not recorded in the documents before 1740, according to Hublos. Planting around Berqayl is probably later than in some other regions of the *wasat* area such as Beqarzla, Qantara, as well as in Baino and 'Akkar al 'Atiqa. Tamimi and Bahgat comment on the olive trees in Berqayl in 1917. Hublos, *Ta'rikh*, pp. 141–2.

One man of *fellah* descent said that Abboud and beys like him had 'torn up the olive trees from the time of the Bani Sayfa and planted new groves'. (The Bani Sayfa were a powerful force in Akkar from the middle of the sixteenth century until their final loss of local power in 1640. See Kamal Salibi, 'The Sayfas and the Eyalet of Tripoli', 1579–1640, *Arabica*, Vol. 20, 1973, pp. 25–52.) This is a very powerful image of a change of the social and political landscape, and marks a radical break in historical narrative. 'Abboud' becomes a transforming figure, uprooting the past and creating a different order.

13. Hublos gives the figure of 4,000 hectares irrigated out of a total of 25,000 on the whole *sahel* area at the beginning of the French Mandate. Irrigated land was far more valuable than non-irrigated and fetched much higher prices. See Hublos, *Ta'rikh*, p. 148.

14. The Arabic word used locally for a grove of lemon or orange trees is *jeneine*, not *karm*.

There are risks in the early stages of a newly planted grove of disease and of destruction by extreme cold. There were stories of large amounts of money being lost when a whole grove of young trees was wiped out by disease, and of the bringing in of outside specialists as (expensive) advisors. The owner must be prepared to invest considerable sums of capital and to wait for five years or so before he begins to show profits. The gardens also need proper irrigation and drainage, which was relatively rare on the plain of Akkar until the 1960s, and it was necessary to grow windbreaks of trees such as poplars around the gardens as protection against the often strong winds that sweep across the plain from the north and west.

Land planted in trees, whether almond, apple, olive or orange, is called *mansub*. It was regarded as the most valuable kind of investment in agriculture because of the possible market returns, and was only rivalled at the time of my fieldwork by a growing awareness, to which I have already referred, of the profitability of producing vegetables all-year round under plastic for the Gulf and Saudi markets. This, too, required considerable initial investment to carry forward on a reasonable scale.

15. Hublos, *Ta'rikh*, p. 140. He indicates that *portugal* oranges began to replace the mulberry trees around 1903 and that they were quickly recognized as far more profitable.

16. I am here referring to Max Weber's construction of an ideal type, and not to an ideal.

17. 'Take it' is an emphatic assertion which is striking in this case precisely because it uses extremely clipped and economic means to perform a dramatically significant act of unexpected exchange. As Dixon says, it serves 'to focus attitudes which have been growing throughout a whole discourse' Peter Dixon, *Rhetoric*, London\New York: Methuen, 1971, p. 43.

18. Gérard Genette, *Figures of Literary Discourse*, (trans. Alan Sheridan), Oxford: Basil Blackwell, 1982, pp. 47–8.

19. No one could remember what the previous name of the grove had been.

20. The mayor's account can be read as saying 'look what sort of ancestors we had – they could participate in this extraordinary world of name and honour', even as he points to the implications for later generations.

21. I am particularly grateful to Robert Smith for his discussion of this dimension of the narrative, as well as his critical reading of this chapter as a whole.

22. I should note that I have written out what he said in the order of topics discussed as I wrote them down at the time in a conversation which I left to his direction. I had asked to come to his reception room to talk about his father but beyond indicating that general interest I did not pose other questions, though I am sure that he noticed cues of interest on my part and had his own ideas of what concerned me.

23. The cemetery of the sheikhs or holy men of Haizouq and Mashha, all from the clan of the Zu'abis, lay just outside the villages and was much visited. It was very unusual for a child to be taken to his mother's village for burial. Indeed, this is the only case I know of from Berqayl. The religious weight and prestige of the mother's family clearly counted very highly with Beit Khalid Ali and this burial was a significant acknowledgement of deference to the celebrated father of Khalid Ali's third wife, Sheikh Ahmad Shakir. The baby daughter was buried in Berqayl and it does not appear that any consideration was given to her being taken to Mashha. As always, the male is the vehicle of public signs of relationship and 'respect'.

24. The material gathered here is derived from a long conversation with the mayor, interspersed with contextual detail supplied at various other times about members of the family. We met quite often at his reception room in the course of my fieldwork, a reception room that in the evening was rarely empty.

He began by saying that his oldest brother, Ahmad, who had died quite young and was unmarried, had been in school with him. They had one teacher for everything and they had been first and second in class. The boys had three examiners, and everything was in French. 'I know how to write "give him five shunbuls of maize and put him to work on them", and that's it', he said.

The mayor had left school at fifteen and took over the house when his mother died. He had had six or seven years in school and 'it was all in French' he repeated, with a disgusted expression. The place was just a shop. The government started building the new school in 1963 and finished in 1964. The old place had been a three-room establishment maintained by Muhammad Bey al Mustafa for six years or so before, or maybe ten.

For a year and a half he had been responsible for the upkeep of his father's house and then his father married again, this time to the daughter of the most celebrated sheikh of Akkar, Sheikh Ahmad Shakir (who had died some years before; the mayor's mother was still alive at the time of my fieldwork). The mayor himself had married in 1956 when he was about twenty-five years old and his wife was twenty-four. She was a younger sister of his father's third wife. In 1959 his father died at about seventy-three years old (he was therefore born around 1886). In 1962 the government had instituted the baladiya and the ra'is's list had won.

25. See Figure 2 for Beit Abd al Latif Abd as-Salam genealogy.

26. Another informant, the mayor's FFBSS, doubted that Ali had sold off the land at Tall Hayat. 'Our grandfathers did not sell down on the plain', he insisted. 'The children must have done it.' In his view 'the grandfathers' represented the generation of acquisition and building of social position. The succeeding generation was the one he blamed for the loss of property.

27. We can easily imagine that these men might be described by descendants as murafiqin carrying out their duties of supporting their lord with bravery and fearlessness.

28. It was impossible to say to what degree this 'madness' related to the killing of his relative and served to diminish collective responsibility for the bloodshed since he was thus defined as outside the social pale and his relatives would not, at least in theory, be appropriate targets for revenge killing. Groups will grasp at such culturally available options to 'classify out' problematic characters, and sometimes a man who was killed was called 'asocial, an animal', thus absolving the killer, again in theory, from punitive action. The move down to the plain, to Tripoli, or the more radical step of emigration abroad, a taking of a distance at once geographical and symbolic, also serves to clear a situation of great cultural and social confusion.

When I was collecting the genealogy the mayor mentioned neither his 'mad' paternal uncle nor the victim. Selective genealogical amnesia was pressingly at work. There were no conventions or rules men could invoke when bloodshed occurred within a beit since any revenge was bound to concentrate the violence within the same group yet further. The risk of mutual annihilation was ever-present.

29. This anomalous relationship was socially censored and passed over in silence. There was a link of service to the beys as the husband also worked for them as an attendant and khawli.

30. 'Mad' in his case was held to mean a derangement of the senses rather than the asocial or dangerous 'craziness' sometimes used to refer to others. (See the narrative of Abu Marwan below, pp. 144–7, for an account of this latter form of classification.)

31. The mayor's brother Muhammad, who worked closely with him in running their lands, spoke of their father in typical terms employed for men of social standing in the past: 'The patron of a manzul, a keeper of fine horses. He puts his nargileh in its place and everyone comes to him. He lives as he wishes.' Of their grandfather Ali he said: 'He carried his lance. He was a man of value.' In that generation the lance and the sword were the weapons of horsemen and cavaliers. In both, the nargileh was a sign of social status and a mark of the man of true social weight being 'at his ease'. The dialect word he used for his grandfather was sharquta, and when I looked puzzled and asked for the meaning he glossed it as nimr, a tiger. The intransitive verb form, sharqata, means to spark or glitter (like a fire) and evocatively conveys the image of the heroic figure as flash of fire or leaping flame. See Barthélemy, Dictionnaire Arabe-Français, fasc. 2, p. 388. 'In those days', he went on, 'they were young men, the real flower of youth, all your height [I am 1.82m tall], but broad-shouldered [I am not]. They'd wrap their headdress (kewfiyya) round their heads, bind the cummerbund (zinnara, the long black waist-wrap men used to wear) about their waists and strike with the staff, and no doctor would be able to do anything.' Such phrases were often-heard formulae in characterizations of 'true men in those days'.

It should be said that this brother was an expert in the elaborations of etiquette and complimentary phrases, something beyond the ra'is's abilities. Muhammad's role was to shower guests with all the proper, most flowery phrases and epithets.

32. Accident, too, played a part. The teenage son of number 27 on the Beit Ibrahim chart was killed when he and another boy were fooling around with a pistol. The other pulled the trigger after a mock threat to 'execute' his friend, and the gun went off, putting a bullet through the teenager's brain. There had instantly been meetings of the elders of the descent group of all Beit Abd as-Salam to decide compensation and the boy responsible was handed over to the authorities who jailed him for several years. (He was still in jail when I was in the village, and we visited him; one of the beys for whom he had worked gave him a monthly allowance, a quite typical arrangement. The lord wanted him as a bodyguard when he came out.)

An additional problem was that the teenager was the son of the man whose sister had been one of the wives of Khalid Ali, the man thus being mother's brother to the mayor and his brothers and a constant visitor to the Marouche where the victim's family lived. He continued to visit regularly and he maintained cordial, though not close relations with the father of the dead boy. One man related to the ra'is (FFBSS) said to me disapprovingly that the father of the victim was 'weak'. It was shameful to allow the mother's brother to come to the area – there was blood between them, accident or no accident. It was *'aib*, shame. Others endorsed the complicit normalization of relations and acted as if there were no cause for any disruption of links, and no fear that in the future one of the victim's still small brothers might grow up with different ideas.

33. The boy who had accidently killed his friend was described, as men who get involved in killing so often are, as 'wild' and 'crazy'. When I returned briefly in 1983 he had become the prosperous owner of a jerrycan-making plant in the village and had other interests in Tripoli where he had lived since coming out of jail. He only visited the village occasionally and told me that he 'hardly knew anyone there any more', a remark he repeated more than once. This spatial distancing from social relations and the immediate scene of an act of blood occurred in not a few of the cases discussed in this book. The city still served its conventional role as a place of (relative) safety.

9. Fellahin and Famine

1. He was, as I would see it, an example of that social 'madness' which was often identified with being an outlaw as a permanent condition of life, for that meant he had no relationship to a lord who would mediate with the law to secure his pardon. (See, in contrast, the narrative of Abu Juwad below.) He is a different type-case of the man alone, for such a one 'lives in the mountain' and is beyond the restraints of society.

2. This is a local version of the many state document complaints about the endemic 'lack of security' in the region of Akkar in the Turkish and French period. It is unclear quite what relationship this man may have had with the beys or whether his shooting of someone from Beit Haddara and evasion of arrest was the reason for his being an outlaw.

3. The phrase Abu Marwan used, *anhas wahid fi'd-dunya*, is difficult to translate. The verb form *n–h–s* means bringing ill-luck or misfortune upon someone, and the form *anhas* would signify someone with a greater capacity than others to do that. Colloquially, something on the lines of 'the most miserable bastard in the world', or 'the most difficult son of a bitch', perhaps gets nearest to the sense.

4. Those who die on the pilgrimage have the status of martyr, *shahid*, and are transported directly to Paradise.

5. I am thinking here of lines of argument developed in David Warren Sabean's perceptive and stimulating work on early modern Germany, and particularly of his discussion of *herrschaft* and violence. See David Warren Sabean, *Power in the Blood: Popular Culture and Village Discourse in Early Modern Germany*, Cambridge: Cambridge University Press, 1984, pp. 22–7.

6. Grandfather, *jidd*, used here in a general sense for 'ancestor' and not meaning his father's father.

7. *Ba'l* land produces fruits and crops without irrigation, using only natural watering by rain.

8. The two decades before the First World War saw the highest rates of migration to the United States, Brazil and Argentina from Syria and Lebanon. Most immigrants in the first decade of this century were joining friends of family who were already abroad. It was not at all unusual, however, for migrants to return after a number of years. See Alixa Naff, *Becoming American: the early Arab Immigrant Experience*, Carbondale, IL: Southern Illinois University Press, 1985; also Kohei Hashimoto, 'Causes and Consequences of International Migration: the Case of Lebanon, 1888–1939', D. Phil. thesis, Oxford University, 1992, 1912 and 1913 were the highest years for the arrival of immigrants in Argentina, and there was a precipitous drop from the 19,542 arriving there in 1913 (5,309 left in the same year) to the 5,142 who came in 1914. The First World War put a stop to emigration to Latin America for the duration. The greatest concentration of migrants from Syria and Lebanon was found in Buenos Aires, the hajj's place of settlement. See I. Klich, '*Criolos* and Arabic speakers in Argentina: an uneasy *pas de deux*, 1888–1914', in Albert Hourani and Nadim Shehadeh (eds), *The Lebanese in the World*, London: I.B.Tauris, 1992.

9. R. Tamimi and M. Bahgat, *Wilayat Beirut*, Beirut: Matba'a al Iqbel, 1916 (republished 1979), p. 250.

10. No word ever came to the village of the fate of these men. They simply never came back and were assumed to have been killed or to have died.

11. We can see here the other side of the Mandate officers' concerns for enumeration, classification, registration and ordering discussed in Chapter 6.

12. Suleiman Franjieh was a strong-arm man from one of the leading Maronite clans of the town of Zghorta. He eventually became the President of Lebanon in 1970, a post he held for one term, until 1976.

13. This chauffeur is the man wounded in the first incident recounted in the next chapter.

14. Ali Abd al Karim was a deputy for one electoral period only. He had a reputation for great 'generosity', distributing a lot of money and doing a great deal for people. During the elections of 1972 men would mention his name nostalgically, saying it was a great pity that he had not known how to draw in money as well as he had given it out – that was the reason they gave for his limited political success. By the time I met him he had lost much of his standing and was regarded as a peripheral figure. He had a political quarrel with the leading notable of Beit Abd as-Salam who had introduced me to the governor of the northern governorate and the chief military officer of Akkar. The notable was a supporter of Bashir al Osman, but I think there were additional reasons for their mutual hostility. When Ali Bey and I were introduced in the governor's office it turned out that he wanted to attack me as an English spy, 'just like a major who had been here in the war', he said. I was not at all prepared for the virtually open allegations, which were a way of putting pressure on the person he saw as my local protector. The latter claimed that Ali Bey was trying to put the frighteners on me to get some money out of it by blackmailing me, but there was no other evidence for this explanation. Neither the governor nor the military commander showed any real interest in his barely veiled charges and I never heard anything more of it. Had he still been a deputy no doubt they might have felt obliged to treat the matter differently.

15. *Deir* is the Arabic word for convent or monastery.

16. *Bi'r* means well or spring. This etymology of the name of the village was quite common and men would sometimes debate whether the name Berqayl referred to the spring or to the presence of a monastery as this informant said.

17. This is an example of the name of the olive grove being coupled with that of the original owner, in this case a very important agha. In this version, Sheikh Osman was effectively dispossessed of it against his will by Abboud. The sheikh's grandsons vigorously denied such a possibility. Their grandfather, they proclaimed, had been 'head of Beit Abd as-Salam' and totally independent. He had never been linked with any of the beys, let alone had land taken from him.

18. Hence the noun form *mur'ib*, terrifying, causing fear and dread. This folk etymology of the name of the beys was quite common and made perfect social sense.

19. There was another side to this policy. Incorporation of fellahin qabadays might also be used by the beys, as I have said, to undermine the agha monopoly of positions as companions and privileged men of violence.

10. Gallous Story or Dirty Deed

1. *Dabah* in this kind of context takes on a particular force. It may, like other terms, be used ironically, in jesting, or simply to mean that a person has been really 'done over'.

2. I never discovered whether there had been any open or veiled suggestion that a negotiated settlement might be reached at this stage. I suspect that at this stage of the fieldwork I had already too much absorbed the narratives as simply 'true' to take a distance from them. In other words, I probably did not conceive of such a possibility because the way of telling what happened seemed to exclude anything but what was told. I no longer saw, if I ever had, the silences and censored possibilities. The rhetoric persuaded me.

3. During my fieldwork a university teacher who had returned to his home village in Akkar from his residence in America was murdered in revenge for a killing that had taken place during his absence. He had had nothing to do with the bloodshed and there was much local dispute as to whether his murder was justified or not. Some argued that as the most 'valuable' member of the family he was a legitimate target; others strongly disputed it. The same debate arose over a young bey who killed one of the agha family, most of whose members lived in Tripoli. Some men argued strongly that the bey's brother represented the best choice as target on the ground that as an educated man with a degree he was 'gold' whereas the killer was merely 'silver'. My own views were asked for, and I said that it seemed to me that the man who pulled the trigger was the obvious person for vengeance.

4. In fact, on the death of his first wife, Abdallah's father had married her sister who had born him the three boys. There was thus a double link between the families.

5. Sulh is often translated as 'peace', but I think that the word 'truce' might be more accurate, certainly in this kind of situation. There was no sense of finality about the process. No one thought that the quarrel would be ended nor that relations would be restored by the mediation. Rather, the reputation of the descent group notables was engaged to guarantee that the truce be kept and to act as a public, consensual warranty for the agreement. Men would hope that no further violence would be committed and that time would lead to a slow renewal of relations.

6. The diya, or *haqq al qatil*, the right of the murdered/killed.

7. Women and young children were, in principle, excluded from this realm of male violence. In any case they were unlikely to go into areas which were defined as problematic. If they did, for whatever reason, their status as socially invisible or insignificant was sufficient protection and embarrassment could be avoided. To kill a woman in such circumstances, at that time in Lebanon, would have been regarded in the village with horror. Women might be killed where men held that they had polluted the family by illicit sexual activity. Cases of such killing, of sisters by brothers, certainly occurred and were reported

in the press as a customary type of crime. But I am not aware that such a killing had ever happened in Berqayl.

8. One reason why I was told this story is that I made the gaffe of referring to Abdallah in front of one of Ali's brothers who became a friend. The teenage agha who was with me, and who 'did not count' since he was not a mature male and not from the fractions of Beit Abd as-Salam most closely implicated in the killing, was deeply shocked. The brother was able to use my ignorance and status as outsider as a reason for not responding. The story was explained to me by the teenager, and then by others in private, one-to-one conversations. Occasionally, men of one of the agha groups would hint at it if some circumstance related in some way to the implications of the sequence of events, but usually he would simply say: 'You know, of course, about ...? and his voice would trail off, leaving me simply to nod my head quickly. We would then carry on in the conversation.

To my embarrassment and horror, however, I made the same gaffe some months later when, in a casual and teasing aside about the unpredictability of someone else's behaviour (whom I was gossiping about in a very relaxed way with my friend, Ali's brother), I compared the subject of our conversation to Abdallah. My sense of mortification was all the greater because an apology would of course only increase the attention drawn to what should have remained under the thickest curtain of silence. The difference between learning a rule, and having a set of practices as part of one's taken-for-granted universe of presuppositions could not have been more painfully clear. The friend carried on the conversation with unbroken grace, though I had hit on the most vulnerable part of his social identity.

9. I enquired of one of my informants when he was telling me the story whether the aghas had considered paying the diya in instalments over time. 'What do you think this is?' I was tartly asked. 'A car sale?'

10. It also meant that I could not elicit accounts from members of the fellahin families since the whole subject was shameful and not to be raised.

11. It was said of him: 'He has thrown off the pollution of Allah from his back.' This is a literal translation of a very problematic phrase which I wrote down in Arabic as I heard it: *rama janabat allah 'an dohruh*. This might be taken to mean roughly that 'he has got rid of the pollution of the blood insult', and might usually be read as referring to his ridding the family of the shame of the wounding of one of their members by the killing of Ali Bashir. If this interpretation is the right one, it implies that Abdallah somehow felt he had made himself free of the pollution of blood without God's power; that he did not seek to be purified by proper ritual and custom; and that he was in fact disregarding God's law. *Janaba*, a term in Islamic law for men or women in a state of serious impurity and not ritually cleansed for the performance of prayer, is, in this context, associated with violence and bloodshed.

12. Two of my acquaintance, who were wanted by the law, often commented to me, in front of Abdallah among others, how they never spent the night in the village because it was then that the armed police, who would not risk a daytime entry, might surprise them, tipped off by someone who had his own interest in seeing them out of the way. Young men sometimes teased the two men in a barbed way with the chance of such betrayal if they thought they could get away with it. No one would think to taunt Abdallah, but he shared in the outlaws' sense of the dangers of the night.

11. Marching in the Wrong Direction

1. Sharaf would also apply to male sexuality if a male were sexually penetrated by another. One man joked that: 'Your sharaf is any hole you can get into.'

2. Higher-status aghas whose lives as hunters, armed companions and independent

small landholders would avoid such talk as, in the first place, being of an inappropriate genre for a man of honour; and, in the second place, because they defended the bey's reputation as a whole as emblematic of an order they too incarnated. One or two, none the less, were prepared to say that he had become zalim, or that sometimes things happened in those families ... Occasionally there were arguments with adult sons, who had effectively taken over social pre-eminence and had their own children, if the old men felt that the beys were being denounced or slandered by talk of this nature. That did not necessarily stop their sons.

3. The man who is penetrated by the other is held to be feminized and not to be a true man. The penetrator is not held to be 'homosexual'. The relationship or act is not in principle one to be talked about, but a nod, a wink and a grin convey the message.

A man of agha descent, whom I knew very well and who had spent a couple of years in Kuwait as a chauffeur, once told me with astonishment about the rich Kuwaiti woman whose driver he had been. She had used him as a stud, and he gave a very funny parody of their shared ecstasies, a performance which was much appreciated by a couple of young aghas who were present. The point of the story, however, was not merely to play out his role as teller of scabrous tales, buffoon, and marginal figure, all of which he did with gusto. It was rather that this woman had suddenly turned on him when he had spoken to her in less than the totally appropriate manner demanded of the etiquette of a complete social inferior, using the second person feminine singular rather than the higher-status plural form. In his version she brutally called him to heel: 'Don't imagine just because you fuck me that you can dare to talk to me like that. One more example and you are finished.' Since, according to him, she could have had him thrown out of the country instantly without any wages, or indeed arbitrarily jailed, the threat was very real. 'Can you credit that?' he said to us, eyebrows raised and arms widespread in astonishment.

4. The bey was thus represented as becoming perverse as he moved into the classi-fication of 'old man', and not as always having been so.

5. Such a story was one to be alluded to or murmured rather than spoken out in front of any but the closest cronies. A man concerned with his status and the proprieties of social maturity would not discuss such matters. A man not so concerned, of course, might wilfully break the constraints of etiquette. Thus an (agha) outlaw who also drank a great deal – another violation of a local interdiction which even men who were known to drink in Tripoli or Beirut observed in the village – once made a great story to me out of the old lord's supposed commands. He looked at his first cousin and neighbour, a man of very low standing in the family who had always been a worker and later supervisor with the beys, and said to me with a mischievous air something like: 'You know what used to happen between this bastard here and the old lord?' 'Don't believe it, ustaz', said his cousin laughing already. 'The bey used to shout out to him, come here you, and take him round the corner and drop his pants for a quick one.' Both men laughed, and the other reiterated his 'don't believe him', treating the whole thing as a joke. 'Oh yes, just shout for him, you there, come here ... and off he'd go.' It was quite clear that the outlaw was using the license of his public discredit to say the discreditable, and to the visitor to the village who should not be addressed on such topics. This, he seemed to say, was what *really* used to go on, a very typical trope.

6. There were certainly hints among adolescent aghas that particular individuals had sexual liaisons with the young beys in which they 'rode' their masters. This was something they and their friends might know about, but it was never spoken of in a public forum and there were those who disapproved. Their everyday behaviour with the young bey was marked by all the signs of respect and deference appropriate to the standing of the particular family and individual involved. Such 'suppressed' and concealed sexual acts seem to me to complement the image of the old lord's demands of his servants and bodyguards.

7. The phrase commonly used is *akhadha bitashlif*, literally 'he took her by abduction'. Shallaf is a term current in Akkar and as far as I am aware is used exclusively for the abduction of women, nearly always in an account of how a particular marriage came about. Barthélemy gives the more general *enlever* and *arracher* as a third meaning without any more specific reference (A. Barthélemy, *Dictionnaire Arabe–Français. Dialectes de Syrie: Alep, Damas, Liban, Jérusalem*, Paris: Librarie Orientaliste Paul Geuthner, 1936, Vol. 2, p. 404). Denizeau has *'enlever (une jeune fille)'* as a second meaning (Claude Denizeau, *Dictionnaire des Parlers Arabes de Syrie, Liban et Palestine*, Paris: Editions G.-P. Maisonneuve, 1960).

8. Few villages in the Qayta' had more than one phone, sometimes located in the baladiya, if there was a separate baladiya building, or in a shop. Thus everyone tended to know of any communications.

9. Erving Goffman, 'On cooling the mark out', in A. Rose (ed.), *Human Behaviour and Social Processes*, London: Routledge and Kegan Paul, 1962, p. 505.

10. M. Gilsenan, 'Word of Honour', in R. Grillo (ed.), *Social Anthropology and the Politics of Language*, London: Routledge, 1989, p. 197.

11. The richest man and leading notable of Beit Abd as-Salam had complained sarcastically to me that if even my companion, 'that nobody', could go off and buy one then what were men of standing to do? He, the notable, would have to purchase some new and expensive model to reassert his pre-eminence, though when he had purchased his own Czech rifle several years before there hadn't been another one in the whole village. Now any son of a dog could get one.

12. M. Gilsenan, 'Lying, honor, and contradiction', in Bruce Kapferer (ed.), *Transaction and Meaning*, Philadelphia, PA: ISHI, 1976, p. 216, note 25.

12. Joking, Play and Pressure

1. The citation is taken from Raymond Jamous's reflections on honour as a way of giving sense to life through the confrontation with death as a violence rather than a 'natural fact'. Honour, he says, takes form in action and defines both the identity of persons and of collectivities as the specific forms of the exchange of violence: 'De ce fait, elle est le lieu de la relation ou tout se joue constamment sur les limites qui distinguent, séparent, opposent, mais qui aussi permettent de se reconnaître, d'être dépendants les uns des autres par cette fascination de la mort violente' (p. 176). Raymond Jamous, 'De quoi parlent les fusils?', in *L'honneur. Image de soi ou don de soi: un idéal équivoque* (Série Morales), No. 3, March 1991, Paris, Éditions Autrement, pp. 176–89.

2. *'arraq* is a dialect word used in the context of putting pressure on someone, giving someone a bad time, making him sweat. See Barthélemy, *Dictionnaire Arabe–Français*, fasc. 3, p. 523. Stanley Brandes has investigated the place of joking, the playing of pranks, skits and forms of play in terms of fear and aggression in his *Metaphors of Masculinity: Sex and Status in Andalusian Folklore*, Philadelphia: University of Pennsylvania Press, 1985 (especially Chapters 6 and 7, pp. 97–136 and Chapter 9, pp. 159–76). The major themes of his material are quite different from my own since they focus on the power of women to emasculate, the voracious sexual appetite of women, the male fear of being cuckolded and the quality and size of male genitals. (p. 100).

3. In the context of the village, verse played no part in confrontation. This was not because men did not appreciate poetic challenges. The largest and most enthusiastic audiences in the very few houses owning a television were always for the weekly programme in which *zajal* contests between two pairs of poets were featured, with much commentary and appreciation of the skill of the individuals. But the extemporization of poetry in this mode was never used in the dai'a. There was no living tradition of authoring poetry, or of

individual and collective extemporization at weddings or celebrations, and no hero boasted of his exploits or confronted his enemies in verse.

The television programme gave access to skilled performances, but also at the same time mediated and reinforced cultural disprivilege. The audience watched eagerly and commented with delight on an especially telling word play or riposte. Yet the context of the elegantly suited performers seated behind the table covered with bottles of drink and decorations signified another world of social honour, the world of the cultural and social centre, not one in which the peripheral villagers could possibly share except through the mediation of the screen.

4. When I returned for three days to the village in 1983 one of the sahras I attended was dominated for some time by the telling of jokes and by verbal contesting. One man, himself with a reputation both as a good man to have on your side in a fight and as a bit of a clown, a thief and a fantasist, stalked majestically from the room saying that this was not a 'real' sahra. Everyone there was spoiling it, he fulminated, by indulging in this mode of interaction at the expense of more 'serious' forms.

5. The washing table reference is to the table on which the corpses were ritually washed after death, around which the young men often made a zikr. It was normally kept at the old lower mosque just by the entrance, while the open coffin in which all the dead were carried to their graves was propped up against an outside wall.

6. The *arba'in* is the fortieth day after a death, the final occasion on which people gather to pay respects to the family. It marks the end of the mourning period and is well attended by those having any links at all with the deceased's kin.

7. Christ (in Arabic, 'Isa) is honoured as a prophet in the Islamic tradition. He is believed to have been born of the Word of God 'cast' into Mary. His death by crucifixion was 'prevented by a change of resemblance', an obscure phrase in the Quran, Chapter 4, verse 157. See "Isa', in H.A.R. Gibb and J.H. Kramers (eds), *Shorter Encyclopaedia of Islam*, Leiden: E.J. Brill, 1953, p. 173.

8. Neither he nor anyone else in the village had formal religious training.

9. We can see again in this episode how important it is to get all the odds in your favour before you begin such a piece of play. As in other contexts, you humiliate those you think can be humiliated.

10. I had not anticipated this kind of contest and was quite unprepared for the switch of frame that Abu Ali accomplished, all the while seeming to remain strictly within the appropriate modes of behaviour at a funeral. Having taken on what I assumed was the appropriate demeanour and attitude, I was also socially thrown by the occasion and it took me some time to grasp what was happening.

11. He was the father of Nabil who became involved in the scuffle on the school bus in Tripoli. The family had no electricity and very bare furnishings. Abu Nabil was a man of a very 'sweet' and gentle temperament and men of his section of Beit Abd as-Salam and maternal relatives quite often came to his house for an evening in winter, though his modest income meant some real strain on the budget in terms of tea, sugar and cigarettes. I felt that their favouring his house was related to the fact that he had no political role or claims to status and never showed an inclination at all to indulge in competitive behaviour. He 'stayed at home, relaxed', and thus constituted a kind of neutral ground appropriate for the easy informality that is supposed to characterize a sahra. The sheikh ash-shebab used his sahras as one of his arenas of mobilization of the young men.

12. Fattan is used to mean someone who causes discord in a group, informs on others or denounces someone to another or to the authorities. Such a figure gets his sense of power from setting people against each other and is not to be trusted. *Fitna*, dissension, has important connotations in Islamic terms as being one of the major dangers threatening

the *umma*, the Islamic community. Cognate meanings include 'fascinating, captivating, enchanting; tempter, seducer' (see Wehr's *Dictionary of Modern Arabic*, p. 696).

13. The word rabb, meaning lord or God, is used in all sorts of boasting formulae, such as *'ana rabb ad-dai'a kullha'*, 'I am the lord of the whole village'. It may be used at the height of a serious dispute, or in jaqmara and play, as here. *'Sabbati fuq ad-dai'a kullha'*, 'my shoe is on the whole village', meaning 'everyone here is under my control', is a grandilo- quent phrase that is frequently used and has the same rhetorical function.

14. The shopkeeper who took messages from the single telephone in the village frequent- ly sent off one of the children to inform whoever was wanted of what had been said. The room for garbled accounts and a kind of game of Chinese Whispers was considerable.

15. Men grow up with the game genre in which young boys try to fool one another with announcements of some major event, the point being to take in the opponent and then triumphantly reveal that one has been lying all along and that the victim 'ate it'. These exercises in momentary dominance and in concealment of true meaning and intention continue in adult form. Oaths on the Quran or the Prophet or 'by Him who created the world' are rhetorically used but carry no weight, at least in these contexts, and are regarded as typical ploys.

Phrases that were not in my experience used except in the truthful mode and which were employed when one really did need to convey the verity of a message or situation were *"an jadd*, 'seriously', *wahyat abuk*, 'by your father's life', or *wahyat ibnak*, 'by your son's life'.

16. It was thought that it would be impossible to marry him, a harsh judgement on any male.

17. Basita and malish are both treated as socially 'neutral' and neutralizing terms. They are conventionally employed in efforts to defuse situations of public anger or dispute, and are spoken in a low and placatory tone, as if the speaker is not actually making an inter- vention at all. Spoken by a senior man the words may have some effect. Should a junior try to calm a senior, on the other hand, it may only serve to fan the flames of rage. A young man of Beit Abd as-Salam dared to half whisper 'basita' in an endeavour to calm an elder, who was violently shouting imprecations at his sons during a dangerous confrontation between the village as a whole and the army and the police, and in front of the qaimaqam. He was rewarded with a devastating verbal onslaught before which he literally slumped back against the wall with his chin on his chest as if physically beaten. The sons and he slunk home, eyes down and white faced.

18. 'Turning on the television' was his phrase for masturbation, and 'we went to the cinema' stood for sexual intercourse. He would gravely and knowingly say to me, after a searching look at a young man present, 'he's turned on the television, *ustaz Mikhail*'. There would follow a whole battery of lubricious looks around the company, the phrase repeated with a lingering relish, and perhaps a one-line 'song': 'when we dangled the bucket down the well, my head turned with the force of it'. This seemed to give him the hugest pleasure and was much repeated. He was not unknown to bellow the line down from the balcony of his house having 'gone to the cinema', and there would be protests from the women in the neighbouring houses of his two brothers at the shamefulness of such behaviour.

Masturbation was joked about by the adolescents, who sometimes would accuse one of their number to see if they could embarrass him. One victim said to me very earnestly while they were joshing him: 'It's not true ustaz. It just happened by itself', an innocent remark which earned him hoots of laughter. One young man, known for his malicious pressuring of others, made barely veiled and amused but bullying references to catching one of his younger first maternal cousins masturbating one day out in one of the fields, to the victim's furious embarrassment as his father was present in the room. 'Well, what did

I catch you doing Abd al Basit? Out there alone? The shame, the shame! I won't say what it was', and so on. I was not aware of other sexual references used in 'pressure'.

19. Thus a religious sheikh related to the mayor for preference always sat on a sheepskin on the floor leaning back on cushions in the place of honour, his close associates around him. Of the rest of the company, some continued to use the couches and chairs while others moved down to the same level if they felt it inappropriate to be sitting at a higher level above him in the position of the superior. The etiquette was uncertain, and when he was invited to mulids in other houses he was usually expected to sit in an armchair and no sheepskin was provided since this was not an article that people regarded as a part of their social universe and they did not seem to make any cultural investment in notions of 'tradition'.

20. Inkassar is a word much used in verbal confrontations. When two young men are jousting verbally the phrase '*fik tkassarna anta*?!' ('think someone like you could defeat me?!'), said with vast scorn, is a usual refrain.

21. Hostility to card games was powerfully expressed by the most prestigious local sheikh who was also a leading member of the Zu'abi Sufi *tariqa* (he was himself from the Zu'abi family). I did not expect to find religious reference brought into cards and incorporated in the play of desecration. A card session in a lord's manzul showed how mistaken my assumption was. A known joker figure, to whom I have often referred and who was a servant of the bey, used the licence of his status to full effect after winning at tarnib. The audience was made up for the most part of the shebab of the aghas, though one or two seniors looked on in amusement. The other three players were young men in their early twenties. One of the losers was the fifth son of the bey himself, a young man devoted to café and discotheque life in Beirut or Tripoli and with a penchant for sexual innuendo which some murmured went further than just talk. It was to him that the joker directed the pantomime of the rhythms of the zikr (in classical Arabic *dhikr*), a Sufi ceremony in which the backwards and forwards movements of the participants easily lend themselves to erotic parody by anyone so inspired. Since the authentic ritual involves the regular chanting of certain of the Names of God, the sexuality of the hugely exaggerated pelvic thrusts could be accompanied by ecstatic cries of 'Allah! Allah!' and 'Hu! Hu!' (lit. 'He', one of the major Names used in Sufi 'remembrance' rituals). The performer climbed onto the tables and chairs (literally walking on another convention, that of 'furniture' and status), chanting all the while and gyrating in paroxysms of sexual desire. We were all reduced to tears of laughter. He had additional freedom, for this particular bey had little time for the sheikhs and their practices, regarding them with cynical amusement and Sufis with the contempt due to the lowest orders. I am certain, on the other hand, that the joker would never have parodied the movements of prayer which all accepted without question as fundamental to religion and with no class or status aspect.

13. The Perils of Display

1. Slavoj Zizek, *The Sublime Object of Ideology*, London: Verso, 1989, pp. 196–7.
2. For a treatment of his role as buffoon see the Coda.
3. When I returned for three days in 1983 to the village both phrases were used in reminiscence of my time there ten years before. The comic narratives were part of the framework of memory and were repeated, to great amusement and pleasure.

14. A Killing in the Street

1. It is also the word used for 'slamming on the brakes' of a car and conveys a very strong physical motion, often imitated when recounting an episode.

15. The Challenge of Work and Wages

1. Pierre Bourdieu, *Algeria 1960*, Cambridge: Cambridge University Press, 1979, p. 40.

2. The Arabic word used is *dakhal*. It is also used of the government 'entering' into the election process to influence the outcome through activities ranging from money payments through intimidation to outright ballot rigging. This power of course implied the capacity to block the efforts of others to bring in their people. It might also mean throwing those appointed by a rival out of their posts when the opportunity arose. Thus after the election of 1972 Suleiman al Ali, the powerful Akkari landlord who had finally returned to elective office after many years out of the Assembly, was said to have dismissed the government service employees 'entered' by his defeated rival Bashir al Othman. The latter had brought in many from his own village of Bebnine and technically they were supposed to have job security. Men said that a large delegation from Bebnine had gone to see al Ali hoping to keep their jobs and to say that they only suppported Bashir because they were from his village and not out of any spirit of opposition to the victor. The new Minister had been courteous and assured them that their futures were safe with him. Three days later he sacked the lot. This story was told with some *schadenfreude* and amusement as testimony to al Ali's ruthless use of power to damage the interests of opponents and advance his own.

3. On one occasion I appeared in the village wearing a new pair of shoes I had bought in Bata's shop in Tripoli. The young agha who had been with me immediately drew the attention of everyone in his maternal uncle's reception room to the shoes and to their price, to my embarrassment but no one else's. One of the older men squashed him by saying authoritatively that he had seen one of the beys who had shoes that had cost four lira more. He also commented unflatteringly on the style. The young man was emphasizing his privileged attachment to me in the traditional way of 'talking me up', in this case by stressing the cost of my shoes. His senior put him in his place, refuted the idea that we had a special relationship, and refused also to show himself impressed by my pattern of consumption compared to others with which he was familiar. Though such articles were not at all in his mode of dress, he, like his peers, was expert at assessing money value and making judgements accordingly. It was quite common for beys to be subject to the same direct appraisal.

The emphasis on the price paid extended to formal invitations to restaurants, a rare occasion for anyone in the village. I had invited a friend to lunch in a small Beirut restaurant known for the quality of its meat – essential on such an occasion – and was slightly surprised when he insisted on pocketing the bill. He later produced it at a sahra back in Berqayl to show exactly how much I had paid to establish what a high class of invitation I had issued, and how I valued him. He not only made the invitation to himself a reminder that others had not been invited, thus vaunting his special status with me, but he turned the sum of money into a kind of challenge. He implicitly defied anyone else to assert that they could claim to have been taken to such an expensive meal, for the bill was nearly a month's salary for one of the lower paid wakils or drivers.

4. President Nasser, regarded locally as the great champion of Arab and, in the Lebanese context particularly, Sunni Muslim identity, had died in 1970. His speeches were much admired, though I think that only two people actually had tape recordings of some of them. His portrait in an ornamental frame stood on side tables in several houses but was never on the walls (any more than was that of any political leader). That would have been too overtly 'political' and a pretext for anonymous letters to the intelligence bureau or the governorate alleging doubtful loyalties to the state. In a frame, and perhaps side by side with a picture of King Hussein, it was acceptable. Though both men represented very

different ideological currents and were frequently opposed, they could be accommodated literally within the same frame as 'real qabadays', true men of honour and power, courageous and tough. That was certainly the standard term used in reference to the two leaders. It might also be used of persons as disparate as 'Sheikh' Pierre Gemayal, the leader of the Phalangist party which had no supporters at all in this Sunni Muslim area, and the Israeli military commander Moshe Dayan. Both were held to have the qabaday qualities of ruthlessness and single-minded pursuit of the interests of their own groups.

Um Kulthum was an almost legendary Egyptian female singer and an enormous star throughout the Arab world. In this context she too represented an attachment to 'Arab (and Egyptian led) nationalism'.

Wall pictures taken from calendars were becoming popular, though previously only the occasional framed verse of the Quran or a photo of a now dead patriarch had hung on the walls, and then only in a few of the more recently built agha houses. The concept of 'decoration' was not familiar, save for the external form of strings of lights hung round a house façade when the owner returned from the Pilgrimage. By the time of my fieldwork it was not unusual to find the stag in the Scottish glens picture, photographs of the Bolshoi corps de ballet taken from a magazine, or views of Swiss mountains pinned up in a small reception room, together with framed photographs of the owner and, for example, passport pictures of his two sons in the army.

5. Quoted in M. Gilsenan, 'Lying, honor and contradiction', in B. Kapferer (ed.), *Transaction and Meaning*, Philadephia, PA: ISHI, 1976, p. 213.

6. Heavy sticks, '*asan*, pl. '*usiy*, were the classic weapon for low-level violence and featured in many stories of what might be colloquially called a good 'doing over' or 'thumping'. When someone said with amused or grim relish that a man needed a good beating, *biddu ya'kul qatl*, the reference was often to sticks rather than fists. Such incidents were frequently related in a comic register, the howls of the victim being heavily parodied, vigorous arm movements performed and syllables such as 'dob, dob, dob' used for the thumping of the staff on the chastised figure. Staffs did not have the honorific associations of lance or gun, though the older companions say they used them on occasion to discipline some unruly labourer, or even to clout a bey who was getting above himself.

The level of physical violence below the staff was the flat of the hand: 'I gave him a couple of cuffs', men would say, imitating their actions with pantomimes of heavy slaps on either side of the head. (The Arabic word used was *kaff*.) Again, there was a comic and slightly derisory note to accounts of this nature. The infringement of the other was of a condescending kind, the slap being at the furthest remove from an exchange through the medium of guns, when blood was at stake.

7. I should add that the opposing party would also have the rhetorical option of justifying themselves on their side later for not responding at the same level. In such a situation people would expect them to say that their opponent had suddenly produced a rifle and was ready to use it ,so they could do nothing with anyone so crazy as to take a gun against people for no reason.

8. The Arabic phrase used for driving someone off was *ridd wahed* (literally, turn someone back).

9. I was later told by the cousin who declined to resign in solidarity that Abu Nabil had gone down to the school with his troublesome son to try to find out what had happened and to affect a reconciliation. Nabil had hurled the bus keys on the director's desk as a flamboyant gesture of resignation, and his father had stalked from the room in exasperation at this display which made his mission quite impossible. In his own house and before a public wider than his sons, of course, he was obliged to support his eldest son to the hilt.

This detail justified the cousin's refusal to resign in solidarity. It established Nabil's foolishness and the way in which he had spoilt his own father's attempt to mediate with the school director. It also illustrates how narratives are dynamically constructed, added to, commented upon and attacked at different levels in different arenas.

10. In the event the baladiya elections were not held and the beginning of the war in 1975 effectively suspended them for the duration of hostilities and beyond.

11. It is no accident that the young man who had been so mischievous with his peers was the maternal nephew of the mayor and hitching his star to his uncle's wagon, as well as trying to keep in with the sheikh ash-shebab to maximize his chances of work and election profits on both sides.

12. It might be argued that villagers were more acutely aware of the full social resonance of the moment than was the director herself. She probably had very little awareness of the values of those she could so confidently put in their place beyond a stereotypical notion of 'rural folk'.

13. I was present when the outlaw sang one of Muhammad Abd al Wahhab's (the great Egyptian composer and singer) songs for Nabil's father and three or four young men one afternoon in Abu Nabil's room. His voice still had an element of the much-valued 'sweetness' about it that hinted at the quality that had once been so admired. He was the only man of all Beit Abd as-Salam who had been known as a singer at all, and performed still with some art. I noted that Abu Nabil had tears running down his face and asked him whether it was the song that had so moved him. He replied that he wept because the outlaw was 'dead', *meyyit*, and the young men looked very affected. I should recall the occasion in which the desperate situation of the makhlu' who had just been shot by a Palestinian and might be dying brought a confession of tears from my friend who said 'it was terrible that he should die that way'. I think that the dominant element was not 'the person himself' for whom my friend actually had no trust or regard at all, but for the whole form of narrative life which was being constructed as having led to such an end, bereft of any social worth or credit.

Men might show feeling in tears that came suddenly to their eyes in response to a sudden stimulus of emotion: for example, in a situation such as the one I have described, or when being told of a beautiful or moving dream, or listening to a recitation of particularly valued lines of poetry. Some men were spoken of as being 'liberal of their tears', *dam'a sakhiya*, meaning that they instantly reacted in this way to these kinds of moments in which some form of art and harmony were created in beautiful language or expression. This sign of emotion was not thought unmanly or feminine. It was as if particular experiences were held to evoke an intense response to which a man might quite properly react, not with sobbing, but with the eyes flooding with tears.

On large-scale, public, collective occasions, however, men were reprimanded for weeping, and others would say sharply that it was 'shame' or 'like women'. Thus at a funeral, for example, where grief was the dominant and defining emotion, other men would speak quite roughly to close male relatives who cried in the procession carrying the coffin to the cemetery. They should 'be men' and not 'behave like women'. Yet at the same time this reprimand had a ritual dimension. For others would always be ready to support the mourners who might show signs of being scarcely able to walk, or whose faces might be crumpled with emotion, their shoulders shuddering.

16. Horsemen on Tractors

1. Men were, or claimed to be, very well informed about the incomes of virtually everyone in the village, how many days a year they were in work, and what, if anything, they were doing on the side.

2. This shifting from job to job as a driver-mechanic was quite typical. Another man of Beit Abd as-Salam, in the twenty-month period of my fieldwork, drove a bulldozer on the airport job, ran an 'unofficial' taxi to the plain and to Syria, operated a tractor ploughing on the plain, and finally went around shops in Tripoli selling sweets for a big company.

3. The word chauffeur has of course been taken into Arabic from French. Most terms to do with car mechanics were direct adaptations from the French – *debraillage*, *frein*, and so on.

4. See Chapter 3 for details of occupations.

5. The term was also used by men who got to know each other in the army, or by a schoolboy of his friend. It distinguished a particular kind of respected outsider with whom one had a relationship that it was appropriate to mark by a formal invitation, an *'azima*, to the house.

6. Men often used the word *ta'ab* as sufficient explanation of why they had 'stopped', *battal*. It has a connotation of being weary, exhausted and fed up. 'A job was too much drudgery or hardship, so I walked away' was the sense of many remarks. Nothing obliged him to remain working unless the conditions suited him.

7. This might happen in other settings. One young man, a half-brother of the *ra'is al baladiya*, returned to the village a few weeks after going down to Tripoli to work in a small furniture-making business, and gave his angry seniors the same minimal explanation. Another, giving an account of why he had left a job in a workshop, just said 'I was ill'. He stuck to this obstinately, despite the exhortations and angry comments of his father and others, but told me privately that 'there wasn't much for him to do anyway'. This kind of refusal of arrangements made by families for sons to find wage work was common, and a source of much discussion and denunciation.

8. See M. Gilsenan, 'Law, arbitrariness and the power of the lords of North Lebanon', *History and Anthropology*, Vol. 1, Pt. 2, 1985, pp. 381–98.

9. We joked endlessly about it: had he tried oil? Or thought of putting in some petrol? Perhaps it needed some electrics? We even performed an imitation of a Sufi *dhikr* round the engine one day while he sang the appropriate hymns, since we decided that only divine intervention could get the wretched thing to move. It was a long time before it dawned on me that, at some stage impossible no doubt to define, the fact that the car was always in pieces at the back of the house, and that he would always have to work on it had become the whole point. (See Plate 7.)

10. This happened with anyone who owned a machine. Only two brothers had garages where they kept machines, the rest either took motors apart in the yard or moved indoors. It was quite common to go to the house of the man organizing the work at the airport or on construction sites to find seven or eight men there with engine parts all over the floor of the manzul, together with tool kits and all the necessary equipment. Indeed, the public space of the house was mainly used for this collective work, which entailed its own socializing patterns and job hierarchy. Everyone would get tea throughout the day, and a little food. If the work took place outside tools were sometimes put down in the dust, which later clogged up the working parts.

11. The phrase 'sheikh ash-shebab' was often used of a man as flattery or as a compliment to his standing in the community and it is a phrase used throughout Lebanon. It might also, of course, be used ironically of someone who was held to think himself a great

deal more important that others did. Young beys were routinely so addressed in forms of elaborate etiquette, though there might well be knowing looks and quick grins if it looked as though the addressee was lapping up the praise.

12. This was not an uncommon occurrence. Nadim had bought a Volvo for use as an unofficial taxi and had to return it for the same reason, a particularly mortifying blow given the way in which he had flashed around in it with the maximum of show.

13. Men said of him that 'he wanted to show himself', *biddu yizhur halu*.

Coda

1. T. Nagel, *Mortal Questions*. Cambridge: Cambridge University Press, 1979, p. 13.

2. G. Simmel, *The Sociology of Georg Simmel*. Ed. Kurt H. Wolff. New York: The Free Press, 1950, p. 310.

3. I employ again Alasdair MacIntyre's formulations (see Chapter 4).

4. This term is the Ottoman one for standard-bearer. One man gave a local Arabic etymology of *bairaq* as flag and *dar* as house, hence standard of the house.

5. This man was probably in his eighties at the time of my fieldwork. He had built an imposing house of two floors and many rooms above one of his olive groves and facing Berqayl from across the valley. A sword with gold hilt and scabbard hung on his wall, a mark of honour from Abboud Bey. He dressed always in the older style, and sent his sons abroad for education. Reputedly a 'millionaire', he was the best example of how an individual murafiq could rise materially and in social status through his service to a major landlord. Everyone accepted as true the story that he had for years been the secret lover of a lord's sister, and this narrative was retold as one of love, and also as one of influence.

Bibliography

Achard, E. 'La plaine d'Akkar', *L'Asie Française*, 23 (1923): 63–9.

Akarli, E. 'Abdulhamid II's attempt to integrate Arabs into the Ottoman system', *Palestine in the Late Ottoman Period: Political, Social and Economic Transformation*. Ed. D. Kushner. Jerusalem/Leiden: Yitzhak ben Zvi/E.J. Brill, 1986, 74–89.

— *The Long Peace: Ottoman Lebanon, 1861–1920*. London: Centre for Lebanese Studies and I.B.Tauris, 1993.

Al Mudiriya al 'Amma, Statistical Bureau, Beirut, 1965.

Anon. 'Khatar ath-thawra fi 'Akkar', *As-Sayyad*, 22 August 1974.

Anon. 'La famine au Liban et l'assistance française aux Libanais pendant la grande guerre (1915–1919)', *L'Asie Française*, supplément, février 1922, pp. 3–14.

ash-Shidyaq, Tannus bin Yusuf. *Akhbaru'l 'ayyan fi jabal lubnan*. Beirut: 1954.

Baaklini, A. *Legislative and Political Development: Lebanon 1842–1972*. Durham, NC: University of North Carolina, 1976.

Barthélemy, A. *Dictionnaire Arabe–Français. Dialectes de Syrie: Alep, Damas, Liban, Jérusalem*. 6 vols. Paris: Librairie Orientaliste Paul Geuthner, 1935–1969.

Bongie, C., *Exotic Memories: Literature, Colonialism and the Fin de Siècle*. Stanford, CA: Stanford University Press, 1991.

Bourdieu, P. *Algeria 1960*. Cambridge, Cambridge University Press, 1979.

Bowen, J. 'Narrative form and political incorporation: changing uses of history in Aceh, Indonesia', *Comparative Studies in Society and History*, 31:4 (1989): 671–93.

Brandes, S. *Metaphors of Masculinity: Sex and Status in Andalusian Folklore*. Philadelphia, PA: University of Pennsylvania Press, 1985.

Bruner, E.M. 'Introduction: the opening up of anthropology', *Text, Play and Story: The Construction and Reconstruction of Self and Society*. Ed. E.M. Bruner. Illinois: Waveland Press Inc., 1988.

Catroux, General. *Deux missions en Moyen-Orient, 1919–1922*. Paris: Plon, 1958.

Chevallier, D. *La société du Mont Liban à l'époque de la révolution industrielle en Europe*. Paris: Librairie Orientaliste Paul Geuthner, 1971.

Clifford, J. *The Predicament of Culture: Twentieth-Century Ethnography, Literature and Art*. Cambridge, MA: Harvard University Press, 1988.

Dahir, M. *Ta'rikh lubnan al ijtima'i, 1914–1926*. Beirut: Dar al Farabi, 1974.

Denizeau, Cl. *Dictionnaire des parler arabes de Syrie, Liban et Palestine (Supplément au Dictionnaire arabe–français de A. Barthélemy)*. Paris: Éditions G.-P. Maisonneuve, 1960.

Detienne, E. *The Creation of Mythology*. Chicago: Chicago University Press, 1986.

Dixon, P. *Rhetoric*. London/New York: Methuen, 1971.

Donon, J. 'La question foncière en Syrie et au Liban: les réformes réalisées depuis l'établissement du mandat français', *L'Asie Française*, 23 (1923): 22–8.

— 'La rescision des ventes de guerre au Liban', *L'Asie Française*, No. 198 (Janvier 1922): 16–21.

Ducousso, D. *L'Industrie de la soie en Syrie et au Liban*. Beirut: Imprimerie Catholique, 1913.

Early, E.A. 'Catharsis and creation: the everyday narratives of Baladi women of Cairo', *Anthropological Quarterly*, 58:4 (1985): 172–81.

Gavin, C.E.S. *Imperial Self-Portrait: The Ottoman Empire as Revealed in the Sultan Abdul Hamid II's Photographic Albums.* Cambridge, MA: Harvard University Press, 1988.

Genette, G. *Figures of Literary Discourse.* Trans. Alan Sheridan. Oxford: Basil Blackwell, 1982.

Ghazzal, Z. *L'Économie politique de Damas durant le XIXè siècle: structures traditionnelles et capitalisme.* Damascus: Institut français de Damas, 1993.

Gibb, H.A.R. and Kramers, J.H. (eds) *Shorter Encyclopaedia of Islam.* Leiden: E.J. Brill, 1953.

Gilsenan, M. 'Lying, honor and contradiction', *Transaction and Meaning.* Ed. B. Kapferer. Philadelphia: Institute for the Study of Human Issues, 1976, pp. 191–219.

— *Recognizing Islam.* London: Croom Helm, 1982.

— 'A modern feudality? Land and labour in North Lebanon, 1858–1950', *Land tenure and social transformation in the Middle East.* Ed. T. Khalidi. Beirut: American University of Beirut, 1984, pp. 449–63.

— 'Law, arbitrariness and the power of the Lords of North Lebanon', *History and Anthropology,* 1 (1985): 381–400.

— 'Sacred words', *The Diversity of the Muslim Community.* Ed. A. Al Shahi. London: Ithaca Press, 1987, pp. 92–8.

— 'Word of Honour', *Social Anthropology and the Politics of Language.* Ed. R. Grillo. London: Routledge, 1989, pp. 193–221.

— 'Nizam ma fi: discourses of order, disorder and history in a Lebanese context', *Problems of the Modern Middle East in Historical Perspective: Essays in Honour of Albert Hourani.* Ed. J. Spagnolo. Reading: Ithaca Press, 1992, pp. 79–104.

Goffman, E. 'On cooling the mark out', *Human Behaviour and Social Processes.* Ed. A. Rose. London: Routledge and Kegan Paul, 1962.

Haqqi, Isma'il Bey. *Lubnan: mabahith 'ilmiyya wa ijtima'iyya.* 2 vols. Ed. Fouad Bustani. Beirut: 1970.

Harré, R. 'Language games and texts of identity', *Texts of Identity.* Ed. J. Shotter and K.J. Gergen. London/Newbury Park: Sage Publications, 1989.

Haut Commissariat de la République Française en Syrie et au Liban. *La Syrie et le Liban en 1921.* 2 vols. Paris: 1922.

Herzfeld, M. *The Poetics of Manhood: Contest and Identity in a Cretan Mountain Village.* Princeton, NJ: Princeton University Press, 1985.

Holmes, D. *Cultural Disenchantments: Worker Peasantries in Northeast Italy.* Princeton, NJ: Princeton University Press, 1989.

Hourani, A. and Shehadeh, N. *The Lebanese in the World.* London: I.B.Tauris, 1992.

Hublos, F. *Ta'rikh 'Akkar al idari wa'l ijtima'i wa'l iqtisadi, 1800–1914.* Beirut: Dar al Ha'ira, 1987.

Hudson, M. *The Precarious Republic: Political Modernization in Lebanon.* New York: Random House, 1968.

Huvelin, P. 'Que vaut la Syrie?', *L'Asie Française,* supplément, décembre (1921): 1–50.

IRFED Mission. *Étude préliminaire sur les besoins et les possibilités de développement du Liban.* 7 vols. n.d. (Published in 1960–61 by Ministère de Plan as *Besoins et possibilités de développement du Liban.*)

Jammous, R. 'De quoi parlent les fusils?', *L'honneur: image du soi ou don de soi, un idéal équivoque.* Série morales. Paris: Éditions Autrement, 1991.

Karpat, K. *Ottoman Population, 1830–1914: Demographic and Social Characteristics.* Madison, WN: University of Wisconsin Press, 1985.

Khalidi, R. 'Society and ideology in late Ottoman Syria: class, education, profession and confession', *Problems of the Modern Middle East in Historical Perspective: Essays in Honour of Albert Hourani.* Ed. J. Spagnolo. Reading: Ithaca Press, 1992, pp. 119–31.

Khalidi, T. (ed.) *Land Tenure and Social Transformation in the Middle East.* Beirut: American University of Beirut, 1984.

Khoury, P.S. *Urban Notables and Arab Nationalism: The Politics of Damascus 1906–1920*. Cambridge: Cambridge University Press, 1982.

Klich, I. '*Criolos* and Arabic speakers in Argentina: an uneasy *pas de deux*, 1888–1914', *The Lebanese in the World*. Ed. A. Hourani and N. Shehadeh. London: I.B.Tauris, 1992, pp. 243–4.

Lane, E.W. *Manners and Customs of the Modern Egyptians*. Everyman Edn. London: J.M. Dent and Sons, 1908.

Latron, A. *La Vie rurale en Syrie et au Liban: étude d'économie sociale*. Beirut: 1936.

Lefort, C. *Democracy and Political Theory*. Trans. David Macey. Oxford: Polity Press, 1988.

Longrigg, S.H. *Syria and Lebanon under the French Mandate*. Oxford: Oxford University Press, 1958.

Luquet, J. *Le mandat A et l'organisation du Mandat français en Syrie*. Paris: Éditions de la Vie Universitaire, 1923.

— *La politique des Mandats dans le Levant*. Paris: Éditions de la Vie Universitaire, 1923.

MacIntyre, A. *After Virtue: A Study in Moral Theory*. 2nd edn. London: Duckworth, 1985.

Mantran, R. and Sauvaget, J. *Règlements fiscaux ottomans: les provinces syriennes*. Beirut: Adrien-Maisonneuve, 1951.

Martin, R.P. *The Language of Heroes: Speech and Performance in The Iliad*. Ithaca, NY: Cornell University Press, 1989.

Meo, L.T. *Lebanon: Improbable Nation. A Study in Political Development*. Bloomington, IN: Indiana University Press, 1965.

Messara, A. *La structure sociale du parlement libanais, 1920–1970*. Beirut: L'Université Libanaise, 1971.

Ministère du Plan, République Libanaise. *Besoins et possibilités de développement du Liban*. 2 vols. Beirut, 1960–61.

Ministére des Ressources hydrauliques et électriques, 'La situation foncière dans la plaine d'Akkar'. Beirut, 1972.

Mumford, S.R. 'Emplotment of historical narratives in the Nepal Himalayas', *Identity, Consciousness and the Past: The South Asian Scene*. Ed. H.A. Seneviratne. Special issue series of *Social Analysis*, 25 (1989): 53–63.

Naff, A. *Becoming American: The Early Arab Immigrant Experience*. Carbondale, IL: Southern Illinois University Press, 1985.

Nagel, T. *Mortal Questions*. Cambridge: Cambridge University Press, 1979.

Nasr, S. 'La transition des chiites vers Beyrouth: mutations sociales et mobilisation communautaire à la veille de 1975', *Mouvement communautaires et espaces urbains au Machreq*. Beirut: CERMOC, 1985, pp. 87–116.

Owen, R. 'The economic history of Lebanon 1943–1974', *Towards a Viable Lebanon*. Ed. H. Barakat. London: Croom Helm, 1988, pp. 27–41.

Rabbath, E. *L'Évolution politique de la Syrie sous Mandat*. Paris: Marcel Rivière, 1928.

Reilly, J.A. 'Status groups and propertyholding in the Damascus hinterland, 1858–1880', *International Journal of Middle East Studies*, 21 (1989): 517–39.

Sabean, D.W. *Power in the Blood: Popular Culture and Village Discourse in Early Modern Germany*. Cambridge: Cambridge University Press, 1984.

Salibi, K. 'The Sayfas and the Eyalet of Tripoli, 1579–1640', *Arabica* 20 (1973): 25–52.

— *A House of Many Mansions: The History of Lebanon Reconsidered*. London: I.B.Tauris, 1988.

Sanlaville, P. 'L'Évolution de la plaine du Akkar', *Hannon: Revue Libanaise de Géographie*, 1 (1966): 71–82.

— 'Les régions agricoles du Liban', *Revue de Géographie de Lyon*, 44 (1969): 47–89.

Schatkowski Schilcher, L. 'The famine of 1915–1918 in Greater Syria', *Problems of the Modern Middle East in Historical Perspective: Essays in Honour of Albert Hourani*. Ed. J. Spagnolo. Reading: Ithaca Press, 1992, pp. 229–58.

Seurat, M. 'Le quartier de Bab Tebbane à Tripoli (Liban): étude d'une "asabiyya urbaine"',
Movements communautaires et espaces urbains au Machreq. Beirut: CERMOC, 1985, pp. 45–86.

Shihab, Emir Haidar. *Luban fi 'ahd al umara' al shihabiyin*. 2 vols. Ed. A. Rustum and F.
Bustani. Beirut: 1933.

Shotter, J. and Gergen, K.J. (eds) *Texts of Identity*. London/Newbury Park: Sage Publications,
1989.

Simmel, G. *The Sociology of Georg Simmel*. Ed. Kurt H. Wolff. New York: The Free Press,
1950.

Smith, B.H. 'Narrative versions, narrative theories', *On Narrative*. Ed. W.J.T. Mitchell.
London/Chicago: University of Chicago Press, 1981, pp. 209–32.

Stickley, T. and Sadr, K. 'Land tenure in Lebanon', Department of Agricultural Economics,
Faculty of Agricultural Sciences, American University of Beirut, 1972.

Tamimi, R. and Bahgat, M. *Wilayat Beirut*. Beirut: Matba'a al Iqbal, 1916 (republished 1979).

Touma, T. *Paysans et institutions féodales chez les druses et les maronites du Liban du XVIIè siècle à
1914*. Beirut: L'Université Libanaise, 1971.

Vaumas, E. de. 'La répartition de la population au Liban: introduction à la géographie
humaine de la République Libanaise', *Bulletin de la Société de Géographie d'Egypte*, 26 (1953):
5–75.

Wagstaff, J.M. 'A note on some nineteenth-century population statistics for Lebanon', *Bulletin
of the British Society for Middle Eastern Studies*, 13:1 (1986): 27–35.

Wehe, H. *A Dictionary of Modern Written Arabic*. Ed. J. Milton Cowen. Wiesbaden: Otto
Harrassowitz/London: George Allen and Unwin, 1966.

Weulersse, J. *Le pays des Alaouites*. 2 vols. Tours: Arrault et Cie, 1940.

— *Paysans de Syrie et du Proche-Orient*. Paris: Gallimard, 1946.

White, H. *Tropics of Discourse: Essays in Cultural Criticism*. Baltimore, MD/London: Johns
Hopkins University Press, 1978.

Wright, G. *The Politics of Design in French Colonial Urbanism*. Chicago: Chicago University
Press, 1990.

Yazigi, N. *Risala ta'rikhiya fi ahwal lubnan fi 'ahdihi al iqta'i*. Harisa: Matba'a al Qiddis Bulus,
1936.

Zamir, M. 'Population statistics of the Ottoman Empire in 1914 and 1919', *Middle Eastern
Studies*, 17 (1981): 85–106.

— *The Formation of Modern Lebanon*. London: Croom Helm, 1985.

Zizek, S. *The Sublime Object of Ideology*. London: Verso, 1989.

Theses

Atiyah, N.W. 'The attitude of the Lebanese Sunnis towards the state of Lebanon'. Ph.D.
thesis, 2 vols., University of London, London, 1973.

Gates, C.L. 'The formation of the political economy of modern Lebanon: the state and
the economy from colonialism to independence, 1939–1952'. D.Phil. thesis, Oxford
University, Oxford, 1985.

Hashimoto, K. 'Causes and consequences of international migration: the case of Lebanon,
1888–1939', D.Phil. thesis, Oxford University, Oxford, 1992.

Hlaihel, A. 'Étude de géographie physique appliquée à l'aménagement dans une region du
Akkar', thèse 3è cycle, Université de Lyon III, Lyons, 1982.

Maalouf, W.D. 'Factors associated with effectiveness of the result demonstration method
in promoting adoption of fertilizer practices by wheat farmers in Baalbeck and Akkar
Counties, Lebanon'. Ph.D. thesis, Cornell University, Ithaca, NY, 1965.

Naoufral-Giappesi, M.-F. 'Contribution à la connaissance de la région du Akkar, Liban', thèse 3è cycle, University of Paris, Paris, 1978.

Rothenberger, J.E. 'Law and conflict resolution, politics, and change in a Sunni Muslim village in Lebanon'. Ph.D. thesis, University of California, Berkeley, CA, 1970.

Zakhlur, F.T. 'Ta'rikh 'akkar as-siyasi wa'ill iqtisadi wa'il ijtima'i, 1908–1943' ('The political, economic and social history of Akkar, 1908–1943'). Ph.D. thesis, University of Saint Joseph, Beirut, 1984.

Archives

Archives Militaires de Vincennes, 24 C3 Levant, 1917–1939.

Ministèrè des Affaires Etrangères (MDAE), Série E–Levant, 1918–1929, sous série Syrie–Liban–Cilicie. Paris.

U.S. Archives Collection, Centre for Lebanese Studies, Oxford.

Index

al Abboud, Muhammad, 3–22, 23, 29, 30, 37, 53, 66, 89, 108, 132, 151, 154, 155, 168, 250, 255, 309; as character in father's narrative, 36; as metaphor of political order, 34, 35; as narrative, 60, 94; coffin of, 29, 30, 31, 32, 33, 35, 36, 37, 221, 299, 309 (as figure of power, 35, 36, 37; unburied, 30, 35, 187); construction of, 34; fear of, 8; killing of, 33, 35, 36, 109, 173, 175, 295; palace of, 29, 34, 35, 36, 45, 66, 305 (as figure of power, 35; burning of furnishings, 309); vengeance for, 258; widow of *see* widow of Muhammad al Abboud

Abd al Hamid, Said, 90

Abd al Latif, Ibrahim, 48

Abd al Qadir, Khalid Bey, 51, 52, 62, 93

Abd ar-Razzaq, Abboud, 8, 9, 11, 20, 30, 35, 46, 51, 52, 60, 61, 64, 65, 78, 83, 84, 85, 86, 87, 88, 91, 93, 94, 103, 106, 107, 109, 120, 123, 136, 144, 146, 152, 153, 154, 250, 261, 267, 291, 300

Abd as-Salam, Ahmad Abd al Latif, 149

Abd as-Salam, Hassan, 292–5

Abdallah, a revenge killer, 177–86; marginality of, 180, 181; visited in hospital, 184; wounding of, 183, 186

Abdo, 241, 242, 243

Abdullah, Ahmad Khalid, 23, 24, 25, 27, 31

Abdullah, genitor of Beit Selim, 145

Abu Abduh, 306, 308; and his hajj, 233–6

Abu Adnan, 91

Abu Ahmad, of Beit al Qaddur, 135–7, 138

Abu Ali, 86, 87, 115

'Abu Ali', an *agha*, 209–11

Abu Faiz, 106

Abu Hassan, Hajj, 89

Abu Juwad, Walid, 150–6, 169

'Abu Khaldun', 258

Abu Khalid, 127, 284

Abu Marwan, narrative of, 144–7

Abu Nabil, 217, 220, 284, 290

Abu Osman, 284

Abu Walid, 53–4

abuse and insult *see* insults

Achard, E., 80

adami (decent man), 115, 185, 188, 195, 199, 258, 276

Adham Bey, 130

adultery, 191

agha, as courtesy term, 4, 135

aghas (*aghawat*), xi, 5, 21, 31, 44, 47, 50, 59, 65, 86, 102, 119, 138, 139, 140, 194, 220, 236, 240, 246, 247, 248, 254, 265, 266, 268, 269, 283, 293, 294, 301, 302, 303; decline of, 278; flaw in identity of, 116; genealogy of, 47; relations with *beys*, 135, 250–1, 255, 260; relations with *fellahin*, 88–9, 89–94, 122, 145, 159–88, 304; selling of land, 106; tricking of, 134

agrarian reform, 99

Agricultural Bank, 82

agricultural machinery, 291, 292

agricultural workers, 50, 98

agriculture, 38, 41, 43, 50, 67, 72, 81, 94, 99, 104, 110, 137; capitalist, 16, 94; changes within, 102; organization of, 120

Ahmad, an *agha*, 159–60, 250–3, 261

Ahmad, grandson of Ibrahim Abd as-Salam, 129

Ahmad, maternal cousin of Tariq, 284

Ahmad, Said, 89

Ahmad, uncle of Abu Marwan, 144

'aib (shame), 192

airport of Beirut, construction work on, 259, 282, 283, 284, 288, 289, 296

akhbar (news), 164, 187

Akkar, xi, 4, 13, 14, 24, 25, 26, 32, 68, 80, 93, 98, 99, 266, 293, 301, 306; administrative division of, 38; as absence, silence and disorder, 69–76; as case of underdevelopment, 98; as contested space, 15; as obstacle to modernity, 67; as 'other', 38–42; as peripheral zone, xiii, 17; as prosperous area, 79; deficiencies of, 100; population